Looking East from Kenmore Square to Boston with Logan Airport in the Background

Looking West from Logan Airport toward the City

Looking Southwest to Boston from Charlestown

Permission courtesy of Mr. Tony Cammarata who is an expert aerial Boston photographer. Mr. Cammarata's studio is Aerial Boston Photographers located in Lexington, Massachusetts.

The views are (i and ii) looking east from Kenmore Square and west from Logan Airport, respectively. Furthermore, view (i) is the Backbay area noted for the extensive and early use of landfill reclamation technology in the New England area. View (iii) is looking southwest to Boston from Charlestown.

CITY
AND
COUNTRY

CITY
AND
COUNTRY

Edited by
Laurence S. Moss

BLACKWELL
Publishers

ISBN 0-631-228845
ISBN 0-631-228853 (P)
ISSN 0002-9246

CONTENTS

CITY AND COUNTRY

Editor's Introduction

This group of essays and case studies was gathered in two steps. First, during the Fall of 1999, a call for papers was circulated electronically and also published in a number of important scholarly journals. The net was cast wide so as to recruit scholars from several disciplines and on several continents. The papers that follow are testimony to our success at recruiting interesting work. Second, I journeyed through the many proposals, identifying a group of papers that if passed by our referees might work well together and with other essays already accepted. My goal has been to provide a coherent and thought-provoking issue. I think that this collection is both interesting and interdisciplinary as its title suggests.

Initially, I expected a spate of papers on the contrasts between the psychological "lifeworld," both in the modern city where space is scarce and in the modern countryside where it is not. Indeed, the title for this volume, "City and Country," was borrowed from an important essay written by the social reformer Henry George and published in his text *Social Problems* (George 1953 [1883], pp. 234–240). In 1883, George complained that "the cities grow, unwholesomely crowding people together till they are packed in tiers, family above family, so are they [also] unwholesomely separated in the country" (1953 [1883],

American Journal of Economics and Sociology, Vol. 60, No. 1 (January, 2001).

p. 236). Several papers in this volume examine the processes by which cities grow and how current public policy, both in the areas of zoning and town planning, respond to this process. The coauthored paper by Professors Nathan B. Anderson and William T. Bogart explain that in the monocentric city of the nineteenth century, the main employment center was the central business district (CBD). With the polycentrism that now characterizes most of the cities of the contemporary world, the main employment centers have expanded from the historic CBD and ended up located near highway crossings and the like. Their paper demonstrates a novel statistical method for identifying these employment centers, which are essential for the analysis of polycentrism. In another paper, Professors David L. McKee and Yosra A. McKee summarize and extend Joel Garreau's notion of edge cities. Edge cities grow up around older metropolitan areas and supply mostly economic services such as accounting, advertising, and legal advice. Are edge cities a global phenomenon or simply part of the American lifestyle?

One of the most important global regularities in all economics if not in all social sciences is Zipf's law. According to Zipf's law, the number of cities with a population size greater than some number, say, S, is inversely proportional to S itself! But not only for cities and towns? Zipf's law holds for the size distribution of firms in any industry as Professor Knudsen carefully shows for Denmark. Professor Thorbjørn Knudsen claims that this is "one of the outstanding empirical success stories in economics." But why does this law hold true in so many contexts? What impersonal, unintended, market-like processes could produce such an awesome empirical reality? Using insights provided by R. Gibrat and X. Gabaix, Knudsen is able to show that when growth is a dynamic stochastic process of a particular sort, Zipf's law is the unintended outcome. Knudsen's paper breaks new ground, as does the above-mentioned paper by Professors Anderson and Bogart which also discusses the relevance of Zipf's law to the distribution of intrametropolitan employment centers.

Professor Mark Jelavich tries to determine whether or not durable goods manufacturers have a preference for locating in rural areas rather than metropolitan areas. This comparison is also carried out for non-durable manufacturers, which are found to have locational preference for rural areas. The single factor that seems to shape locational preferences is state taxation. The fact that public policy interventions can produce measurable patterns of economic development is a topic that several of our contributors emphasize in their essays. Professor Thomas L. Daniels tries to reconcile what some might term "opposite approaches" toward trying to influence urban growth and urban sprawl. Land value taxation discourages idle land speculation and creates an incentive for getting land back into use. At the same time, efforts are underway to remove land from commercial development to provide open spaces and even public spaces where community life can flourish. Can the two approaches be reconciled? Professor Daniels tries to do so in his paper.

The relevance of land value taxation to modern methods of infrastructure improvement has been asserted time and time again by Henry George enthusiasts. I am delighted that Mr. H. William Batt shows us a specific example of how land value taxation can work. He examines how a well-traveled stretch of the New York state highway system near Albany, New York could have been financed differently and more equitably than it was financed. Assessments of betterments charged against the huge changes in land valuation caused by the new highway constructions would have provided more than enough financing for the highway without having to dip down into the general tax fund for the whole state. By taxing what the followers of Henry George have termed the "unearned" capital gains and preventing the unjust enrichment of the political speculators, far greater fairness could have been introduced into the New York state tax system.

Professor Carol E. Heim offers a case study of Phoenix, Arizona, where the planners have tried to outsmart the natural and unobstructed processes that lead to urban sprawl. Her work contrasts nicely with Professor Gura Bhargava's piece on the legendary city of Lloydminster. Lloydminster is the only city in Canada that straddles two different Canadian provinces with radically contrasting ideologies about individual responsibility and collective action. The contrasting mental spaces of the inhabitants produce measurable differences in industry, housing, and social relations. Professor Bhargava offers an extended case study of this most unusual urban development.

The American city known as Kansas City, Missouri has experienced most of the typical and expected effects of postwar urban economic development. Professor Kevin Fox Gotham tells the story of Kansas City, but with a careful eye toward the role that private-public initiatives have played in shaping the segregation of the urban population along racial lines. The key actors and organized interests who helped shape this development extend far beyond faceless federal bureaucracies, as Professor Gotham points out in his paper.

While all economic growth and development occurs in space that is either in urban or rural areas, the source of this growth is frequently creative thinking translated into inventions first and innovations second. Researchers Professors Norman Sedgley and Bruce Elmslie have tried to endogenize the growth process by appreciating the role that innovative ideas can play in the growth process. In their paper, Sedgley and Elmslie tell the story of innovative success as measured by the cross-section patent statistics associated with the various states in the United States by directly taking notice of the clustering of populations. This is the sort of phenomena—a positive feedback situation helping to expand the economy—that Alfred Marshall described as "localized industries" in his *Economics* (Marshall 1961 [1890], p. 271). Sedgley and Elmslie might have them renamed "creative discovery districts." Their point is that one needs to take notice of these areas in order to help illuminate the growth process as it has occurred in the United States. This paper, by linking congestion, agglomeration and innovative success, opens the door for a new and original approach to modeling the growth process.

There is a great deal of "economic geography" in this special invited volume. According to Professor Paul Krugman, the whole field of economic geography covers "the location of production in space" (Krugman 1991). Krugman goes on to claim that traditional orthodox trade theory ignores the importance of space and, as a result, economists "normally model countries as dimensionless points within which factors of production can be instantly and costlessly moved from one activity to another, and even trade is usually given a sort of spaceless representation in which transport costs are zero for all goods that can be traded" (Krugman 1991, p. 2). Those of us with advanced degrees in economics know that Krugman's complaints have a great deal of validity. The texts that we were assigned and made to study for our examinations really did not produce an economics in space. Still, the possibility exists that the broader economics literature may contain a great deal more about the economics of location and space than the "normal" teaching of the required canon recognizes. That is why the several historical papers in this volume are so timely and help clarify some of the impressions shared by Krugman and others.

Professor Stephen J. Meardon directly engages Krugman. By carefully analyzing the scholarly work of Gunnar Myrdal and François Perroux, much can be learned about the fate of some of the leading ideas in economics. Myrdal saw the appreciation of agglomeration economies as directly linked to a rejection of traditional or classical economics. Perroux wanted to intergrate the ideas of power and domination into a body of economic analysis that seemed to leave no room for these phenomena. Both economists wished to devise a new economic geography but not in the fashion recommended by Krugman and others, which relies so heavily on rational choice and the solution of equations. The standard techniques may indeed distort the empirical phenomena of agglomeration and cumulative expansion that are linked to the importance of location and space.

Once we look for predecessors they are sure to turn up. One important example is none other than Henry George, who as early as 1879 showed himself a pioneering student of the phenomena of agglomeration. Whereas many other writers had failed to put their insights into a coherent framework, George succeeded quite dramatically, pioneering what Professor John Whitaker declares "significant extensions to the classical theory." I am delighted to offer in this volume Whitaker's ingenious reconstruction of George's growth theory as it was presented in Book IV of *Progress and Poverty*.

We also have a suggestive chapter on European or continental economic thinking and its linkages to the important problem of city and country. I was delighted when Professors Jürgen G. Backhaus and Gerrit Meijer submitted this piece. They review some of the most important German language writers, including Henrich von Storch, Gustav Schmoller, Werner Sombart, and Wilhelm Roepke. Perhaps because of these thinkers' location nearer to the eastern border of Europe, they were more attentive to the evolutionary development of cities on open plains and the like. Each writer emphasized a different problem in the development of cities. Von Storch wrote for the Russian monarch and urged that the busy cities in Russia assume a greater role in promoting the rise of wealth and culture in the countryside. Schmoller took careful notice of the consequences of industrialization. Sombart pushed the analysis toward an actual theory of the city, and Roepke counseled about what sorts of government interventions were suited to a human and just community. Still, when the city of Marl was engineered by the German government, the phenomenon of mass boredom—somewhat overlooked by the earlier writers—reared its ugly head. The Backhaus-Meijer paper invites further discussion and comment. I was also happy to include the paper by Daniel Block and E. Melanie DuPuis, which nicely emphasizes the historical importance of Heinrich von Thünen's *Isolated State* on various subfields of academic study, including geography, agricultural economics, and sociology. Each of these historical papers breaks new ground.

Our final section is entitled "The Transformation of the City in the 21st Century." It contains two essays that, in my opinion, help us imagine new directions for the city in the twenty-first century. The first paper is by Professors Rolf D. Cremer, Anne de Bruin, and Ann Dupuis. They document the successful "sister-cities" concept now operating between a city in China and another in New Zealand. This is a practical and exciting way to facilitate urban well-being and cultural exchange and to bridge the global-local divide. It is simple to connect other people in this way and the town mayors enjoy the glamour and travel associated with its implementation. By sending the sports teams back and forth between the cities to compete, sponsoring joint cultural exhibitions and events, and entering into many multicultural collaborative arrangements of lasting value, the world really gets to be a smaller place and cities connect with one another in a more varied space of mental images and ideas.

Finally, Dr. Fred E. Foldvary reminds us of the discussion of how things can be changed in more radical ways still. Henry George's favorite subject—radical reform to alleviate poverty—has not been forgotten more than a century later. There is no person more qualified than Dr. Foldvary to imagine how a city of the future based on voluntary exchange can evolve. He suggests that a purely voluntary city is not science fiction or idle fantasy but something within our reach. It means extending Batt's plans for highway financing into a large scale and fundamental doctrine of "benefits based" public finance. Foldvary finds case-based evidence available to support the practicality of these suggestions toward radical reform and argues his position well.

This issue was a delight to put together and I want to thank all the people involved, especially the staff at Blackwell Publishers for agreeing to run this special invited issue of the *AJES* as a separate free-standing book as well as part of Volume 60 of the *American Journal of Economics and Sociology*.

References

George, Henry. (1953 [1883]). *Social Problems*. New York: Robert Schalkenbach Foundation.
Krugman, Paul. (1991). *Geography and Trade*. Cambridge: MIT Press.
Marshall, Alfred. (1961 [1890]). *Economics*. London: Macmillan

PART I

Historical Perspectives on the Agglomeration Approach to Economic Growth

American Journal of Economics and Sociology, Vol. 60, No. 1 (January, 2001).
© 2001 American Journal of Economics and Sociology, Inc.

Henry George and Classical Growth Theory

A Significant Contribution to Modeling Scale Economies

By JOHN K. WHITAKER *

ABSTRACT. It is widely recognized that the analysis of economic growth in Henry George's *Progress and Poverty* was considerably influenced by the British classical tradition, especially the writings of Adam Smith, David Ricardo, and John Stuart Mill. What has been less clearly perceived is that George made significant extensions to the classical theory. This paper's aim is to provide an interpretation, and to some extent a "rational reconstruction," of George's positive analysis, largely leaving aside the striking normative lessons he drew from it. George's unsatisfactory treatment of capital is disposed of in Section I, while Section II—the core of the paper—follows George's lead in aggregating capital and labor into a single productive factor which is employed in a given natural environment. Section III adds the complication of improvement in the arts of production, and Section IV deals briefly with George's views on land speculation. Section V assesses, comparing George with his contemporary Alfred Marshall.

HENRY GEORGE (1839–1897) is widely regarded as a mediocre amateur economist who absorbed—perhaps too well—the general ideas of the British classical school as to the effects of growth on factoral income distribution, and built thereon a social reform movement reflecting a largely outmoded view of the world. There can be little doubt that in writing *Progress and Poverty*, first published in 1879,[1] George was strongly influenced by the classical economists, especially Adam Smith, David Ricardo, and John Stuart Mill, as well as by the views of Thomas Robert Malthus on population. (Subsequently he was to claim

* John Whitaker is the Georgia Bankard Professor of Economics in the Department of Economics at the University of Virginia, Charlottesville Virginia 22903: e-mail jw9s@virginia.edu. His interests center on the history of economic thought since 1850, especially the life and work of Alfred Marshall. The present paper draws heavily on Whitaker 1997, 1998, while providing a fuller documentation from George's writings.

American Journal of Economics and Sociology, Vol. 60, No. 1 (January, 2001).

affinity with the Physiocrats, but that was more retrospective affiliation than formative influence.) George's claims that land was rightly the property of all and pure rent an unearned and undeserved individual income echoed a long tradition, also associated with the classical school, especially James Mill and his son John Stuart, and rather naturally incited by classical rent theory. What distinguished George's proposals and helps account for the worldwide furor they raised was his call for "expropriation now" by the immediate punitive taxation of pure Ricardian rent without compensation to landowners.

However, my concern here is not with George the social reformer, propagandist, and political activist, but with George the economic theorist: that is, not with the normative aspects of his thought but with the positive ones. I hope to show that his modeling of the economic growth process in *Progress and Poverty* went well beyond the classical paradigm and displayed considerable ingenuity, innovativeness, and analytical skill. In particular, he took spatial aspects into account, in a way giving him some claim to be regarded as a significant contributor to spatial economics. His analytical performance was, of course, not without flaws. In particular, his treatment of capital remains problematic and I propose to dispose briefly of that facet of his thought before expounding his analysis in the context of a two-factor setting involving only land and labor. This, as will be seen, follows a line of simplification suggested by George himself. It allows the exposition to be sharpened and focused on essentials.

I

The Problem of Capital

ON THE PLUS SIDE, George deserves considerable credit for breaking away from the unsatisfactory wage-fund idea that all wages have to be advanced during the gestation period of any production process from a previously accumulated store of *finished* workers' consumption goods—perhaps a relic of a propensity of earlier writers to treat all production as synchronously yielded by an annual harvest cycle and all wages as immediately consumed. George recognized clearly the possibility of a balanced-flow situation in which production starts for any good are undertaken at a steady rate in time and current consumption requirements are met by the output emerging from a just-maturing previous start. Maintained stocks of *finished* consumer goods are then required only for precautionary purposes to bridge unexpected *changes* in equilibrium flow levels. This by now common conceptualization, clearly stated (without reference to George) by Alfred Marshall (1888), was firmly indicated by George in 1879 (pp. 71–9).

When it came to the question of how production yield at the no-rent margin was divided between labor and capital, George's treatment became sketchy and elusive, although with intriguing hints of marginal-productivity thinking. He alluded vaguely to the productivity of time in biological growth processes, but argued more significantly that capital was simply "labor stored up in matter" and that with free competition the "natural relation between interest and wages" required that both direct and stored-up labor obtain "equal returns to equal exertions" (pp.198–9). This led to his main proposition: wages and interest tend to remain in fixed ratio, rising and falling together, for "if wages fall, interest must also fall in proportion, else it becomes more profitable to turn labor into capital than to apply it directly" (p.199). This proposition could hardly refer to the relation between the wage rate and the interest rate and is best interpreted in terms of the absolute shares in output accruing to labor and capital. Even so, it gives no scope to the productivity of waiting and the need to compensate it, or to changes in the relative supplies of labor and capital.[2] But his proposition greatly simplified George's enquiry by freeing it from any further discussion of the distribution of income between labor and capital and by focusing attention on the distribution between land and labor-allied-with-capital—both labor and capital being equally oppressed by a rise in the share of output claimed by landowners. Thus:

> the primary division of wealth in distribution is dual, not tripartite. Capital is but a form of labor and its distinction from labor is in reality but a subdivision, just as the division of labor into skilled and unskilled would be (p.203).

George recognized that he had now

> reached the same point as would have been attained had we simply treated capital as a form of labor, and sought the law which divides the produce between rent and wages; that is to say, between the possessors of

the two factors, natural substances and powers, and human exer-
tion—which two factors by their union produce all wealth (p.203).

The simplification to two productive factors that George suggests here
will be adopted from now on, allowing the inadequacies of his treatment of capital to be bypassed. There is one important proviso, however. The harmony George discerned between the interests of labor
and capital applied only under free competition. *Monopolized* capital
was as inimical to the interests of labor and competitive capital as was
the private ownership of land. Indeed, George's tendency, following a
common nineteenth century practice, to refer to the private ownership
of land as "land monopoly" even when control was fragmented drew
the parallel even more tightly.[3] The elimination or control of monopoly and protectionism, and the active promotion of free competition
became important subsidiary planks in George's policy platform.[4] But
he saw monopolistic distortions largely as epiphenomena resulting
from an undue concentration of wealth and power whose ultimate
source lay in the "great problem" posed by private land ownership
(see p.193). The problems posed by concentrated capital will not be
pursued further here.

II

The "Great Problem"

FOR GEORGE THE "GREAT PROBLEM" was to diagnose the fundamental
causes of "the increase of want with the increase of wealth" (as the
subtitle to *Progress and Poverty* put it) that he saw manifested in the
world around him. The secular aspects of his diagnosis, our concern
here,[5] are set out in Book IV of *Progress and Poverty* which is entitled
"Effect of material progress upon the distribution of wealth." George
here drew heavily upon the classical theory of growth and distribution, accepting its adverse distributional implications for labor but ve-
hemently disputing its pessimistic prognosis for overall living standards, even in the absence of sustained technical progress.

George in effect discussed the problem in a macroeconomic
two-factor setting, with "land" standing for all aspects of the physical
environment and "labor" for all forms of human effort devoted to production. Rather than restrict rent creation to primary production, as

Ricardo had done, George worked with an aggregative concept of output as a whole, arguing that all production draws to some extent on appropriable aspects of the physical environment (pp. 168–70). He followed Ricardo, however, in identifying the competitive real wage rate with the "average produce of labor at the margin of cultivation" (p. 206), which represented "the produce which labor can obtain at the highest point of natural productiveness open to it without the payment of rent" (p. 213). But he departed sharply from the pessimistic Malthus-Ricardo tradition by introducing two general classes of scale economy. These take effect even if there is no improvement in "the arts," in which term George includes both "improvements in the arts of production and exchange" and "improvements in knowledge, education, government, police, manners, and morals, so far as they increase the power of producing wealth" (p. 228).

The first scale effect reflects increased possibilities for specialization of tasks and functions as the labor force grows: "increased population, of itself, and without any advance in the arts, implies an increase in the productive power of labor. . . . with every additional pair of hands which increasing population brings, there is a more than proportionate addition to the productive power of labor" (p. 232), an increase which applies to all labor, not just the incremental addition.

The second scale effect reflects agglomeration economies arising as the density of economic activity in urban centers increases. These economies do not raise the productivity of all labor, but only of that employed on the specific pieces of land that are the site of urban development. Population growth, by increasing such agglomeration economies, "brings out a superior power in labor, which is localized on land—which attaches not to labor generally, but only to labor exerted on particular land; and which thus inheres in the land as much as any qualities of soil, climate, mineral deposit, or natural situation, and passes, as they do, with the possession of the land" (p. 235).

Increased urban concentration not only increases efficiency in production and exchange of tangible goods, but also makes possible provision of otherwise unattainable amenities and services, all of which should be reflected in the overall measure of output. George's famous account (pp. 235–42) of the evolution of a tract of land from vacant prairie to bustling urban center makes these points unforgettably: loss of peace and rural solitude was something that he—a city dweller at heart—gave little heed to.

The growth of urban population, itself driven by an overall growth in population and economic activity, increases the productive power of urban land in a way "equivalent to the multiplication of its original fertility by the hundred fold and the thousand fold" (p. 241). Thus it is that "the lands which yield the highest rent, are not lands of surpassing natural fertility, but lands to which a surpassing utility has been given by the increase of population" (p. 242). This increasing of land rent by urban agglomeration was for George the most important influence raising the share of rent in total output, an effect which he justly believed had been neglected hitherto by "political economists" (p. 243).[6]

Population growth with a fixed land endowment inevitably forces marginal production to take place under conditions less well endowed by nature than before. This may involve recourse only to more distant and inconvenient sites rather than to land of inferior intrinsic quality.[7] In any case, workers at the no-rent margin will operate under worse conditions. However, increased productivity accruing to all workers from the specialization effect as population grows may still prevent output per worker at the no-rent margin from falling, the greater individual efficiency of the marginal worker compensating for a less propitious working environment.

Despite this, the added benefits new workers create for *other* workers through the increased-specialization effect and the benefits they create by enhancing agglomeration economies fail to accrue to them. By George's assumption that competitive wages are determined by the *direct* output contribution that a worker makes at the no-rent margin, these benefits are in effect treated as uncompensated external benefits. They accrue not to the additional workers who create them but to the already active workers whose efficiency is raised and to the landlords who are the residual claimants to the benefits of increased urban agglomeration.

The existence of specialization and agglomeration economies made it seem quite possible—even likely—to George that population growth could increase output per head overall, even without any "improvement in the arts" occurring, a conviction which underlay his fervent anti-Malthusianism. But growth in output per head did not guarantee that labor would share in the gains due to population growth. Despite increased national prosperity, there would, George claimed, at best be a decline in labor's share of output and at worst an absolute decline in its living standards.

A simple formalization will help to illustrate these points more clearly. The level of total output, Q, as a function of total labor input, L, assumed proportional to population, may be approximated as

$$(1) \qquad\qquad Q = A(L)[F(L) + B(L)]$$

Here A(L) reflects the increased-specialization effect,[8] B(L) reflects the increased output arising from urban agglomeration, and F(L) represents the standard way in which land limitation exerts a diminishing-return effect.[9] The following qualitative restrictions apply (primes denoting derivatives)

$$(2) \qquad\qquad A', B', F' > 0 > F''$$

It is evident that these qualitative restrictions are consistent with the possibility that output per head, Q/L, may rise as population and labor force grow, despite the presence of diminishing returns to land.

The real wage rate, w, at any level of L is given by the derivative of Q with respect to L, holding A(L) and B(L) constant since extra labor is not compensated for creating specialization and agglomeration economies for other individuals. Thus

$$(3) \qquad\qquad w = A(L)F'(L)$$

which may rise or fall as L increases, depending upon the balance between increase in average labor efficiency and diminishing return to extra labor of constant efficiency. This is argued by George in the following terms:

> Let us suppose land of diminishing qualities. The best would naturally be settled first, and as population increased production would take in the next lower quality, and so on. But as the increase of population, by permitting greater economies, adds to the effectiveness of labor, the cause which brought each quality of land successively into cultivation would at the same time increase the amount of wealth that the same quantity of labor could produce from it. . . . If the relations of quantity and quality were such that increasing population added to the effectiveness of labor faster than it

compelled a resort to less productive qualities of land, though the margin
of cultivation would fall and rent would rise, the minimum return to labor
would increase (p.233).

Even if the real wage rate fell, labor's *absolute* share of output, wL,
might rise, although even it could fall if the onset of diminishing returns to land is very severe. In any case, an increase in the agglomeration effect, B(L), will have no effect upon labor's absolute share of
output, but it will lower the *relative* share received by labor.

Absolute rent is given by

(4) $R = Q - wL = A(L)[F(L)-LF'(L) + B(L)]$

so that (in abbreviated notations)

(5) $dR/dL = (A'R/A) + A(B'-LF'') > 0$

which implies that absolute rent must increase as L does. The *relative*
share of labor is given by

(6) $wL/Q = (LF'/F)/(1+B/F)$

It is well known that for the class of diminishing-return production
functions like F(L) the elasticity LF'/F may rise or fall with L, although
remaining less than unity. If it rises with L, and if B/F falls with L (or
does not rise too rapidly) as is logically possible, then labor's relative
share will rise as L increases, belying George's claim that a reduction is
inevitable. A rapid growth in agglomeration economies makes his
claim more likely, however.

Even before introducing agglomeration economies, George had
claimed that "increase of population, as it operates to extend production to lower natural levels, operates to increase rent and lower wages
as a proportion, and may or may not reduce wages as a quantity:
while it seldom can, and probably never does, reduce the aggregate
production of wealth as compared with the aggregate expenditure of
labor, but on the contrary increases, and frequently largely increases
it" (p.234). But although he thus formally claimed only the necessity of
relative immiserization of labor, he was prone to take a darker view
and to slip into assuming the likelihood of *absolute* immiserization: for

example, "in spite of the increase of productive power, wages constantly tend to a minimum which will give but a bare living" (p.282).[10]

George saw immiserization as the consequence of inappropriate human institutions, not of the inescapable niggardliness of nature as Malthus had claimed. The contrast between rising output per head and the deteriorating position of labor gave fire to his proposal to tax away the rent of land. However, the public revenue thus raised was to be devoted only to public purposes, not redistributed to individuals. Since a continuing decline in the competitive real wage rate would remain a possibility even after the regime change, the question of whether improved public facilities could permanently preserve living standards while wages were falling should have been addressed. But George was prone to a rosy view of his proposed new regime, in contrast to his dark view of the existing one.

III

Will "Improvement in the Arts" Offer an Escape?

THE DISCUSSION HAS RESTED SO FAR on the restrictive assumption that no advances occur in the arts of production, exchange, or social organization. It would appear that such advances might help ameliorate the position of workers, even under a regime of private land ownership. However, George, by a clever but hardly defensible restriction, severely narrowed this potential escape route. He supposed in effect that improvement in the arts always takes a labor augmenting character, turning one worker into the equivalent of more than one worker but otherwise leaving production conditions unchanged. Thus, "the effect of inventions and improvements in the productive arts is to save labor—that is, to enable the same result to be secured with less labor, or a greater result with the same labor" (p.244). It follows that improvements in the arts tighten the grip of the natural-resource constraint in the same manner as would population growth. The return at the margin to a worker of given efficiency must be lowered, but the typical worker is now more efficient, so that the effect on the real wage *per worker* is ambiguous.

The effects of improvement in the arts are analyzed most simply by assuming that population stays constant, due perhaps to "an extensive circulation of Annie Besant's pamphlets" (p.249). In that case:

as invention and improvement go on, constantly adding to the efficiency of labor, the margin of production will be pushed lower and lower, and rent constantly increased, though population should remain stationary. . . . Whether, in any particular case, the lowering of the margin of production lags behind or exceeds the increase in productive power, will depend, I conceive, upon what may be called the area of productiveness that can be utilized before cultivation is forced to the next lowest point (p. 251).[11]

This passage may be formalized by assuming that, with constant population, production function (1) may be re-expressed as

$$(7) \qquad Q = G(L.E); \ G'>0>G''$$

where E is the number of units of labor of standard efficiency represented by an individual worker.[12] Advance in the arts increases E. The competitive real wage *per worker*, w, is now given by the notional change in output resulting from an extra worker. Thus:

$$(8) \qquad w = \frac{\partial Q}{\partial L} = EG'(L.E)$$

so that G'(L.E) which equals w/E is the wage of a hypothetical worker of efficiency E = 1. With L constant, an increase in E lowers G'(L.E). The overall effect on w will be an increase if G' falls in smaller ratio than E increases, and so on.

Rent is now given by

$$(9) \qquad R = Q - wL = G - LEG'$$

It must increase as E does since

$$(10) \qquad \partial R/\partial E = -L^2EG''>0$$

Though perceiving the effect on workers of an advance in the arts as ambiguous, George was again prone to take the dark view of actual prospects.[13]

IV

The Role of Land Speculation

GEORGE OBSERVED THAT RISING LAND RENTS and land values due to population growth or improvement in the arts would induce land speculation in a regime of private land ownership. He argued that speculatively held land would—at least in North America—tend to be kept out of productive use, further tightening the effective natural-resource constraint on production (see pp. 251–60). While his argument is logically satisfactory, its premises might be questioned. In any case, for this effect to tighten the resource constraint progressively, as George assumed (p.259), continual expansion of speculative land holding would be necessary. The anti-social nature of all speculative withholding of land from production might also be questioned. In an evolving economy, a site may have a profitable use in prospect for which the time is not yet ripe, yet temporary use in the interim may require too large a sunk investment to be justifiable. Exhaustible resources raise a similar issue more pointedly. Glimmerings of thinking along these lines might be discerned in George's observation, apropos of vacant lots in a rapidly growing city, that "[t]hese lots, some of them extremely valuable, are withheld from use, or from the full use to which they might be put, because their owners, not being able or not wishing to improve them, prefer, in expectation of the advance of land values, to hold them for a higher rate than could now be obtained from those willing to improve them" (p.257). But the thought was not pursued.

George believed that his proposed "single tax" would virtually eliminate the incentive for speculative landholding, producing a major relaxation of the natural resource constraint on production (pp. 436–8). What he again failed to emphasize was that the resulting one-time improvement in labor's position might be undermined by a continuing adverse wage trend.

V

Closing Remarks

I HOPE TO HAVE DEMONSTRATED THAT George in 1879 showed more ability and innovativeness as an economic theorist than is usually admitted, and that *Progress and Poverty* has claims to be regarded as a significant contribution to the analysis of economic growth. If one compares the thinking of George and Marshall about the macroeconomics of growth and distribution at this time it is not clear that the advantages lie wholly on Marshall's side. Both attempted to extend the classical model so as to incorporate scale economies and both struggled to correct and improve the classical theory of distribution. As to the former, it is true that Marshall was more aware than George of the need to reconcile scale economies with the persistence of competition, but he had hardly resolved the matter in 1879, and perhaps never did. George, on the other hand, deserves credit for his pioneering treatment of the economies of agglomeration, richer than Marshall's rather sketchy treatment of external economies. When it came to breaking with the classical theory of distribution, George escaped the more easily from wages-fund preconceptions, but Marshall's vestigial marginal productivity theory of 1879 pointed to a more satisfactory treatment of capital and interest than George was ever able to achieve.[14]

George was of course entirely self taught as an economist and perhaps too confident in his own power of thinking through intricate economic and social issues. This, together with the grandiosity of his ambitions, left him open to easy criticism. The economists of his day gave him a largely hostile reception, paying little heed to the economic-theoretical component of his work. For this and other reasons he failed to advance as an economic theorist in the years following 1879. Since his era historians of economics have tended to perpetuate the neglect of *Progress and Poverty*'s contribution to economic theory despite full awareness of George's significance as social critic and reformer.

Notes

1. *Progress and Poverty: An Inquiry into the Causes of Industrial Depressions and of Increase of Want with Increase of Wealth* was published privately in 1879, the first commercial edition appearing in 1880 with many subsequent editions, none significantly changed from the 1879 version. References here are to the frequently reprinted 50th anniversary edition (George 1929) to which all unspecified page references below refer and where the chapters most heavily drawn upon have the following page ranges: I.4(71–9), III.2(165–72), III.3(173–9), III.6(204–17), IV.2(230–43), IV.3(244–54), IV.4(255–60).

2. In defense of George it can be noted that he viewed capital as a fungible component of the broader stock of wealth accumulated by saving and not as a given magnitude devoted inelastically to production.

3. See, for example, p. 412. It should be stressed that George did in fact analyze land rent in Ricardian fashion, assuming free competition among many landowners.

4. George (1886) gave special emphasis to these matters but they had already been dealt with emphatically in *Progress and Poverty*.

5. George also placed considerable stress on the immiserizing effects of persistent business cycles but this facet of his thought will not be pursued here.

6. It can hardly be claimed that the possibility of scale or agglomeration economies had gone unnoticed—the writings of Adam Smith, Edward Gibbon Wakefield (on whom see Kittrell 1973), and the American protectionists led by Henry Carey are enough to refute such a claim. George's contribution was rather to fit these notions skillfully into a coherent macroeconomic framework with results strikingly different from those of the classical growth theory derived from David Ricardo.

7. See pp. 256-8. This point helps explain the apparent anomaly of an obsession with natural-resource limitations being bred in the vastness of the American West.

8. George hints at the implied assumption that increased efficiency is output augmenting: "If population be doubled, land of but 20 productiveness may yield to the same amount of labor as much as land of 30 productiveness could before yield" (p. 232).

9. To justify (1) assume that it holds only for $L>M$ (fixed) and that all agglomeration effects occur on lands where the M highest-yielding workers are employed. Then $A(L)B(L)$ is the output of the M workers employed on this land (increasing with overall labor force, L, due to specialization and agglomeration economies despite the fixity of the land area involved) while $A(L)F(L)$ is the output of the other L-M workers who work under the less propitious conditions where diminishing returns are significant and no agglomeration economies arise.

10. George, discussing rent, asserted, "I am using wages not in the sense of a quantity, but in the sense of a proportion" (p. 216) but did not adhere consistently to this usage. By implication he defined the real wage rate in terms of command over output as a whole, including a full share of manufactures and services. Had he assumed that workers predominantly consume primary products, whose relative prices rise as the natural-resource constraint tightens, his claim for adverse effects on labor could have been strengthened. He viewed the bare minimum to which real wages might be driven as a conventional subsistence level, suppressing population growth.

11. George continues (pp. 251–2) with a numerical example. Output per man at the margin is initially 20, but worker efficiency increases by 10 percent. If the output at the margin of a unit of labor *of the old efficiency* now falls to 18 (that is by 10 percent) when released workers have been re-employed, then the real wage is unchanged. If the fall is only to 19 the real wage increases by 5 percent. Any fall in the marginal yield raises rent, however.

12. To obtain (7) from (1), replace F(L) by F(L.E), treating A(L) and B(L) as

constants, on the reasonable assumption that specialization and agglomeration effects are unchanged if population is unchanged.

13. As George recognized (p.252), workers could always protect themselves collectively from a cut in real wages by reducing labor supply sufficiently to keep L.E constant.

14. On Marshall's early work on distribution and growth see Donoghue (1995) and Whitaker (1974).

References

Donoghue, Mark. (1995) "Classical Remnants in Marshall's Early Theory of Distribution," *European Journal of the History of Economic Thought*, Vol. 2 (Autumn), pp. 355–74.

George, Henry. (1886) *Protection or Free Trade*. New York: George.

George, Henry. (1929) *Progress and Poverty: Fiftieth Anniversary Edition*. New York: Robert Schalkenbach Foundation.

Kittrell, Edward R. (1973) "Wakefield's Scheme of Systematic Colonization and Classical Economics," *American Journal of Economics and Sociology*, Vol. 32 (January), pp.87–111.

Marshall, Alfred. (1888) "Wages and Profits," *Quarterly Journal of Economics*, Vol. 2 (January), pp. 218–23.

Whitaker, John K. (1974) "The Marshallian System in 1881: Distribution and Growth," *Economic Journal*, Vol. 84 (March), pp.1–17.

———. (1997) "Enemies or Allies? Henry George and Francis Amasa Walker One Century Later," *Journal of Economic Literature*, Vol. 35 (December), pp.1891–1915.

———. (1998) "Henry George on the Location of Economic Activity," pp.174–84 of Michel Bellet and Corine L'Harmet (eds), *Industry, Space and Competition: The Contribution of the Economists of the Past*. Cheltenham UK: Edward Elgar.

Modeling Agglomeration and Dispersion in City and Country

Gunnar Myrdal, François Perroux, and the New Economic Geography

By STEPHEN J. MEARDON[*]

ABSTRACT. The "new economic geography" is a recent body of litera-ture that seeks to explain how resources and production come to be concentrated spatially for reasons other than the standard "geo-graphic" ones. Unlike alternative explanations of the geographic dis-tribution of industry, the literature is not interdisciplinary. The new economic geography lies well within economics proper: it is an off-spring of international trade theory, with models characterized by in-creasing returns, factor mobility, and transportation costs. The models explain the distribution of industry in terms of the opposition of an ag-glomerating force, the interaction of transportation costs and increas-ing returns to scale, with a dispersing force, commonly the interaction of transportation costs and a partially fixed input or output market.

Some authors outside the new economic geography (e.g., Martin 1999) have criticized it as simplistic, irrelevant, or passé. They claim it employs overly abstract analysis, prioritizes mathematical technique over realistic explanation, and is reminiscent of the much earlier works of Gunnar Myrdal and François Perroux—in comparison to which, however, it falls short.

This paper investigates the similarities and differences between the new economic geography and the work of Myrdal and Perroux, who in the previous special issue of this journal were ranked by Zafirovsky (1999, pp. 596, 598) as among the leading twentieth century economic

*Stephen J. Meardon is assistant professor of economics at Williams College. His re-search interests include the history of economic thought, international trade theory, geographical economics, and Latin American area studies. A recent article authored by him and Craufurd Goodwin, "The International Dimension of American Economic Thought," appeared in Malcolm Rutherford (ed.), *The Economic Mind in America: Es-says in the History of American Economics*, Routledge, 1998.

American Journal of Economics and Sociology, Vol. 60, No. 1 (January, 2001).

sociologists. I examine how the techniques of analysis and intuitive explanations of agglomeration compare between these economic sociologists and the new economic geographers. The paper highlights what has been gained and what has been lost by the new economic geographers, who generally eschew interdisciplinary study.

IN THE PAST DECADE "the new economic geography" has emerged as a means of thinking about and modeling the spatial agglomeration of economic activity. Questions emblematic of the literature are, "Why, as late as 1957, was 64% of U.S. manufacturing employment concentrated in the Northeast and Eastern Mid-West?" (Krugman 1991b, p. 12), or "Why, as late as 1980, was 40% of Mexico's manufacturing employment concentrated in Mexico City?" (Krugman and Livas 1996, p. 138). The questions are answered in terms of interactions between just a few variables and parameters: transportation costs, a production technology featuring increasing returns to scale, and productive factors that are partly fixed and partly footloose.

Questions about the spatial arrangement of markets were not, of course, alien to economics prior to the new economic geography. In the past fifty years (not to mention the past one hundred and fifty) spatial questions have been central to some subdisciplines of economics, among them urban economics and regional science, whose practitioners outnumber the new economic geographers and continue to disseminate their own work in widely circulating scholarly journals. Claims that the new economic geography makes new forays into uncharted territory—or, as more commonly argued (e.g. Krugman 1995), partly charted but subsequently lost territory—are overstated.[1]

Nevertheless the models of the new economic geography have brought greater attention to spatial questions than was previously afforded in general interest economics journals. The models have awakened interest particularly among international economists, for whom one might think spatial questions would come naturally, but who instead have a longstanding tradition of modeling "wonderlands of no spatial dimensions."[2] Indeed it is by way of international economics that the new economic geography has found its way into the general interest journals, not vice versa. The "new international trade theory" of the 1980s gestated the new economic geography of the 1990s, and the latter bears the former's distinguishing features. Both employ the metaphor of a system of simultaneous equations to represent the interdependence of quantities and relative prices; both use the same technical tricks to make increasing returns to scale compatible with equilibria in which firms enter freely and make zero profits. Undoubtedly it is the new economic geography's use of these tools, not only understandable but *de rigueur* to mainstream economists, that has allowed it to attract widespread attention.

Naturally, attention has incited criticism. Among the most vocal critics are social scientists outside the mainstream of economics, whose largely methodological critiques could just as well be applied to other classes of models in economics. They are applied with particular force to the new economic geography, however, because the fragmentation of geographical economics along methodological lines in the mid-twentieth century left numerous alternative ways of thinking about the subject.[3] Whatever methods the new economic geography brings to bear, it is said they obscure rather than illuminate the relevant determinants of geographical location; whatever insights the new economic geography offers, it is said they were expressed earlier and more profoundly. As Paul Krugman has paraphrased the complaints of his critics, "it's obvious, it's wrong, and anyway they said it years ago" (Gans and Shepherd 1994, p. 178).

Perhaps the most pointed and detailed critique has been made by Ron Martin (1999), a geographer skeptical of the applicability of the simultaneous equations metaphor to the essential questions of geographic location. The metaphor is inapt, he argues, because it is too simplistic, abstracting from factors of paramount importance:

> Now, clearly, there are aspects of economic development in general, and spatial agglomeration, in particular, that do lend themselves to mathematical representation and modelling. But there are also severe epistemological and ontological limits to such a narrow approach. For one thing, it means that "messy" social, cultural, and institutional factors involved in spatial economic development are neglected. Since these factors cannot be reduced to or expressed in mathematical form they are assumed to be of secondary or marginal importance and, as Krugman puts it, are "best left to sociologists." But it is precisely the social, institutional, cultural and political embeddedness of local and regional economies that can play a key role in determining the possibilities for or constraints on development, and thus

why spatial agglomeration of economic activity occurs in particular places and not others (Martin 1999, p. 75).

One might read the preceding quotation as an argument that, given the present state of the discipline, economics is not the appropriate field in which to study the spatial arrangement of markets. If the new economic geography's methods are necessary to make mainstream economists pay attention to spatial questions, then maybe the social sciences were better off when more economists ignored the questions. The appropriate forum for discussing markets in geographic space is one where the debate will be centered on institutions, history, politics, and culture—aspects, as Martin (ibid., p. 77) puts it, "of *real* places." Perhaps the proper forum is geography; perhaps it is economic sociology.

Yet if the problem with the new economic geography is that it is not enough like economic sociology, there is an apparently incongruous fact to be explained. Two earlier authors whom new economic geographers claim as their progenitors are Gunnar Myrdal and François Perroux[4]—both of whom Zafirovsky (1999, pp. 596, 598) identifies in the previous special issue of this journal as pioneers of economic sociology. Two sets of questions spring to mind. In what terms did Myrdal and Perroux frame their explanations of agglomeration or dispersion of markets, and what conceptual tools did they use? Notwithstanding the ancestral claims of the new economic geography, how does the literature differ from the work of these two economic sociologists—and what has been gained, and what has been lost?

I

The New Economic Geography

In trying to answer the questions posed above I will work backwards, beginning by defining the new economic geography more carefully and then considering the older works of Perroux and Myrdal in contrast.

As I define it—and as I believe most others intend, however latently, to use the term—the new economic geography is a literature employing models that:

1. are of a general equilibrium nature, in that they consist of a sys-

tem of equations wherein prices and quantities are determined simultaneously, firms enter freely and make zero profits in equilibrium, and economy-wide resource constraints are specified;

2. feature increasing returns to scale production technologies, providing a rationale for the concentration of production in locations that may differ from the initial locations of productive factors;

3. employ a monopolistically competitive market structure, usually (but not necessarily) the Dixit and Stiglitz (1977) formulation, to overcome the difficulties in obtaining criteria (1) and (2) simultaneously;

4. have a spatial geometry that is not only expressed in notation ($x_{i,j}$ denotes good i produced in region j), but also is implicit in the parameterization of the model. For example, locations 1, 2, and 3 could be assumed to form an isosceles triangle in geographic space if transport costs between all three pairs, in any direction, are equal;

5. allow at least one productive factor to be mobile between locations, so the rationale of spatial concentration can be realized and the initial locations of productive factors can be altered.

The works that meet these criteria are sufficiently numerous to deserve some kind of collective name; yet at the same time they are sufficiently few, and written by sufficiently few authors, that Krugman (1998a) appears more comfortable referring to the new economic geography as a "genre" rather than a "subdiscipline." By far the most widely discussed article that meets the criteria is Krugman (1991a), which is cited 220 times by articles indexed by the SSCI.[5] Other influential contributions—whose citation counts, however, differ from the latter's by an order of magnitude—have been Krugman and Venables (1995: 49 citations), Krugman (1993: 38 citations), Venables (1996: 33 citations), Fujita and Krugman (1995: 28 citations), and Puga and Venables (1996, 1997: 7 and 10 citations). Fujita, Krugman, and Venables (1999) recapitulated the methods and insights of the literature produced thus far in a book, as Helpman and Krugman (1985) did for the new trade theory.

Articles about the economics of geographical space that ask different questions, use different methods, or generally have a different flavor than those cited above tend to meet some but not all of the definition's five criteria. A couple of examples should help illustrate the point. August Lösch's (1950) model has an explicit spatial geometry as in criterion (4), and is, in a sense, a general equilibrium system—albeit not in the sense of (1). Within any firm's market area, other firms are assumed not to enter. The system determines quantities of goods, their prices, and the spatial dimensions of hexagonal market areas that are *assumed to be* spread evenly throughout the geographical plane. Lösch's model thus addresses the geographical breadth of markets but not their uneven concentration.

A less well known example of spatial modeling that is in some respects closer to the new economic geography, but still distinctly different from it, is found in Bruce Benson and James Hartigan's (1984, 1987) models of spatial competition. Their models were intended to wed Lösch to the emerging "new trade theory" models of Brander (1981) and Brander and Krugman (1983), whose own purpose was to explain the ubiquity of intra-industry trade (also known as "reciprocal dumping" or "cross-hauling"). A compelling theoretical explanation of intra-industry trade was a paramount objective of new trade theorists, who observed the phenomenon empirically but could not make sense of it within the confines of the Heckscher-Ohlin model. Brander and Krugman explained intra-industry trade using a model in which Cournot-competing firms in two nations served the consumers of both nations; Benson and Hartigan extended this model to make space more explicit: consumers were assumed to be distributed along a line whereupon domestic and foreign producers were located at the ends and the national border was located somewhere in the middle. Transportation costs had to be incurred to ship goods to consumers in proportion to their distance from producers. Intra-industry trade was therefore likely to be observed near the border, where substantial transport costs would be incurred in shipments from *either* domestic or foreign producers.

Benson and Hartigan's extension thus allowed them to maintain the intra-industry trade result of other new trade theorists while locating their model in a slightly more real (one-dimensional rather than no-dimensional) spatial setting. Incorporating space also allowed them to address topics other than intra-industry trade, namely the spatial distribution of the effects of a tariff on the real incomes of consumers. Relating their work to the new economic geography, it would appear they met criteria (2) and (4). They missed (1) only because in their free-entry version of the model there is no economy-wide resource constraint. They did not meet (3) or (5). This is not to suggest however that their work was somehow less evolved than the new economic geography. But, they did not at all aspire to write in that genre, not only because it did not exist at the time, but also because, like Lösch, they wished to address different questions.

The same is true of products of the new trade theory, many of which resemble the new economic geography even more closely than Benson and Hartigan's models. Indeed there are some works—notably by Krugman (1980), Avinash Dixit and Victor Norman (1980, ch. 9), and Elhanan Helpman (1981)—that meet all the criteria but (5). These too are addressed to different questions, however: again, chiefly intra-industry trade and other consequences to international trade of increasing returns to scale. Like the models of Lösch and Benson and Hartigan, then, it would be inappropriate to lump these in with the new economic geography. At this point, though, it is important to note that we are now considering literature from which the new economic geography differs by little more than a tweak of the model and a change of emphasis. In fact that is precisely how the new economic geography evolved.

In sum, the five criteria listed previously for the definition of the new economic geography serve not only in themselves to distinguish the literature from others; in addition they reflect the questions towards which the literature is directed, which also distinguish it from others. Many other "spatial" works, though they employ models that are similar in many respects, do not share the new economic geography's concerns: their models are intended to help explain market areas, or spatial competition, or intra-industry trade. The new economic geography asks instead: aside from the usual "geographical" determinants like rivers and mountains, what determines the spatial agglomeration or dispersion of economic activity?

The first step towards answering the question is to define "agglomeration" in the context of the model. Agglomeration is taken to mean that more monopolistically competitive firms are located in one region than in another. Increasing returns to scale at the firm level implies that each monopolistic competitor will be the sole producer of its own variety, which it can choose to produce in one region or another. If firms agglomerate in one or a few regions, they do so impelled by pecuniary externalities that arise from the interaction of increasing returns with transportation costs between regions.

Suppose for illustration that there are two regions situated at the ends of a line, the length of which is given by the transportation costs between the regions (so that our model meets criterion 4). Consumers, who are also laborers and who can move between regions (criterion 5), derive utility from two types of goods. One good is produced perfectly competitively using land, endowed equally to each region, and labor; the other good is produced in numerous varieties by monopolistic competitors (criterion 3, and by implication criteria 2 and 1) using labor alone. Assume initially that the number of laborers and the number of monopolistically competitive firms is divided evenly between the regions. To begin with, then, there is no agglomeration.

Suppose now, though, that a new profit opportunity in one region induces entry there of an additional monopolistically competitive firm and hence production of an additional variety. That region now becomes more agglomerated relative to the other region. More importantly, pecuniary externalities may cause the agglomeration to grow cumulatively.

The pecuniary externalities function as follows: the consumer price index decreases in the agglomerated region relative to the other region, because consumers in the more agglomerated region now do not have to pay transport costs for the majority of the varieties they consume. Nominal wages increase in the more agglomerated region because, as a result of the additional firm's entry, there is greater aggregate production and thus greater demand for labor. Higher nominal wages eliminate the profit opportunity that the firm entered to exploit, but meanwhile something has changed: with a lower price index and higher nominal wages, real wages are now higher in the more agglomerated region than in the less agglomerated region. This induces laborers to migrate to the more agglomerated region; once they have done so, nominal wages there decrease. At given prices, however, lower nominal wages imply additional profit opportunities. So there is entry of additional firms in the more agglomerated region, which sets the same process in motion once again.

The limit of cumulative agglomeration is determined by the degree to which the agglomerating force is balanced by a dispersing force. In this example, the dispersing force is comprised of the laborers who choose to stay behind in the less agglomerated region, motivated by its abundant land.[6] They demand the varieties produced in the monopolistically competitive sector, so there remains a motive for the producers of some varieties to locate near them. The dispersing force is greatest with either very high or very low transportation costs: with very high transport costs the dispersed output market can only be served with very dispersed production; with very low transport costs there will be little incentive for laborers to move in the first place, because the consumer price index will not differ much between regions—and the more laborers remain dispersed, the more production will be dispersed.

The model described above differs only slightly from the one in Krugman's (1991a) influential paper.[7] Indeed, most work in the new economic geography consists of theoretical wrinkles on the preceding story. There is some, however, which also endeavors to be a bit more applied: one example is Krugman and Livas (1996), who view Mexico through the lenses of the new economic geography, attempting "to explain why so much population and industry concentrated in Mexico City in the first place" (p. 138). Their basic set-up is similar to the model described above insofar as the Dixit and Stiglitz monopolistically competitive market structure underlies everything, fulfilling criteria (1) through (3). The geometry that fulfills criterion (4) is different, though: there are three regions situated at the apexes of an isosceles triangle pointed upwards, the uppermost apex representing the United States and the lower two representing Mexican regions. Moreover, while labor is mobile between the two Mexican regions, allowing the model to meet criterion (5) in the same fashion as the model described above, the dispersing force is different: in this case, bearing in mind the reality of Mexico City, it is the cost of congestion in the more-agglomerated region that constitutes the dispersing force, not a partially dispersed output market.

The model's insight is that the high tariff barrier maintained by Mexico prior to 1986 may have played a role in promoting excessive agglomeration in Mexico City. Cut off from the United States, immense agglomeration in one of the two Mexican regions was practically inevitable. Under free trade, firms would have wanted to locate wherever they could serve the U.S. market more cheaply; but as it happened, given high trade barriers, they wanted to serve the Mexican market—which was to be found wherever Mexican firms had already located.

The insights the model shares with others in the new economic geography are the cumulative logic of agglomeration once it gets started; the possibility of multiple equilibria, meaning that if there is to be agglomeration it could just as well be in one region as in another; and given the latter possibility, the dependence of the actual equilibrium on initial conditions or "history." Mexico City rather than Puebla is Mexico's primal city, in other words, not because of contemporary advantages to Mexico City's geographical location (to the contrary!), but because of a small difference in the cities' relative sizes that appeared in the late nineteenth century and then expanded cumulatively and spectacularly.[8]

The question of whether these insights into agglomeration are profound, relevant, and novel—or instead "obvious, wrong, and anyway they said it years ago"—remains to be addressed. If not a definitive answer, an advantageous perspective can be gained by comparing the approaches of Gunnar Myrdal and François Perroux to the same subject.

II

Perroux

ZAFIROVSKY (1999, P. 596) LISTS FRANÇOIS PERROUX'S *Économie et Société* (1960)[9] among the works of a "distinct economic school (in France) guided by the premises of economic sociology," namely the premise that economic behavior is "embedded in institutions, norms, and values." Of course few economists would disagree that such factors are important, but nevertheless most have proved willing, for the sake of mathematical modeling, to set them aside or make severe simplifying assumptions about their influence. François Perroux (1903–1987) was an exception. His analysis, not only in *Économie and Société* but throughout his oeuvre, was based on the belief that neoclassical economics has consigned itself to irrelevancy because it abstracts away from the most important aspects of economic behavior. One of the most fundamental and omnipresent characteristics of market interactions, claimed Perroux, is asymmetry of power between the actors. Asymmetrical power relations are present in interactions between similar decision making units—whether individuals, firms, regions, or nations—just as commonly as between dissimilar units. In this way Perroux's ideas about regional agglomeration stemmed from his economic sociology: to him, regional agglomeration resulted from, and was itself a manifestation of, power exercised in geographical space.

One might then wonder wherein lies the affinity of new economic geographers for his work. And one might wonder all the more given Perroux's long-running critique of general equilibrium modeling in the tradition of Léon Walras, Vilfredo Pareto, and Gustav Cassel, since modeling in that tradition constitutes criterion (1) of the new economic geography.

The critique of general equilibrium modeling lay at the foundation of Perroux's work throughout his career (1970 [1950], p. 93; 1963 [1960], pp. 66–73; 1967 [1965], p. 15–19; 1983, pp. 61–65; 1988b, pp. 82–86), and is expressed succinctly by an aphorism Perroux appropriated from Oskar Morgenstern: "there is no road from L. Walras to reality" (1988b, p. 83). Specifically, the reliance of the standard general equilibrium model on assumptions of perfect competition and atomistic agents constitutes an unacceptable departure from the real world, which is characterized by imperfect competition and agents' exercise of power or submission to coercion:

> Ingeniously constructed, it does away with all *activity* by any human *agent*; the decision-maker could be replaced by a robot which records the price and can accordingly make the necessary adjustments in the use of the quantities available. Although *this* particular, so-called general, equilibrium is now challenged by seasoned economists from all over the world, it is still a model that is commonly taught, reformulated in various mathematical styles, but left intact as regards its basic structure. And *that* very structure is essentially misleading for the crucial reason that it assumes that things and goods are ordered by allegedly neutral market forces instead of

allowing for human activity, for people's ability to change and to change their material and human environment (1983, p. 63).

The critique was intended to clear the stage for the positive contribution of Perroux: a "new theory of interdependence" characterized by "deviation from the pattern of perfect competition" and "rejection of the idea of considering individuals to be annihilated." He proposed to reconstruct general equilibrium theory "starting with the agents or 'actors' and active units" (1983, pp. 69-70).

Rejecting Walrasian general equilibrium and starting afresh did not mean, however, rejecting all existing models and mathematical methods. Perroux approved of Edward Chamberlin's theory of monopolistic competition (going so far as to write the preface to Chamberlin's French edition) because within the model of interdependent producers, each of which exercised market power, he saw some of "the tools we need, in order gradually to integrate, in a rigorous and realistic theory, the facts of economic inequality, economic power, and irreversible economic influences, which cannot be assimilated to the analysis of pure and perfect competition" (1955 [1953], p. 138). And while Chamberlin did not lay out a mathematical general equilibrium formalization of monopolistic competition, Perroux perceived changes in mathematical economics that made such a formalization possible:

> The most notable change has been the shift from the somewhat discredited mathematics taken over from Lagrange's classical mechanics to topological mathematics, following G. Debreu and K. J. Arrow. The former describes the movement in space of indeformable objects and their halting (point of equilibrium when two equal and contrary forces are applied to them). The latter admits of spaces lending themselves to contraction, expansion and deformation and representing the operations of economic agents; it describes the successive equilibria while setting limiting conditions; it amplifies all the models of monopolistic competition, while retaining all they have to teach us (1983, p. 186).

Trying to impart the feel of the sort of model he had in mind, a model of interdependence among 'active units,' Perroux (1962 [1960], ch. 2; 1967 [1965], ch. 1) took a basic static general equilibrium model as point of departure. Considering a profit function for a firm employing n inputs,

$$\Pi = P_v Q - p_1 q_1 - p_2 q_2 , \ldots, - p_n q_n$$

he posited several such firms (or other units) which, rather than taking market prices as given and choosing optimally their output, instead find themselves subject to an external power that imposes the prices they face or the output they produce:

> a power (C) imposes, for example, the *quantity* . . . that must be sold by unit U_1 [indicated by a "+" above the variable]:

$$\Pi_1 = P_{v1} \overset{+}{Q_1} - p_1 q_1 - p_2 q_2 , \ldots, - p_n q_n$$

or, for example, the price of inputs purchased by U_2:

$$\Pi_2 = P_{v2} Q_2 - \overset{+}{p_1} q_1 - \overset{+}{p_2} q_2 , \ldots, - \overset{+}{p_n} q_n$$

or, for example, the price of the product sold by U_3:

$$\Pi_3 = P_{v3} \overset{+}{Q_3} - p_1 q_1 - p_2 q_2 , \ldots, - p_n q_n$$

> It is possible to conceive of diverse combinations [of C's influence on the subordinate units] and translate them into this notation (1967 [1965], p. 18. Author's translation.).

Diagrammatically, Perroux depicted the relationships between C, U_1, U_2, and U_3 as shown in Figure 1.

Explaining further, he wrote,

> The preceding implies an action that is *asymmetric* and *irreversible* during a time period. The action extends from C towards U_1, U_2, . . . , U_n, and not in the opposite direction. . . . This asymmetric action admits gradations: from total domination of C over a unit (U_1, U_2, . . . , U_n), to a *very limited influence* exercised by C over one of the units (ibid., pp. 18-19).

Following Perroux's rejection of the Walrasian model and his call for a new model of interdependence to replace it, the exposition above can be frustrating to read. It is not, after all, a replacement. There is no way to measure, for example, the response of U_2 to changes in its input prices—much less the response of U_3 to U_2's response. Exercises in comparative statics or dynamics are impossible because the model is not specified mathematically; rather it is described textually with the aid of some algebraic notation. That by no means invalidates Perroux's

Figure 1

Domination of "active unit" C over units U_1, U_2, and U_3.

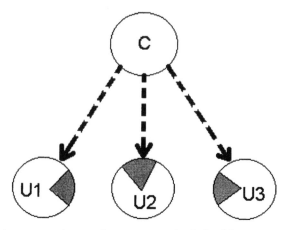

Author's reproduction from Perroux (1967 [1965], pp. 18–19).

ideas, but he leaves the reader expecting something more revolution-ary: a mathematically specified general equilibrium model that fulfills the same functions as the Walrasian model, but in addition captures the exercise of market and extra-market power that the Walrasian model entirely misses. The reader never finds it.

Nevertheless Perroux's ideas of power and domination became quite influential, reaching the apex of their popularity in the 1960s. At that time, insofar as the ideas were embodied in the concepts of "growth poles" and "development poles," they were adopted enthusiastically by regional planners (Parr 1999, p. 1195). As Perroux defines the concepts, for given sets of units (whether agents, firms or industries),

> the *growth pole* is a set that has the capacity to induce growth of another set ("growth" being defined as a lasting increase in the dimensional indica-tor); the *pole of development* is a set that has the capacity to engender a dia-lectic of economic and social structures whose effect is to increase the complexity of the whole and expand its multidimensional return (1988a, p. 49).

The link between domination and the growth pole or development pole is "l'industrie motrice," the propulsive industry. Because units exercise asymmetric effects upon one another, some hold the ability, as they expand, to induce expansion in others. Whereas in general competitive equilibrium firms are interdependent through prices alone, in Perroux's system "the profit of a firm is a function of its output, of its inputs, and of the output and inputs of another firm" (1970 [1955], p. 96). And this is true not only of firms: "what has been said of the interrelations between firms can also be said of the interrelations between industries" (ibid., p. 96). Industries that generate profit opportunities in other industries as they expand are "propulsive industries," constituting "poles" of growth in economic space.

In discussing propulsive industries Perroux refers explicitly to Tibor Scitovsky's 1954 article "Two Concepts of External Economies." In the article Scitovsky distinguishes between *technological* externalities, wherein the output and factor utilization of one firm enter the production function of another firm, and *pecuniary* externalities, wherein the output and factor utilization of one firm affect the profits of another firm but *do not* enter its production function (Scitovsky 1954, pp. 145–146). Perroux's language immediately before his citation of Scitovsky, describing a relationship between one firm's profit and other firm's output or inputs, but not necessarily a direct functional link between one firm's output and another firm's output or inputs, indicates that he was thinking of pecuniary externalities in particular. A growth pole, then, could be defined alternatively as a center in economic space from which growth is spread among industries through pecuniary externalities.

The use of "economic space" rather than "geographical space" in the definition of growth poles is deliberate. Perroux insisted that the pecuniary externalities generated by a propulsive firm or industry might be circumscribed in "banal" geographical space, or they might not be (1950, pp. 95-96). Regional agglomeration was supposed to be just one special case of the growth pole concept, and regional planning just one of its applications.

But due to enthusiasm for the concept among regional planners, agglomeration became its *predominant* application. Jaques Boudeville (1966) was an influential author who employed "regional operational models," including regional input-output matrices, in an effort to develop the regional application of growth poles. Boudeville furthermore advocated the implementation of planned poles in France by means of regionally targeted investment in public services and financial incentives to private industry. Outside of Perroux's home territory, Harry W. Richardson and Margaret Richardson (1975) discussed generally similar growth pole strategies in Chile, Peru, Venezuela, Colombia, Bolivia, Argentina, Brazil, and Mexico. A volume edited by Kuklinski (1972) includes chapters applying the growth pole concept to regional policy in Canada, India, Libya, Poland, Sweden, and Tanzania. The appeal of the regional application of growth poles was world-wide—and owed much to the intellectual framework it provided for state planning that would have happened, in some fashion, one way or another. "Growth poles," wrote Friedmann and Forest (1988, p. 117), "emerged as the central planning doctrine."

Research and advocacy of planned regional poles expanded from the 1960s through the mid-1970s. During the research program's ascendancy, insufficient attention may have been paid to the question of whether planned poles were equivalent to poles that had evolved independent of planning, or for that matter whether poles could be planned successfully in the first place (Parr 1999, p. 1198). These matters of confusion and others contributed to disappointment with growth pole strategies in the mid to late 1970s, which in turn led to a decline in the influence of the growth pole concept.[10]

Perroux, however, became ever more interested in the regional application of his ideas. Shortly before his death he prepared an essay (Perroux 1988a) for a conference held in his honor on regional economic development. This essay may be the most complete exposition he made of the geographical application of growth poles.

To demonstrate "in a first approximation" an application of the growth pole concept in geographical space, Perroux posits a large multinational firm operating in a developing country either on its own or through a subsidiary. Inside of the firm's territorial space, T, it acts within an "operations space" and, more narrowly, a "decision space." The multinational firm shares its territorial space with agricultural units, small industries, commercial shops, local public services, and individuals. Market interactions between the multinational and selected subsets of the smaller units are called "itineraries," or channels; they are represented by arrows (running from the dominant to the dominated units) in Perroux's "diagram of channels," shown in Figure 2. The main transport and communication routes also appear in the diagram.

What does figure 2 reveal, and how does it tie into the rest of Perroux's thought? As he explains it,

> This diagram places in opposition: A development which will mainly bene-
> fit the big firm and the agglomerated area, and a development which will
> benefit the whole population. The big firm has extensive and intensive re-
> lations with the exterior: with its head office if it is a subsidiary, or with its

Figure 2

Diagram of channels for "Territory T."

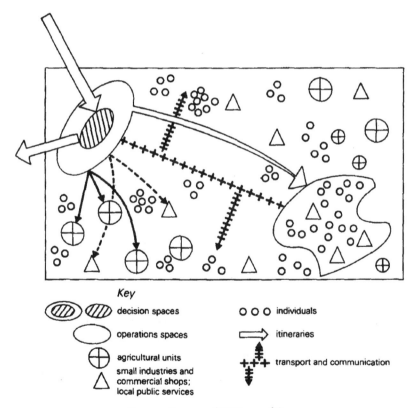

Source: Perroux (1988a, p. 62).

main partner if it is an associated company; therefore, we shall say that in order to develop the entire population on the whole territory, we must define and then implement interior exchange channels (1988a, p. 63).

Perroux has in mind using government action to turn the "growth pole" that the multinational firm represents, and the territorial agglomeration of selected individuals and commercial units that interact with it, into a "development pole" that benefits units not initially included in its itineraries. The action may be as simple as the creation or improvement of lines of transportation and communication. It may be implemented in a number of different ways, including "the spontaneous agreement of the big firm," "the rational consent of the big firm to direction by the authorities," "methodical negotiation between the firm and the authorities," or "constraining pressure" applied to the big firm by the political authorities (ibid., p. 64).

Very well, but does this vision of dominant firms, growth poles and agglomeration constitute a *theory*? The reader might once again be left with the feeling of getting something less than he was promised. Perroux was dogged by such perceptions throughout his career, notwithstanding his ever more emphatic dissent: "contrary to hasty and superficial statements, it can be said that the pole of development is situated within an already articulated and coherent general theory" (1988b, p. 54). Benjamin Higgins (1988, 32) leaves no doubt that Perroux was highly respected by many of his peers, and notes that he was nominated several times for the Nobel prize. Higgins also (ibid., p. 46) cites H. W. Spiegel's assessment of him as "the only living economist who developed a theoretical system rivaling conventional equilibrium analysis." Yet Higgins and Spiegel's assessments do not represent a clear consensus. There are others who would agree with Mark Blaug (1964, p. 563): "unfortunately, the theory is unsatisfactory . . . , being in principle non-falsifiable: it is simply a slogan masquerading as a theory."

The debate will not be settled here. Whether penetrating theory or pretentious slogan, Perroux's work on regional agglomeration can be characterized as emphasizing the role of pecuniary externalities generated by the activities of dominant units, as well as asymmetries of power among units. The sociological nature of the work lies primarily in the latter facet.

III

Myrdal

UPON AWARDING GUNNAR MYRDAL (1898–1987) the 1974 Nobel Prize for Economic Science jointly with Friedrich von Hayek, the Royal Swedish Academy of Sciences referred to three of his works: *The Political Element in Economic Theory* (1954 [1932]), *An American Dilemma* (1944), and *Asian Drama* (1968).[11] The books, regarding respectively the value premises of economic theory, poverty among black Americans, and underdevelopment in south Asian countries, are more closely related than their titles and their disparate dates of publication would seem to indicate. Like Perroux, Myrdal persisted throughout his career in criticizing mainstream economic thought and developing a theoretical concept that could not be exposited within the mainstream. Also like Perroux he applied his concept to numerous areas of study, of which spatial agglomeration was just one, and he did so in a manner that reached beyond economics into sociology and the study of institutions. Of the three books cited by the Nobel committee, *The Political Element* expresses most comprehensively Myrdal's critique of neoclassical economics, while *American Dilemma* and *Asian Drama* represent two applications of his theoretical concept.

The concept was that of "cumulative causation": the possibility that changes in a given variable in the social system will "not call forth countervailing changes but, instead, supporting changes, which move the system in the same direction as the first change but much further" (Myrdal 1957, p. 13). The concept is basically that of the "vicious cycle" or "virtuous circle"—and so, stated in its most basic terms and without a broader context, is of course not an idea for which Myrdal sought priority.

Myrdal acknowledged Knut Wicksell's influence in turning his thoughts towards cumulative processes. In *Monetary Equilibrium* (1939), Myrdal both criticized and developed Wicksell's theory of business cycles, subjecting the theory to an "immanent criticism" that renovated its edifice while maintaining its foundation (1939, p. 31). The foundation was Wicksell's notion of the cumulative causation of the cycle. As Myrdal relates the theory (ibid., pp. 24–28), if the money rate of interest were to deviate negatively from what is defined as the "natural" rate of interest, firms would be encouraged to accumulate capital. In addition the present discounted value of firms' future receipts would rise, increasing the value of their capital stock and encouraging "more roundabout processes of production," implying yet more reallocation of resources from direct production of consumption goods towards production of capital goods. This would raise the relative prices of consumption goods, raising entrepreneurs' price expectations and further increasing capital values—which would encourage yet more capital accumulation, and so on. A negative difference between the money rate of interest and the natural rate of interest would thus spur a cumulative economic expansion.

Following his critique and elaboration of Wicksell's theory, Myrdal began to discern cumulative causation in variables far removed from questions of business cycles. In 1937 Myrdal was invited by the Carnegie Foundation to undertake a comprehensive study of the "negro problem" in the United States, the results of which he published in 1944 as *An American Dilemma*. Once more, as in *Monetary Equilibrium*, his analysis was couched in terms of cumulative processes:

> White prejudice and discrimination keep the Negro low in standards of living, health, education, manners and morals. This, in its turn, gives support to white prejudice. White prejudice and Negro standards thus mutually "cause" each other. ... If either of the factors change, this will cause a change in the other factor, too, and start a process of interaction where the change in one factor will continuously be supported by the reaction of the other factor. The whole system will be moving in the direction of the primary change, but much further. This is what we mean by cumulative causation (1944, p. 76).

His analysis in *American Dilemma* revealed an additional characteristic of Myrdal's approach which became more visible in his work thereafter. He believed, as one author put it, that "there were no 'economic' problems, but rather that society's problems were complex and not simply economic, sociological, political, or psychological" (Angresano 1997, p. 61). An adequate diagnosis of problems might entail reaching into all of these fields and more, and in all of them the principle of cumulative causation would very likely be applicable (ibid., p. 90).[12] Myrdal's application of the principle to regional issues commenced, at the latest, during his tenure from 1947 to 1957 as Executive Secretary of the United Nations Economic Commission of Europe. His experience there informed the material he drew together for a set of lectures published in 1957 as *Economic Theory and Under-Developed Regions*[13] (Agresano 1997, p. 70), and influenced also his later writings in *Asian Drama* (1968) and *The Challenge of World Poverty* (1970).

In these three books Myrdal showed how cumulative causation was fundamental in explaining international and interregional disparities of income. As such disparities are reflections of agglomeration of production and wealth in geographical space, and insofar as Myrdal did not confine himself *solely* to explaining differences between nations with arbitrary frontiers, but rather viewed space more seamlessly, it can be fairly said that he developed a theory of spatial agglomeration even if he did not use the term.

On the international level, Myrdal explained that "[b]y circular causation and cumulative effects, a country superior in productivity and incomes will become more superior, while a country on an inferior level will tend to be held down at that level or even to deteriorate further—as long as matters are left to the free unfolding of market forces" (1970, p. 279). He discussed the cumulative mechanism in terms of a tension between the "backwash effects" of international trade and capital flows that promote inequality, and the "spread effects" that mitigate it. The backwash effects consist of "internal and external economies" (ibid., pp. 279–80): economies of scale and the growth of knowledge through innovation, which tend to raise agricultural productivity, allow manufacturers to economize in the use of raw materials, and encourage entrepreneurs to develop substitute products for the exports of underdeveloped countries. (As an example of the operation of backwash effects Myrdal cited the invention and marketing of synthetic coffee [ibid., p. 41], which reduced the rich countries' demand for one of the underdeveloped countries' key exports.) The spread effects, on the other hand, consist of the purchase of domestic inputs by foreign investors in underdeveloped countries, as well as the transfer of skills and the "spirit of enterprise." Because foreign investments in underdeveloped countries often take the form of "enclave economies" which employ no domestic resources other than low-skilled labor, and as poor countries are often torn by racial strife and cultural differences that hamper the transfer of skills and entrepreneurism, the backwash effects commonly overwhelm the spread effects (ibid., p. 282). Indeed, the greater the disparities that already exist between trading countries, the more likely are the backwash effects to dominate, widening cumulatively the disparities.

The same mechanism, claimed Myrdal, operates on an interregional level:

> We can see these effects of the working of the market forces also within a country. A "growing point" established by the location of a factory or any other expansional move, will draw to itself other businesses, skilled labor, and capital. It will by the same token have backwash effects that keep down or even impoverish out-regions, if the spread effects are not strong enough. This theory is confirmed by the observable tendency for poorer countries to have greater regional differences in income than richer countries (ibid., p. 280).

Furthermore, if the "cumulative causation" view of regional agglomeration is correct, then one could say that the foremost reason for the great disparities between rich regions and poor regions is just that long ago, perhaps by accident, there had arisen small disparities:

> [W]ithin broad limits the power of attraction of a [commercial] center today has its origin mainly in the historical accident that something was once started there and not in a number of other places where it could equally well or better have been started, and that the start met with success. Thereafter the ever-increasing internal and external economies—interpreted in the widest sense of the word to include, for instance, a working population trained in various crafts, easy communication, the feeling of growth and elbow room, and the spirit of new enterprise—fortified and sustained their continuous growth at the expense of other localities and regions where, instead, relative stagnation or regression became the pattern (1957, p. 27).

This "accidental" view of regional disparities resulting from cumulative causation lent both practical guidance and moral force to Myrdal's policy proposals to counteract them. For practical effect the greatest policy changes would have to take place in the underdeveloped countries, where "strategic variables" such as corruption in the public sector would have to be targeted to catalyze the cumulative process in the opposite direction (1970, pp. 241-52). Yet the developed countries, too, had a substantial role to play: they had a moral imperative to support a "welfare world" in which they would not only extend aid, but also relax their trade barriers without expecting the underdeveloped countries to reciprocate (ibid., pp. 292–301). The moral imperative was not rooted in the observation that the developed countries' relative wealth was a "historical accident," but was surely made more persuasive by it.

The root source of the moral imperative was neither more nor less than a value premise: "the egalitarian ideal" (ibid., p. 294). Myrdal admitted that while he could investigate and explain the likely economic consequences of his policy prescriptions, the question of whether or not they *should* be followed was not an economic question: "*this is, at bottom, a moral issue*" (ibid., p. 301. Myrdal's italics).

It might seem that in touching on moral issues we stray from Myrdal's theory of agglomeration. But in fact one his more important points, which he made in *The Political Element* early in his career and continued to stress thereafter, was that the economist can not separate his value premises from his economics; the best he can do is state his value premises explicitly. The consequences of *not* doing so, Myrdal believed, are observable (if one looks very carefully) in neoclassical economics—and his theory of agglomeration was inextricably related to his critique of neoclassical economics.

To Myrdal, many of the common assumptions of neoclassical economics were "analytical ideal types" that tended to "turn all too easily into political ideals" (1954 [1932], p. 104). Competitive firms and the representative utility-maximizing agent, he thought, were useful devices in the neoclassical theory of price formation, which was "harmless as it stands" (ibid., p. 88); the problem was that those who developed the theory, W. S. Jevons, Léon Walras, Carl Menger, and Eugen von Böhm-Bawerk, sought to use their individualistic value theory to construct, purportedly without normative preconceptions, a more sweeping theory of social value. As evidence Myrdal quoted Jevons's definition of the essential problem of economics: to find, for a given population, "the mode of employing their labor which will maximize the utility of the produce" (ibid., p. 17). To the extent that Jevons and others found the political principle of economic liberalism to solve the social utility maximization problem, Myrdal asserted that they must have committed a fallacy: political principles governing people with heterogeneous value systems can *never* be inferred without premises regarding whose values are to be prioritized.

In Jevons's case the fallacy lay in the assumption of interpersonal comparison of utilities. To the contrary, claimed Myrdal, utilities can not be compared interpersonally; therefore, an analysis that assumes the opposite and concludes with an endorsement of economic liberalism has really just stumbled unwittingly into its own normative preconceptions—certainly not any meaningful conclusions (ibid., p. 88). Thus, with respect to the extension of neoclassical economics to a theory of social value,

> [w]ith great theoretical ingenuity nothing more was accomplished than an elaborate formulation of tautology based on circular definitions. It was the function of this very complicated modern theory of value . . . to mask the specific logical errors which permit the inference of political norms (ibid., p. 16).

Myrdal believed the same to be true of the neoclassical trade theory elaborated by Eli Heckscher and Bertil Ohlin. Here it was the "unrealistic assumption of stable equilibrium" that was the culprit, having "opened the way for the ideological predilections that since classical times have been deeply embedded in all economic theory but particularly in the theory of international trade" (1970, p. 277). Neoclassical trade theory *began by looking* for a stable equilibrium—and found it, with factor price equalization, under free trade. The theory would lead one to believe that international inequalities would be mitigated, and under certain conditions entirely eliminated, by free trade. According to Myrdal that conclusion was invalid, constituting no more than "*a bias—opportune to the people in developed countries*" (ibid., p. 278. Myrdal's italics.). He argued, as we have already seen, that the theory was false: free trade as well as capital flows tended to *increase* international inequalities by a process of cumulative causation. The predominant trade theory was thus just convenient intellectual cover for the value premise, unstated and perhaps held unconsciously, that the rich countries should continue to benefit at the expense of the poor.

In part because the predominant trade theory was opportune for developed countries it was perpetuated, in one form or another but substantively intact, from the classics through the twentieth century. And because the theory proved so durable in spite of its weaknesses, Myrdal's development of the concept of cumulative causation was more revolutionary than a basic statement of it would have it seem. The concept was integral to a comprehensive critique of the substance, method, and value premises of neoclassical economics, with which cumulative causation was fundamentally incompatible. Having demonstrated the incompatibility, Myrdal applied the concept to numerous subjects of interdisciplinary social science research.

In sum, Myrdal's theory of agglomeration was part of a holistic alternative research program. Its main components were a critique of predominant economic theory, the development and interdisciplinary application of the concept of cumulative causation, and the proposal of public policies intended to reduce international, interregional, and even interracial inequalities—all founded upon explicitly stated value premises.

IV

Comparing the Approaches

THE INITIAL QUESTIONS OF THIS ESSAY remain to be resolved: how is it that the new economic geographers claim economic sociologists like Myrdal and Perroux as their progenitors, while at the same time their work is criticized for lacking the characteristics of economic sociology? What does the new economic geography have in common with Myrdal and Perroux, what does it add to them, and what does it lack entirely?

To his credit, Krugman (1999) has confronted the new economic geography (and the new trade theory) with similar questions, albeit vis-à-vis Bertil Ohlin rather than Myrdal and Perroux. Having posed the question "Was it all in Ohlin?", Krugman answers "no"—although with qualifications and with genuine appreciation of Ohlin's work. Krugman finds that Ohlin anticipated the new economic geography's focus on the centrality of increasing returns to international trade and factor movements. He finds Ohlin to have lacked, however, the new literature's appreciation of the importance of imperfect competition, the distinction between equilibria and optima, and the idea of discontinuous change from one equilibrium to another.

The preceding sections of this essay are intended to show that the new economic geographers share common ground with Myrdal and Perrroux in the ideas of cumulative causation driven by pecuniary externalities, the multiplicity of equilibrium agglomeration sites, and the importance of initial conditions or "history" in determining the actual equilibrium. What the new economic geographers have that Myrdal and Perroux lack are neoclassical methods: methodological individualism embodied in utility maximizing consumers and profit maximizing firms, whose behavior is represented algebraically in a system of equations. But, the contributions of the new economic geography beyond Myrdal and Perroux are more limited than its contributions beyond Ohlin. The preceding sections have shown that the first two items in Krugman's list—the centrality of imperfect competition and the distinction between equilibria and optima—can also be found in Myrdal's and Perroux's works.

This would seem to support Ron Martin's assertion that the new economic geography offers nothing new and valuable beyond the work of older authors whom it faintly echoes. "To economic geographers," Martin writes,

> the industrial agglomeration models of the 'new economic geography' generate a dull sense of 'déjà vu.' There is a long tradition of using externalities, increasing returns and cumulative causation in urban and regional analysis (Martin 1999, p. 70).

Worse, because of its alignment with the methodological approach of mainstream economics, he claims that the new economic geography represents *retrogression* from the earlier authors. For there are "severe epistemological and ontological limits to such a narrow approach. For one thing, it means that 'messy' social, cultural and institutional factors involved in spatial economic development are neglected" (ibid., p. 75).

Even with the evidence at hand, though, there are counter-arguments to this negative assessment of the new economic geography. One might say that even if the new economic geography were no more than a mathematical formalization of old ideas, that alone would be sufficient for it to be useful and to represent progress. One might accept the point that the new economic geography is very abstract, but disagree that it abstracts from what is most important. Moreover one might argue that the practice of abstraction, even (indeed especially) to extreme lengths, is necessary to communicate insights to colleagues who stand ready to build upon the work. In fact, feeling the heat from his critics, Krugman makes exactly these arguments. He acknowledges that the public as well as economists themselves benefit substantially from economic argumentation written in clear English *without* mathematics; however, he adds,

> professional economists have another task: to communicate with each other, and in so doing to help economics as a discipline progress. In this task it is important for your colleagues (and students) to understand *how* you arrived at your conclusions, partly so that they can look for weak points, partly so that they may find other uses for the technical tricks you used to think an issue through (1998b, p. 1835).

It is interesting to think where Myrdal and Perroux would take sides in this argument. We have already seen that Perroux sought a mathematical formulation of his ideas, and even held great hopes for models of monopolistic competition (1955 [1953], p. 143) that drive the results of the new economic geography. Nor was Myrdal hostile to mathematical modeling so long as the math represented reasonably well, rather than distorted (as he believed was commonly the case), the social phenomenon or question:

> Neither is [my] approach "adverse to models." Model building is a universal method of scientific research, in the same way that quantifying knowledge is a self-evident aim of research. But to construct models in the air, out of uncritically conceived concepts that are inadequate to reality and not logically consistent, and so pretend to knowledge when none has been established, does not represent scientific progress; it comes nearer to being an intellectual fraud (1970, p. 24).

It is clear that critics like Martin consider the new economic geography to be exactly such an example of "models in the air." The new economic geographers of course disagree, but their empirical evidence of the relevance of their work is still in its infancy. The difficult question of how to go about testing the models empirically has still not been answered definitively: Donald Davis and David Weinstein (1999) and Gordon Hanson (1997) have made attempts, but the terrain is still new and uncertain.

Absent convincing and abundant empirical tests of the models, it seems likely that despite Myrdal's and Perroux's acceptance of mathematical modeling in general, they would look somewhat askance at the new economic geography. Perroux would object that it doesn't represent the asymmetries of power that are observable in the real world: firms in the Dixit and Stiglitz model of monopolistic competition, after all, are symmetric. Myrdal would probably object as well; like Martin, he would likely argue that in most circumstances non-economic factors are too important to omit from the analysis, even in the worthy interest of abstraction. He made a similar point in *The Challenge of World Poverty*:

> My main point is that, while in developed countries an analysis in purely "economic terms" . . . may make sense and lead to valid inferences, . . . in underdeveloped countries this approach is simply not applicable, except at the price of making the analysis irrelevant and grossly faulty (1970, p. 10).

This essay has been intended to sort through the apparently inconsistent claims to the mantle of Myrdal and Perroux by new economic geographers and their critics outside of economics. But to suggest in conclusion that Myrdal and Perroux might not have approved of what the new economic geography has done in their names is not necessarily to criticize its models. The suggestion is more germane to a criticism of the new economic geography's self-crafted history than a criticism of the models themselves. New economic geographers should take care in their historical sketches to acknowledge, if not agree with, the reasons why those whom they claim as ancestors avoided their methods.

Notes

1. In a recent exchange in the *International Regional Science Review*, for example, Paul Krugman (1996) and Vernon Henderson (1996) debated the differences between the new economic geography and the "neoclassical urban systems" literature. The differences that emerged are neither as obvious nor as great as the reader of Krugman's sketches of the historical background of the new economic geography might expect.

2. The expression is originally Walter Isard's (1949, p. 477).

3. The splintering of geographical economics into several scholarly communities, each asking different questions and employing different methods, is the subject of Meardon (2000).

4. Others cited as progenitors are Paul N. Rosenstein-Rodin and Albert

Hirschman. Among several discussions of the new economic geography that refer to Myrdal and Perroux, two are Krugman (1995) and Ottaviano and Puga (1998).

5. Citations data were obtained from the Social Sciences Citation Index on-line database, consulted in August 2000.

6. An underlying assumption is that laborers are mobile not only between regions, but also between the perfectly competitive and monopolistically competitive sectors within each region. The migration of labor to the monopolistically competitive sector in the more agglomerated region must therefore raise the land-to-labor ratio in the perfectly competitive sector in the less agglomerated region, and hence raise the marginal product of labor there. It is in this sense that the workers who stay behind are motivated by abundant land. There could never be a *complete* exodus of laborers to the more agglomerated region, because in that case the marginal product of labor in the vacated region would be infinite.

7. In Krugman (1991a), a portion of the laborers remain dispersed simply by assumption, not because of fixed and dispersed endowments of land.

8. See Garza (1985, p. 97).

9. Hereafter Perroux (1962 [1960]). Apart from his very few articles and books that appeared originally in English, I will cite the Spanish and English translations of Perroux's work.

10. Parr (1999) provides a thorough guide to the rise and fall of the growth pole concept in regional planning.

11. The Nobel committee referred to these works in his biographical sketch (RSAS 1974a).

12. His interdisciplinary approach was cited specifically by the Nobel committee in its press release announcing him the winner of the 1974 prize (RSAS 1974b).

13. Published in the United States, also in 1957, as *Rich Lands and Poor*. I will cite the U.S. version.

References

Agresano, James. 1997. *The Political Economy of Gunnar Myrdal: An Institutional Basis for the Transformation Problem*. Lyme, NH: Edward Elgar.

Blaug, Mark. 1964. "A Case of Emperor's Clothes: Perroux' Theories of Economic Domination." *Kyklos* 17: 551–64.

Bocage, Ducarmel. 1985. *The General Economic Theory of François Perroux*. Lanham, MD: University Press of America.

Davis, Donald and David Weinstein. 1999. "Economic Geography and Regional Production Structure: An Emprirical Investigation." *European Economic Review* 43(2): 397–407.

Dixit, Avinash and Victor Norman. 1980. *Theory of International Trade: A*

Dual, General Equilibrium Approach. Cambridge, U.K.: Cambridge University Press.

Dixit, Avinash and Joseph Stiglitz. 1977. "Monopolistic Competition and Optimum Product Diversity." *American Economic Review* 67 (3): 297–308.

Friedman, John and Yuon Forest. 1988. "The Politics of Place: Toward a Political Economy of Territorial Planning." In B. Higgins and D. S. Savoie, eds., *Regional Economic Development: Essays in Honor of Francois Perroux.* Boston: Unwin Hyman.

Fujita, Masahisa and Paul Krugman. 1995. "When is the Economy Monocentric? Von Thunen and Chamberlin Unified." *Regional Science and Urban Economics* 25 (4): 505–28.

Fujita, Masahisa, Paul Krugman, and Anthony Venables. 1999. *The Spatial Economy: Cities, Regions, and International Trade.* Cambridge, MA: The MIT Press.

Garza, Gustavo. 1985. *El Proceso de Industrialización en la Ciudad de México, 1821-1970.* México, D.F.: El Colegio de Mexico.

Hanson, Gordon H. 1997. Increasing Returns, Trade, and the Regional Structure of Wages. *Economic Journal* 107: 113–33.

Helpman, Elhanan. 1981. "International Trade in the Presence of Product Differentiation, Economies of Scale and Monopolistic Competition: A Chamberlin-Heckscher-Ohlin Approach." *Journal of International Economics* 11 (3): 305–40.

Helpman, Elhanan and Paul Krugman. 1985. *Market Structure and Foreign Trade.* Cambridge, MA: The MIT Press.

Henderson, J. Vernon. 1996. "Ways to Think about Urban Concentration: Neoclassical Urban Systems versus the New Economic Geography." *International Regional Science Review* 19 (1,2): 31–36.

Higgins, Benjamin. 1988. "François Perroux." In B. Higgins and D. J. Savoie, eds., *Regional Economic Development: Essays in Honor of François Perroux.* Boston: Unwin Hyman, pp. 31–47.

Higgins, Benjamin and Donald J. Savoie. 1988. "Appendix: The Main Publications of François Perroux." In B. Higgins and D. J. Savoie, eds., *Regional Economic Development: Essays in Honor of François Perroux.* Boston: Unwin Hyman, pp. 385–410.

Isard, Walter. 1949. "The General Theory of Location and Space-Economy." *Quarterly Journal of Economics* 63 (4): 476–506.

Kirat, Thierry and Christophe Sierra. 1998. "Economic Space, Institutions, and Dynamics: A Revisitation of François Perroux." In Michel Bellet and Corine L'Harmet, eds., *Industry, Space and Competition: The Contribution of Economists of the Past,* pp. 107–121. Northampton, MA: Edward Elgar.

Krugman, Paul. 1980. "Scale Economies, Product Differentiation, and the Pattern of Trade." *American Economic Review* 70: 950–59.

———. 1991a. "Increasing Returns and Economic Geography." *Journal of Political Economy* 99 (3): 483–99.

————. 1991b. *Geography and Trade*. Cambridge, MA: The MIT Press.

————. 1993. 1st Nature, 2nd Nature, and Metropolitan Location. *Journal of Regional Science* 33 (2): 129–44.

————. 1995. *Development, Geography, and Economic Theory*. Cambridge, MA: The MIT Press.

————. 1996. "Urban Concentration: The Role of Increasing Returns and Transport Costs." *International Regional Science Review* 19 (1,2): 5–30.

————. 1998a. "Space: The Final Frontier." *Journal of Economic Perspectives* 12 (2): 161–74.

————. 1998b. "Two Cheers for Formalism." *The Economic Journal* 108 (November): 1829–36.

————. 1999. "Was it all in Ohlin?" Paper presented for the centennial celebration of Bertil Ohlin, Stockholm. Accessible from Paul Krugman's web page, http://web.mit.edu/krugman/www/ohlin.html.

Krugman, Paul and Raul Livas. 1996. "Trade Policy and the Third World Metropolis." *Journal of Development Economics* 49 (1): 137–50.

Krugman, Paul and Anthony Venables. 1995. "Globalization and the Inequality of Nations." *Quarterly Journal of Economics* 110 (4): 857–880.

Kuklinski, Antoni R., ed. 1972. *Growth Poles and Growth Centers in Regional Planning*. The Hague: Mouton & Co.

Lösch, August. 1954 [1944]. *The Economics of Location*. (English translation by William H. Woglom and Wolfgang F. Stolper of *Die räumliche ordnung der wirtschaft*, 2nd revised ed.) New Haven: Yale University Press.

Martin, Ron. 1999. "The New 'Geographical Turn' in Economics: Some Critical Reflections." *Cambridge Journal of Economics* 23 (1): 65–91.

Meardon, Stephen. 2000. "Eclecticism, Inconsistency, and Innovation in the History of Geographical Economics." In R. Backhouse and J. Biddle, eds. *Toward a History of Applied Economics*. Durham, N.C.: Duke University Press, pp. 323–357.

Myrdal, Gunnar. 1954 [1932]. *The Political Element in Economic Theory*. (English translation by Paul Streeten *of Das Politische Element in der nationalökonomischen Doktrinbildung*.) Cambridge, MA: Harvard University Press.

————. 1939. *Monetary Equilibrium*. London: William Hodge & Company.

————. 1944. *An American Dilemma: The Negro Problem and Modern Democracy*. New York: Harper & Brothers.

————. 1957. *Rich Lands and Poor*. New York: Harper & Brothers.

————. 1968. *Asian Drama: An Inquiry into the Poverty of Nations*. New York: Twentieth Century Fund and Pantheon Books.

————. 1970. *The Challenge of World Poverty: A World Anti-Poverty Program in Outline*. New York: Vintage Books.

Ottaviano, Gianmarco and Diego Puga. 1998. "Agglomeration in the Global Economy: A Survey of the 'New Economic Geography'." *The World Economy* 21 (6): 707–31.

Perroux, François. 1950. "Economic Space: Theory and Applications." *Quarterly Journal of Economics* 64: 89–104.

———. 1955 [1953]. "The Theory of Monopolistic Competition—A General Theory of Economic Activity." (English translation by Krishnan Kutty of Perroux's preface to the French translation of E. H. Chamberlin's *Theory of Monopolistic Competition*, Paris: Presses Universitaires de France.) *The Indian Economic Review* 2 (Feb.): 134–43.

———. 1962 [1960]. *Economía y Sociedad: Coacción - Cambio - Don.* (Spanish translation by X. Cornudella of Perroux's *Économie et Société: Contrainte - Échange - Don*, Paris: Presses Universitaires de France.) Barcelona: Ediciones Ariel.

———. 1967 [1965]. *Tecnicas Cuantitativas de la Planificación.* (Spanish translation by José M. Muntaner Pascual of Perroux's *Les Techniques Quantitatives de la Planification*, Paris: Presses Universitaires de France.) Barcelona: Ediciones Ariel.

———. 1970 [1955]. "Note on the Concept of Growth Poles." (English translation by Linda Gates and Anne Marie McDermott of Perroux's "Note sur la Notion de 'Pole de Croissance'," *Economie Appliquée* 7: 307–20.) In David L. McKee, Robert D. Dean and William H. Leahy, eds., *Regional Economics: Theory and Practice.* New York: The Free Press, pp. 93–104.

———. 1979 [1948]. "An Outline of a Theory of the Dominant Economy." (English translation by Sylvia Modelski of Perroux's "Equisse d'une Théorie de l'Economie Dominante," *Economie Appliquée* 1 (2,3): 245–84.) In George Modelski, ed., *Transnational Corporations and World Order: Readings in International Political Economy.* San Francisco: W. H. Freeman and Company, pp. 135–54.

———. 1983. *A New Concept of Development: Basic Tenets.* London: Croom Helm.

———. 1988a. "The Pole of Development's New Place in a General Theory of Economic Activity." In B. Higgins and D. J. Savoie, eds., *Regional Economic Development: Essays in Honor of François Perroux.* Boston: Unwin Hyman, pp. 48–76.

———. 1988b. "Peregrinations of an Economist and the Choice of his Route." In B. Higgins and D. J. Savoie, eds., *Regional Economic Development: Essays in Honor of François Perroux.* Boston: Unwin Hyman, pp.77–90.

Polenske, Karen R. 1988. "Growth Pole Theory and Strategy Reconsidered: Domination, Linkages, and Distribution." In B. Higgins and D. J. Savoie, eds., *Regional Economic Development: Essays in Honor of François Perroux.* Boston: Unwin Hyman, pp. 91–111.

Puga, Diego and Anthony Venables. 1996. "The Spread of Industry: Spatial Agglomeration and Economic Development." *Journal of the Japanese and International Economies* 10 (4): 440–464.

———. 1997. "Preferential Trading Arrangements and Industrial Location." *Journal of International Economics* 43 (3–4): 347–368.

Richardson, Harry W. and Margaret Richardson. 1975. "The Relevance of Growth Center Strategies to Latin America." *Economic Geography* S1:163–178.

Royal Swedish Academy of Sciences (RSAS). 1974a. "Gunnar Myrdal." http://www.nobel.se/economics/laureates/1974/myrdal-bio.html.

Royal Swedish Academy of Sciences (RSAS). 1974b. Press Release—The Sveriges Riksbank (Bank of Sweden) Prize in Economic Sciences in Memory of Alfred Nobel: Economics Prize for Works in Economic Theory and Inter-Disciplinary Research. . 09 October 1974.

Scitovsky, Tibor. 1954. "Two Concepts of External Economies." *Journal of Political Economy* 62 (2): 143–51.

Venables, Anthony. 1996. "Equilibrium Locations of Vertically Linked Industries." *International Economic Review* 37 (2): 341–59.

Zafirovsky, Milan. 1999. "Economic Sociology in Retrospect and Prospect: In Search of its Identity within Economics and Sociology." *American Journal of Economics and Sociology* 58 (4): 583–627.

City and Country

Lessons from European Economic Thought

By JÜRGEN G. BACKHAUS and GERRIT MEIJER*

ABSTRACT. The article concerns some European thought on the issue of city and country. We discuss the contributions of Henri von Storch, Gustav von Schmoller, Werner Sombart, Wilhelm Röpke, and Friedrich Hayek and attempt to translate these theories into practice in documenting the case of the city of Marl.

Introduction

This short essay is devoted to discussing theoretical issues of city and country in German economic literature. We give five examples of original and often overlooked classical contributors.

I

Henri von Storch:[1] Culture, City, Country and Culture of Development

IN INSISTING THAT POLITICAL ECONOMY IS ABOUT the wealth of nations broadly conceived, where wealth includes the stock of knowledge, abilities, and decency that is part of the cultural heritage and needs a continuous nurturing, Storch goes far beyond Adam Smith in integrating the theory of social goods into the system of political economy.[2] Any book needs to be read in its context, of course. Since this massive work had been prepared for the sole purpose of instructing the Russian Crown Prince and his brother,[3] one could believe that its emphasis on culture reflected aspects of the students' character. Although this is not inconceivable, the competing and not incompatible interpretation should prevail: that Storch took the opportunity of the rela-

* Prof. Dr. Jürgen G. Backhaus has been a Professor of Public Economics at Maastricht University since 1986. In 1994 he founded (with Frank H. Stephen) the *European Journal of Law and Economics*, of which he is the managing editor. Dr. Gerrit Meijer has been an Assistant Professor of Public Economics at Maastricht University since 1989. His interests include Friedrich Hayek and Wilhelm Röpke.

American Journal of Economics and Sociology, Vol. 60, No. 1 (January, 2001).

tive leisure (of having to instruct only these two students) to work out a fresh approach to political economy that took full advantage of the then available knowledge,[4] yet substantially improved upon it. Whereas the Austrian Crown Prince Rudolph in 1867 received just 15 lectures on political economy from Carl Menger (Streissler and Streissler 1994), the main point of which appears to have been to impress upon the young Crown Prince the futility of governmental attention to economic affairs, the Russian Crown Prince and his brother received a very different type of instruction from Storch. Here the emphasis was on Russia's vast natural resources and the desire for and feasibility of economic development, as well as an emphasis on cultural progress in order to alleviate the permanent dependence on foreign ideas and influences. Since Storch was, unlike Carl Menger later, an equally patient and impassioned instructor, rendering his ideas in clear prose, much of what he argues has retained a stunning freshness. Most of the problems he addresses have certainly not gone away during the almost two centuries that have followed.

The book[5] itself has a fascinating history related to the core part of this argument. Storch had corresponded with Jean-Baptiste Say and even secured him a knighthood in the order of Saint Volodomir.[6] Say, apparently without sufficient prior consultation, proceeded to publish the text in French, amended by extensive and, in part, very critical footnotes. The criticism was aimed at the core of the argument, the importance of the so-called "unproductive" part of the economy, in Smith's unfortunate phrase. Storch, infuriated by Say's translation, wrote a long essay on the measurement of national wealth that was published as the fifth volume of the text, which had previously been published in four bound volumes.

Storch's *Cours d'Économie Politique* (1823) is organized in two parts. Part I entitled *Theory of the Wealth of Nations* contains eight books and is concerned with the production of wealth (Book 1); the accumulation of wealth and funds (Book 2); the primitive distribution of wealth (Book 3); the circulation or secondary distribution of wealth (Book 4); the "numéraire," where this money is defined as first serving the purpose of unit of account and second having an although insignificant use value (Book 5); credit (Book 6); consumption (Book 7); and the natural progress of the wealth of nations (Book 8). The big

TERMS AND METHODS OF THOSE DOCTRINES WHICH COMPOSE POLITICAL ECONOMY

POLITICAL ECONOMY

POLICY

This is to be divided according to the three subjects which compose political economy, i.e. the constitution of the state, its external security and its internal security, of which prosperity is the most important aspect:

Constitutional political economy

Foreign affairs

Internal affairs

1. Civil and penal legal science
2. Science of economic and financial legislation

SOCIAL SCIENCE

Sources on which political principles can be based:

International laws of nations

Universal human rights

Universal private law

Political economy

POSITIVE SCIENCES (in support of policy)

These positive sciences allow the applications of the principles derived before:

Positive public law

Positive international law   } As supported by

Positive private law   historical and

Economic and financial   statistical evidence

legislation

surprise is Part II, which consists of just two books and is entitled *Theory of Civilization*. Book 1 enumerates the elements of civilization, the importance of the so-called internal goods including health, education, taste, customs, religious sects, and certainty and leisure, all the way to a complete theory of taxation. The second book of *Theory of Civilization* deals with the progress of civilization, adding the dynamic part. The work concludes with chapters on the influence of wealth on immaterial labor, the influence of civilization on industry, the mutual complementarity of wealth and civilization, and the real conclusion that equilibrium is constituted as a national prosperity when civilization and production of wealth grow in tandem. This remarkable work apparently never circulated in Russia. It was published in German and, in the 1823 and 1824 editions, in France, marketed through the same publisher in Leipzig and London. It is bound in five volumes. Volumes I through III contain the ten books just mentioned. Volume IV contains the table of contents and Jean Baptiste Say's extensive notes, which infuriated the author to such an extent that the publisher had to add Volume V. This last volume is a restatement of the example of measuring the wealth of a particular nation in terms of both its material wealth and its immaterial wealth, to which Part II (Books 9 and 10) had been devoted. Again, we have the specter, as in the cases of Jakob[7] and Schlözer,[8] of an enormous inspiration born in Russia, a sensible and sincere attempt to deal squarely with the Russian conditions and adapt Central European insight to it; yet with hardly any influence in Russia itself, although it produced extensive reverberations in Central Europe.[9]

Before looking at the specifics of Storch's argument, it is important to study his terms and approach. After all, any author should be interpreted on his own terms.

As we can see, Storch emphasizes the distinction between general principles and the individual manifestation of behavior. In economics, it is a general principle that man, guided by his desire to improve his lot, is willing to save, and that means that he will reduce his current consumption in order to provide for his future satisfaction (Cours, p. 22).[10] If we happen to observe some people who behave differently, that does not disprove the basic principle. He then continues:

[T]he facts from which political economy derives its general laws are of a moral nature: They are the result of the working of human nature. Man is himself the maker of his wealth and his civilization; it is him who uses those to serve his needs and pleasures; in the same way, all occurrences which are related to his wealth and civilization are equally based on the human nature, they can only be explained by reference to her. From this follows a very important observation which substantially weakens the analogy which we have found between the natural sciences and political economy. The natural sciences are based on physical facts, and these are susceptible to rigorous appreciation, they therefore belong to the precise sciences; political economy, on the other hand, as it is based on moral facts, that is results which stem from the abilities, the needs and the choices of men, can under no circumstances be subject to a precise calculation, they remain within the domain of the moral sciences.[11]

In Storch's writings we can discern an approach to political economy that probably began with Wolff (Backhaus 1998). Political economy remains located in the moral sciences, closely interconnected with law, and its emphasis is clearly on institution building and on wealth creation through the building of institutions and the teaching of prudent behavior. Man is portrayed as having a duty to exploit his physical and moral endowments with prudence and care in the interest of the future. The task is seen as merging nature and culture, country and city.

At the center of Storch's concern is the vastness of the Russian countryside, as opposed to the relatively small number of cities and the relatively small part of the population residing in the cities. The aristocracy derives its income (essentially the land rent) from the agricultural estates, yet resides in the cities where this rental income is consumed. It is essentially used for luxury consumption and the entire industry of crafts and manufacture is geared towards these consumption patterns. Industrialization is rare and innovation in agricultural production hardly exists. Since the land rent is constantly diverted to the consumption of city dwellers, there is hardly any investment emanating from the city to the country, and even more importantly, very little investment in the infrastructure.

It is here that Storch's third sphere of economic activity, the cultural sphere, becomes particularly important. Russia's large natural riches can only be tapped if, on the one hand, there is an entrepreneurial spirit interested in such expansive activity and, on the other hand, technology in the form of human skills and knowledge as well as tools and machines can be brought to bear on the development process. Finally, given the large distances separating the different parts of Russia from one another and notably from the cities, a means of communication must be established to help integrate the country and the city. Storch thought primarily of the use of the natural waterways combined with an extensive system of canals, similar to the development strategy of Frederic II (Backhaus 1999). We can summarize this section by saying that the relationship between city and country in Storch's vision of a development strategy against the background of Tsarist Russia is clearly the focal point of his *Theory of Civilization* (i.e., the third pillar of his economic edifice). This strategy builds by identifying the cultural sector as the crucial nexus of developmental activity. While cities can be identified as the centers of culture in terms of entrepreneurship, skills and learning, and technological knowledge, the key to development lies in bringing the country closer to the city through a systematic reduction of the costs of transportation by using the natural endowments of waterways and expanding upon them.

II

Gustav von Schmoller: Urbanization and the Social Problem

GUSTAV (VON 1908) SCHMOLLER (1838–1917) also identified the relationship between city and country as the key to his research program. However, in his case he had to deal with the results of industrialization rather than ways of getting it started, which had been Storch's original problem. As a consequence of the massive industrialization in the cities, the rural population flocked to them in search of work and a better life. The sudden swelling of these industrialized cities led to the formation of a rootless proletarian underclass such as we today see in contemporary China. Schmoller took this part of Marx's analysis seriously, and took even more seriously the political consequences of Lasalle's campaigns on the communist platform.[12] With Germany recently having been politically unified in 1871 and with the process of industrialization in full swing, this process of industrialization threatened to endanger the new political state if, as Marx had predicted and wished and Lasalle was active in bringing about, class formation led to class struggle. Instead of trying to reverse the process so as to create more employment in the country (internal colonization) or trying to export population growth and social conflict into new territories (external colonization), Schmoller identified the city as the center of growth, the cause of the increasing proletarization he saw in the absence of effective protection against the major risks of life. He identified these major risks as the loss of the ability to work due to accident, the loss of a major breadwinner, and the loss of the ability to work due to old age. Given the large numbers involved and the still miniscule size of the insurance market, a market solution for these risks in the sense of market-based insurance was not yet available. However, once a basic compulsory insurance had been established, Schmoller felt that the private market would step up in order to offer additional protection. Hence, he proposed and ultimately accomplished through Prince Bismarck's political initiatives a compulsory insurance system covering the effects of work related accidents, support of widows and dependents upon the death of the major breadwinner, and provisions for retirement. The system was based on actuarial principles and received no support from taxation. It was further based in the different industrial sectors under state supervision, but not run by the state. Thus, for instance, the costs of accidents in mining had to be borne by the mining industry, and the performance of the different enterprises were reflected in the premiums. Hence, the system was also used to improve the protection of the insured.

Schmoller's focus on the city took other forms as well. For instance, he was concerned about the availability of sufficient housing of good and sanitary quality and proposed city zoning so as to encourage large cooperative complexes of residential housing with sufficient open space and inner city park areas. Many sanitary measures can be enumerated, but the major message should be clear. In order to facilitate mass agglomerations and enable industrialization, the major risks of life of the newly arrived city dwellers—who had left their cushioned existence in agriculture—had to be brought about through modern solutions of insurance. This required a state impulse to activate credit and insurance markets, which in turn was the prerequisite for further industrialization.

III

Werner Sombart: The Theory of Rents and
the Theory of the City

WERNER SOMBART (1858–1941) CAN RIGHTFULLY BE CLAIMED as the pioneer of the economic theory of the city. In brief, he stated that the city can prosper if its authorities succeed in attracting the landlords to reside in the cities, bringing their land rent into the city and feeding it into entrepreneurial ventures. He then goes on to show that besides aristocratic entrepreneurship, various other forms can be encouraged to exist. This, however, is not the focus of our attention in this essay. As we are interested in the social policy implications of economists' thinking about the relationship between country and the city, a different aspect of Sombart's theorizing needs to receive our attention. As we noted in the previous section, Schmoller (who was Sombart's teacher) had focused on three basic risks in the life of a working class family as they flocked towards the city. Conspicuously absent in the original set of legislation was unemployment insurance. This was to follow many years later. Yet as the world economic crisis unfolded in the early 1930s, the state run system of unemployment insurance remained woefully insufficient, and a private alternative was obviously not available for the large number of working class people. Surely, the risk is not insurable in the wake of a cumulative world crisis. In this historical context, Sombart went out to support Keynesian employment measures which, based on a multiplier and accelerator effect, could be credit financed, as they would subsequently pay for themselves. The emphasis was on productive labor-intensive investment by all levels of government (Backhaus 1989). Sombart added a relevant twist for our topic of country and city in economic theory, suggesting measures of internal colonization. The long term unemployed should be given the chance to receive a small farm in exchange for their unemployment benefits. That would provide them with a decent level of self-sufficiency and in addition, as skilled labor transferred to the country, allow for the industrialization process in the countryside to be cushioned against major economic crises. Here, we see a complete reversal, from an attempt to develop insurance markets where actuarial risks can be assessed, to using the sufficiency economy as the ultimate form of insurance against the vicissitudes of international crises, but not with the intention of blocking further industrialization. This apparent paradox of an anti-modern strategy of modernization will reappear in our fourth example.

IV

Wilhelm Röpke: The City as the Center of Civilization

WILHELM RÖPKE (1899–1966) was a very special economist. His program of economic and social policy includes four supplementary groups of measures (Röpke 1946 [1944], pp. 69–87, 97–98, 100; 1943 [1942]):

1. There have to be measures to create and maintain the institutions which make possible an economic order based on competition (*Wettbewerbsordnung*). This is the policy of economic order (*Rahmenpolitik*).

2. Furthermore, he wants to interfere in the economic process. This Röpke calls *Marktpolitik*. Together with the *Rahmenpolitik* it forms the positive economic policy he advocates. Röpke develops two criteria of rational economic policy, on the basis of which he distinguishes between permissible and non-permissible interventions.

The first criterion is the one of *Anpassungsinterventionen* (adjustment interventions) versus *Erhaltungsinterventionen* (status quo interventions). Changes in the data of economic process often bring painful adjustment processes for the subjects involved. The government can respond in three ways: it can do nothing; it can stop the adjustment process; or it can accelerate and soften the adjustment processes. The first reaction means laissez faire. The second leads to *Erhaltungsinterventionen* (status quo interventions), resisting the dynamic working of price formation. The third point of view leads to adjustment interventions which serve to soften the adjustments and help the weak groups in their struggle for existence. Through that adjustment support the market mechanism's working is not affected. It is precisely the intention to come across with measures which make the adjustment process less painful and quicker. Röpke mentions agriculture, handicraft, the small firms, and the laborers as groups which deserve to be considered for adjustment interventions.

The second criterion is that of compatiblity and non-compatiblity (conforming and non-conforming). With each measure one has to ask oneself whether the instrument used is or is not compatible with the market economy. Compatible instruments do not abolish the working of price formation, but insert as new data in the economic process. On the other hand non-compatible instruments will block the working of price formation.

3. Measures which together form the economic-social structure policy and try to change income and property distribution, size distribution of firms, and distribution of the population over city and country and over agriculture and industry. They concern the social conditions of the market economy. This means promotion of the medium and small firms and property formation (particularly in the form of houses with gardens) in order to fight proletarization and massification (congestion). The policy has to be focused on distribution of industry and deconcentration in industry. In this context Röpke speaks of economic humanism.

4. Finally, a policy has to be pursued which is focused on the creation of a structure of society in which the market economy can prosper. This (the so-called *Gesellschaftspolitik*) has been strongly neglected by the liberals of the past century. To combat massification (congestion) and proletarianization, stimulation of agriculture and handicraft and distribution of the location of industry are necessary. The measures under (3.) and (4.) are very important, even essential, elements in Röpke's program.

V

Röpke on Town and Country Planning

WITH REGARD TO PHYSICAL TOWN AND COUNTRY PLANNING Röpke is an optimist. Here the pricing process via the markets can only give a partially satisfactory solution. The problems of town and country planning cannot be resolved by competition alone: land as a place of location has to be distributed among different economic activities. Planning concerns a balanced distribution of population over towns and country and a balanced distribution over industry and agriculture.

Röpke (1946 [1944], pp. 284–294; 1943 [1942]) thinks the spread of industry and population is essential to fight proletarianization and congestion (massification). Therefore decentralization and deconcentration of industry is necessary, as is the breaking up of large land holdings in agriculture.

The objective is to improve the quality of life and the living and working environment *(Vitalpolitik)*. Of course, in a highly developed culture there have to be cities as centers of political, economical, societal, and spiritual life along with country life.

The cities which developed over the last two centuries, now forming our contemporary cities, are not the normal or natural form, but are highly pathological by way of their monopolistic centralization (e.g., Paris), their abnormal and extreme size, and their sociological structure, making them centers of congestion, proletarianization, and devitalisation.

The formation and expansion of gigantic cities has to be counteracted. The break up of the big city is one of the most important objectives of the reform of society—decentralization is the objective. Although the formation of suburbs is an advancement, it is not the correct method of decentralization. It is only a decentralization of sleeping quarters, and gives rise, among other issues, to increased traffic problems. The big city still remains the center of work and other business and cultural activities.

Röpke pleads for small towns as an alternative to the big city. Smaller towns of about 50,000 to 60,000 inhabitants have to be aimed for. They have to be combined as far as possible with a policy of restoration of property in the form of family houses with gardens. This would be genuine decentralization. Decentralization of living through the restoration of property in the form of individual houses with gardens is necessary since the conditions for family life are embedded in nature.

The house and garden would give family members a place to live as well as enabling them to provide themselves with products created during (un)voluntary leisure, as an occupation besides their usual and often not satisfying jobs. In this way both overseeable communities (in which political decisions can be influenced by all citizens at the lowest level) and the natural conditions of human life can be created.

These measures of *Gesellschaftspolitik* and economic-social structure policy for giving the market economy a sound social structure belong partly to planning for competition or *Rahmenpolitik* and partly (e.g., town and country planning) to *Marktpolitik*. They are also a form of social policy that has the objective of making people more independent and thus self-reliant. The state intervenes to give its members a better living and working environment. It also intends to make them more independent of the vicissitudes of life and the market and to give the individual some degree of privacy in mass society. It is a new form of social policy, and at the same time *Vitalpolitik*.

Röpke also calls upon consumers and entrepreneurs, architects and technicians, and others to do their utmost to find solutions to decentralize and deconcentrate firms and to spread the population over many smaller cities and the countryside. Here housing policy and the policy of property formation are very important. These ideas were formed against the background of contemporary developments in Germany.

VI

Hayek on Town and Country Planning

IN HIS *CONSTITUTION OF LIBERTY* (1960) Hayek (1899–1992) devoted an entire chapter to the problems of housing and town planning (Chapter 22). Hayek's ideas on this subject were influenced by those developments in England that he observed while living in London from 1930 to 1950. He was critical of England's policies, especially the policy of the Labor government after the Second World War. It tried to solve problems by direct interference with prices and quantities, such as rents of houses. In this way the price system was prevented from solving the housing problem.

Hayek pointed out that this is also the case with public housing and building subsidies. They have similar results as rent restrictions unless they are carefully limited in scope and method. Public housing (and subsidized housing), he concluded, can thus at best be an instrument of assisting the poor. This, however, has the inevitable consequence of making those who benefit dependent on government to a degree that would be politically very serious if they constituted a large part of the population. Like any assistance to an unfortunate minority, such a measure is not irreconcilable with a general system of freedom. But it raises very grave economic and political problems that should be squarely faced if it is not to produce dangerous consequences.

Hayek also discussed the problem of the slums and the problems raised by the fact that in the close contiguity of city living the price mechanism reflects only imperfectly the benefit or harm to others that a property owner may cause by his actions (the neighborhood effects). In order that the market may bring about an efficient coordination of individual actions, both individual owners and the authorities controlling communal property should be enabled to take into account the more important effects of their actions on other property. Then the price mechanism will function as it should. Since the price mechanism is an imperfect guide for the use of urban land, the framework of rules will have to be both more detailed and more adjusted to particular local circumstances than is necessary with other kinds of property. This type of town planning is part of the effort to make the market mechanism more effective (planning for competition). There is another type that dispenses with the price mechanism and replaces it by central direction (planning against competition) (Hayek 1961 [1944], chapter 3).

Most measures of town planning will influence the value of private property. Some property values will rise, others will fall. The measures have to be beneficial in the sense that the total benefits exceed the losses. Hayek pleads for charging the owners of properties that rise in value and compensating the owners of properties that fall in value. The planning authority has this as its task, but would have only the right of expropriation at fair market value.

After discussing some other minor problems, Hayek at the end of the chapter writes about the problems related to the location of industries at a national scale. Here again the price mechanism works imperfectly. But the price mechanism works favorably, because it takes all available information via the prices into account. It is more than doubtful whether a central planner could do better.

VII

A Case in Point: The City of Marl

THE CITY OF MARL (Lowinski 1964; Schüpp 1963) became a town in 1936. It is situated in Nordrhein-Westphalen, in the Ruhr-area, on the Lippe-Seitenkanal (subsidiary channel), in the Kreis (county of) Recklinghausen.

Marl's origin and development was part of the historical development of the region and had no relation to the national-socialist movement, since the national-socialist movement had no specific ideas about town and country planning. Originally the territory consisted of old villages, agricultural landscape, and forests. It has become an important industrial center for coal mining since 1906 and for chemical industry (Hüls A) since 1938. Its inner harbor is in the West-Dattelnkanal. The national-socialist period had its influence on the implementation of plans that had already been a long time in preparation and execution. This influence existed mainly in retarding Marl's development in many respects; as the national-socialist economy became more and more a war economy, there were other priorities for which time and money were needed.

The city center was built in the post-war period. After the reconstruction period there followed the *Wirtschaftswunder* (economic miracle) associated with Ludwig Erhard, the German Minister of Economic Affairs. The economic and social policy that he followed (Erhard 1962; Hohmann 1977) was inspired by Röpke's ideas (Erhard 1968), as well as in the field of town and country planning.

In the 1950s, 1960s, and 1970s, the city created several cultural institutions: a theatre, a school of music, and a museum for contemporary sculpture, with a collection which included works by Oscar Zadkine and Max Ernst. The museum is accommodated in the so-called *Glaskasten* (Box of Glass) (1979). The city has a modern town hall, which was built between 1958–1965 under the direction of the Dutch architects Van den Broek and Datema. Other modern buildings are the *Paracelsusklinik* (built under the direction of the architect W. Hedebrand during 1953–1967) and the *Herz Jesu Kirche* built in 1958–59, in cubistic style.

The authors we have discussed here were concerned with the consequences of industrialization. They saw urbanization, congestion (massification), and proletarianization. People left the countryside and the agricultural sector. A process of centralization and concentration took place in all spheres of human society. Schmoller proposed to fight proletarianization by a compulsory insurance system for the vicissitudes of life in an industrialized and urbanized society. Moreover, he was in favor of zoning and the provision of sufficient housing of good and sanitary quality. Sombart stressed the problems related to unemployment, especially in the light of a possible world crisis. He was in favor of labor-intensive investment by all levels of the government. Moreover, he wanted a balance between the town and the countryside by reversing the process of urbanization, congestion, and proletarianization. He proposed to combine small farming with industrialization. In this way, self-sufficiency could counterbalance the consequences of an economic crisis. Similar more elaborated ideas can be found in the writings of Röpke. He stressed decentralization and deconcentration in economic and political life. Hayek's ideas, although worded differently, have a fundamentally similar character and scope.

In the case of Marl, all the elements mentioned by these authors can be found: a balance between agriculture and industry, embedding in nature, zoning in order to create a balance between work and recreation. Facilities for a rich cultural and political life are available. The town hall is the center for local democracy. Political and economic decentralization and deconcentration are consequently sought after, in accordance with the subsidiarity principle. A social policy in the sense of a *Vitalpolitik* is in a large measure realized. Nevertheless, people in Marl do not seem to be happy there. What is the reason for this?

In his book *A Humane Economy* (1960, chapter 2), Röpke gives a thorough analysis of mass society. From his analyses of its origin and consequences we can learn that the diagnosis as well as the therapy is difficult. He is of the opinion that the crisis has even become worse during the third quarter of the twentieth century.

The citizens of Marl accidentally came together in their new town. They and their families have their historical roots in the original villages. New citizens came in with all kinds of backgrounds, mostly from larger cities in the neighborhood. The new town development also had to absorb an overwhelmingly large number of refugees from very different areas of the German East and Southeast. These new refugees had already lost their sense for nature and tradition and were the victims of proletarianization, congestion, and devitalisation.

According to Röpke, mass society is characterized by boredom, mechanized life, concentration, breaking with the past and the decline of cultural traditions, degeneration of liberal democracy in mass democracy (which is accompanied by inflation), mass culture, degeneration of federalism, the mass state (which has influence on the social structure of society and results in urbanization, industrialization, and proletarianization), an increase of nervous disorders, the welfare state with its mass relief (which lowers individual responsibility and erodes the functions of small communities such as charity organizations and the family), mass education, mass health care, mass tourism, and in general organization and concentration in all fields of life.

Only as far as society changes in the direction of market economy and decentralization and deconcentration will there be chances for improvement. More important still is the awareness of the causes of massification (congestion) and proletarianization by all those concerned. As long as this is not the case, only small steps in the right direction can be made, as demonstrated by the case of Marl.

Conclusion

In this short essay, we have tried to introduce the reader to treatments of the topic of city and country which are not generally available to the English-based scholar (with the exception of Hayek and, partially, Röpke). Each author deserves a fuller treatment. We hope to have paved the path to such a more complete treatment with this introductory attempt.

Notes

1. Heinrich F. von Storch (1766–1835).
2. Adam Smith, *An Inquiry into the Nature and Causes of the Wealth of Nations,* London: Everyman, 1910.
3. Their Imperial Highnesses, Grand Dukes Nicholas and Michael.
4. He became a member of the Academy of Sciences in 1796; this meant that he had full access to the internationally available literature in addition to

his studies in Jena and Heidelberg. He also remained active in the Academy; when he died in 1835 he was serving as its vice president.

5. Henri Storch, *Cours d'Économie Politique*, Paris : Aillaud, 1823.

6. This means that the Tsar, at the behest of Storch, had ennobled Say.

7. Ludwig Heinrich (von 1816) Jakob (1759–1827).

8. Christian von Schlözer (1774–1831).

9. Both the French and German versions of the book circulated widely. The German version is still in print.

10. Please note that Storch uses a very broad notion of utility. He says, "retrencher sur ses jouissances actuelles pour se ménager des jouissances futures."

11. "Les faits dont l'économie politique déduit ses lois appartiennent à l'ordre moral: ils sont le résultat de l'action de la nature humaine. L'homme est lui-même l'artisan de sa richesse et de sa civilisation; c'est lui qui les fait servir à ses besoins et à ses jouissances; ainsi, tous les phénomènes que ces objets nous présentent sont fondés sur la nature humaine, et ne peuvent s'expliquer que par elle. Ceci conduit à une observation importante, et qui affaiblit l'analogie que nous avions trouvée entre les sciences naturelles et l'économie politique. Les premières étant fondées sur des faits physiques, qui sont susceptibles d'une appréciation rigoureuse, appartiennent au domaine des sciences exactes; l'économie politique, au contraire, étant basée sur des faits moraux, c'est-à-dire sur des faits produits par les facultés, les besoins et la volonté de l'homme, n'est point soumise au calcul, et rentre dans le domaine des sciences morales." At this point, overshooting the argument, Jean-Baptiste Say adds a long footnote pointing out that even in physics there are areas which evade efforts at precision. In this sense, he says, physics and political economy are similar.

12. Karl Marx and Friedrich Engels, *The Communist Manifesto: Collected Works, vol. VI*, London, 1975.

References

Backhaus, Jürgen G. (ed.) (1998). *Christian Wolff and Law and Economics: The Heilbronn Symposium*. Hildesheim: Olms Verlag.

———. (1989). "Werner Sombart's Theory of the Business Cycle," in Donald A. Walker (ed.), *Perspectives on the History of Economic Thought*, vol. 2, pp. 3–22. Aldershot: Edward Elgar Publishing Ltd.

———. (1999). "Land Rents and Ecological Crisis: The Case of the Oder River Valley," *American Journal of Economics and Sociology*, vol. 58, no. 2, April, pp. 249–252.

Erhard, Ludwig. (1962). *Deutsche Wirtschaftspolitik*, Düsseldorf/Vienna: Econ Verlag, Frankfurt/Main: Knapp.

———. (1968). "Gedenkrede," in *In Memoriam Wilhelm Röpke*, Reden gehalten anläßlich der akademischen Gedenkfeier der Rechts- und Staatwissenschaftlichen Fakultät der Philipps-Universität Marburg zu Ehren ihres Mitglieds am 3., pp. 9-21. Juli 1967, Marburg: N.G. Elwart Verlag.

Hayek, Friedrich A. (1961 [1944]). *The Road to Serfdom.* Chicago: University of Chicago Press.

———. (1972 [1960]). *The Constitution of Liberty.* South Bend, IN: Gateway Editions Ltd.

Hohmann, K. (ed.) (1978). *Ludwig Erhard Erbe und Auftrag: Aussagen und Zeugnisse,* Eine Veröffentlichung der Ludwig Erhard-Stiftung e.V., Düsseldorf/Vienna: Econ Verlag.

Lowinski, H. (1964). *Städtebildung in Industriellen Entwicklungensräumen,* Recklinghausen: Verlag Aurel Bongers.

Marx, Karl and Friedrich Engels. (1975). *The Communist Manifesto: Collected Works,* vol. VI, London.

Röpke, Wilhelm. (1943 [1942]). *Die Gesellschaftskrisis der Gegenwart,* Erlenbach-Zürich: Eugen Rentsch Verlag.

———. (1946 [1944]). *Civitas Humana,* Erlenbach-Zürich: Eugen Rentsch Verlag.

———. (1960). *A Humane Economy. The Social Framework of the Free Market.* South Bend, IN: Gateway Editions, Ltd.

Schmoller, Gustav. (1878). *Staats- und sozialwissenschaftliche Forschungen,* since 1878 126 Monographs

———. *(1879). Die Straßburger Tucher- und Weberzunft. Urkunden und darstellungen nebst Regesten und Glossar. Ein Beitrag zur Geschichte der deutschen Weberei und des deutschen gewerbechts von 13.–17. Jahrhundert,* Strasbourg, Trübner.

———. (1884–87a). *Wirtschaftliche Politik Preußens im 18. Jahrhundert.*

———. (1884–87b). *Wirtschaftliche Politik Preußens im 18. Jahrhundert,* J.f. G.V.

———. (1889a). *Die Tatsachen der Arbeitsteilung.*

———. (1889b). *Das Wesen der Arbeitsteilung und der sozialen Klassenbildung.*

———. (1890). *Zur Sozial- und Gewerbepolitik der Gegenwart (Reden und Aufsätze).*

———. (1890–93). *Die geschichtliche Entwicklung der Unternehmung.*

———. (1892). *Acta Borussica. Denkmäler der Preußischen Staatsverwaltung im 18. Jahrhundert,* since 1892 14 vols.

———. (1898a). *Über einige Grundfragen der Sozialpolitik und Volkswirtschaftslehre,* Leipzig: Duncker & Humblot.

———. (1898b). *Umrisse und Untersuchungen zur Verfassungs-, Verwaltungs- und Wirtschaftsgeschichte besonders des Preußischen Staates im 17. und 18. Jahrhundert,* Leipzig: Duncker & Humblot.

———. (1901). "Simmel's Philosophie des Geldes," *Jahrbuch für Gesetzgebung, Verwaltung und Volkswirtschaften im Deutschen Reich,* 25 (3), pp. 799-860.

————. (1978 [1900]). *Grundriß der allgemeinen Volkswirtschaftslehre*, 2 volumes, Berlin/Leipzig: Duncker & Humblot.

Schüpp, N. (1963). *Von Dörfern zur Stadt*, Düsseldorf: Rudolf Stehle.

Smith, Adam. (1910). *An Inquiry into the Nature and Causes of the Wealth of Nations*. London: Everyman.

Sombart, Werner. (1909). *Socialism and the Social Movement*, translated from the 6th (enlarged) German edition with introduction and notes by M. Epstein. London: J. M. Dent & Co.

————. (1913 [1911]). *The Jews and Modern Capitalism* (Die Juden und das Wirtschaftsleben). Translated by M. Epstein.

————. (1902/1927/1928). *Der moderne Kapitalismus*, I, II, 1902: I (rev.) 1916; II (rev.) 1917; III, 1927; I–III, 1928. Berlin: Duncker & Humblot.

————. (1929). "Economic Theory and Economic History," *The Economic History Review*, 2, 1–19.

————. (1930a). "Capitalism," *Encyclopaedia of the Social Sciences*, vol. III, 195-208.

————. (1930b). *Die drei Nationaloekonomien: Geschichte und System der Lehre von der Wirtschaft*. Munich, Leipzig: Duncker & Humblot,.

————. (1932). *Die Zukunft des Kapitalismus*. Berlin: Buchholz & Weisswaage.

————. (1933). "Zum Problem der Arbeitsbeschaffung," *Die Wirtschaftswende*, special issue, no. 2.

Storch, Henri. (1823). *Cours d'Économie Politique*. Paris: Aillaud.

Streissler, E. and M. (eds.) (1994). *Carl Menger's Lectures to Crown Prince Rudolph of Austria*. Aldershot: Edward Elgar.

Making the Country Work for the City

Von Thünen's Ideas in Geography, Agricultural Economics and the Sociology of Agriculture

By DANIEL BLOCK and E. MELANIE DuPuis*

ABSTRACT. Geography, as the discipline responsible for describing the organization of space, has developed several ways of dealing with the phenomenon of the central city and its surrounding hinterlands. One of the most prominent of models used is von Thünen's Isolated State, a predictive model of how rural hinterlands organize agricultural production in relation to an urban center. Despite today's globalized food provisioning system, there are still some agricultural commodities that remain in U.S. city hinterlands. The most prominent of these is milk. The spatial organization of dairying is therefore a topic in which von Thünen's notions of centrality are still pertinent. In addition, outside of geography, his ideas had a significant effect on the agricultural economists who formulated dairy marketing policy. This paper will examine von Thünen and notions of centrality in the formulation of dairy policy in the United States. His contribution has been very important to agricultural economists and agricultural geographers but less important to sociologists of agriculture, who see the spatial organization of food production around cities due as much to contingent, local political outcomes as to law-like notions of central-

*Daniel Block is an Assistant Professor of Geography at Chicago State University. He received his Ph.D. from UCLA in 1997. His dissertation, "The Development of Regional Institutions in Agriculture: The Chicago Milk Marketing Order" examines the role of urban and rural groups in the development of dairy regulation in the United States. His recent paper, "Purity, Economy, and Social Welfare in the Progressive Era Pure Milk Movement," was named by the Oxford Symposium on Food and Cookery as one of the best writings in food history for 1999. E. Melanie DuPuis is an Assistant Professor of Sociology at the University of California-Santa Cruz. She received her Ph.D. from Cornell in 1991. She is the co-editor of *Creating the Countryside : The Politics of Rural and Environmental Discourse*, and has published numerous articles on the sociology of dairy production and milk consumption. Her forthcoming book, *Nature's Perfect Food: Milk and American Identity* (NYU Press), is a social and economic history of milk and the idea of perfection in the United States.

American Journal of Economics and Sociology, Vol. 60, No. 1 (January, 2001).

ity. Comparative historical method in sociology has been particularly useful in determining the role of predictive models and contingency in determining the spatial organization of milksheds.

I

Introduction

GEOGRAPHY, AS THE DISCIPLINE RESPONSIBLE for describing the organization of space, has developed several ways of dealing with the phenomenon of the central city and its surrounding hinterlands. One of the most prominent models used is von Thünen's Isolated State, a predictive model of how rural hinterlands organize agricultural production in relation to an urban center. Von Thünen's thesis was that around a lone market city in the middle of a featureless plain, crops with high transportation costs and intensive uses of land would be produced nearer the market than would other types of crops. Whether or not a farmer grew a particular crop depended on his or her distance from the market. Distance determined land value and transportation costs and therefore the margin of profit from a particular enterprise needed to be sufficient to pay these costs. As a result, agricultural production organized itself as "rings" of lowering production intensity around central cities.

In today's global food system, von Thünen's model seems a bit quaint: suburbs surround our cities and much of our high value agricultural foods come from the Central Valley of California or from around the world. Nevertheless, there are still some agricultural commodities that remain in city hinterlands. The most prominent of these in U.S. society today is milk. Despite a continuing lengthening of the trip milk makes to the consumer, especially with current merger craze making dairy farmer cooperatives into national organizations, most American cities still have in their vicinities a dairy "milkshed." This was predicted by von Thünen, who stated: "Next to fruit and vegetables, milk is a prime necessity for the Town; and as this is a difficult and costly product to transport and is . . . highly perishable, milk too will be produced in the first ring" (1966 [1826], p. 9).

The spatial organization of dairying is therefore a topic in which von Thünen's notions of centrality are still pertinent. His ideas have had a significant effect on dairy marketing policy. This paper will examine von Thünen and notions of centrality in the formulation of milksheds and dairy policy in the United States. Our main purpose is to use the study of milksheds and dairy policy to view the manner in which the Isolated State theory entered three academic fields: geography, agricultural economics, and sociology. Geographers turned to von Thünen as a predictive model for land use around cities. Most interestingly for us, however, recently uses and interpretations of von Thünen within geography have themselves become objects of study (Barnes 1998). Agricultural economists used von Thünen both as a framework to understand observed trends and as a prescriptive policy model upon which to build dairy policy (Cassels 1937; Gaumnitz and Reed 1937). However, sociological notions of centrality have not always followed the precepts of predictive models. Instead, sociologists have looked more at social relationships between the city and the country. As a result, sociological studies tend to point to aspects of spatial organization that are the result of local, contingent historic social relationships, not economic efficiency. From this perspective, von Thünen's spatial boundaries between particular kinds of dairy production are as much the product of economic margins as they are the product of political outcomes. Comparative historical method in sociology has been particularly useful in determining the role of predictive models and contingency in determining the spatial organization of milksheds.

II

Von Thünen and Geography

GEOGRAPHERS HAVE FOUND THE VON THÜNEN RING MODEL both attractive and repulsive. Its attractiveness is based on its simplicity and the fact that many land use patterns around cities seem to be predicted by the model. However, this simplicity is also seen as repulsive. Some geographers complain that the model becomes too simple to use by concentrating almost exclusively on the results of competitive land markets which push more accessible, low transport cost land near a central city into intensive uses, by ignoring history and by assuming a featureless plain.

In 1962, geographer Michael Chisholm published *Rural Settlement and Land Use*, an entire chapter of which was devoted to a description of von Thünian location theory. In this chapter, Chisholm laid out the basic precepts of the theory and made a number of observations. He noted in particular that the isolated state theory was an ideal that would not exactly predict situations but could be widely applied to studying land use patterns in a variety of situations. Chisholm states that Von Thünen "was at pains to make it clear that his particular findings had no claim to universality. But, he claimed, the method by which these results were obtained could be applied generally" (Chisholm 1962, p. 21). These ideas—the fact that von Thünen presented an ideal, a general model that shows how land use should, but probably will not exactly, be organized—formed the center of inquiry for much quantitative revolution research. The publishing of an edited version of von Thünen's *Isolated State* in English in 1966 led to a further flowering of excitement among geographers of the period searching for general economic theories that attempted to explain patterns within the cultural landscape. For instance Peet, who used a von Thünen-based model for the spatial expansion of nineteenth century agricultural zones, states:

> In constructing the model complicating factors were assumed away, providing a laboratory in which the interplay between a small number of essential causal influences and their relations with certain effect could be studied. In particular this model provided a mechanism in which changing technical and economic inputs could be linked with evolving geographical patterns of production (1969, p. 300).

The attraction was thus, that the theory simplified the world by concentrating on the effects of one primary variable, transportation costs, on the location of agricultural production. Von Thünen himself accomplished this by creating the idea of the economic margin. In his view, land use areas were bounded by "margins" where one use became more cost-effective than another (Samuelson 1983). Given von Thünen's thesis, Peet could attempt to explain how these factors may have changed historically and explain changes in the location of production. Use of the von Thünen model, or derivatives of it, continue to this day among quantitative geographers (see, for example, Wang and Guldmann 1997; Hill and Smith 1994; Asami and Isard 1989; Kellerman 1989a, 1989b).

Even in 1966, however, the limitations of the model were accepted. Harvey, for instance, admits "von Thünen's analysis is basically descriptive rather than normative" and does not explain changes over time or the possible effects of economies of scale (1966, p. 363). Despite this, he promotes the model because it made marginal economics geographical. In the years since, these limitations, in particular the fact that von Thünen ignored changes over time, have often been mentioned, but the model survives in importance in the minds of geographers and is a main subject of beginning economic geography courses. The most likely reason for this is that von Thünen rings actually appear to exist in many cases. For instance, cities are often surrounded by a dairy ring. Von Thünen rings are one of the few very easily understandable models in geography that truly appear to explain a pattern in the world, even if the model is primarily descriptive and does not give much idea about how exactly this pattern came to be or what might happen to it in the future. Harvey made this argument in *Social Justice and the City* (1973), arguing that social scientists are attracted to models such as the Isolated State because they appear to be empirically relevant.

Barnes (1998), following Haraway (1997) and Latour (1987), comments on the manner in which von Thünen's model, in particular the concentric zone diagram showing agricultural land use rings of decreasing intensity with distance from the city, has been "fetishized" within economic geography. Barnes argues, based on the work of Barnbrock (1974) and Harvey (1981), that von Thünen's concept of the frontier wage, the "just reward" for work done that, if paid, would ensure worker harmony, leads to a more complete understanding of von Thünen's work. This sense of harmony was also von Thünen's vision of the isolated state in general, "constructed not just an isolated state, but an ideal one" (Barnes 1998, p.101). The rings were "less a description of how the world is, but how it should be once social harmony was realized" (Barnes 1998, p.101). The idea that the isolated state was not just descriptive but also prescriptive is emphasized by Barnbrock, who writes that for von Thünen "the Isolated State is the 'true' representation of the final end mankind should strive for." He further quotes von Thünen, who states "in the Isolated State . . . we have in mind only the final goal" (Barnbrock 1974, p. 61). Harvey points out, however, that this was an essentially conservative goal. Through the imposition of the frontier wage and a more harmonious land use pattern, "class conflict and social polarization" would be minimized within German society (1981, p.9). The lesson learned by neo-classical economists, Harvey argues, was that "economic science could seek and spell out principles of social harmony without appeal to the political economy of the spatial fix" (1981, p.9).

Specific discussions of milksheds among geographers are somewhat limited, but reflect disagreement about the applicability of the von Thünen theory. Loyal Durand was a mid-twentieth century economic geographer who spent his career documenting the dairy regions of the United States. Durand did not often address the von Thünen theory by name, but accepted a transportation-cost based theory as the prevailing theoretical idea on the location of fluid milksheds, which often had some explanatory power. He acknowledged, however, that milksheds were very rarely, if ever, near-perfect circles around cities and discussed specific reasons for the variances from the model in specific locations (Durand 1964, 1952). Lewthwaite, discussing the location of cheese production in Wisconsin, references Cassels (1937), an agricultural economist who refers to von Thünen specifically, and states: "This economic law undoubtably helps explain some features of the geographical pattern," but not "so closely as one might expect" (1964, p. 98). Atkins (1987) studying nineteenth century dairying around London, finds a distinctly un-Thünen-like landscape, not at all in a ring around the city, and often within the city itself.

The use of von Thünen's ideas within geography highlights the conflicts within a discipline that strives both to find regularity in the world and to explain the patterns seen in specific places. The Isolated State theory is attractive because it one of the few easily understood location theories for which empirical examples can be easily drawn. Of course, these examples are never absolutely correct and often seem overly simplistic. Barnes' (1998) analysis of von Thünen and the social construction of von Thünen's theory within economic geography particularly helps us understand the use of von Thünen within agricultural economics. The idea that von Thünen's theories were not just descriptive but also prescriptive more closely parallels the attitudes of the agricultural economists, who were searching not just to describe land use but often also to restrict it in order to build a more harmonious dairy economy.

III

Von Thünen and Agricultural Economics

VON THÜNEN'S IDEAS HAVE LONG BEEN INTEGRATED into agricultural economics, sometimes explicitly and other times less so. Specifically, von Thünen seems to have had the most influence during the creation of the federal milk marketing order system in the 1930s and 1940s, when academic agricultural economists were faced with the challenge of devising pricing systems for fluid milk delivered to particular markets.

Before the 1930s, von Thünen's ideas appear to have been little discussed among dairy economists., Clyde L. King, a Wharton economist who was the author of many early pricing plans and the first chief of the dairy section of the Agricultural Adjustment Administration (AAA), does not makes no mention of von Thünen in his 1920 book *The Price of Milk*. However, he does state that the price of fluid milk must be placed competitively above that of butter and that "there is a limit to the distance that whole milk can be regularly transported to market" (1920, p. 95). Ohio State University agricultural economist Ray Erdman, in his 1921 book *The Marketing of Whole Milk*, also does not mention von Thünen, but extensively discusses the concept of the "milk zone" around cities and discusses the expansion of this zone in a manner which recalls von Thünen's land rent surface, where more central land have higher rents. "These new producers," Erdman writes, "are operating on somewhat lower priced lands and hence can frequently produce milk somewhat more cheaply" (1921, p. 52).

In 1933, agricultural economists, many of whom now worked for the government, were asked to devise the rules for the first milk marketing agreements, the predecessor of the federal milk marketing order programs. From the start these programs had a distinctly geographic component. The federal government would agree to regulate a milkshed when asked to do so by the farmers providing milk to a particular city. The idea of the "milk zone" was thus inherent in the conception of the milk marketing agreements themselves. The question was, however, what the boundary of the zone was to be. Faced with this question, dairy economists appear to have studied von Thünen more explicitly.

It is probable that dairy economists knew of von Thünen before this time. Alfred Marshall refers to von Thünen in *Principles of Economics* and specifically mentions the monopoly rent which can evolve from a company possessing transportation cost advantages within an area where quality differences between the products of particular companies are difficult to discern (1891 [1890], p. 475). In a recent summary of the correspondence of Marshall, John Whitaker notes that Marshall, "drawn from the experience of administering his own estate," claimed to have been "considerably influenced" by Thünen (Whitaker 1996, p.xliv). In 1928 an English translation of a German article on von Thünen's theory of intensity was published in the *Journal of Farm Economics* (Krzymowski 1928). In the 1930s, however, the use of von Thünen's ideas became much more explicit, becoming part of the theoretical support for government involvement in milk markets. A preeminent dairy economist, John D. Black, in a book discussing the involvement of the AAA in the dairy industry, uses a von Thünen-like diagram showing bid-rent curves and concentric milk, cream, and manufacturing zones (Black 1935). Despite the obvious connection, Black does not mention von Thünen specifically here but does in a later agricultural economics textbook in which he states that milk prices follow "the von Thünen principle that producer and use are distributed in zones outward from the consuming center" (1953, p. 423). Black also acknowledges the assistance of John M. Cassels, a Harvard economist who published *A Study of Fluid Milk Prices* in 1937. Cassels refers specifically to von Thünen's isolated state, uses a concentric zone diagram, and states, "The cost of shipping a given quantity of milk in fluid form being greater than the cost of shipping its equivalent in the form of cream, it will naturally be shipped from points nearer to the market than those from which cream is shipped" (1937 [1976], p. 20). He then discusses each zone in more detail, including a discussion of the effect of changes in demand on the size of the zones, and gives quantitative examples. Cassels shows that the milk of closer producers is more valuable to distributors than milk further away, thus causing the zoning. A similar diagram is shown in Krzymowski (1928).

The importance of Cassels' account is that he uses von Thünen to link milk marketing areas to marginal economics. In other words, what King (1920) and Erdman (1921) and others had merely observed, that fluid milk tended to be produced in a zone surrounding cities, while less perishable dairy products were produced further away, was now supported by a theory that presented these conditions as the "ideal." This ideal was also stated, perhaps more importantly, in a report published by the Department of Agriculture and written by the chief of the dairy section and a senior economist. Gaumnitz and Reed (1937) include a chapter on "The General Theory of Milk Pricing," in which they do not refer specifically to von Thünen, but conclude:

> In many areas it is economical to manufacture dairy products at some distance from the market and transport them to market in product rather than fluid form. In such cases the supply area will tend to be zoned, with the bulky and more perishable products, such as fluid milk, produced in the zone or zones nearer the city and the manufactured dairy products produced in more distant zones (p. 106).

The particularly interesting thing about this report is that it goes on to specifically discuss the type of regulation suggested by this theory. This is particularly important since Gaumnitz was the head of the AAA dairy section at the time and was in charge of creating pricing systems for the milk marketing order programs. These programs set minimum prices paid to producers and were quickly being put into place in many areas of the country at the time. As they write, "Thus the theory presented explains the development of the classified-price plan of selling milk" (p.107) and "it would appear possible to approximate that the price for any given volume of milk . . . should be by taking the farm price of milk in alternative uses at the point at the outer edge of the milkshed from which it would be necessary to bring milk in order to secure the desired supply, adding thereto the cost of transporting the milk to the city" (p.108).

The use of these general theories to both justify and provide a theoretical basis for U.S. dairy pricing continues to the present day. Later writings on dairy pricing restated the von Thünenesque "ideal." University of Illinois professor Roland Bartlett, who helped formulate the Chicago pricing plan, stated in a note on milk marketing areas, "The theory of von Thünen supplements that of Marshall by relating the size of a marketing area to goods of different values. Milk has a relatively low specific value and a high degree of perishability. . . . It therefore tends to be produced close to the consuming center . . ." (1952, p. 2). Beal and Bakken (1956) discuss concentric milk, cream, butter, and cheese zones being produced under a system of free competition, and then discuss the manner in which regulation may affect this situation. Bailey (1997), in a section entitled "Theory of Milk Marketing," again shows a concentric zone diagram and a graph of price versus distance. Both reference the Gaumnitz and Reed report.

Manchester (1983), a longtime U.S. Department of Agriculture economist, claims that "inherent instability" results from the ring model. Production around a central city should consist of three regions: an "inner ring" of producers for the fluid milk market; an "outer ring" of producers who sell their milk to manufacturers of butter, cheese, and other products; and a "middle ring" of producers who sell their milk to the fluid market only during periods of high prices. The "inherent instability" results from the middle ring. Because it is generally in the producers' interest to secure a constant buyer for their milk, producers near the outer part of the middle ring may enter into permanent contracts with manufacturing plants, which may further shortages in the city, or producers near the inner portion of the ring may decide to ship all of their milk to the city, which will accentuate spring flush periods. This problem was earlier mentioned by Black (1935) and has been cited as a reason for government involvement in fluid milk pricing. "Under these conditions," states Manchester, "only a monopoly coordinator can achieve a solution that is equitable to all producers and approaches the least-cost situation" (1983, p. 7).

Von Thünen-like models thus appear to form both the theoretical backbone supporting the development of pricing systems used in federal milk marketing orders and a theory-based reasoning for their existence. In order to understand the manner in which they were applied, however, we need to study the context in which this application occurred. A first point is that this context was extremely political. The milk marketing laws were not merely put into place to bring order to the dairy economy but also to support farmer prices. "It is clearly the intention of the Agricultural Adjustment Act to raise farm prices, even at the cost of larger expenditures by consumers," admitted one agricultural economist (Waite 1935, p. 101).

A second point is that von Thünen's theories fulfilled the need for an ideal through which agricultural economists, suddenly in policy positions, could model a better world, just as Harvey (1981) and Barnbrock (1974) suggested. While the writings of the time vary greatly in the importance placed on theoretical and applied research, the general theme is towards the development both of the "ideals" discussed above and of the applications of those ideals. For instance, in a review of Cassels' book, dairy economist W. P. Mortenson states that Cassels' theoretical discussions "will outlive the rest of the book" but "value of the analyses . . . turn on whether or not the assumptions made are so far removed from the situation existing in real life as to virtually divorce the theory from the practical issues involved" (1937, p. 968). Cassels himself states:

> Even before the old regulations of the Mercantilist period had been entirely cleared away it became apparent that the job with which society was confronted was not simply one of demolition, but was one of reconstruction, that implicit faith could not be placed in the guidance of any 'invisible hand' and that the real problem to be tackled was the development of a new set of rules for the carrying on of economic activity which would be more appropriately adapted to the changing conditions of a dynamic age (1938, pp.189–190).

These statements should be viewed within the context of the Department of Agriculture in the 1930s, a place in which the support for direct government involvement in the economy was immense. This can be seen in the statements of USDA officials to the American Farm Economics Association during the period. In 1933, Assistant Secretary Rexford Tugwell looked forward to a more prosperous "planned rather than muddled" future (1934, p.55). Secretary of Agriculture Henry A. Wallace, rallying the troops at the annual meeting in 1935, derided laissez faire economics for obtaining "a grim satisfaction prophesying disaster to the interferences with economic laws by governments and others," and further stated that a second group of economists believed that

> governments, corporations, and other institutions are continually modifying the time, place and manner of action of economic laws. They may rec-

ognize the remorselessness of certain economic laws as much as the classical economists, but they are much more strongly of the belief that it is
possible for human institutions to be pointed more consciously in the direction of harmonious working with economic laws (1936, pp. 2–3).

While all agricultural economists certainly would not have agreed with
Wallace's assessment of laissez faire economics, the idea that their
task was to create a world which more closely approximated that of
the "ideals" and which functioned in a manner which created a more
harmonious society seems to have been accepted by most. Economists such as Black and Cassels used neoclassical economics, particularly von Thünen, to discover the ideals, and believed that government could help adjust markets to more closely approximate these
ideals (Johnson, 1992). As Harvey (1981, 1974) argues, von Thünen's
Isolated State was a precursor of this attitude.

IV

Sociological Notions of Centrality

LIKE GEOGRAPHERS AND AGRICULTURAL ECONOMISTS, sociologists have also
generalized about the relationship between urban centers and their
rural "hinterlands." While these notions are intrinsically spatial, they
most often occur in the classical sociological literature as a temporal
distinction between modern and traditional ways of life. The basic
concern of classical sociology – the transition from feudalism to capitalism – did not explicitly spatialize the distinction between tradition
and modernity, although Marx, Max Weber, and Durkheim all associated the advent of modernity with the rise of cities (Marx and Engels
1978 [1848]; Durkheim 1964 [1893]; Weber 1978 [1922]). The work of
Ferdinand Tönnies is explicitly in this vein. In his book *Gemeinschaft
und Gesellschaft* (1957 [1887]), Tonnies associates the countryside
with a particular way of life that is substantially different from city
life. Subsequent sociological writers continued this framework, looking at rural inhabitants as "folk society" (Redfield 1947) and urbanism
as "a way of life" (Wirth 1938). Geography's preoccupation with centrality, when overlaid with sociology'concern with large-scale historical change, made "modernity" and "centrality" inextricably linked.

Yet, unlike von Thunen's countryside organized simply to trade with the city, sociological views of rurality exphasized aspects of its social organization that did not solely derive from the needs of the center.

Because social theory temporalized ahistorical geographical concepts, it also allowed for a loosening of the assumption of homogenous time. As a result, certain sociologists brought to the fore the social context in which macro forces "worked." From this viewpoint, the spatial relationships between the city and the countryside were not simply law-like but also social and contingent, bringing in notions of power, culture, and human decision making.

Despite these differences in approach, sociological notions of centrality were often treated as predictive and normative models of social change. Like agricultural economists, applied sociologists involved in Third World rural development projects emphasized law-like macro forces affecting temporal change and spatial organization and translated these ideas into policies that worked to reinforce these trends. These projects worked to "get agriculture moving" (Mosher 1996) primarily as a way to feed growing city populations. For example, adoption-diffusion theories of technological change in agriculture focused on the diffusion of productivity-enhancing technological innovations from university centers to expectant farmers (Rogers and Shoemaker 1971). The categories used to describe farmer responses to technological change were explicitly normative, defining these farmers in terms of their response to central actions: those who adopted technology quickly were called "innovators" while those who didn't were called "laggards" (Griliches 1957) As a result, the economic idea of hinterlands spatially organized in terms of the economic efficiency of production for the city became intertwined with sociological notions of "marginality" (Park 1928), defined as rural and agricultural activity not organized around this goal.

In contrast, sociologists and social historians working in the comparative tradition of Max Weber (1978 [1922]), have emphasized contingent, localized, social phenomena over macro-economic trends.Weber's essay "Capitalism and Rural Society in Germany," exemplifies the extent to which his intellectual program differed from that of von Thünen. In this essay, Weber examines the reasons why agriculture in the eastern part of Germany is organized around extensive production while agriculture in the western part of the nation was more intensive. Like von Thunen, his question has to do with explaining differences in agricultural intensity. Yet, his answer has little to do with the spatial location of farming in reference to cities. Weber focuses on the differences in history and culture of each region, particularly differences in the relationship between farmers and landowners. From this point of view, city/country relationships involved struggles and negotiations between the inhabitants of these areas, struggles that affected spatial organization.

Recent approaches to studies of rural and urban life have included textual studies of changing representations of city and country in professional and popular parlance (Williams 1973; Marx 1977; DuPuis and Vandergeest, 1996). Like comparative history, textual studies emphasize less law-like notions of centralityand tend to see the city-country distinction as both terrain and idea (Bell, 1992).

How do we reconcile the more law-like notions of centrality with those that see city/country relationships as the product of social contestation? To examine the relationship between macro forces and local politics, sociologists have turned increasingly to comparative social history as a method (Skocpol and Sommers 1980; McMichael, 1990). From a comparative historical perspective, von Thünen's assumption of harmonious and conflict-free relations between city and country do not and cannot exist; they are as much a fiction as his flat and featureless plains. Comparative history focuses on the bumpy terrain of politics and society, bringing in notions of power, culture and human decision-making.

Interestingly, a number of scholars concerned with relating the universal and the contingent in agriculture have turned to the study of dairy regions. Because milk production has remained in the rural hinterland of cities, comparative histories of city milksheds enable the researcher to both test the predictiveness of von Thunen's model and to examine the contingent local forces that lead to less universal, predictable, "harmonious" spatial relationships.

For example, Gilbert and Akor's (1988) comparative study of California and Wisconsin dairying shows that California's dairy industry has become significantly more intensive than Wisconsin's due to ecological, cultural and political factors related to the Los Angeles' milkshed. DuPuis' (1993; forthcoming) comparison of New York, California, and Wisconsin milksheds showed that spatial boundaries between zones of dairy production in these states were as much a product of political interests as they were of law-like forces. States without urban milksheds pursued a less industrial model of dairying in their agricultural extension policies. Schwartzweller and Davidson's comparison of Upper and Peninsula and lower Michigan dairy regions shows how the Upper Peninsula region, at the edge of the urban milkshed, became more economically marginalized over time. Cruise and Lyson (1991) compare two dairy communities in Western New York State and show that differences in dairy practices are related to the presence or absence of support institutions. Pritchard (1996) looks specifically at the role of cooperatives in influencing the spatial organization of dairy markets in the United States and Australia.

Block and DuPuis' (2000) comparative historical study of New York and Chicago milksheds explicitly addresses von Thünen's model and shows that the "efficient" boundary between dairy zones has often been the product of political struggles whose outcomes have varied according to region. For example, in Illinois, farmers retained some political power and were therefore able to pursue more aggressive policies to restrict milksheds. In New York, with a politically dominant urban populace interested in cheap food supplies, farmers were unable to restrict market boundaries within the state, although they were better able than Illinois to restrict out of state supplies.

The politics of urban milkshed boundaries continues today with the implementation of the Northeast Dairy Compact, an agreement between New England states to give higher milk prices to farmers serving their market. Midwest congressional representatives assailed the Compact as a restriction on trade (*Congress Daily*, July 30 1999), while New England representatives presented it as a way to save family dairy farms in the region (*Economist*, August 8 1998). While the Compact was recently expanded to allow New York and other Mid-Atlantic states to join, "big-city opposition" has defeated New York state legislation approving its membership because, according to the *Economist*, "cities feared the Compact would make milk more expensive, and of course it has" (p. 29). Von Thünen's model, for all its predictive power, could not have predicted this current set of contentions over milkshed boundaries.

V

Conclusion

IN THIS STUDY, WE COMPARE the use of von Thünen's Isolated State theory in three disciplines—geography, agricultural economics, and sociology—as it relates to the spatial organization of dairy farming. We find that von Thünen's theory has been most explicitly used by geographers, who were attracted to it as a locational theory at a time when they were searching for such theories. The analysis of the social adoption of the Thünen theory by geographers leads us to a similar analysis of agricultural economics, in which von Thünen's ideas, while not being as explicitly mentioned as within geography, nevertheless had a great influence on the economic theory behind government dairy pricing programs. Finally, among agricultural sociologists who examine the structure of the dairy industry, von Thünen's theories have been the least used. This is partially because sociology is more temporal than spatial, but also because sociological analysis tends to be more open to contingency and political power as key factors in both temporal change and spatial organization. Comparative historical methods enable sociologists to test the predictiveness of macro theory and local, contingent historical forces, especially political power relationships between the city and the country in particular regions.

Comparative historical methods enable researchers to look at particular spatial configurations as the product of both large-scale forces and local, contingent politics. Such comparisons enable power and political agency to come to the front of the story. In these cases, the forces described by von Thünen that even today organize milksheds around a city remain a part of the story, but only one part. Comparing actual places to the universal ideas expressed in geographical models enables researchers to gain a greater understanding of both politics and macro forces in the organization of space.

A comparison of the disciplinary use of a theory allows us to understand more about the disciplines themselves. Von Thünen's ideas became popular in geography and were used in agricultural economics because they fit specific desires within those disciplines at a particular time. Geography was searching for locational models. Agricultural economics needed to find an "ideal" upon which to base milk marketing policy. The use of von Thünen within these disciplines is a fine example of how a theory can be discovered, used, become part of the accepted knowledge of a discipline, and sometimes greatly affect public policy.

References

Asami, Tasushi and Walter Isard. (1989). Imperfect Information, Uncertainty and Optimal Sampling in Location Theory: An Initial Reexamination of Hotelling, Weber, and Von Thünen. *Journal of Regional Science* 29(4): 507–521.

Atkins, P. J. (1987). The Charmed Circle: von Thünen and Agriculture around Nineteenth Century London. *Geography* 72(2):129–139.

Bailey, Kenneth W. (1997). Marketing and Pricing of Milk and Dairy Products in the United States. Ames, IA: Iowa State University Press.

Barnbrock, Joern. (1974). Prologomenon to a Methodological Debate on Location Theory: The Case of von Thünen. *Antipode* 6(1): 59–66.

Barnes, Trevor. (1998). Envisioning Economic Geography: Three Men and their Figures. *Geographische Zeitschrift* 86(2): 94–105.

Bartlett, R. W. (1952). Theory and Practice of Establishing Milk Marketing Areas. University of Illinois Department of Agricultural Economics, Agricultural Economics Reports 2895.

Beal, George Max and Henry H. Bakken. (1956). *Fluid Milk Marketing*. Madison, WI: Mimir Publishers.

Bell, Michael. (1992). The Fruit of Difference: The Rural-Urban Continuum as a System of Identity. *Rural Sociology* 57: 65–82.

Black, John D. (1953). *Introduction to Economics for Agriculture*. New York: Macmillan.

———. (1935). *The Dairy Industry and the AAA*. Washington, DC: The Brookings Institution.

Block, Daniel and E. Melanie DuPuis. (2000). Rings of Contention: Politics, von Thünen, and the Fluid/Manufacturing Milk Boundary around Chicago. Paper presented at the annual meeting of the Association of American Geographers, Pittsburgh, PA. April.

Cassels, John M. (1937 [1976]). *A Study of Fluid Milk Prices*. Harvard Economic Studies 54. Reprinted 1976. New York: Arno.

———. (1938). The Future of Milk Control. *Journal of Farm Economics* 20: 188–195.

Chisholm, Michael. (1962). *Rural Settlement and Land Use*. 1st edition. London: Hutchinson and Co.

Congress Daily A. (1999). "Judiciary Subpanel Extends Northeast Dairy Compact." (July 30).

Cruise, James and Thomas Lyson. (1991). Beyond the Farmgate: Factors Related to Agricultural Performance in Two Dairy Communities. *Rural Sociology* 56:41–55.

DuPuis, E. Melanie. (Forthcoming). *Nature's Perfect Food: Milk and American Identity*. New York: NYU Press.

———. (1996). *Creating the Countryside: The Politics of Rural and Environmental Discourse*. (Philadelphia: Temple University Press).

———. (1993). Sub-National State Institutions and the Organization of Agricultural Resource Use: The Case of the Dairy Industry. *Rural Sociology* 58(3): 440–460.

Durand, Loyal Jr. (1964). The Major Milksheds of the Northeastern Quarter of the United States. *Economic Geography* 40(1): 9–33.

———. (1952). The Migration of Cheese Manufacture in the United States. *Annals of the Association of American Geographers* 42(4): 263–282.

Durkheim, Emile. (1964 [1893]). *The Division of Labor in Society*. New York: Free Press.

Economist. (1998). "A Contented Moo." 348(8080):28–29. Aug. 8.

Erdman, Henry E. (1921). *The Marketing of Whole Milk*. New York: Macmillan.

Fairburn, Miles. (1999). Social History: Problems, Strategies and Methods.

Gaumnitz, E. W. and O. M. Reed. (1937). *Some Problems Involved in Establishing Milk Prices*. DM-2 Marketing Information Series. Agricultural Adjustment Administration, U.S. Department of Agriculture. Washington D.C.

Gilbert, J. and R. Akor. (1988). Increasing Structural Divergence in United States Dairying-California and Wisconsin Since 1950. *Rural Sociology* 53(1): 56–72.

Griliches, Z. (1957). Hybrid Corn: An Exploration in the Economics of Technical Change. *Econometrica* 25: 501–522.

Haraway, Donna J. (1997). Modest Witness@SecondMillenium. FemaleMan©MeetsOncoMouse™. New York: Routledge.

Harvey, David. (1981). The Spatial Fix-Hegel, von Thünen, and Marx. *Antipode* 13(3): 1–12.

———. (1973). *Social Justice and the City*. Baltimore: Johns Hopkins.

———. (1966). Theoretical Concepts and the Analysis of Agricultural Land-use Patterns in Geography. *Annals of the Association of American Geographers* 56(2): 361–374.

Hill, Ron and Derek L. Smith. (1994). Is Von Thünen Alive and Well? A Transport-Cost Surface for South Australian Wheat. *Australian Geographical Studies* 32(2): 183–190.

Johnson, Glenn L. (1992). Philosophic Foundations of Agricultural Economic Thought from World War II to the Mid-1970's. in Martin, Lee R, ed. *A Sur-*

vey of Agricutultural Economics Literature, vol. 4, pp. 971–1037. Minneapolis: University of Minnesota Press.

Kellerman, A. (1989a). Agricultural Location Theory 1: Basic Models. *Environment and Planning A* 21(10): 1381–1396.

———. (1989b). Agricultural Location Theory 2: Relaxation of Assumptions and Applications. *Environment and Planning A* 21(11): 1427–1446.

King, Clyde L. (1920). *The Price of Milk.* Philadelphia: The John Winston Company.

Krzymowski, Richard. (1928). Graphical Presentation of Thuenen's Theory of Intensity. Translated and annotated by P. G. Minneman. *Journal of Farm Economics* 10: 461–481.

Latour, Bruno. (1987). *Science in Action: How to Follow Scientists and Engineers through Society.* Cambridge, MA.: Harvard University Press.

Lewthwaite, Gordon R. (1964). Wisconsin Cheese and Farm Type: A Locational Hypothesis. *Economic Geography* 40(2): 95–112.

Manchester, Alden C. (1983). *The Public Role in the Dairy Economy: How and Why Governments Interfere in the Milk Business.* Boulder, CO: Westview.

Marshall, Alfred. (1891). *Principles of Economics,* 2nd edition. New York: MacMillan. First edition published 1890.

Marx, Karl. (1978 [1848]). *The Communist Manifesto.* Pp. 469–500 in Tucker, Robert C. (Ed.) *The Marx/Engels Reader.* New York: Norton & Co.

Marx, Leo. (1977). *The Machine in the Garden.* London: Oxford University Press.

McMichael, Philip. (1990). Incorporating Comparison within a World-Historical Perspective: An Alternative Comparative Method. *American Sociological Review* 55 (3): 385–397.

Mortenson, W. P. (1937). Review of *A Study of Fluid Milk Prices* by John M. Cassels. *Journal of Farm Economics* 19: 967–970.

Mosher, Arthur Theodore. (1966). *Getting Agriculture Moving; Essentials for Development and Modernization.* New York: Praeger.

Park, Robert. (1928). Human Migration and the Marginal Man. *American Journal of Sociology* 33(6): 881–892.

Peet, J. R. (1969). The Spatial Expansion of Commercial Agriculture in the Nineteenth Century: A von Thünen Interpretation. *Economic Geography* 45: 283–301.

Pritchard, W. (1996). Shifts in Food Regimes, Regulation, and Producer Cooperatives: Insights from the Australian and US Dairy Industries. *Environment and Planning A* 28 (5): 857–876.

Redfield, Robert. (1947). The Folk Society. *The American Journal of Sociology* 52(4):293–308.

Rogers, Everett and F. Floyd Shoemaker. (1971). *Communications of Innovations: A Cross-Cultural Approach.* New York: The Free Press.

Samuelson, Paul A. (1983). Thünen at two hundred. *Journal of Economic Literature* 21: 1468–1488.

Schwarzweller, Harry K. and Andrew P. Davidson. (1997). Perspectives on Regional and Enterprise Marginality: Dairying in Michigan's North Country. *Rural Sociology* 62 (2): 157–179.

Skocpol, Theda and Somers, Margaret. (1980). The Uses of Comparative History. *Comparative Studies in Society and History* 22(2): 174–197.

Tönnies, Ferdinand. (1957 [1887]). *Community and Society: Gemeinschaft und Gesellschaft*. (East Lansing, MI: The Michigan State University Press).

von Thünen, Johan Heinrich. (1966 [1826]). *Von Thünen's Isolated State*. ed. Hall, Peter. Oxford: Pergamon Press. First published 1826 as *Der isolierte Staat Beziehung auf Landwirtschaft und Nationalökonomie*. Hamburg: Perthes.

Tugwell, Rexford G. (1934). The Place of Government in a National Land Program. *Journal of Farm Economics* 16(1): 55–69.

Waite, W. C. (1935). Economic Bases and Objectives of Public Regulation of the Milk Industry. *Journal of Farm Economics* 17: 101–108.

Wallace, Henry A. (1936). Farm Economists and Agricultural Planning. *Jounal of Farm Economics* 18: 1–11.

Wang, F. and J-M Guldmann. (1997). A Spatial Equilibrium Model for Region Size, Urbanization Ratio, and Rural Structure. *Environment and Planning A* 29(5): 929–941.

Weber, Max. (1978 [1922]). *Economy and Society*. Berkeley, CA: University of California Press.

———. (1978 [1922]). "The City" in *Economy and Society*. Berkeley, CA; University of California Press.

Whitaker, John K. (1996). *The Correspondence of Alfred Marshall, Economist*, vol. 1: Climbing, 1868–1890. New York: Cambridge University Press.

Williams, Raymond. (1973). *The Country and the City*. New York: Oxford University Press.

PART II

New Research on Size, Geography, Specialization and Productivity

American Journal of Economics and Sociology, Vol. 60, No. 1 (January, 2001).
© 2001 American Journal of Economics and Sociology, Inc.

Agglomeration and Congestion in the Economics of Ideas and Technological Change

By NORMAN SEDGLEY and BRUCE ELMSLIE

ABSTRACT. Urban economists have long recognized that space is economically important. Evidence of the importance of urban agglomeration and the offsetting effects of congestion are provided in a number of studies of productivity and wages. Little attention has been paid to this evidence in the economic growth literature. The new growth research focuses on technological change. We extend the production function for new ideas common to this research in a way that allows for congestion and agglomeration in innovation and test the hypothesis that these forces are important in explaining innovation. Strong evidence is found that agglomeration and congestion are important in explaining the vast differences in per capita patent rates across US states. This suggests an important new agenda in linking studies of urban economics with the rapidly advancing field of endogenous growth.

I

Introduction

THE PURPOSE OF THIS PAPER is to extend the idea of agglomeration and congestion effects from regional and urban economics by drawing a link between this literature and the new models on the economics of ideas common to the new growth research. Empirical evidence from urban economics, regional economics, and economic geography suggests that agglomeration and congestion effects have an important im-

Norman Sedgley, Department of Economics, Sellinger School of Business and Management, Loyola College in Maryland, Baltimore, MD 21210 and Bruce Elmslie, Reginald F. Atkins, Associate Professor, Department of Economics, University of New Hampshire, McConnell Hall, Durham, NH 03824, Phone: (603)862–3347, Fax: (603)862–3383, e-mail: bte@hopper.unh.edu.

The authors thank Ross Gittell, Michael Goldberg, Torsten Schmidt, and Stanley Sedo for helpful comments. The usual caveats apply.

American Journal of Economics and Sociology, Vol. 60, No. 1 (January, 2001).

pact on productivity differences across economies. While most of these studies measure the scale of production by the absolute size of the economy (the size of the population being most common) as many growth studies do, Ciccone and Hall (1996) are an exception. They show that population density across US States is important for explaining differences in productivity levels across states. Their analysis, however, suggests that agglomeration effects are much stronger than congestion effects. While their analysis is entirely static, it does suggest an important extension of the dynamic endogenous growth models.

Within the new endogenous growth theory there is a focus on the economics of ideas. This approach has proven useful to many wishing to understand the economics of innovation and technological change. These models, in their simplest form, suggest a scale effect: *ceteris paribus* a large economy innovates and grows at a faster rate than smaller economy. This unique implication is found to be at odds with the evidence (Helliwell and Chung, 1992; Jones, 1995a).

The absence of the scale effects suggested in these models concerns growth theorists. These scale effects tend to arise due to relaxed resource constraints and, therefore, a lower cost of innovation in a larger economy. An absence of these scale effects does not rule out the possibility of agglomeration and congestion having an important role to play in the new growth literature. The lack of evidence of scale effects, however, has caused the new growth literature to move in a direction that removes all notions of scale from the models. We believe new growth theory is overlooking some important and interesting evidence concerning the role of agglomeration and congestion in the production of new ideas and the dynamics of economic growth.

Our empirical analysis of agglomeration and congestion differs from past investigations. We use a direct measure of innovative outcomes as our dependant variable. Typically, researchers look for agglomeration and congestion in productivity measures. While these forces are well documented, little attention has been paid specifically to evidence of agglomeration and congestion in the production of new ideas. The production function for new ideas is at the heart of endogenous growth in much of the new growth research. The link between measures of innovation and productivity growth is well documented.

Studies by authors such as Abramovitz (1986), Amable (1993), Fagerburg (1988, 1994), Verspagen (1991), Sedgley (1998), and Sedgley and Elmslie (2000) demonstrate that differences in innovation as measured by patenting statistics are important in explaining differences in productivity growth.

We give the *density* of economic activity an explicit role in a model where growth is driven by the production of new ideas and test the implications using state level data available from the US Federal Government. Our formulation allows us to gain some insight into how important agglomeration economies and congestion effects are for understanding the economics of ideas and innovation.

Section II reviews the related literature. Section III develops a theoretical reformulation of the production function for new ideas that allows for congestion and agglomeration in a straightforward way. Section IV describes the data collected for the research and empirical estimates are outlined in Section V. Section VI draws some final conclusions and suggestions for further research.

II

Related Literature

PACK (1994) CONVINCINGLY argues that there are very few true tests of endogenous growth theory. One of the salient implications of endogenous growth models is the prediction of scale effects, large economies innovate faster than small economies, *ceteris paribus*. Some empirical studies look for scale effects, typically adding the size of the population to the list of explanatory variables within the neoclassical framework (See for example Helliwell and Chung, 1992). The evidence does not strongly support the existence of scale effects.

This evidence receives a good deal of attention from growth theorists. Grossman and Helpman (1994) refer to scale effects as a "counterfactual implication" of endogenous innovation models. This concern over the apparent non existence of scale effects caused some researchers to reformulate endogenous growth theory in an attempt to free the models from the prediction of scale effects (Lucas, 1988). Others have argued in favor of a more aggregate and long term view of the impact of scale. Kremer (1993) looks at population growth and advances in technology from "one million BC to 1990." He argues that the appropriate scale of interest is global. Kremer states:

> The model's implications for growth theory are clearer. Most models of endogenous technological change imply that all else equal, higher population spurs technological change. This result, I believe, is not due to any quirk of modeling....Endogenous growth theorists have dismissed the population implications of their models as empirically untenable. This paper suggests that we should take them seriously (Kremer, 713–714).

Barro and Sala-I-Martin (1995) note that all these caveats tend to blur the empirical implications of endogenous growth models. This, they argue, makes it difficult to test these models with macroeconomic data (Barro and Sala-I-Martin, PP151). It is fair to say that researchers working in the area of endogenous growth view scale effects as a nuisance. Scale implications are either ignored or models are reformulated to dispel all implications that scale impacts growth.

The apparent absence of these scale effects does not imply, however, that the concentration of economic activity has no role to play in the economics of innovation. The division of labor will allow for efficient innovation of new products once the basic needs of the local economy are met[1]. This division of labor and concentration of economic activity will increase productivity, a fact that has been recognized in the area of urban economics. Beeson (1987), for example, reports evidence of the importance of urban agglomeration in determining productivity levels across states. The ideas surrounding urban agglomeration are potentially of great importance for endogenous growth theory, though the link has not been fully appreciated by most growth theorists.

Evidence of the importance of urbanization and the concentration of economic activity on productivity measures is well documented. Glaeser (1992, 1995) estimates growth equations and links changes in employment growth, wage growth, and worker productivity across US cities to agglomeration, measured again by population levels. Segal (1975) reports that larger cities in the United States have a total factor productivity advantage over smaller cities. Soroka (1994), however, does not find the same relationship between productivity and city size in Canada. In an important article Ciccone and Hall (1996) study the relationship between differences in worker productivity across US states, and the density of economic activity. Density, in their words, is high when "there is a large amount of labor and capital per square foot"(Ciccone and Hall, 1996; 55). They find that the density of employment is a more important explanatory variable for differences in productivity levels than the size of the economy.

In terms of testing the implications of endogenous growth models, scale effects arise because resource constraints are relaxed, leading to lower costs of product innovation. To the extent that labor markets are defined geographically it can be argued that population density is of interest. Agglomeration might include these types of scale effects. Actual agglomeration is likely to include other factors such as external economies in knowledge spillovers and transport networks (including the transport of new ideas). Jaffe, Trajtenberg, and Henderson (1993) who show that patent citations are geographically linked to the area where a patent is filed, providing important evidence of spatial considerations in knowledge networks. These factors will tend to increase labor's marginal product and wages in high-density areas. Evidence of these effects is provided in some of the studies cited above. These forces together with labor market pooling effects are developed as far back as Marshall (1920).

III

A Theoretical Reformulation

It seems obvious that sustained long run growth must in some way depend on technological change and that the determination of the rate technological change rests well within the sphere of economics. Economists since Solow (1957) have recognized the importance of technological change. The rate of technological change, however, was treated as exogenous or as a result of unintended externalities until more recent theoretical advances allowed economists to easily model internal economies of scale and imperfect competition in a general equilibrium setting (Dixit and Stiglitz, 1977). Authors such as Romer (1987, 1990), Agion and Howitt (1992, 1998) and Grossman and Helpman (1991) pioneered models where the private incentive to innovate results from profit opportunities in the imperfectly competitive sector of the economy.

While the micro foundations of these models differ slightly from one author to the next, they lead to the same basic reduced form. The details are of little importance here and we will follow Jones (1995b) in concentrating on the reduced form of the models. Allow output to be produced with the following production function:

(1) $$Y = K^{\alpha}(AL_Y)^{1-\alpha}$$

where Y is aggregate output, K is the capital stock, L_Y is the supply of labor used to produce aggregate output and A is Harrod neutral level of technology. A doubling of L_Y and K will double output. A doubling of L_Y, K and A will more than double output, leading to rising per capita output over time. This stems from the basic non-rival and non-excludable nature of ideas in the production function for aggregate output.

The growth of A is endogenized in these models by interpreting K as an index of (nondurable) intermediate goods and indexing the level of technology to the number of such available goods. While Y is produced under conditions of perfect competition, intermediate goods follow a monopolistically competitive market structure. Traditionally the models assume labor is used to produce new ideas with the existing stock of knowledge through the following production function for new ideas:

(2) $$\frac{A}{A} = \delta L_A^{\lambda}$$

where δ is a parameter determining the productivity of labor in research. The traditional scale effect is immediately clear. The growth rate of technology is proportional to the level of population used in the research sector. Since L_A is a constant fraction of L the growth rate of technology is directly proportional to the level of population. Furthermore, it is well known that in a steady state the growth rate of per capita output will be equal to the rate of technological change:

(3) $$\gamma_y = \frac{A}{A} = \delta L_A^{\lambda}$$

where y denotes per capita output and γ is used to denote a steady state growth rate.

Jones's often cited critique of the model is based on the simple observation that, in a steady state, L_A is a constant fraction of the available supply of labor L, where $L = L_A + L_Y$ is the economy's resource constraint. Therefore the growth rate of output per capita is predicted to rise at the rate of population growth. This argument ignores the possible offsetting effects of congestion. Once agglomeration and congestion are allowed into the model it is clear that much of the existing literature on endogenous growth is ignoring important variables and relationships in an attempt to explain the absence of scale effects.

Consider the following modification of equation (3).

(4)
$$\frac{\dot{A}}{A} = e^{\phi(L/s)} L^\lambda \varepsilon$$

Where the productivity of labor in research, $\delta = e^{\phi(L/s)}$, depends on the concentration of economic activity, s represents space and L/s represents the concentration of economic activity within the economy. ε is a random disturbance attached to the discovery of new ideas.

Within this formulation we assume ϕ is nonlinear in L/s. The formulation should capture the idea that the productivity of labor in the production of new ideas is related to agglomeration and congestion. Furthermore, agglomeration economies are likely to be most important when L/s is low. Congestion economies might begin to set in right away, but are unlikely to dominate the positive effects of agglomeration until a critical level of population density is reached. We assume that ϕ' is positive and diminishing for low values of L/s. $\phi' = 0$ at some optimal population density, L^*/s. Beyond the optimal population density congestion economies tend to dominate, implying ϕ' is negative. This theoretical reformulation could have important consequences for understanding the economics of innovation and endogenous growth.

To motivate the empirical discussion we must have an equation in observable variables. The problem with equation (4) is that the level of knowledge, A, is difficult to measure. We can rearrange equation (4) as:

(5)
$$\frac{\dot{A}}{L} = e^{\phi(L/s)} A L^{\lambda-1} \varepsilon$$

Our desired properties for ϕ can be captured by assuming the following quadratic form.

(6) $\phi(L/s) = a_0 + a_1(L/s) + a_2(L/s)^2_2$, $a_0 \geq 0$, $a_1 > 0$, $a_2 < 0$

Inserting equation (6) into equation (5) and taking logs provides an empirical framework.

(7)
$$\log\left(\frac{\dot{A}}{L}\right) = a_0 + a_1(L/s) + a_2(L/s)^2$$
$$+ \log(A) + (\lambda - 1)\log(L) + \log \varepsilon$$

We can proxy the dependant variable with a per capita patent rate while adding measures to the list of independent variables in order to control for differences in the initial level of knowledge, A, which apply to patenting over some time period.

IV

Data

THE DATA COLLECTED FOR THIS PAPER spans the years 1970 to 1996. Data is collected for each of the 48 continental United States and the District of Columbia. One advantage of studying growth across states is the fact that US states are more institutionally and culturally homogeneous than a diverse sample of countries. Furthermore, factors of production flow more easily across state boundaries than internationally and US states certainly share a common capital market. Another convenience in studying state growth is the relative abundance of data. Data is collected in a systematic and methodologically identical manner across all states. A list of variables and descriptions is presented in Table 1.

The considerations outlined above suggest an exciting opportunity to test the implications of growth theory. An average patent rate per 10,000 workers within the state (PAT) is used as a proxy for the dependant variable. Data on patents is collected from the US Patent and Trademark Office while employment data is collected from the Bureau of Economic Analysis Regional Economic Information System (BEA REIS). Patents, while an imperfect measure of knowledge creation, are an output measure. Given the likely significance of knowl-

Table 1.

Variables

PAT = Average patents per 10,000 workers

LQHTI = Location quotient in high technology manufacturing industries.

POP = Population level (measured in thousands).

POPD = Population density (persons per square mile)

RDU = Average federal govenrment university R&D expenditures per worker.

SCHOOL = Educational attainment, percent of population with four or more years of college.

AGE 0–24 = Percentage of the total population between the ages of 0 and 24.

AGE 24–64 = Percentage of the total population between the ages of 0 and 64.

AGE 65+ = Percentage of the total population age 65 and over.

edge spillovers across industries it is important to use an economy wide measure of the patent rate. Regional and industry specific knowledge as well as any unmeasurable spillovers of knowledge between regions and industries should be captured in an aggregate patent rate. One potential problem with the patent variable is the lag between the time an innovation is made and the time at which a patent is ultimately granted. Fortunately, a close examination of the data reveals that the states where innovative activity occurs most heavily changes little over time. Therefore, similar results are likely regardless of the period for which the variable PAT is calculated.

As for agglomeration, congestion, and scale effects, data from the Bureau of the Census on population (POP) and population density in (POPD) at the start of the growth period are used. Also from the Census Bureau are measures of human capital. This data includes a measure of the proportion of the population with four or more years of college at the start of the growth period (SCHOOL) and data on the age structure of the state at the start of the period.

Persson and Malmberg (1996) report that the initial age structure is important to subsequent growth. In particular, they report that growth across US states is positively related to the percentage of the population in the age group 25 to 64. The age structure captures an important element of human capital implied in learning by doing models, elements not likely to be captured in the SCHOOL variable. To calculate the age structure variable, the relative frequency of a state's population is broken down as follows: AGE 0–24, AGE 25–64, and AGE 65 +. This information is collected from the US Census Bureau's Population Division. The variable AGE is then calculated as:

$$(8) \qquad AGE = \frac{(AGE25 - 64)}{(AGE0 - 24 + AGE65)}$$

A greater value of AGE is expected to increase the growth rate in productivity.

Variables included in the empirical investigation on the determinants of the rate of innovation include average federal government research and development (R&D), expenditures per worker at universities (RDU). This data is included to control for a state's university R&D infrastructure. Data on Federal Government R&D expenditures are available from the National Science Foundation. Employment data are, once again, extracted from the BEA REIS.

A location quotient for high technology manufacturing industries at the beginning of the period (LQHTI) is calculated as a location quotient in the combined industries of Industrial Machinery and Equipment (SIC 35), Electronic and Other Electric Equipment (SIC 36), and Instruments and Related Products (SIC 38). These industries are chosen based on American Electronic Association's (AEA) high technology manufacturing industry definition. The location quotient measures the ratio of the percentage of state employment in high tech industries to the national percentage of employment in these industries. It is expected that a high concentration in high tech industries will lead to a higher rate of innovation. Employment data used to calculate LQHTI is from the BEA REIS.

V

Empirical Results

WE ESTIMATE EQUATION (7) in the most direct way possible. It is common in the growth literature to condition a growth measure (PAT in this case) averaged over some time period on the initial or starting values of the independent variables. This insures causation runs in one direction since the future cannot cause the past (or present). The data shows that there is a great deal of variation in innovation across states. Average patents per 10,000 workers over the 1970 to 1995 period ranges from a high of 12.43 in Delaware to a low of 0.83 patents per 10,000 workers in Mississippi. The average across all states is 3.53. Other noteworthy states include New Jersey with an average of 9.41, and Massachusetts with an average of 6.40. States with low levels of innovation include Arkansas with an average of .98 and The District of Columbia with an average of 1.05. States also differ remarkably in terms of population density, suggesting that agglomeration and congestion in innovation may help explain the vast differences in innovative activity across states. The density of population per square mile ranges from 9,982 in DC to a low of 4.7 in Wyoming. The average density of population across US states in 1990 was 366.7 persons per square mile.

The empirical specification of equation (7) is:

$$(9) \qquad Log(PAT)_i = a_0 + X_i\alpha + a_1 POPD_i = a_2 POPD_i^2$$
$$+ (\lambda - 1)\log(POP_i) = Y_i{}'\theta + \varepsilon_i$$

Where X is a vector of regional dummy variables. Dummy variables are included for the Northeast, Midwest, and Southern regions. The rate of patenting is conditioned on the congestion and agglomeration variables POPD and *POPD²* as well as the scale variable POP. Y represents a vector of variables included to control for differences in the level of knowledge and technology. These variables include measures of a state's R&D infrastructure (in industry and at universities) as well as variables to account for differences in human capital.

Notice that we expect the coefficient on log (POP) to be between zero and minus one. If we find that this is the case, the data are consistent with traditional scale effects. The decrease in the per capita patent rate suggested by a larger population is at least partially offset by a larger number of new ideas generated through a relaxed resource constraint. Y, the vector of additional variables that are potentially important for explaining rates of innovation through differing initial levels of knowledge or technology, includes measures of human capital, federal government support of research activities within the state, and the concentration of a state's economy in high technology industries. This model is estimated for the periods 1970–1980, 1980–1990, 1990–1995, and 1970–1995. Parameter estimates are provided in Table 2.

There is evidence of heteroskedasticity associated with each specification of equation (9). This problem, if left uncorrected, biases the estimated standard errors of the parameter estimates and renders any attempt to make valid inferences impossible. The variance is modeled in a general form using White's consistent estimator of the variance-covariance matrix. [2] This method corrects the bias in the variance-covariance matrix and provides consistent estimates of the standard errors. All models are estimated using the method of maximum likelihood.

Referring to Table 2, POP is a measure of absolute scale. It is included to test the hypothesis of scale effects as they relate to the size of the economy. It is clear that the population level is not significantly related to the per worker rate of innovation in a state's economy. The value of the coefficient on the variable is essentially equal to zero and it is not significant in each specification of the model. This is true across the various model specifications and time periods. The evidence suggests it is essentially equal to one and increases in population are matched proportionally by increases in $\dot{A}$ and, therefore, have no impact on per capita patent rates.

Population density and its quadratic suggest population density is positively related to innovation, but there are diminishing returns. Glaeser (1988) links the speed of the transport of ideas to population density, but notes that congesting forces can create costs for the local economy in terms of increased commuting costs, pollution, crime, and poverty. Both variables are highly significant in each regression reported in Table 2. Model specification 3 for the 1970–1995 period, for example, suggests diminishing absolute returns will set in when population density reaches a level of 5,496 persons per square mile.[3] This is a figure far greater than the 1990 population density figures reported for all states. The closest region is the District of Columbia whose pop-

Table 2.

Parameter Estimates

	1970–1980			1980–1990		
	1	2	3	1	2	3
popd	.17383E-02*	.15447E-02*	.90762E-03*	.12477E-02**	.11293E-02**	.90638E-03**
	(.6675E-03)	(.578E-03)	(.2793E-03)	(.5801E-03)	(.5278E-03)	(.3587E-03)
popd²	-.14104E-06*	-.12409E-06*	-.7917E-07*	-.12537E-06**	-.10835E-06**	-.92834E-07**
	(.551E-07)	(.485E-07)	(.2331E-07)	(.5715E-07)	(.5247E-07)	(.3655E-07)
Log(pop)	.1903	.5603E-01	-.55662E-02	.19771	.89261E-01	.6295E-01
	(.1205)	(.127)	(.1027)	(.130)	(.1145)	(.1054)
Log(RDU)		.21681**	-.10061		.1632***	.14062E-01
		(.1036)	(.8874E-01)		(.905E-01)	(.1013)
Log(LQHTI)		.24761*	.30491*		.25099*	.29315*
		(.677E-01)	(.5985E-01)		(.7826E-01)	(.8004E-01)
Log(SCHOOL)			1.8013*			1.0026*
			(.4146)			(.3806)
Log(AGE)			2.2458**			1.2896***
			(1.037)			(.7441)
F	6.91*	7.5*	13.48*	7.37*	7.38*	8.04*
ADJ RSQR	.42	.52	.72	.44	.52	.59

Note: Standard errors in parenthesis. Standard errors based on White's estimator of the variance-covariance matrix. Two tailed tests: * significant at 1%, ** significant at 5%, *** significant at 10%. All regressions include regional dummy variables.

ulation density fell from 12,321.6 persons per square mile in 1970 to 9,882.8 persons per square mile in 1990.

The impact of population density is large in all specifications. For example, again in specification 3 in Table 2, 1970–1995, a population density one standard deviation greater than the mean leads to a rate of innovation 3 patents per 10,000 workers greater, holding other factors constant[4]. The data tell a similar story across other specifications of the model and across all time periods. The evidence suggests that agglomeration and congestion has an important impact on innovation.

The location quotient in high technology manufacturing industries is also very important. Looking once again at specification three in Table 2 for the full 1970 to 1995 period the estimated parameters suggest that a location quotient one standard deviation greater than the mean translates to an average patent rate per 10,000 workers 1.7 higher[5]. It is noteworthy that the impact of being one standard deviation beyond the mean in population density has nearly twice as great an impact on patents as being one standard deviation beyond the mean in high technology industries.

Model specification two and three in Table 2 include measures of human capital. It is no surprise to see median years schooling having an important positive impact on innovative activity over the period the entire time period from 1970 to 1995. From the 1970's through the 1990's the significance and magnitude of the importance of the educational attainment of the population has remained stable. In the 1970's one standard deviation of educational attainment (2.3%) caused the patent variable to increase in magnitude by 1.04. This effect was 1.02 in the 1990 to 1995 sample. The additional human capital variable measuring learning by doing through the age of the population is always positive, as expected, and is significant at a 5% confidence level in the 1970's, significant at 10% in the 1980's and for the full 1970 to 1995 time period. The 1990 to 1995 model shows a lower influence of the age structure of the economy on innovation than in earlier time periods. For the full quarter century a one-percent increase in the percentage of the population of prime working age increases the per capita patent rate by 1.7%.

The research and development expenditures at universities are generally positive and significant until the human capital variables are included. Adding the human capital tends to increase the estimated impact and significance of the location quotient in high technology industries while diminishing the importance of the R&D measure. Schooling of the population may be capturing the influence of university R&D infrastructure as well as human capital. The results show the importance of controlling for R&D infrastructure and human capital. The signs and magnitudes of each variable seem quite plausible and in line with intuition as well as the model. Furthermore, the model appears to explain a good deal of the variation in innovation across states. For the full 1970 to 1995 period the explanatory variables explain 76% (the adjusted R-squared of .70 is reported in the table) of the variation in patents per 10,000 workers from the mean for US states.

The data used in producing the results in Table 2 can also be used to estimate a balanced panel data model, thus allowing for more degrees of freedom and more precise estimates. Re-write equation (9) as:

(10)
$$Log(PAT)_{i,t} = a_1 POPD_{i,t} + a_2 POPD^2_{i,t}$$
$$+ (\lambda - 1)\log(POP_{i,t}) = Y_i{}'\theta + \varepsilon_{i,t}$$

Allow

(11)
$$\varepsilon_{i,t} = u_i + \gamma_t + v_{i,t}$$

where $E[v_{i,t}] = 0$ and $VAR[v_{i,t}] = \sigma^2_{i,t}$ where the variance is expressed in a general form to allow for the heteroscedasticity apparent in the data. Substituting equation (11) into equation (10) yields:

(12)
$$Log(PAT)_{i,t} = u_i + \gamma_t + a_1 POPD_{i,t} + a_2 POPD^2_{i,t}$$
$$+ (\lambda - 1)\log(POP_{i,t}) = Y'_{i,t}\theta + v_{i,t}$$

Equation (12) represents a two way error components model. We estimate equation (12) using weighted partitioned least squares. The results are reported in Table 3. The benefit of this exercise is a substantial increase in our degrees of freedom (147 observations versus 49 observations). Though we estimate individual fixed effects for each

Table 3.

Panel Estimates: Two Way Error Component Model

	1	2	3
popd	.11427E-02*	.15475E-02*	.15671E-02*
	(.2095E-03)	(.2543E-03)	(.2680E-03)
popd2	-.52835E-07*	-.81477E-07*	-.83088E-07*
	(.1023E-07)	(.1296E-07)	(.1387E-07)
Log(pop)	.91403*	.17276	.18675
	(.1861)	(.2584)	(.2659)
Log(RDU)		.16938	.18285
		(.1704)	(.1842)
Log(LQHTI)		.65242*	.66037*
		(.1061)	(.1108)
Log(SCHOOL)			.66088E-01
			(.2565)
Log(AGE)			-.30692
			(.8175)
F	353.545*	411.904*	484.063*
ADJ RSQR	.95	.96	.95

Note: Standard errors in parenthesis. Based on weighted partitioned least squares where
Two tailed tests: * significant at 1%, **significant at 5%, ***significant at 10%.

state and time period our degrees of freedom more than double in each specification of the model.

Results are reported for each of the specifications outlined in Table 2. The F test reported is a test of the null hypothesis that the cross sectional unit fixed effects and the time period fixed effects are jointly equal to zero. The results are qualitatively very similar to Table 2. The main differences are the significance of population in specification one. This variable becomes insignificant, however, when the R&D infrastructure variables, LQHTI and RDU, are included in the model. All coefficients are of the expected signs. Like the earlier estimates the concentration in high technology is a more important control variable than the Federal R&D measure. Another salient feature of the fixed effects model is that the fixed effects appear to be capturing, in part, the impact of human capital. The inclusion of age and school lower the adjusted R-squared and neither is significantly different from zero.

Comparing model specification three in Table 3 with model specification three in Table2 for the 1970–1995 period shows that the optimal population density increases to 9,940. We cannot estimate the model directly for cities due to a lack of data concerning the dependant variable for SMSAs. The actual scale of the economy used in estimation is of little consequence as long as knowledge spillovers within the economy are reasonably complete. It is worthwhile noting that the population density of New York City was 23,671 in 1992. The next largest measured density for a city was San Francisco with 15,609 followed by Jersey City with 15,341. Other noteworthy cities include Chicago (12,185), Boston (11,398) and Philadelphia (11,492). There are no other cities with a density over 10,000 persons per square mile. Given the importance of agglomeration in innovation it is not surprising to see areas such as New York, Boston (Rt. 128) and San Francisco (Silicon Valley) emerging as leaders in innovation and patenting.

This model demonstrates that the rate of innovation and inventive activity varies greatly across states and is strongly related to the geographic concentration of innovative activity. The rate of innovation depends historically on the human capital and on the percentage of the population who are working aged. Population density, concentrations of high technology industries and the industrial structure of the economy are also important determinants of local innovation.

VI

Conclusion

THERE IS NOT ENOUGH EFFORT directed at understanding the links between urbanization, cities, innovation and growth. One major goal of this paper, therefore, is to formulate a model that directly tests the potential importance of the ideas of urban agglomeration and congestion as they relate to innovation and the economics of ideas. Looking for evidence of agglomeration by accounting for the spatial density of economic activity we find strong evidence that rates of innovation are significantly higher when resource constraints are relaxed through a greater concentration of economic activity. More theoretical work concerning the mechanisms linking agglomeration, innovation, and economic growth is required.

It may be the case that evidence of scale effects has been eluding growth theorists because they have not fully appreciated what urban economists and economic geographers have known for some time—that space is economically important. We believe this to be the most reasonable and fruitful interpretation of the results presented in this chapter, and it suggests many fascinating avenues for future research. The evidence from many urban studies suggests that accounting for the density of economic activity might provide for further insights to the economics of innovation, technological change, and growth.

The empirical evidence suggests that, while congestion effects are present, agglomeration tends to dominate congestion up to a population density of approximately 10,000 persons per square mile. The only urban areas in the US with such a high level of density include New York City, Boston, San Francisco and Jersey City. Many of the areas typically thought of as being centers of innovation clearly benefit heavily from the urban agglomeration effects estimated in this paper. Again, Boston, San Francisco, New York, and Jersey City are good examples. This evidence fits in well with studies of agglomeration and congestion in productivity levels. Ciccone and Hall (1996) also report evidence of agglomeration and congestion using state level data. As in this study they report agglomeration effects that strongly outweigh congestion.

Extending models of innovation common to the new research on economic growth holds the most promise for understanding the nature of technological differences across economies and differences in economic growth. Combining this framework with the literature concerning economic geography and recognizing the importance of spatial considerations and urbanization in determining growth rates holds the greatest promise for understanding the economics of growth. Empirically understanding the forces at work in the so called "agglomeration effect", and linking these forces back to dynamic models of economic growth and innovation is an important next step.

An increased understanding of the nature and causes of growth, innovation, industry concentration, and the role of knowledge spillovers will require thoughtful theoretical extensions of endogenous innovation models. The literature in this area, and economic geography provides the most fertile ground for the future of this research.

Notes

1. Economic models rarely include a geographical component. In some cases this seems to pose little or no problem. In the case of growth models, however, it may be a more significant shortcoming. Perhaps this shortcoming is partially responsible for the confusion surrounding the empirical validity of scale effects in economic growth. Kremer's (1993) measure of scale (world population) can be seen as a rough proxy for world population density since the earth certainly has a finite amount of space available. Of course, more land is inhabited today than in 10,000 BC and there may be room for further land development. Regardless of these trends it seems obvious that global population density has increased with global population. Cross-country studies do not account for this spatial component Kremer unwittingly includes.

2. White's consistent estimator of the variance covariance estimator is, in matrix notation, $\Sigma = (X'X)^{-1} \Sigma_i e_i^2 x_i x_i' (X'X)^{-1}$, where e_i is the ith least squares residual (White, 1978).

3. This is calculated using partial regression coefficients such that $(.73369E - .03) = 2(.66684E - .07(POPD))$.

4. One standard deviation in POPD is 1,752.9. Using the point estimate $(.73369E - .03)1,752.9 - (.66684E - .07)1,752.92 = 1.1$, $EXP(1.1) = 3$

5. The standard deviation in LQHTM for this time period is .584 and the point estimate of interest is .27471, .16=.584*.27471, EXP(.16)=1.17.

References

Abramovitz, Moses (1986) "Catching Up, Forging Ahead, and Falling Behind," *Journal of Economic History*, 46, 2, 386–406.

Aghion, Philippe and Peter Howitt (1992) "A Model of Growth through Creative Destruction," *Econometrica*, 60, 2, 323–351.

Aghion, Philippe and Peter Howitt (1998) *Endogenous Growth Theory*, The MIT Press, London, England.

Amable, Bruno (1993) "Catch-Up and Convergence: A Model of Cumulative Growth", *International Review of Applied Economics*, 7(1), 1–25.

American Electronics Association (1997) Cyberstates: A State by State Overview of the High-Technology Industry.

Barro, Robert and Xavier Sala-I-Martin (1995) *Economic Growth*, McGraw-Hill, New York.

Beeson, Patricia (1987) "Total Factor Productivity Growth and Agglomeration Economies in Manufacturing, 1959–73," *Journal of Regional Science*, 27, 2, 183–199.

Ciccone, Antonio and Robert Hall (1996) "Productivity and the Density of Economic Activity," *American Economic Review*, 86, 1, 54–70.

Dixit, Avinash and Joseph Stiglitz (1977) "Monopolistic Competition and Optimum Product Diversity," *American Economic Review*, 67, 3, 297–308.

Fagerburg, Jan (1988) "Why Growth Rates Differ", *Technical Change and Economic Theory*, Francis Pinter, London, 432–457.

Fagerburg, Jan (1994) "Technology and International Differences in Growth Rates", *Journal of Economic Literature*, XXXII, 1147–1175.

Glaeser, Edward (1998) "Are Cities Dying?," *Journal of Economic Perspectives*, 12, 2, 139–160.

Glaeser, Edward, Hedi Kallal, Jose' Scheinkman and Andrei Shleifer (1992) "Growth in Cities," *Journal of Political Economy*, 100, 6, 1126–1152.

Glaeser, Edward, Jose' Scheinkman, and Andrei Shleifer (1995) "Economic Growth in a Cross Section of Cities," *Journal of Monetary Economics*, 36, 117–143.

Grossman, Gene and Elhanan Helpman (1991) *Innovation and Growth in the Global Economy*, MIT Press, Cambridge.

Grossman, Gene, and Elhanan Helpman (1994) "Endogenous Innovation in the Theory of Growth", *Journal of Economic Perspectives*, 8, 23–44.

Helliwell, John and Alan Chung (1992), *Convergence and Growth Linkages between North and South*, NBER Working Paper No.3948

Jaffe, Adam, Manuel Trajtenberg, and Rebecca Henderson (1993) "Geographic Localization of Knowledge Spillovers as Evidenced by Patent Citations," *Quarterly Journal of Economics*, CVIII, 3, 577–598.

Jones, Charles (1995a) " R&D Based Models of Economic Growth," *Journal of Political Economy*, 103, 759–784.

Jones, Charles (1995b) " Time Series Tests of Endogenous Growth Models," *Quarterly Journal of Economics*, 110, 495–525.

Kremer, Michael (1993) "Population Growth and Technological Change: One Million B.C. To 1990", *Quarterly Journal of Economics*, 108,3,681–716.

Lucas, Robert Jr. (1988) "On the Mechanics of Development Planning", *Journal of Monetary Economics*, 22, 1, 3–42.

Marshall, Alfred (1920) *Principals of Economics*, Macmillan Publishers, London.

Persson, Joakim and Bo Malmberg (1996), "Human Capital, Demographics and Growth across the US states 1920–1990", Unpublished Manuscript.

Romer, Paul (1987) "Growth Based on Increasing Returns Due to Specialization," *American Economic Review*, 77, 2, 56–62.

Romer, Paul (1990) "Endogenous Technological Change", *Journal of Political Economy*, 98, S71-S102.

Sedgley, Norman (1998) The Role of Industrial Innovation in Growth and Convergence Across US States, Doctoral Dissertation, University of New Hampshire.

Sedgley, Norman and Bruce Elmslie (2000) "Convergence and the Aggregate

Production Function," Unpublished Manuscript, University of New Hampshire.

Segal, David (1976) "Are There Returns to Scale in City Size?, " *The Review of Economics and Statistics*, 58, 3, 339–350.

Solow, Robert (1957) "Technical Change and the Aggregate Production Function," *Review of Economics and Statistics*, 39, 312–320.

Soroka, Lewis (1994) "Manufacturing Productivity and City Size in Canada, 1975 and 1985: Does Population Matter?," *Urban Studies*, 31, 6, 895–911.

Verspagen, Bart (1991) A New Empirical Approach to Catching Up or Falling Behind", *Structural Change and Economic Dynamics*, 2, 2, 359–380.

Zipf's Law for Cities and Beyond

The Case of Denmark

By Thorbjørn Knudsen*

Abstract. Zipf's law for cities is one of the most conspicuous and robust empirical facts in the social sciences. It says that for most countries, the size distribution of cities must fit the power law: the number of cities with populations greater than S is inversely proportional to S. The present paper answers three questions related to Zipf's law: (1) does the Danish case refute Zipf's law for cities?, (2) what are the implications of Zipf's law for models of local growth?, and (3) do we have a Zipf's law for firms? Based on empirical data on the 61 largest Danish cities for year 2000, the answer to (1) is NO—the Danish case is not the exception which refutes Zipf's law. The consideration of (2) then leads to an empirical test of (3). The question of the existence of Zipf's law for firms is tested on a sample of 14,541 Danish production companies (the total population for 1997 with 10 employees or more). Based on the empirical evidence, the answer to (3) is YES in the sense that the growth pattern of Danish production companies follows a clean rank-size distribution consistent with Zipf's law.

Prediction in economics, and in the social sciences generally, is a rather scarce commodity (Reder 1999) and perhaps an unattainable ideal (Aumann 2000). According to Aumann, the value of a good theory lies in its usefulness in structuring reasoning and, therefore, one empirical fact to be cited in favour of a theory is its diffusion in some population of scientists. In other words, the more use of a particular theory, the better. As Reder notes, economists tend to place higher value on technique than content; clever theoretical ideas are valued over the assiduous gathering and careful presentation of data. And since mainstream

* The author is at the University of Southern Denmark, Main Campus: Odense University, School of Business and Economics, Department of Marketing, Campusvej 55, DK5230 Odense, Denmark. E-mail: tok@sam.sdu.dk. I appreciate inspiration and comments from Rabah Amir, Laurence S. Moss, and two anonymous reviewers. All remaining errors were produced without any help.

American Journal of Economics and Sociology, Vol. 60, No. 1 (January, 2001).

economics, in any case, has a sufficiently flexible theoretical basis to rationalize contrary empirical facts also, data do not play the prominent role they do in the natural sciences. As important reasons for the gap between theory and applied work, Reder points to the rather low status of empirical facts and the tendency to use the term "prediction" when "retrodiction" would be more suitable (pp. 27–29). In contrast to this generally disappointing state of affairs (see, e.g., Reder 1999), there exists one exceptional case, a notable empirical success story in which theory must bow to facts. This case is Zipf's law for cities, which has important implications for the admissibility of theoretical growth models. In economics one very rarely finds empirical relationships which deserve to be called laws. Zipf's law for cities, however, is one of the most conspicuous empirical facts in economics and in the social sciences in general (Brakman et al. 1999). It is surely an outstanding empirical regularity deserving the status of an experimental law (Gabaix 1999).

According to Zipf's law, the growth pattern of cities almost everywhere follows the power law—the number of cities with populations greater than S is proportional to $1/S$. Put differently, if we rank a sample of cities according to population size, and then place the log of the size on the X-axis and the corresponding log of the rank on the Y-axis, there should appear a straight line with slope −1. Should the numerical value of the slope exceed 1, cities are more dispersed than predicted whereas a slope less than one indicates that cities are more even sized than the prediction. Suprisingly, we actually see a slope of about 1 when data on American metropolitan areas are used. Both Gabaix (1999) and Krugman (1996) obtained a slope of −1.005 (std.dev. 0.010) and an R^2 of .986 for the 135 American metropolitan areas listed in the Statistical Abstract of the United States for 1991. Similar results have been reported for most countries in contemporary times (Rosen and Resnick 1980). The support of Zipf's law for previous periods has included samples of cities in India (Zipf 1949), China (Rozman 1990), the Netherlands (Brakman et al. 1999) and the United States (Krugman 1996; Zipf 1949).

Although most evidence corroborates Zipf's law, some evidence has been reported which seems to refute the prediction of a slope of −1. Thus, Brakman et al. (1999) compare data from the Netherlands in 1600, 1900, and 1990 and, despite a very good fit for all three regression models (R^2= 0.96 or better), obtain estimates that deviate from the slope of −1 predicted by Zipf's law. In their study, only data for 1900 fit this prediction. Both the estimates for 1600 and 1990 obtain a lower value, indicating that cities are more even-sized than predicted. Inspired by this deviation, we have sampled data to test the Danish case for the year 2000. Since Denmark and the Netherlands are both small countries and to some extent comparable in development, it is interesting to ask if the Danish case will show yet another deviation from Zipf's law for cities.

At this point it should be noted that Zipf's law is a special case of what is known as the rank-size distribution, which states an inverse linear relationship between the logarithmic size of a city and its logarithmic rank without any constraints on the slope. In the study of size distributions of firms, the term "Pareto distribution" is often used synonymously with the term rank-size distribution (see, e.g., Ijiri and Simon 1977). Furthermore, Zipf's law, or rather the rank-size distribution, applies to a much wider number of phenomena than size distributions of cities (Zipf 1949). For example, rank-size distributions have been shown to fit empirical observations of relative income (Zipf 1949), the relative size of business firms (Ijiri and Simon 1977), the number of biological species per genus (Zipf 1949) and the relative frequency of a word (Estoup 1916; Zipf 1935, 1949; Irmay 1997). Moreover, Irmay (1997) showed that Zipf's law is approximately equal to Benford's (1938) logarithmic distribution of first significant digits in a table of numbers. That Zipf's law fits size distributions of cities and business firms, relative frequencies of large texts of words (in several languages) and can account for first digits in various tables of numbers begs a second question: What is the explanation for Zipf's law and why do we see it in the case of cities?

The present paper suggests that, in view of the great success of Zipf's law in accounting for the growth of cities, it is not only possible but also plausible that the growth of firms may follow Zipf's law or at least a modified version of it. Note that the related proposition that size-distributions of firms can be explained by the Gibrat assumption has previously met strong criticism (Schmalensee 1989; Sutton 1999) and has, perhaps wrongly, been rejected. Thus, the third question to be addressed in the present paper is: Does the empirical evidence on asset distributions of business firms follow Zipf's law?

We address all three questions in turn. Due to the importance of the third question, we test it on data for what is a complete sample of all Danish production firms with 10 or more employees for 1997.

Zipf's Law for Cities: The Danish Case

WILL THE DANISH CASE SHOW yet another deviation from Zipf's law for cities? As noted by Brakman et al. (1999), this question may, due to its attention to a specific member of the the the family of rank-size distributions (with slope −1), obscure the more interesting question whether some rank-size distribution will fit the city-size distribution of Denmark. Nevertheless, it is a curious fact that Zipf's law at present holds true in the United States. Clearly, it would be interesting if this were the case also in Denmark, since that would indicate some generality in the underlying dynamics of city growth across countries.

In accordance with Brakman et al.'s reservations, we expect some rank-size distribution to hold for the case of Denmark but would be surprised if Zipf's law was supported. That is, when the log of the size is placed on the X-axis and the corresponding log of the rank is placed on the Y-axis, there should appear a straight line. However, it would be surprising if its slope turned out to be −1, at least if we consider that the geographical size of Denmark is comparable to the Netherlands where Brakman et al. estimated a slope well below −1 as predicted by Zipf's law.[1]

Contradicting Brakman et al.'s scepticism, Gabaix (1999) has showed that Zipf's law can be viewed as the unique steady state distribution arising from Gibrat's law (originally stated in Gibrat 1931). Gabaix further showed that city size processes may converge to Zipf's law within a relatively short period of time (100 years) in dynamic urban systems. Thus, even very young urban systems may satisfy Zipf's law as, for example, empirical evidence on U.S. cities in 1790 has shown (Zipf 1949, cf. Gabaix 1999). So, if Gabaix is right, the Dutch case is an exception, and we should therefore expect Zipf's law with an exponent close to 1 to hold in the Danish case.

The more fundamental issue that the empirical evidence on Zipf's law and other rank-size distributions point to is the underlying cause for variation in the size of cities. Thus, for regional economists, the question of why cities vary in size is a fundamental one. There has been much progress in understanding the role, existence and growth of cities (Brakman et al. 1999) and Zipf's law plays an important role as a very tight constraint on the admissible models of local growth (Gabaix 1999). In short, any theoretical explanation for the growth of cities should, according to Gabaix, be consistent with Zipf's law or, according to Brakman et al., at the very least satisfy some rank-size distribution. In the following section, we shall address this issue. In the present section, we now turn to the Danish case as illustration of Zipf's law.

To avoid terminological confusion, we use Brakman et al.'s (1999) useful distinction between Zipf's law and rank-size distributions. Thus, equation (1), below, shows Zipf's law for cities and equation (2) shows the more general rank-size distribution.[2] The log-linear version shown in equation (3) was used for empirical estimation reported in the present paper. R_j refers to the rank of city j and S_j is its size. C and K are country-specific parameters to be estimated and E is the error-term.

(1) $$R_j S_j = C, \qquad j = 1, 2, ..., N$$

(2) $$(R_j)^K S_j = C, \qquad j = 1, 2, ..., N$$

(3) $$ln(R_j) = C - K \, ln(S_j) + E_j \qquad j = 1, 2, ..., N$$

We obtained a sample for of the 61 largest cities in Denmark for 2000 from the Danish Statistical Bureau. Equation four shows the estimates obtained for the Danish sample.

(4) $$ln(R_j) = 13.82 - 1.056 \, ln(S_j) + E_j \qquad j = 1, 2, ..., 61$$

$$(0.027)$$

The standard error of the estimate is in parentheses and the R^2 is 0.962, a value that indicates a good fit. Additionally, the estimated slope is reasonably close to -1.[3] According to equation (2), a useful interpretation of this finding is that the observed distribution for Danish cities is a specific instance of the rank-size distribution where the probability that the size of a given city is larger than some *S* is proportional to $1/S^K$ with *K* approximately 1 (Gabaix 1999). However, as can be seen in Figure 1, the largest Danish town, Copenhagen, as well as some mid-range towns deviate from the linear prediction. A plausible explanation is simply that capitals are peculiar objects driven by unique political forces (Ades and Glaeser 1995; Gabaix 1999). Therefore, the deviation of the Danish capital Copenhagen from the linear prediction is the exception to be expected.

As can be seen from Figure 1, there is a smaller deviation which lies in the range of about 10.2 to 10.9 for $\ln(S_j)$. Thus there are more medium-sized cities in Denmark than predicted by Zipf's law and it is this effect which is responsible for raising the exponent *K* slightly above 1. A further but even smaller deviation is that (the many) Danish cities

Figure 1

The 61 largest Danish cities, year 2000: X: ln(size), Y: ln(rank).

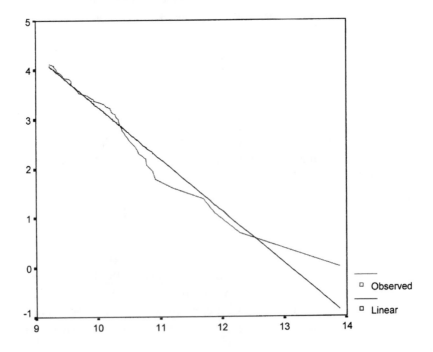

with a population less than 27,000 (ln(S$_j$)<10.2) has an exponent less than 1. So, according to Zipf's law, there are too few small Danish cities (with 27,000 inhabitants or less), a finding that is consistent with data for the United States (Gabaix 1999). In the following sections, we shall return to an explanation provided by Gabaix (1999) for this phenomenon.

The important point to convey here is that the empirical data for the size distribution of Danish cities for 2000 provides yet another reasonable fit with Zipf's law. This statement must be supplemented with the observation that two of the three most important deviations from the linear prediction observed in the Danish case have also been reported to be present in other studies (Gabaix 1999). In sum, according to the Danish case of Zipf's law for cities for year 2000, there is no grounds for concluding that we have encountered a refuting case.[4]

Explaining Zipf's Law for Cities

ZIPF'S LAW IS ONE OF THE OUTSTANDING EMPIRICAL success stories in economics and in the social sciences in general. We have seen that the Danish case is consistent with its prediction. Not only is Zipf's law an empirical success story, it also has a rather surprising empirical regularity. What could be the explanation for the large number of empirical studies that arrive at these results? Or is the attention to Zipf's law as a specific realization of the rank-size distribution, as Brakman et al. suggest, unwarranted since the exponent is likely to reflect both time- and sample-specific variation?

From the viewpoint of social theory, the problem with Zipf's law is its experimental character. As Brakman et al. note, we still do not have a proper understanding of the underlying explanation for its observed empirical regularities. Many explanations can produce Zipf's law and many have been proposed (Carroll 1982). This is not the place to review the wide range of explanations given for Zipf's law. Rather, we shall concentrate on the most important ones. According to Gabaix (1999), arguably the two most successful models have been Steindl's (1965) and Simon's (1955) path-breaking and now classic works. We shall therefore briefly consider the rationale for Zipf's law offered by these models as well as some difficulties which have been pointed out as limits to their plausibility.

We first consider Steindl's model (1965) in which existing cities grow at a rate G and new cities are born at a rate V. Accordingly, the size distribution of cities will follow a power law with exponent $K=V/G$ such that the number of cities with size greater than S will be proportional to S^{-K} (Gabaix 1999). This explanation is clearly problematic since it demands the implausible condition $V=G$ to be satisfied. For example, this condition is clearly violated in the Danish case as well as for most other mature urbane systems where we observe $V<G$ (Gabaix 1999).

Simon's (1955) model is, according to Gabaix (1999), the most successful stochastic growth model for Zipf's law; however, it is not without its difficulties. Briefly, in Simon's model, migrants will form a new city with probability P and will go to an existing one with probability $(1-P)$. Since P is proportional to the size of the city, this model generates the familiar power law but now with the steady state exponent $K=1/(1-P)$. There are two major difficulties with this model. As pointed out by Krugman (1996), the speed of convergence to Zipf's law is infinitely slow (since this requires P very close to 0, which again requires that existing cities are infinite at the limit). The second problem, pointed out by Gabaix (1999), is the model's implication that the rate of growth of the number of cities has to be larger than the growth rate of the population of the existing cities, a consequence which is refuted by empirical data.

Were it not that empirical data repeatedly show an exponent close to 1, both Steindl's and Simon's models would be possible contenders as an explanation for size distributions of cities. Note here that Simon's model, as Gabaix points out, may be viewed as a special case of Steindl's model, with the steady state exponent $K=V/G=1/(1-P)$. The two models, however, imply competing empirical predictions. According to Steindl's model, $K<1$ (since $V<G$ for most urban systems) whereas Simon's model suggests $K>1$. One solution is the approach taken by Brakman et al. who view the exponent of 1 as a special case. Arguably, a more attractive solution is the one provided by Gabaix's model, which delivers Zipf's law as the limit of a stochastic process whose assumptions are consistent with empirical observations.

Now, consider Gabaix's (1999) model, which has a number of young migrants deciding in which city (populated by a number of seasoned agents) to locate. The agents maximize wage w_t and amenities a_t (which are independent and identically distributed), so the equilibrium of "utility adjusted" wages will be the same across cities ($w_t\, a_t = u_t$). Given that the increase in population of city i is ΔN_t and that agents die with probability P_d, the normalized growth G_t of city i will be:

(5a) $$G_t = \Delta N_t/N_t = f'^{-1}(u_t/a_t) - P_d,$$

As can be seen, Gabaix's model of city growth is an expression of what is commonly known as Gibrat's law, which simply states that growth is scale-invariant and independent of initial size, i.e., $G_{t+1} = S_{t+1}/S_t$. Since Gabaix's model implies a common and size-independent variance, it is necessary to justify this implication. This is done by assuming that the total variance of the growth rate $q^2(S)$ can be broken down into three components of which only one is size-dependent:

(5b) $$q^2(S) = q^2_{policy} + q^2_{region} + q^2_{industries}/S,$$

It is thus assumed that the variance (but not the *level*) of the city-specific provision of public goods is size-independent and that regional shocks affect all cities of the region equally. Whereas policy and regional shocks are seen as size-independent, the shocks experienced by a city's industries should, according to Gabaix, depend on size. Again, this assumption seems reasonable because larger cities may hedge the industry-specific growth risk by diversifying their industrial portfolio. All this boils down to the needed justification that the variance of the growth process is size-independent at least for large cities (since for a large S, $q^2_{industries}/S$ tends to 0). Thus, cities in the upper tail of the size distribution should follow Zipf's law whereas small cities should deviate from it, a point which, according to the previous section, was supported by the data on Denmark.

Armed with the justification for constant variance of the growth process, Gabaix then develops a stochastic version of the equation for city growth simply by taking the continuous limit of equation (5a), which gives

(5c) $$dS_t/S_t = md_t + qdB_t,$$

Here B_t is reflected Brownian motion (random walk with a barrier) which depends on the model parameters shown in equation 5(a) (u_t, a_t, $P_{d,}$). The expected growth in normalized size m is the difference between the growth rate $G(S)$ of city with size S_t and the mean growth rate ($m = G(S)-G_{mean}$). We are now in a position to convey Gabaix's central result, which is that Zipf's law necessarily emerges as the steady state size distribution. In terms of the above model (5c), for $S_t >$ S_{min} and $dS_t = s_t\ max[md_t + qdB_t, 0]$, Gabaix shows that the distribution converges to a Zipf distribution with exponent $K = 1/(1-S_{min}/S_{mean})$. Thus, when the minimal allowable city size tends to 0, K tends to 1 from above. According to this result, the existence of some lower barrier will induce city size to be distributed according to the power law. All that is needed for the emergence of Zipf's law, then, is the existence of some repelling force that keeps cities from becoming too small. Having presented the core of Gabaix's model, we shall briefly note that the problem of slow convergence and the possibility of deviations from an exponent of 1 is explicitly dealt with. Thus, Gabaix shows how the convergence to a steady state will be reasonably fast if the variance $q^2(S)$ is not too low and further provides an elaborate and useful analysis of the two possible causes of deviation from an exponent of 1, the mean and the standard deviation of the growth process.

In sum, Gabaix's paper presents a very useful and convincing stochastic explanation for Zipf's law and the necessary emergence of an exponent of 1 within a reasonably short time frame. The model is driven by the condition that the ratio of wages and amenities equilibrate across cities and the (infinitesimal) lower barrier to city size, which helps a size-invariant random walk converge to a power distribution with an exponent of 1 at the limit. It should be noted that Gabaix shows this result to hold for other stochastic processes as well. The crucial point is that a wide range of stochastic growth models may produce Zipf's law from the Gibrat assumption. This result is also surely important for growth models of business firms where Gibrat's law plays an important role (Sutton 1999). We shall return to this issue in the ensuing section, where a complete sample of Danish production companies for 1997 is used to test Zipf's law for business firms. However, first we shall briefly consider Brakman et al.'s model and how it relates to Gabaix's result.

Brakman et al.'s claim that the time-distribution of the exponent will follow an *n*-shaped pattern is clearly at odds with Gabaix's result. So, how does Brakman et al. arrive at this conclusion? Their main point is that the reported structural economic changes rather than random growth underlies the size distribution of cities. This size distribution might well follow the rank-size distribution; however, we should expect the exponent to change over time according to an *n*-shaped pattern. The reason for this shape is that the force of agglomeration has its strongest effect in the industrialization period. For different reasons, spreading forces have relatively higher effects in both the pre- and post-industrialization periods, with the result that small cities will have a tendency to grow more quickly. Therefore, the exponent of the rank-size distribution will peak in the industrialization period. Brakman et al. support this claim with data from the Netherlands which show an exponent of 0.55 in 1600, 1.03 in 1900 and 0.72 for 1990 and further refer to Parr's (1985) results as support for the *n*-shaped time-pattern of the exponent. Then, based on Krugman's (1991a, 1991b) general equilibrium location model, Brakman et al. proceed to develop an equilibrium model of industrial location which can mimic the data observed for the Netherlands. The model is built on reasonable assumptions and, based on simulations, quite successfully reconstructs the historical trends observed for the Dutch case. The value of this simulation exercise lies in its ability to use the parameters found important by economic historians to reproduce the expected effects in terms of the rank-size distribution as a structural outcome of the modelling exercise. A major drawback, however, is that the parameter settings, although plausible, are completely arbitrary. Nevertheless, the question remains whether an exponent of 0.72 presents an unsurmountable difficulty for stochastic models as Brakman et al. claim.

As indicated above, Gabaix's stochastic model has no difficulty in handling this problem. Gabaix's general explanation for an exponent of 0.72 would be that either the mean or the variance of the growth process deviates from Gibrat's law. Thus, Gabaix shows that if a range of cities has a high growth rate, its distribution will decay more slowly than in the pure Zipf case (the exponent will decrease) because small cities constantly feed the stock of big cities. The second cause for a small exponent Gabaix gives is that the variance of the growth process is size-dependent. The data reported by Brakman et al. for the Netherlands does not allow evaluation of these possible alternative explanations for the observed low exponent for 1990. The point is that, at least in principle, Gabaix's stochastic model can account for these deviations as deviations from Gibrat's law.

In sum, we have seen that the puzzling empirical regularity of Zipf's law with exponent 1 can be explained as the expression of the steady state size distribution arising from Gibrat's law. Given that the process has had time enough to reach a steady state (which should be the case for all mature urban systems), deviations from the exponent of 1 may be explained as deviations from Gibrat's law. Alternatively, one may side with Brakman et al. and attempt to account for the expression of power law rank-size distributions as the outcome of structural economic changes. Although the latter approach is very attractive due to its attempt to align with actual historical data, the equilibrium models provided so far essentially rely on rather arbitrary parameter settings. This is not the place to pass a verdict over the comparative value of the two approaches, only to note the differences and some of the associated pros and cons. Having presented the most important explanations for Zipf's law, this paper's next section examines the size-distribution of Danish production companies. Since Zipf's law can be viewed as the outcome of Gibrat's law, it should be interesting to see whether this also holds for the size-distribution of business firms and, if not, whether a deviation from Zipf's law may be explained within the framework of Gabaix's stochastic model.

I

Zipf's Law for Firms?

Since Zipf's law turns out to be the steady state distribution of the familiar Gibrat's law commonly used as a foundation for growth theory, it would not be unreasonable to expect Zipf's law also to hold for the growth of firms. As Sutton (1999) notes however, the development of the empirical literature since Gibrat (1931) has indicated that attempts to make simple generalizations about the shape of firm size distributions have been rather dubious. Sutton's reason for this is that a model of firm growth needs a rational basis. Therefore, a stochastic model has no chance of mimicking an empirical size distribution of business firms. Also, according to Gabaix (1999), the empirical question of size distributions of firms is still unresolved.

Motivated by the insights presented about Zipf's law and the need to access a comprehensive data set of size distributions of firms, we use a sample of Danish production companies for 1997. The sample is made up of the total population of 14,541 firms with more than ten employees. One suspicion regarding the failure of previous empirical tests to support the Gibrat assumption, at least for some industries, is that these failures were due to bias introduced by missing data and/ or industry-specific samples. The obvious way to rule out this problem is simply to use a sample that includes the total population rather than some more or less arbitrarily chosen subset of firms. This is the approach we followed in the present study. Furthermore, in contrast to most previous studies, we use data on assets rather than sales as a proxy for firm size. The reason for this is that we think asset accumulation comes much closer to agglomeration than sales growth does. Again, we use equation (3) to obtain the empirical estimate on basis of the full sample:

(6a) $ln(R_j) = 14.98 - 0.669 \; ln(S_j) + E_j = 1, \; 2, \; ..., \; 14,541$

$$(0.0013)$$

The standard error of the estimate is in parentheses and the R^2 is 0.942, a value that indicates a reasonable fit. The estimated slope clearly seems too far from -1 to warrant any speculation that we have stumbled over yet another instance of Zipf's law. The good fit, however, indicates that the size distribution might well be a rank-size distribution that follows the power law. If we take a look on the plot of the size distribution in Figure 2, below, we see that it has two very distinct parts.

As can be seen from Figure 2, the distribution consists of a first part with almost even-sized small firms (across all industries) and a second part (from about ln size 9.5), which portrays a straight line with negative slope. The linear fit of the second part is striking, as can be seen from the following regression which includes the 13,543 firms (93%) with assets (measured in Danish kroner) equal to or higher than ln(9.5).

Figure 2

The 1997 population of 14,541 Danish production companies with ten or
more employees: X: ln(size), Y: ln(rank).

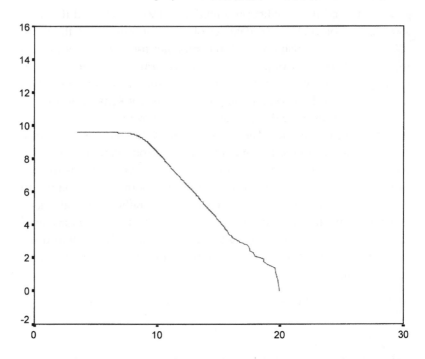

(6b) $ln(R_j) = 15.73 - 0.741 \, ln(S_j) + E_j = 1, 2, ..., 13,543$

(0.0017)

Considering the sample size, the R^2 of 0.985 indicates an extremely
good fit. There is no doubt whatsoever that the size distribution of
Danish production companies excluding the 7% of smallest firms follows a rank-size distribution with exponent 0.741.

This result is quite remarkable in view of the widespread scepticism
towards models of firm behaviour which are merely statistical and not
based on maximizing behaviour (Sutton 1999). Thus Schmalensee
(1989) notes the failure of statistical models such as Ijiri and Simon's
(1977) to provide a satisfactory description of size distributions for

some industries. And as noted by Sutton, there has been a long-standing concern about the theoretical basis of statistical growth models. According to Sutton (1999: 245), most authors now claim only that the size distribution will be skew, but do not specify the extent of the skewness, or its particular shape.

Sutton himself develops a model which characterizes the minimum degree of industry level inequality of firm size. He develops Ijiri and Simon's (1977) model by substituting its Gibrat law assumption with the much weaker assumption that the probability of seizing a new market opportunity is size-independent. By further assuming constant probability that the next market opportunity will be filled by a new entrant, as Ijiri and Simon assumed, Sutton arrives at a benchmark case which defines a limiting Lorenz curve. It is defined in two-dimensional space in terms of the normalized rank k and the k-firm concentration ratio C_k:

(7) $$C_k \geqq k/N \, (1 - ln(k/N)).$$

The point is that this limiting Lorenz curve places a lower bound on firm inequality (in terms of the k-firm concentration ratio). Based on a game-theoretic "island model," assuming strictly independent submarkets, Sutton shows that this result also holds in the presence of strategic effects. That is, the effect of independence *between* submarkets is strong enough to override any strategic effects *within* submarkets so a minimal degree of inequality emerges in the limit. The size distribution obtained from the game-theoretic analysis is at least as unequal as the limiting Lorenz curve. So how does the present paper's very clean result obtained for the size distribution of Danish firms relate to the criticism of the empirical and theoretical failure of statistical models raised by Sutton and others? And how does the obtained evidence for Danish firms compare to Sutton's benchmark case, the limiting Lorenz curve?

The first thing to note is that our findings are consistent with, but much stronger than, the prediction offered by Sutton's model. If we compute the Lorenz curve of the size-distribution of Danish firms in the two-dimensional space used by Sutton, we find that the Lorenz curve bends much further away from the diagonal than predicted. In other words, the inequality of the firms in our distribution is much greater than indicated by Sutton's model. The next thing to note is that the part of the size distribution reported in the present paper, which excludes very small firms, clearly follows a rank-size distribution with exponent 0.741. As can be seen from Figure 2 and the R^2 of 0.985, this is a very clean result. Against widespread claims to the contrary, there is no doubt that, apart from the extreme lower tail, the size distribution of Danish production companies can adequately be summarized by a rank-size distribution. Moreover, the result is obtained on a complete sample of firms with 10 or more employees. A crucial reason for our result may well lie in the breadth of our sample. Previous studies have predominantly used more narrow samples focused on the industry level, which may explain why these studies have failed to obtained similar results. But how can we make sense of the obtained result? And what about the deviation in the lower tail and the slight deviation in the upper tail? Armed with insights provided by Gabaix, some answers to these question can be given.

The failure of statistical models to provide a satisfactory description of size distributions for some industries.

As Ijiri and Simon (1977) note, the observed regularities in business firm size distributions usually fit closely to the Pareto distribution, an outcome that follows from the Gibrat assumption that expected growth is proportional to size. Given the observed regularity, the Gibrat assumption then works as a criterion of admissibility for the class of models that aspire to explain firm growth. It is therefore of great importance if we dismiss the Gibrat assumption. As noted by Schmalensee (1989), statistical models (most based on the Gibrat assumption) have encountered persistent difficulties in providing an adequate description of the size distribution of some industries. Combined with the search for sound economic explanations of size distributions, this led to a widespread dismissal of the Gibrat assumption. The data presented in the present paper, however, suggests that the dismissal of Gibrat's law may have been premature—previous studies have analysed more narrow samples, typically defined in terms of industry. If we accept the reasonable assumption that entry fees vary greatly between industries, the left tail of the distribution, which consists of small even-sized firms, will be unevenly distributed across industries. Accordingly, an industry-level analysis will always fail to confirm Gibrat's law for some industries. The reason for the failure of previous studies may well be due to the fact that population-wide samples have not been used.

Explaining the observed size distribution.

The empirical size distribution of the population of Danish production companies with ten or more employees reported in Figure 2 has three parts. Part 1 consists of small even-sized firms with attained size ln(9.5) or less. This part contains 7% of the population. Part 2 consists of the 93% medium- and large-sized firms with a degree of inequality that shows a very clean fit with the Gibrat assumption— a rank-size distribution with exponent 0.741. Concerning this part of the distribution, Figure 2 shows some deviation from the almost perfect linear fit for the extreme upper tail of the distribution where size is ln(16) or more. We shall refer to this extreme upper tail as part 3 of the distribution and note that it contains the 30 largest Danish production companies. These 30 firms comprise 0.2% of the population in terms of number but in terms of their combined asset mass they account for 73.14% of the population's assets. Now to the outline of an explanation for the observed size distribution. We start with part 2 of the distribution. Since this part has an almost perfect fit with the rank-size distribution, it follows the Gibrat assumption. Hence, the expected growth and the variance of the growth process is size-invariant. In other words this 93% of firms experience the same shocks to the growth process.

(8) $$q^2(S) = q^2_{international} + q^2_{national} + q^2_{regional} + q^2_{industry}/S_, + q^2_{strategy}(S_k)$$

In line with the explanation given for size-independent variance of the growth process, we can break down the total variance into its components. For simplicity, we assume independent variance; however, this assumption is not essential since specifying the relevant interaction terms is straightforward. We may reasonably assume that international, national and regional shocks to the growth process will be experienced independent of firm size. By contrast, since we may adopt the quite reasonable assumption that large firms can hedge against industry-specific risk, we find that the effect of industry specific shocks decrease in size. Finally, we assume that for the m very large firms (rank 1, 2, ..., k-m), firm-specific strategic effects will introduce idiosyncratic variance into the growth process.

Thus, the proposed explanation for the observed size distribution is that the variance of the growth process for very small firms depends on industry-specific effects. With increasing size, these effects gradually trail off. This proposition is consistent with the curve observed in Figure 2 in the size range between $\ln(7.0)$ and $\ln(9.5)$. For part 2 of the size distribution, it is thus proposed that industry-specific shocks to the growth process have a minor effect compared to international, national and regional shocks. That is, excluding the largest 30 firms in the extreme right tail of the distribution, the mean and the variance of the growth process is size-independent. The size distribution observed in part 2 of the distribution is thus consistent with an underlying stochastic process which can be described in terms of equation (5c) as a random walk with a lower barrier, i.e., reflected Brownian motion.[5] Regarding the 30 largest firms found in the extreme right tail of the distribution, we suggest that firm-specific strategic effects of the sort typically studied in theories of industrial organization (see, for example, Tirole 1988) influence the variance of the growth process. Therefore for about 93% of the Danish production companies, their growth process may almost perfectly be described in terms of an underlying dynamic stochastic process which is consistent with the Gibrat assumption.

As observed by Ijiri and Simon (1977), the Gibrat assumption can be derived from the postulate that access to internal and external investment funds is proportional to size, without assuming rational choice as part of the causal mechanism. As we have seen, it is also consistent with a breakdown of variance approach.

According to Gabaix's argument, the exponent of 1 predicted by Zipf's law should emerge as the steady state distribution of Gibrat's law. So, why the deviation from the expected exponent of 1 predicted by Zipf's law? Perhaps the steady state has not been reached yet. Although it is possible that the process is not in a steady state due to ongoing pertubations, the difference beween part 1 and 2 of the observed distribution suggests an alternative explanation. As demonstrated by Gabaix, deviations from a Zipf exponent of 1 can be due to deviation in the expected growth rate and in the variance of the growth process for some range of firms. Both effects will result in an exponent less than 1. If a range of firms has a high growth rate, its distribution will be flatter. This is because the distribution will decay less quickly than in the pure Zipf case since small firms feed the stock of big firms (Gabaix 1999). It is reasonable to assume that the smallest Danish production companies (the 7% contained in part 1 of the observed distribution shown in Figure 2) have a very high expected growth rate, so it is not surprising to observe an exponent of 0.741. A second reason that could explain the observed deviation from the Zipf case, would be that a range of firms had high variance, which, due to the higher mixing of small and large firms, also results in a flatter distribution. Since this effect may well be present in the range of small firms at the extreme left tail of the distribution, there is an additional reason why we observed an exponent that was significantly less than the Zipf case.

In sum, we have presented data for the size distribution of the entire population of Danish production companies with ten or more employees and found a striking fit with the rank-size distribution with exponent 0.741 when the extreme left tail of the distribution was excluded. We presented the data for 1997 but also posess data for the four previous years. The data for the four years prior to 1997 do not show any deviation from the results reported here. Thus for about 93% of the Danish production companies, the growth process may almost perfectly be described in terms of an underlying dynamic stochastic process consistent with the Gibrat assumption. Inspired by Gabaix, we have further provided the outline of an explanation for this result. We propose that the growth process for very small firms depends strongly on industry-specific effects. With increasing size, these effects gradually trail off and what remains is international, national and regional shocks that hit all firms with equal force. Therefore, the variance of the growth process will be size-independent for all but the smallest firms. The few Big Players will, however, show firm-specific deviations due to strategic effects of the sort studied in the theory of industrial organization.

The obtained empirical result is very clean and quite surprising in view of the widespread scepticism towards statistical explanations, in part fed by the failure of previous studies to support the Gibrat assumption for some industries. As already mentioned, the present study suggests that this may well be due to sampling bias. Since the ratio of small firms to each industry is likely to vary due to the costs associated with entry, industry-level sampling and analysis is likely to face some inexplicable cases. To remedy this problem, it is recommended to use population-wide samples, as in the present study, or at the very least to use unbiased cross-industry samples.

Conclusion

THE PRESENT PAPER HAS EXAMINED one of the outstanding empirical regularities of the social sciences, Zipf's law for cities. The empirical data presented for Danish cities for year 2000 showed a Zipf exponent close to 1. This fact, combined with a sufficiently good fit, led to the conclusion that yet again we have encountered a case that is consistent with the prediction of Zipf's law.

We have further conveyed the most important explanations offered for the puzzling fact that city growth follows Zipf's law. According to Gabaix (1999), Zipf's law can be explained as the steady state distribution arising from Gibrat's law. Thus, when a stochastic process follows the Gibrat assumption, it will eventually converge to Zipf's law. And, as Gabaix showed, all that is needed to ensure that convergence will happen sufficiently quickly to make the emergence of Zipf's law plausible is that some impurity be introduced into the process, e.g., in terms of an infinitesimal lower barrier to city size. This result not only holds when city growth is modelled as reflected Brownian motion but also holds for a much more general class of models, namely any Markov process with repelling force. Alternatively, one may side with Brakman et al. (1999) and attempt to account for the expression of power law rank-size distributions as the outcome of specific structural economic changes. Even if this approach is attractive due to its attempt to align theory with actual historical data, such structural models may, as theirs does, suffer from arbitrary parameter settings due to the inclusion of unobservable variables. In sum, the two approaches may best be seen as complementary, each contributing an important facet of explanation.

Nevertheless, there is a crucial difference between Gabaix's stochastic model with its general prediction that city growth will converge to Zipf's law and Brakman et al.'s model devised to mimic the structural changes observed in a specific country. According to Brakman et al. the time-distribution of the Zipf exponent will be *n*-shaped with a peak value of 1 or more. By contrast, Gabaix's model implies that the exponent will converge to 1 unless there is deviation in the mean or variance of the growth process for some range of the distribution. This indicates that one of the most important implications for future research is to obtain better estimates of the time-distribution of the Zipf exponent in order to substantiate the veracity of the competing claims made by Gabaix and Brakman et al.

Inspired by Gabaix's result that Zipf's law can be viewed as the outcome of the Gibrat assumption, we went beyond city growth and examined the empirical size distribution of firms. Our sample included the entire population of Danish production companies with ten or more employees. Excluding the 7% smallest firms, the size distribution (assets) showed a striking fit with the rank-size distribution with exponent 0.741. This result indicates that the growth process of 93% of the Danish production companies can almost perfectly be described in terms of an underlying dynamic stochastic process consistent with the Gibrat assumption.

This result is very clean and, therefore, rather surprising in view of the widespread scepticism towards statistical explanations of size distributions of firms. A possible reason for the failure of previous studies to consistently obtain similar results may well be due to sampling bias. Since the ratio of small firms to each industry is likely to vary due to entry costs, industry-level samples will probably show apparent deviations from the Gibrat assumption, at least for some industries. Since the result obtained in the present study suggests that this problem disappears at the population-level size distribution, the obvious remedy would be to obtain population-level samples or at least unbiased cross-industry samples. Thus, the present study suggests that examination of population-level samples should be high on the agenda of empirical research on the size distributions of firms. It should also be noted that we find assets to be better proxies for size in growth models than the sales data typically used in previous studies (Sutton 1999).

Therefore, it is possible that the very clean empirical result reported in the present study partly reflects this fact.

It is further proposed that the deviation from the Zipf exponent of 1, which should be expected according to Gabaix's model, was caused by the strong influence of industry effects on very small firms. With increasing size, it is argued, this effect gradually trails off and what remains are international, national and regional shocks that hit all firms with equal force. Therefore, the variance of the growth process will be size-independent for all but the smallest firms. A second possible source of deviation from Zipf's law was the strategic interactions of the few Big Players (only 30 firms or 0.2 % of the present sample).

In sum, the present study has raised the implication that a simple stochastic model based on the Gibrat assumption adequately describes the underlying causes of persistent inequality of firm size for most firms. It may thus be premature to dismiss such models despite the scepticism raised by previous authors (see for instance Sutton 1999). Notably, this conclusion is based on empirical data sampled at the population level. Had industry-level samples been used, some industries would have shown a relatively bad fit. The important exception to this conclusion is the growth of Big Players, which may better be understood in terms of the standard tools of the theory of industrial organisation (see e.g., Sutton 1999; Tirole 1988).

Regarding theory, the value of the empirical support for Zipf's law, which may be seen as the steady state outcome of Gibrat's law, lies in the strong bounds placed on the set of models that may be used to explain city and firm growth. One could formulate this condition in terms of an impossibility theorem which states that the set of possible models of population-level city and firm growth should be consistent with Zipf's law in the long run.

Notes

1. Brakman et al. (1999) reports a slope of -0.72 ($R2 = 0.96$).

2. There is some disagreement in terminology here. Gabaix (1999) refers to the rank-size rule, which states an inverse linear relationship between the actual rank and size (the size of the city of rank i varies with $1/i$). For Brakman et al. (1999), the rank-size distribution denotes the inverse linear relation between log rank and log size.

3. The standard deviation is -0.027 and the estimate is -1.056. If we

choose significance level 0.05, it must be rejected that the true estimate is −1.000. But if we choose significance level 0.01, we *cannot* reject that the true estimate is −1.000. Therefore, I say that the estimated coefficient is reasonably close to 1 and conclude that Denmark cannot be viewed as a refuting case.

4. The empirical regularity of Zipf's law raises the question of how cities are defined and why this does not seem to make a difference. In the face of the arbitrary manner in which cities are defined, the persistent regularity of Zipf's law is rather perplexing. The city as a part of its overall Standard Metropolitan Area (SMSA) differs between and within countries. As long as cities are defined so their relative sizes are internally consistent, between-country differences can be handled by the country-specific parameter C in equation (3). Within- country differences could in principle be handled by adding a dummy to equation (3) if necessary, but this is not widely done. But why has this inconsistency in the data not made a big difference in previous estimations? The reason is probably that the estimation of Zipf's law according to equation (3) is very robust regarding variation in relative size if two conditions hold: (1) the ranking of cities must be preserved; and (2) *systematic* bias must not be introduced.

5. This requires redefining models (5a) and (5c) in terms of firms maximizing, for example, market share and quality so the equilibrium of "profit adjusted" market shares will be the same across industries.

References

Ades, A. and Glaeser, E. (1995). Trade and Circuses: Explaining Urban Giants. *The Quarterly Journal of Economics*, CX: 195–228.

Aumann, R. J. (2000). What is Game Theory Trying to Accomplish? In: Aumann, R. J. (Ed.), *Collected Papers*, Volume I: 5–46. Cambridge, MA: The MIT Press.

Benford, F. (1938). *The Law of Anomalous Numbers*. Proceedings of the American Philosophical Society, 78: 551–572.

Brakman, S., Garretsen, H., van Marrewijk, C., van den Berg, M. (1999). The Return of Zipf: Towards a Further Understanding of the Rank-Size Distribution. *Journal of Regional Science*, 39(1): 182–213.

Carroll, G. (1982). National City-Size Distribution: What Do We Know After 67 Years of Research? *Progress in Human Geography*, VI: 1–43.

Estoup, J. B. (1916). *Gammes Sténographiques*. Paris: Gauthier Villars.

Gabaix, X. (1999). Zipf's Law for Cities: An Explanation. *The Quarterly Journal of Economics*, August: 739–767.

Gibrat, R. (1931). *Les Inégalités Économiques*. Paris: Librairie du Recueil Sirey.

Ijiri, Y. and Simon, H. A. (1977). *Skew Distributions and the Sizes of Business Firms*. Amsterdam: North-Holland.

Irmay, S. (1997). The Relationship Between Zipf's Law and the Distribution of First Digits. *Journal of Applied Statistics*, 24 (4): 383–393.

Kooij, P. (1988). Peripheral Cities and Their Regions in the Dutch Urban System until 1900. *Journal of Economic History*, 48: 357–371.

Krugman, P. (1991a). *Geography and Trade*. Cambridge, MA: The MIT Press.

———. (1991b). Increasing Returns and Economic Geography. *Journal of Political Economy*, 99: 483–499.

———. (1996). *The Self-Organizing Economy*. Cambridge, MA: Blackwell.

Parr, J. B. (1985). A Note on the Size Distribution of Cities over Time. *Journal of Urban Economics*, 18: 199–212.

Reder, M. W. (1999). *Economics. The Culture of a Controversial Science*. Chicago and London: The University of Chicago Press.

Rosen, K. and Reznick, M. (1980). The Size Distribution of Cities: An Examination of the Pareto Law and Primacy. *Journal of Urban Economics*, VIII: 165–186.

Rozman, G. (1990). East Asian Urbanization in the Nineteenth Century. In Van der Woude, A. and Shishido, H.(eds.) *Urbanization in History*, pp. 61–73. New York: Oxford University Press.

Schmalensee, R. (1989). Sunk Costs and Market Structure: A Review Article. *Journal of Industrial Economics*, 40: 125–133.

Simon, H. A. (1955). On a Class of Skew Distribution Functions. *Biometrika*, XLII: 425–440.

———. (1979). On Parsimonious Explanations of Production Relations. *Scandinavian Journal of Economics*, 81: 459–474.

———. (1997). Models of Bounded Rationality, Volume 3, empirically Grounded Economics Research, Cambridge, MA: The MIT Press.

Steindl, J. (1965). Random Processes and the Growth of Firms. New York: Hafner.

Sutton, J. (1999). Technology and Market Structure. Theory and History. Cambridge, MA: The MIT Press.

Tirole, J. (1988). *The Theory of Industrial Organization*. Cambridge, MA: The MIT Press.

Zipf, G.K. (1935). *The Psycho-biology of Language*. Cambridge, MA: The MIT Press.

———. (1949). *Human Behavior and the Principle of Least Effort*. Reading, MA: Addison-Wesley.

The Structure of Sprawl

Identifying and Characterizing Employment Centers in Polycentric Metropolitan Areas

By NATHAN B. ANDERSON and WILLIAM T. BOGART*

ABSTRACT. This paper applies a consistent framework to four comparably sized metropolitan areas to identify and characterize their employment centers. Employment centers are identified as places that exceed a threshold employment density and a threshold employment level. They are also characterized as specializing on the basis of location quotient analysis. We find clear evidence of specialization in every employment center in the four metropolitan areas studied. Our interpretation is that what we are observing is a systematic change in metropolitan structure rather than a random sprawling of firms. We also find some evidence that the size distribution of employment centers follows the rank-size rule. This suggests that there is structure not only in the distribution of economic activity among the employment centers but also in their size distribution. Because less than 50 percent of metropolitan employment is within employment centers, future research should focus on understanding the more diffuse employment patterns. The rank-size rule gives some guidance as to the expected size distribution of employment throughout the metropolitan area.

* Nathan B. Anderson earned his B.A. with honors in economics from Case Western Reserve University in 2000. He is currently attending the University of Michigan to obtain his Ph.D. in economics. William T. Bogart is an associate professor of economics and a research associate at the Center for Regional Economic Issues at Case Western Reserve University. His undergraduate urban economics textbook, *The Economics of Cities and Suburbs*, examines the important changes in metropolitan structure in recent years. His current research interests include metropolitan structure, intrametropolitan trade in services, and local government economic development policies. Please address correspondence to Professor Bogart at the Department of Economics, Case Western Reserve University, 10900 Euclid Avenue, Cleveland, OH, 44106–7206. Email can be sent to wtb@po.cwru.edu.

American Journal of Economics and Sociology, Vol. 60, No. 1 (January, 2001).
© 2001 American Journal of Economics and Sociology, Inc.

I

Introduction

The sweeping changes in metropolitan structure in the United States have led many to decry urban sprawl as a blight on the landscape. However, it is possible that much of this metropolitan decentralization has not been sprawl in the sense of random scattering of people and firms but rather a change in structure to reflect changing technology and preferences. A growing literature in urban economics looks for common features of decentralized metropolitan areas.

This paper applies a consistent analytical framework to four comparably-sized metropolitan areas (Cleveland, Indianapolis, Portland, and St. Louis) to identify and characterize their employment centers. Employment centers are identified as places that exceed a threshold employment density and a threshold employment level. They are then characterized as specializing on the basis of location quotient analysis. If decentralization is occurring randomly, then we should find that some or all of the employment centers are not identified as specialized. We find, to the contrary, clear evidence of specialization in every employment center in these four metropolitan areas.

There is also some evidence that the size distribution of employment centers follows the rank-size rule. Theoretical models of urban growth are now expected to generate the rank-size rule for city size distributions. Our finding that the rank-size rule holds for intrametropolitan size distributions suggests that it is possible that similar processes govern the growth and development of the parts of a metropolitan area as govern the growth and development of the metropolitan area as a whole.

II

Identifying Employment Centers

An employment center is an area with both a high density and high quantity of employment. We use the transportation analysis zone (TAZ) as the geographical unit of analysis. A TAZ is composed of one or more census blocks, with the borders being supplied to the U.S.

Census Bureau by the metropolitan planning organization in each metropolitan area. Our data are thus a snapshot of metropolitan structure in 1990. An interesting task for future research will be to link these snapshots (even at ten-year intervals) to better understand the dynamic processes driving metropolitan structure.

The methodology developed by Giuliano and Small (1991) in their study of Los Angeles requires identifying TAZs with dense employment, combining adjacent employment-dense TAZs into groups, and measuring total employment in the groups. An employment center is defined as a cluster of contiguous TAZs, all with gross employment density exceeding some minimum D, and with total employment exceeding some minimum E. McMillen and McDonald (1998) and Bogart and Ferry (1999) use this methodology to study Chicago and Cleveland respectively. Identifying employment centers in this way is quite labor intensive, and most researchers have been content to focus on only one metropolitan area at a time. While understandable, this also reduces our ability to generalize about the experience of other metropolitan areas.

This paper uses a consistent analytical approach on four comparably-sized metropolitan areas. The total employment in the regions served by the metropolitan planning organizations (which can differ from the Census-defined metropolitan statistical area) was 627,358 in Indianapolis, 984,967 in Cleveland, 1,100,811 in St. Louis, and 992,185 in Portland.[1]

We follow Bogart and Ferry (1999) in choosing density and total employment cutoffs of 5,000 employees per square mile and 10,000 total employees. We also use their modification to the Giuliano and Small methodology of adding adjacent TAZs with employment densities of less than 5,000 to prospective employment centers, so long as the employment density for the entire center remains over 5,000. This modification compensates for some quirks in the local definitions of TAZs. For example, boundaries can run down the middle of roads, dividing areas with large employment on either side of the road. Without the correction suggested by Bogart and Ferry, we could incorrectly omit some TAZs from consideration despite their integral connection to the employment center.

III

Diffusion of Employment throughout the Metropolitan Area

The monocentric city model, long the standard approach to studying urban areas, postulated a concentration of employment in the central business district (CBD) with the rest of the metropolitan area devoted to residential use. More recently, polycentric models have extended the monocentric city model to account for the fact that there are multiple centers of employment, while maintaining the assumption that these multiple centers account for the bulk of metropolitan employment.

Anas et al. (1998) summarize previous research that finds that less than half of metropolitan employment is located within employment centers. Much of this research has focused on the large cities of Los Angeles and Chicago and the newer cities of the South and Southwest such as Houston and Atlanta. One contribution of our research is to investigate whether the generalizations made on the basis of these cities are also an accurate depiction of medium-sized cities throughout the United States. Table 1 presents our results on this question. Before turning to the main findings, note that each of the metropolitan areas is found to have between 9 and 11 employment centers. This is an interesting result in its own right, which we will return to when we look at the size distribution of employment centers.

We begin by confirming that the monocentric city model is not ap-

Table 1

CBD and Employment Center Employment as a Percent of
Metropolitan Employment

Metropolitan Area	Number of Centers	CBD Employment as a Percent of Metropolitan Employment	Center Employment as a Percent of Metropolitan Employment
Cleveland	9	16%	31%
Indianapolis	11	17%	46%
Portland	11	27%	52%
St. Louis	10	20%	42%

propriate for describing these metropolitan areas. The CBD represents between 16 and 27 percent of total metropolitan employment, greater than the 10 percent found by Giuliano and Small (1991) for Los Angeles but still substantially smaller than we would expect if the monocentric city model were accurate. This provides further confirmation to the observations by Garreau (1991), Bogart (1998), and others that there have been substantial changes in metropolitan structure that have favored the relative growth of suburban employment centers over the traditional downtown central business district.

However, even the polycentric city model seems to be incomplete as a description of metropolitan employment structure. Only one city, Portland, has as much as 50 percent of its employment concentrated within employment centers. Cleveland's 31 percent is actually smaller than the 32 percent found for Los Angeles by Giuliano and Small (1991). Our results confirm that the large changes in metropolitan structure epitomized by the new "auto" cities of the South and Southwest such as Phoenix and Houston are not confined to those places

Figure 1

Employment Centers in Cleveland

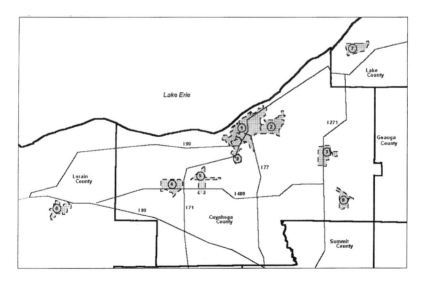

but rather are reflected throughout the United States. In terms of metropolitan structure, Cleveland had become Los Angeles at least as early as 1990, even if the residents didn't realize it.

The maps in Figures 1 through 4 illustrate the employment centers in each of the four metropolitan areas.[2] The employment centers are numbered in order of decreasing employment, and center 1 is the central business district (CBD) in each city. One interesting feature of the maps is the relationship between interstate highways and employment centers. In each city we find that there is almost always a center located near the intersection of interstate highways and that all centers are located in close proximity to an interstate highway. Our maps also demonstrate that the concept of a center/satellite relationship within polycentric cities is a misleading metaphor. Each metropolitan area resists the concept of the CBD as the large nucleus with the rest of the centers as small and dependent satellites. In Portland, two nuclei can be seen, the CBD and the grouping of centers 2, 5, and 3, whose total employment of 133,641 is about 50 percent of the employment in the CBD. St. Louis could boast of having at least three large nuclei. Any ar-

Figure 2.

Employment Centers in Indianapolis

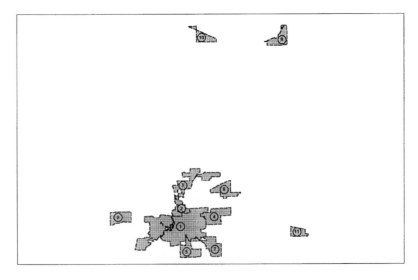

Figure 3.

Employment Centers in St. Louis

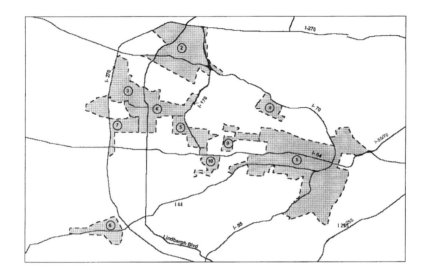

Figure 4.

Employment Centers in Portland

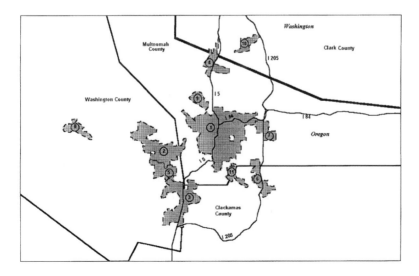

guments of dependence solely upon the CBD are false. These maps confirm the observation made by Rybczynski (1995): it's time to stop assuming that one center necessarily precludes the others.

IV

Specialization of Employment Centers

A COMMON CRITICISM OF metropolitan decentralization is that firms have been scattered throughout the metropolitan area without any pattern.[3] The existence of employment centers mitigates that criticism to some extent, because it provides evidence of significant employment concentrations rather than just diffuse employment. However, if the employment centers themselves are no more than random agglomerations of firms, then some of the efficiency benefits from concentrated economic activity are lost.

Several studies have examined whether suburban employment centers are specialized in production or not. Giuliano and Small (1991) use cluster analysis to divide the 32 centers they find in Los Angeles into five types of centers. Bingham and Kimble (1995) also use cluster analysis to analyze edge cities in Ohio. Bogart (1998) argues that a useful way to characterize a metropolitan area is as a set of small open economies that specialize and trade with each other. Bogart and Ferry (1999) implement this idea by using location quotients to measure the specialization of employment centers, and we follow that approach here.

The location quotient is the sectoral percentage of employment in an employment center divided by the same-sector percentage for the entire metropolitan area. This method describes the specialization of the smaller geography as compared to that of the wider geography.

An alternative interpretation of the location quotient is that it reveals information about trade patterns (Isserman 1980; Knight 1973). If consumption of goods and services in each employment center is proportional to the metropolitan area's sectoral employment composition, then employment centers with relatively high employment in a sector presumably export that sector's output to the rest of the metropolitan area and to the wider economy.

Tables 2 and 3 summarize the results of the analysis, while Tables 4 through 7 provide information on the specific centers in each city.

Strictly speaking, a location quotient greater than 1 in a sector indicates that the employment center specializes in that sector and is a net exporter, while a location quotient less than 1 indicates that the employment center is a net importer. However, in order to better identify areas that were clearly net importers and exporters, we focus on location quotients that are greater than 1.25 or less than 0.75. In other words, we do not identify an employment center as specializing in a sector unless its employment in that sector is at least 25 percent higher than it would be if the center reflected the metropolitan area's employment pattern.

We begin by examining the degree to which employment centers are specialized. Table 2 presents a frequency distribution of the number of specializations in each employment center. The mean number of specializations is 3.4 and the median is 3. The maximum number of specializations found is 7 in downtown Cleveland. There are 18 sectors in the analysis (see Table 3 for specific sectors), so we see that no center is identified as having even half of the possible specializations.

Table 3 approaches the question of whether we can characterize employment centers as being specialized from another direction. The number of centers in each metropolitan area that have a location quotient greater than 1.25 is compared to the number of centers that have

Table 2

Number of Specializations in Centers

Number of Specializations	Centers Having this Many Specializations
1	2
2	6
3	10
4	5
5	5
6	1
7	1

Table 3.

Employment Center Specialization by Sector

Sector	Number of Centers with Location Quotient > 1.25 | Location Quotient < 0.75 (Cleveland)	Number of Centers with Location Quotient > 1.25 | Location Quotient < 0.75 (Indianapolis)	Number of Centers with Location Quotient > 1.25 | Location Quotient < 0.75 (St. Louis)
FFF	1 | 7	2 | 8	0 | 6
Mining	1 | 7	2 | 7	2 | 5
Construction	0 | 3	3 | 3	1 | 4
Nondurable Manufacturing	1 | 3	2 | 4	*4 | 3*
Durable Manufacturing	*5 | 4*	2 | 6	3 | 4
Transportation	2 | 5	1 | 7	3 | 4
Communication and PublicUtilities	1 | 7	3 | 6	1 | 5
Wholesale	*3 | 2*	3 | 6	*4 | 2*
Retail	0 | 5	1 | 2	0 | 10
FIRE	2 | 5	4 | 5	3 | 6
Producer Services	1 | 2	2 | 3	*3 | 2*
ConsumerServices	1 | 6	2 | 3	2 | 5
Entertainment	1 | 6	1 | 4	0 | 7
Health	2 | 4	2 | 3	1 | 7
Education	1 | 6	2 | 4	1 | 8
ProfessionalServices	3 | 4	2 | 3	1 | 2
PublicAdministration	3 | 4	2 | 7	4 | 6
Armed Forces	3 | 4	2 | 9	2 | 8

Note: The first number in each column is the number of employment centers with a location quotient greater than 1.25 in that sector. The second number is the number of employment centers with a location quotient less than 0.75. Numbers in *italics* indicate sectors and cities where there were more centers with location quotients greater than 1.25 than there were with location quotients less than 0.75.

a location quotient less than 0.75. If, as we hypothesize, employment centers are highly specialized in production, then we should find that there are many centers with either relatively high or relatively low location quotients.

The results in Table 3 vary by sector, but there are some consistencies among metropolitan areas. There are four main results. First, there are only five cases (out of a possible 54) of finding more employment centers with a location quotient greater than 1.25 than there are employment centers with a location quotient less than 0.75. In other words, within a metropolitan area there are more "importers" for each sector than there are "exporters."

Second, in most cases the majority of employment centers fall into one of the extremes listed in Table 3. Begin with the first row, FFF (an abbreviation for the Farms, Forests, and Fisheries sector). We see that one center in Cleveland is identified as an exporter while seven are identified as importers. This makes 8 out of 9 employment centers in Cleveland with location quotients above 1.25 (exporters) or less than 0.75 (importers). Similarly, we see 10 out of 11 centers in Indianapolis and 6 out of 10 in St. Louis in these categories for FFF.

Third, there is one sector where a majority of the centers are *not* identified as importers or exporters in all three metropolitan areas — Producer Services. In other words, employment in producer services is relatively evenly distributed among the centers within a metropolitan area. This finding is consistent with producer services being complementary to the production of other goods and services, rather than being an export or import in its own right.

Fourth, there is systematic variation in the number of employment centers that specialize in each sector. For example, only one center of the 30 is identified as specializing in retail and two are found to specialize in entertainment. At the other extreme, ten are identified as specializing in wholesale, ten in durable manufacturing, and nine in public administration.

Tables 4 through 7 identify the employment centers in each metropolitan area along with their specializations. The specializations are listed in decreasing order of total employment, as are the employment centers. The employment centers are numbered in decreasing order of total employment. The downtown of the central city in the metropolitan area is Center 1 in each case. For example, in Table 4 we see that downtown Cleveland has the highest employment in that metropolitan area. The sector in which downtown Cleveland is specialized that has the highest employment is Professional Services, followed by FIRE,

Public Administration, and so on. A complete list of location quotients by employment center is available from the authors on request.

One key feature of Tables 4 through 7 is the calculation of the percentage of employment center employment accounted for by the sectors in which the center is specialized. This again goes to the issue of whether or not it is appropriate to characterize these areas as specialized. While any cutoff is arbitrary, we note that 10 of the 30 centers have over 50 percent of their employment in the sectors of specialization. In addition, all of the employment centers in Cleveland and St. Louis (and 7 of 11 in Indianapolis) have over 30 percent of their employment in the sectors of specialization.

An important question is the extent to which the downtowns in the metropolitan areas are similar. There are at least two dimensions to this question. First, is there a set of sectors in which downtowns tend to specialize? Second, are downtowns less specialized than other employment centers, as might be expected given the earlier monocentric pattern of concentrated employment in all sectors in the central business district?[4]

All three of the downtowns specialize in FIRE, Communications and Public Utilities, and Public Administration. These sectors make intuitive sense. Mills (1992) points out that ambiguous information is best transmitted via personal interaction, and much of the data that banks, insurance companies, and related firms deal in is ambiguous. Further, these firms all need continuous interaction with law firms, which tend to cluster near government buildings such as courthouses. The downtown concentration of public administration employment in part reflects the role of each city in housing local, county, state, and federal government court buildings. Finally, communication and public utilities infrastructures were originally constructed in a monocentric era. Both the infrastructures themselves and the employment needed to operate and maintain them remain focused on the downtown. The fact that both downtown Cleveland and downtown St. Louis are also found to specialize in transportation services reinforces this point.

The evidence on the specialization of the downtown is mixed. The downtowns are less specialized than average, but they are not the least specialized among all of the employment centers. Downtown Cleveland has seven specializations, the most of any center in the three met-

Table 4.

Employment Centers in Cleveland

Employment Center	Total Employment	Employment per Square Mile	Specializations (in order of employment)
1	155,924	15,489	Professional Services, FIRE, Public Administration, Communication and Public Utilities, Transportation, Mining, Armed Forces (44.6%)
2	41,991	10,123	Health Care, Education, Entertainment (57.8%)
3	19,082	5,919	FIRE, Professional Services, Producer Services, Wholesale, Consumer Services (40.9%)
4	18,197	5,336	Durable Manufacturing, Transportation, Professional Services, Public Administration, Wholesale (74.0%)
5	14,650	5,010	Durable Manufacturing (46.5%)
6	13,779	5,204	Durable Manufacturing, Public Administration (31.8%)
7	13,455	5,086	Durable Manufacturing, FFF, Armed Forces (41.6%)
8	12,468	5,105	Health Care, Armed Forces (37.7%)
9	12,152	5,475	Durable Manufacturing, Nondurable Manufacturing, Wholesale (62.9%)

Note: FFF is an abbreviation for Farms, Forests, and Fisheries. FIRE is an abbreviation for Finance, Insurance, and Real Estate. The source of the data is the 1990 Census Transportation Planning Package. The percentage in parentheses at the end of the list of specializations is the fraction of total employment in the center accounted for by those sectors.

Table 5.

Employment Centers in Indianapolis

Employment Center	Total Employment	Employment per Square Mile	Specializations (in order of employment)
1	105,685	5,044	FIRE, Public Administration, Communications and Public Utilities, Mining (31.5%)
2	38,425	17,907	FIRE, Education, Entertainment (25.9%)
3	26,583	5,162	Durable Manufacturing, Public Administration, Armed Forces (41.1%)
4	20,887	5,351	Health Care, Education, Transportation (58.1%)
5	16,849	5,301	Retail, Health Care, FIRE, Armed Forces (50.2%)
6	16,539	5,474	Transportation (21.8%)
7	15,669	5,033	Wholesale, Construction, Producer Services (24.7%)
8	14,367	5,076	Construction, Wholesale, Communications and Public Utilities, FFF, Mining (36.8%)
9	14,123	5,043	FIRE, Producer Services, Wholesale, Consumer Services (38.0%)
10	10,704	5,076	Durable Manufacturing, Nondurable Manufacturing, Consumer Services (44.0%)
11	10,547	6,760	Nondurable Manufacturing, Construction, FFF (22.5%)

Note: FFF is an abbreviation for Farms, Forests, and Fisheries. FIRE is an abbreviation for Finance, Insurance, and Real Estate. The source of the data is the 1990 Census Transportation Planning Package. The percentage in parentheses at the end of the list of specializations is the fraction of total employment in the center accounted for by those sectors.

Table 6.

Employment Centers in St. Louis

Employment Center	Total Employment	Employment per Square Mile	Specializations (in order of employment)
1	224,299	7,854	Nondurable Manufacturing, Communications and Public Utilities, Transportation, Public Administration (38.8%)
2	71,156	5,685	Durable Manufacturing, Transportation (64.5%)
3	37,924	5,240	FIRE, Wholesale, Nondurable Manufacturing, Producer Services, Mining (45.0%)
4	34,427	5,219	Nondurable Manufacturing, Public Administration, Wholesale, Armed Forces (35.1%)
5	27,392	8,127	FIRE, Professional Services, Public Administration, Producer Services, Consumer Services, Mining (60.1%)
6	20,087	5,870	Durable Manufacturing, Transportation, Wholesale (65.4%)
7	15,273	5,814	Health Care, FIRE (57.4%)
8	11,532	5,799	Public Administration, Armed Forces (44.9%)
9	11,131	5,438	Education, Consumer Services (47.5%)
10	10,654	5,968	Durable Manufacturing, Nondurable Manufacturing, Wholesale, Producer Services, Construction (59.9%)

Note: FFF is an abbreviation for Farms, Forests, and Fisheries. FIRE is an abbreviation for Finance, Insurance, and Real Estate. The source of the data is the 1990 Census Transportation Planning Package. The percentage in parentheses at the end of the list of specializations is the fraction of total employment in the center accounted for by those sectors.

Table 7.

Employment Centers in Portland

Employment Center	Total Employment	Employment per Square Mile
1	271,604	9,767
2	56,300	5,026
3	54,496	5,018
4	25,310	6,430
5	22,845	6,203
6	21,788	5,370
7	15,241	5,103
8	13,818	5,386
9	12,684	6,008
10	11,766	5,115
11	11,044	5,387

Note: The source of the data on TAZ boundaries is the 1990 Census Transportation Planning Package, with 1995 employment data from the Portland metropolitan planning organization. Employment by sector is unavailable for Portland at the TAZ level, so it is not possible to calculate location quotients.

ropolitan areas. Downtown Indianapolis and downtown St. Louis both have four specializations. One center in Indianapolis and three centers in St. Louis have more specializations than the downtown.

When we look at the fraction of employment accounted for by the export sectors, the hypothesis of less downtown specialization again receives mixed support. Downtown Cleveland has 44.6 percent of its employment in export sectors, the fifth highest ranking in this category among the nine employment centers in the metropolitan area. Downtown Indianapolis, at 31.5 percent, ranks seventh out of eleven, and downtown St. Louis, at 38.8%, ranks ninth out of ten.

All of the location quotient analysis to this point has been conducted within each metropolitan area. In other words, the focus has been on the specialization of an employment center relative to the rest of the metropolitan area. It is well known that metropolitan areas themselves tend to specialize in production relative to the rest of the country. It is therefore interesting to investigate whether there are any changes in specialization identified when we use all employment in the United States as a benchmark. If a metropolitan area "gains" some previously identified specializations, it is evidence that the metropolitan area is a net exporter in the sector in question, while if it "loses" some specializations we can infer that is a net importer.[5]

In the case of Cleveland, there are two employment centers that have a location quotient greater than 1.25 in Health Care when compared to the United States but not when compared to Cleveland. This indicates that Cleveland is an exporter of health care services to the rest of the United States. Similarly, one additional employment center is identified as specializing in Wholesale using this approach. There are several sectors where Cleveland is identified as a net importer, however. These sectors include Armed Forces (three employment centers' location quotients drop below 1.25), FFF (one center), Consumer Services (one center), Public Administration (one center), and Entertainment (one center).

Indianapolis also displays evidence of metropolitan area specialization. It is a net exporter of Professional Services (two centers), Communications and Public Utilities (one center), Wholesale (one center), and FIRE (one center). Indianapolis is a net importer of Nondurable Manufacturing (one center), Consumer Services (one center), Construction (one center), Mining (two centers), Armed Forces (one center), Transportation (one center), Retail (one center), and Education (one center).

St. Louis has the fewest changes in specialization when the comparison is made to the United States as a whole, indicating that the economy of St. Louis is the most like that of the United States among the metropolitan areas studied here. St. Louis is a net exporter of FIRE (one center), Health Care (one center), and Transportation (one center). St. Louis is a net importer of Mining (two centers), Armed Forces (one center), and Public Administration (one center).

V

Size Distribution of Employment Centers

ONE OF THE BEST-KNOWN AND most robust empirical regularities about city sizes is Zipf's Law, or the rank-size rule.[6] Let a city's population be denoted as **N**, and let **S(N)** equal the number of cities with a population of **N** or greater. In other words, **S(N)** is the "rank" of the city in terms of population. The rank-size rule states that a regression of the logarithm of **S** on the logarithm of **N** will have a slope of -1. This rule has been found to be a reasonable description of the size distribution of cities in a wide variety of places and over a wide range of time periods.

Urban theorists have recently given renewed attention to Zipf's Law as a restriction on the class of acceptable models of urban growth. Models that generate the rank-size rule as a feature have been proposed by Fujita et al. (1999), Gabaix (1999a, 1999b), and Brakman et al. (1999).

Let **N** be the total employment in the employment center, and **S(N)** the number of employment centers in the metropolitan area with employment greater than or equal to **N**. We estimate the following regression. The test of Zipf's Law is whether or not β is equal to -1.

$$ln(S) = \alpha + \beta \, ln(N) + \varepsilon \quad (1)$$

Table 8 summarizes the results of the rank-size rule regression for each of the four metropolitan areas. A coefficient on *ln*(employment) less than 1 in absolute value implies that employment is more concentrated in larger employment centers than predicted by the rank-size rule, while a coefficient greater than 1 in absolute value implies that employment is less concentrated in larger employment centers than predicted by the rank-size rule.

We find that two of the four metropolitan areas have an estimated relation between rank and size of employment centers consistent with the rank-size rule. Interestingly, one of the metropolitan areas where we reject the rank-size rule is Portland, which is well known for its urban growth boundary policy aimed at altering the metropolitan spatial structure.[7] These results are consistent with the idea that employment in Portland is more concentrated in the larger employment centers (especially downtown) than the rank-size rule would predict. We do not have as concise an explanation for the rejection of the rank-size rule in St. Louis.

Rusk (1995) hypothesizes that metropolitan areas that are "elastic" are systematically different than metropolitan areas that are "inelastic."

Table 8.

Rank-Size Rule Regressions

Metropolitan Area	Intercept	Ln(Employment)	Adjusted	Rank-Size R²Rule
Cleveland	9.51	−0.81	0.87	Yes
	(1.08)	(0.11)		
Indianapolis	12.42	−1.09	0.95	Yes
	(0.80)	(0.08)		
Portland	9.29	−0.76	0.95	No
	(0.55)	(0.05)		
St. Louis	9.22	−0.75	0.98	No
	(0.33)	(0.03)		

Note: Standard errors in parentheses. The variable "Rank-size rule" is yes if we do not reject the hypothesis that the coefficient on ln(employment) equals -1 at the 95 percent significance level.

An elastic metropolitan area is one in which the central city can easily annex undeveloped land and in which there is ample undeveloped land within the central city for growth. Two of the metropolitan areas in our study, Cleveland and St. Louis, are categorized by Rusk (1995, Table 2.2, p. 53) as having zero elasticity, his lowest category of five. Portland is ranked as having low elasticity, the second lowest category, while Indianapolis is ranked as having high elasticity, the second highest category. Interestingly, Indianapolis is the only one of the four metropolitan areas to have an estimated coefficient greater than 1 in absolute value in the rank-size rule regression. The earlier analysis did not indicate any other systematic differences in the structure of Indianapolis, contrary to Rusk's hypothesis.

We can use the estimated coefficients from equation (1) to predict the "rank" of the employment center with a total employment of 10,000, which should also be the number of centers in the metropolitan area. This approach predicts eight centers for Cleveland, 11 for Indianapolis, and 10 for both Portland and St. Louis. As we saw in Table 1, there are nine centers in Cleveland, 10 in St. Louis, and 11 in both Portland and Indianapolis. The similarity in the number of centers in the cities is further evidence of a general structure underlying metropolitan change in the United States.

One reason that the size distribution of employment centers is of interest is that it can be used to predict the number and size distribution of geographical areas where there is dense employment but not yet sufficient total employment to exceed the threshold. We refer to areas with employment density greater than 5,000 per square mile but with less than 10,000 total employees as "proto-centers." [8] If there is indeed regularity in the size distribution, then the parameters estimated using the employment centers with more than 10,000 employees should be helpful in predicting the number and distribution of proto-centers.

Table 9 presents summary evidence on the proto-centers in the various metropolitan areas. With the exception of the smaller proto-centers in Indianapolis, the regression in Table 8 is a reasonably good predictor of the number of proto-centers at various employment levels. This is further evidence of systematic structure in the intrametropolitan distribution of employment.[9]

The rank-size rule has been widely accepted as a restriction on acceptable models of aggregate metropolitan growth. The results reported here suggest that a similar criterion should be applied to models of metropolitan structure and the growth of employment centers within metropolitan areas.

Table 9

Size Distribution of Proto-Centers

Metropolitan Area	≥ 10,000 (Predicted/ Actual)	≥ 8,000 (Predicted/ Actual)	≥ 6,000 (Predicted/ Actual)	≥ 4,000 (Predicted/ Actual)	≥ 2,000 (Predicted/ Actual)
Cleveland	8 / 9	9 / 12	12 / 15	16 / 19	29 / 31
Indianapolis	11 / 11	14 / 12	19 / 16	29 / 18	62 / 23
Portland	10 / 11	12 / 11	15 / 16	20 / 21	34 / 35
St. Louis	10 / 10	12 / 10	15 / 13	20 / 18	34 / 28

VI

Concluding Remarks

This paper has demonstrated, using data on four comparable metropolitan areas, that there are substantial regularities in metropolitan structure across the United States. These regularities include the size distribution of employment centers and the extent to which employment centers specialize in production.

An important finding with implications for future research is our confirmation of previous research by Anas et al. (1998) that concluded that less than 50 percent of metropolitan employment is concentrated in employment centers. The research reported here, combined with earlier research by several authors, has given us a good understanding of the economic structure of these employment centers. However, by its very nature, a focus on the centers is inadequate for describing what is happening outside of those centers. The use of location quotient analysis to describe the trading activity of employment centers is suggestive of a fruitful way to approach the more diffuse employment elsewhere in the metropolitan area. Anderson (1999) characterizes suburbs as "trading places" and calculates their imports and exports, identifying substantial economic interactions beyond the employment centers that are the focus of this paper. Further development of this approach and other approaches that develop our understanding of the employment not concentrated in centers is crucial.

Notes

1. The Census Bureau does not collect TAZ employment data for Portland. All employment figures for Portland were obtained from the metropolitan planning organization and are from 1995.

2. The metropolitan planning organizations provided the TAZ maps. The St. Louis highway map was provided by the metropolitan planning organization, while the Cleveland and Portland highway and county boundary maps are from MapInfo. The MapInfo highway map for Indianapolis is incompatible with the TAZ map provided by Indianapolis.

3. Jackson (1985, p. 270) approvingly quotes Lewis Mumford's description of metropolitan structure in the United States as a "formless urban exudation."

4. Anas et al. (1998) take as given that downtowns are less specialized than suburban employment centers.

5. The complete data are available on request from the authors.

6. The seminal work is Zipf (1949). See Fujita et al. (1999) or Gabaix (1999b) for a review of the literature on Zipf's Law as applied to city size distributions.

7. See Knaap and Nelson (1992) for a description and analysis of the Portland urban growth boundary.

8. It is also possible that a geographical area has an employment greater than 10,000 but a density less than 5,000 per square mile. For example, large shopping malls often anchor such an area, as illustrated in Anderson (1999). It is possible that including these types of proto-centers in our analysis would alter the results.

9. In addition to the results reported in Table 9, we also estimated the rank-size rule regression for each metropolitan area using proto-centers that met lower employment thresholds (for example, all centers and proto-centers with total employment greater than or equal to 6,000). Adding the proto-centers did not significantly change the coefficient on employment in the regression, and most importantly, did not alter whether or not we reject the rank-size rule for the metropolitan area. Complete results available on request from the authors.

References

Anas, Alex, Richard Arnott, and Kenneth Small. (1998). "Urban Spatial Structure." *Journal of Economic Literature* 36: 1426–1464.

Anderson, Nathan. (1999). " 'Trading Places': Measuring Trade in Labor Services Among Suburbs in Greater Cleveland." Senior honors thesis, Department of Economics, Case Western Reserve University.

Bingham, Richard, and Deborah Kimble. (1995). "Industrial Composition of Edge Cities and Downtowns." *Economic Development Quarterly* 9: 259–272.

Bogart, William T. (1998). *The Economics of Cities and Suburbs*. Upper Saddle River, NJ: Prentice Hall.

Bogart, William T., and William C. Ferry. (1999). "Employment Centres in Greater Cleveland: Evidence of Evolution in a Formerly Monocentric City." *Urban Studies* 36: 2099–2110.

Brakman, Steven, Harry Garretsen, Charles Van Marrewijk, and Marianne van den Berg. (1999). "The Return of Zipf: Towards a Further Understanding of the Rank-Size Distribution." *Journal of Regional Science* 39: 183–213.

Fujita, Masahisa, Paul Krugman, and Anthony Venables. (1999). *The Spatial Economy: Cities, Regions, and International Trade*. Cambridge, MA: MIT Press.

Gabaix, Xavier. (1999a). "Zipf's Law and the Growth of Cities." *American Economic Review Papers and Proceedings* 89: 129–132.

———. (1999b). "Zipf's Law for Cities: An Explanation." *Quarterly Journal of Economics* 114: 739–767.

Garreau, Joel. (1991). *Edge City: Life on the New Frontier.* New York: Doubleday.

Giuliano, Genevieve, and Kenneth Small. (1991). "Subcenters in the Los Angeles Region." *Regional Science and Urban Economics* 21: 163–182.

Isserman, Andrew. (1980). "Estimating Export Activity in a Regional Economy: A Theoretical and Empirical Analysis of Alternative Methods." *International Regional Science Review* 5: 155–184.

Jackson, Kenneth. (1985). *Crabgrass Frontier: The Suburbanization of the United States.* New York: Oxford University Press.

Knaap, Gerrit, and Arthur Nelson. (1992). *The Regulated Landscape: Lessons on State Land Use Planning from Oregon.* Cambridge, MA: Lincoln Institute of Land Policy.

Knight, Richard. (1973). *Employment Expansion and Metropolitan Trade.* New York: Praeger Press.

McMillen, Daniel, and John McDonald. (1998). "Suburban Subcenters and Employment Density in Metropolitan Chicago." *Journal of Urban Economics* 43: 157–180.

Mills, Edwin. (1992). " Sectoral Clustering and Metropolitan Development." In *Sources of Metropolitan Growth*, E. Mills and J. McDonald (eds.). New Brunswick, NJ: Center for Urban Policy Research.

Rusk, David. (1995). *Cities Without Suburbs, 2ⁿᵈ Edition.* Washington, DC: Woodrow Wilson Center Press.

Rybczynski, Witold. (1995). *City Life: Urban Expectations in a New World.* New York: Scribner.

Zipf, George. (1949). *Human Behavior and the Principle of Least Effort.* Cambridge, MA: Addison-Wesley.

Edge Cities and the Viability of Metropolitan Economies

Contributions to Flexibility and External Linkages by New Urban Service Environments

By DAVID L. MCKEE and YOSRA A. MCKEE*

ABSTRACT. Economists have had little to say concerning the impact of Edge Cities in metropolitan complexes, much less about how they relate to the economy in general. The present paper is aimed at those concerns. It begins with a general overview of the Edge City concept as put forward by Joel Garreau. Following that it discusses metropolitan change in a pre-Edge City format. It then considers Edge Cities in the context of growth poles and discusses their role in providing economic linkages that facilitate change. The intent is to provide a better understanding of the impact of Edge Cities upon host metropolitan areas and the economy at large.

I

A Preliminary Overview

THE EDGE CITY CONCEPT which was put forward by Joel Garreau (1991) offers new insights into forms of urban expansion in and around major metropolitan complexes in the United States. It may hold similar relevance to the understanding of expansion in the metropolitan areas of other advanced nations. Beyond metropolitan expansion per se this concept seems to signal the linkages which impacted areas may have to national economies and beyond. Indeed it appears as though Garreau may have contributed an idea that will aid in the understanding of how various major corporate players are contributing ongoing

*David L. McKee is Professor of Economics in the Graduate School of Management at Kent State University, where he specializes in development economics and economic change. Yosra A. McKee is an adjunct faculty member in economics at Kent State University. Her work on international trade and services, economic integration, and regional development has been included in various professional publications and presentations.

American Journal of Economics and Sociology, Vol. 60, No. 1 (January, 2001).

strength and viability to urban and regional subsets of national economies and to those national economies themselves.

Garreau listed five parameters which demarcate his concept. First of all he saw the Edge City as containing a minimum of five million square feet of leasable office space. In addition to that he saw such configurations as holding at least six hundred thousand square feet of retail space. The centers in question were seen primarily as work locations with populations which expanded during work days, rather than as residential suburbs. Edge Cities would be perceived locally as a single end destination for mixed use-jobs, shopping and entertainment (1991, p. 425). Finally, Garreau saw Edge City sites as having been predominantly rural or residential as little as thirty years ago (p. 425).

It seems as though the Edge City as described by Garreau is related to the emergence of the United States as a service economy. Today seven out of ten new employment opportunities are service-oriented (McKee 1988, p. 15). Service industries are growing in size and importance in the national economy and many services are housed in urban settings. Beyond service industries themselves many positions within manufacturing concerns are occupationally service-oriented.

Insofar as the Edge City as described by Garreau appears to house and nurture what have become leading service-oriented activities in the national economy, it may be an element that continues to link large metropolitan areas to that economy. In a strictly local context, Garreau's vision of millions of square feet of office space may appear to hold an overstated importance. However it appears to be the type of office space that emerges which infuses energy into the areas in question.

Although retailing is important in the Garreau schema, it is far less significant than the office component. Presumably the type of retail activity that is most significant in an Edge City context would be regional malls and shopping centers which service far broader clienteles than what the suburb or jurisdiction housing the retail facilities may boast. It appears unlikely that retail facilities in and of themselves can be expected to generate Edge Cities. However, considered in conjunction with the types of office concentrations described above, they can be expected to strengthen the local or regional impacts of Edge Cities.

The significance of Edge Cities in the national economy appears to be that they represent concentrations of the service pursuits which have become central in importance to that economy. In many cases these pursuits are the service aspects of the operations of major corporations which are not necessarily producing services as their outputs. These types of activities are positioning themselves in locations on the periphery of metropolitan complexes where they can take advantage of urban access while at the same time satisfying spatial and aesthetic requirements.

There is no question that such concentrations impact their metropolitan hosts. They focus attention on the area of the metropolitan region that they have selected. The fact that they represent concentrations of employment opportunities adjusts traffic patterns and generates wide varieties of consumer services needed in the area. They may draw a certain amount of activities away from previous locations within the metropolitan mix. Eventually they may impact residential patterns as well.

In cases where this type of development coincides with the positioning of regional shopping malls, the metropolitan impact of the area will be magnified. Although Garreau alludes to the importance of retailing and entertainment facilities in the Edge City, it is clear that he regards the office and corporate components of his concept as being more significant (1991, pp. 6–7). As long as these components retain their significance they will provide employment opportunities and purchasing power in their selected metropolitan hosts. unlike manufacturing facilities of the production line variety, these corporate facilities may be more resistant to the swings of the business cycle.

These types of development are not the only employment-generating growth patterns in and around major metropolitan areas. Various types of commercial expansion aimed at local needs are still occurring. Commercial strip development has not been rendered redundant by Edge Cities, nor has the regional shopping center in settings that are not Edge Cities in and of themselves. Major manufacturing and corporate distribution centers are growing in importance in the suburbs and open space surrounding metropolitan areas. Although such facilities do not appear to fit the strictest parameters of Garreau's vision, they are nonetheless very important players in metropolitan growth and viability and must be included in any analysis of metropolitan economies.

A careful reading of Garreau suggests that he sees the Edge City as an outgrowth of advances in transportation and communications which have freed both people and activities from the need to focus upon large central cities (1991, p. 32). His Edge Cities are creatures of the metropolitan periphery or of citified rural landscapes accessible to major metropolitan areas. According to Garreau, Edge Cities have emerged or are most likely to emerge near beltways surrounding major metropolitan complexes, near bypasses which were intended to permit traffic to avoid large centers, or perhaps on major access routes to large centers. The last form for the Edge City would be well out beyond the traditional orbit of the urban complex.

II

Metropolitan Change in a Pre-Edge City Context

THE EDGE CITY AS DESCRIBED BY GARREAU is a relatively recent phenomenon. Various forms of suburban development predate it in an historical sense. Commuting to work sites in large central business districts began with street railways and commuter trains and became more flexible with the wider use of automobiles and buses.

Buses and automobiles generated suburban expansion of both residential and commercial varieties. With suburbanization came commercial strip development and the emergence of shopping centers of various sizes in suburban locations. By and large the menu of changes enumerated here predates the phenomenon alluded to by Garreau. Nonetheless many such changing land use patterns have continued to emerge and/or grow in dormitory suburbs, both old and new. Presumably, metropolitan complexes that are experiencing the emergence of Edge Cities are also experiencing ongoing suburbanization of a more traditional variety.

Prior to the emergence of systems of limited access highways in and around major metropolitan areas, the expansion of non-manufacturing activities in those complexes was signaled by more and taller buildings in central business districts and by the emergence of strip development along major access routes. Of course the success of commercial strips led to the emergence of shopping centers and, as suburban populations increased, to malls and regional shopping complexes. These last mentioned forms of suburban retailing and consumer service concentration received further stimulation from the advent of the limited access highway systems.

The advent of those highway systems has also impacted the nature and location of manufacturing and distributional activities. Whereas such activities had been constrained in their locations by rail, and in some cases, water transport, the highways have rendered them more footloose. Their concentration in crowded and constraining urban settings is no longer necessary. As older facilities depreciate, they are being replaced by industrial parks in suburban settings, by free-standing complexes in rural areas (e.g., the Saturn automotive plant), and of course by facilities located abroad. In cases where industrial parks have emerged on the peripheries of major metropolitan areas, they still play active roles in metropolitan labor markets and also contribute to physically configuring their host complexes.

The types of growth or change referred to here hardly constitute a dialectic. Certainly business activities take part in shaping the physical structure of such areas in the way that they position themselves in and around urban areas (McKee 1994, p. 4). However, new activities or new settings for ongoing ventures hardly clean the slate of older endeavors, not to mention the settings that house them. The emergence of strip development and malls do not necessarily signal the demise of the central business district. Although certain activities have left central cities, others are still expanding within them. Strip development has not ceased with the emergence of shopping centers, nor have the latter given way to malls. In the metropolitan mix all of these forms of activity may be growing simultaneously. Beyond them Edge Cities are growing as well and their local, regional, national, and even international roles have not been analyzed.

Garreau himself can hardly be faulted for lack of discussion of the extra-metropolitan roles of the Edge City. He certainly recognized it as a national phenomenon, since throughout his book he identified existing and emerging examples across the United States. However, the identification of Edge City locations raises more questions than answers concerning the extent of their functions.

III

Edge Cities and Pole Theory

PERHAPS A BETTER UNDERSTANDING OF THE EDGE CITY phenomenon can be gleaned by examining it within the framework of growth pole theory. Assessing the impact of various service sub-sectors in a growth pole format is hardly new (e.g., McKee 1988). Certain services have been examined with respect to their potential as vehicles for ongoing growth and prosperity in the modern world. Since Edge Cities, as they have been defined, appear to be the locus of service pursuits or occupationally service-oriented activities within the manufacturing sector, a similar approach may be useful.

Pole theory "attempts to understand change from the point of view of the leadership roles of activities engaged in competitive processes" (McKee 1993, p. 25). Such pursuits are presumed to be influencing the direction and momentum of the economies which house them in accordance with their own strength. In effect pole theory is a form of analysis designed to explain how leading sectors or key industries determine the direction of growth and change (McKee 1991, p. 86).

Francois Perroux, if not the originator of pole theory, was certainly one of its most prominent exponents. He has stated: "Growth does not appear everywhere at the same time, it becomes manifest at points or poles of growth, with variable intensity; it spreads through different channels, with various terminal effects on the whole of the economy" (1970, p. 94). That passage contains a definitive statement of the imbalance which appears to be central to profit-driven economies. Perroux never really emphasized spatial imbalance per se, but imbalances can certainly be spatial as well as structural and temporal. Whether the Edge City has a part in such imbalances remains to be seen.

Space has been a rather confusing element in pole theory. Perroux had several ways of looking at economic space, two of which appear to be pertinent to the current discussion. At one point he referred to economic space as defined by a plan—"the set of relations which exist between the firms and, on the one hand, the supplier of input . . . And, on the other hand, the buyers of output (both intermediate and final)" (1950, p. 95).

It would certainly seem that the view of space alluded to above may assist in the understanding of how Edge Cities are impacting their local or regional hosts, not to mention the national or international economies. Firms that boast facilities in Edge Cities obtain the resources required for their operation from either local markets or beyond. Those same firms supply goods and services to local, regional, or larger markets. The impact of such firms can be measured locally, regionally, nationally, or internationally by what they purchase and what they in turn sell at whatever level.

This type of logic is hardly new to economists or location theorists. In assessing the local (metropolitan) impact of an Edge City, questions must be asked about its labor force, about the space it occupies, and about what it supplies to the local area. Do the activities housed by the Edge City draw workers of varying skills away from pursuits in other parts of the metropolis or do the activities bring in new populations of workers from elsewhere? If the Edge City workforce is not recruited from those already working in the metropolis, the immediate impact should be positive. Of course, a negative employment impact may follow eventually if activities in the Edge City force redundancy upon similar activities predating them in the citiscape. Such questions have destination-specific answers.

In occupying space, Edge Cities impact the geography of metropolitan expansion and place demands upon the existing infrastructure and various urban services. Economists could readily construct the appropriate cost-benefit scenario to assess such impacts. What the Edge City supplies to the local area is most obvious in the realm of retail facilities and consumer services. Of course, once again any toll exacted by Edge City facilities upon previously existing competitors should be assessed.

Additional local impacts may follow if Edge Cities influence the residential pattern of the metropolis. Garreau spoke of Edge Cities as work destinations, enjoying infusions of workday populations. Eventually those employed in the Edge City may want to live in easy access to it. Residential adjustments do not just represent changing land use patterns, but bring with them changes in public service needs and changes in the tax base to supply these needs. Thus, the eventual impact of Edge Cities on the metropolitan mix may be rather extensive.

Unfortunately a mere assessment of such impacts may fall far short of explaining Edge Cities' overall significance.

The question of what Edge Cities supply to the metropolitan area may be more complicated than it first appears. The Garreau parameter with respect to retail space may be the easiest to assess. Six hundred thousand square feet may represent a regional mall of reasonable dimensions or it may represent a combination of facilities. The mall format may be the most visible, attracting consumers from broader areas, including the customers of previously existing facilities. What five million square feet of office space supplies to the metropolitan complex may not be as obvious on the surface. The offices of various service establishments geared to the local community may be included in the mix, but a more important component may be corporate offices with various functions. The business of those offices may involve major linkages and/or customers beyond local metropolitan confines.

Writing in 1984, Thierry Noyelle and Thomas Stanback referred to "the rise of the very large, multiproduct, often multinational corporation—resulting in the multiplication of locally distinct service-like corporate establishments: national headquarters, regional sales headquarters, divisional offices [and] R&D facilities" (p. 3). What those authors were describing signaled the way in which such service-like activities can keep the metropolitan complexes that host them as important elements in the national economy. Another view of space put forward by Perroux may be helpful in understanding the significance of corporate office space housed in Edge Cities. He suggested that economic space could be considered as a field of forces composed of centers or poles "from which centrifugal forces emanate and to which centripetal forces are attracted" (1950, p. 95). If Edge Cities are housing the type of office facilities referred to by Noyelle and Stanback, it may be difficult to ascribe directly to them the centrifugal and centripetal forces under discussion. However, those office facilities are a part of corporate organizations to which the force fields in question are attached. Thus the logic developed by Perroux may apply.

Certain firms and/or industries may have acquired leadership positions in national economies or indeed in the world economy. Aside from being actual leaders on national or world scales, many firms are large enough to be very influential. No one would discount the importance of various Fortune 500 firms, for example, merely because they fail to survive an arbitrary cutoff, aimed at identifying the world's twenty or thirty leading firms in terms of ongoing growth.

It seems safe to suggest that most large multinational firms and perhaps the industries that they comprise exhibit the centrifugal and centripetal forces Perroux alludes to. Because they may have large numbers of spatially and functionally diverse operating units in many nations and jurisdictions, the identification of their force fields becomes a complicated abstract process (see McKee 1991, pp. 86–89).

The steel industry in the United States has been used as an example (McKee 1991, p. 88). In an historical sense most experts would agree that the steel industry played a central role in the industrial establishment of the nation. In the jargon of the pole theorists, it was a key industry. "Today much has changed with respect to the status of that particular industry within the economy of the United States, and it is hardly likely that many would contend that it has retained its earlier stature" (McKee 1991, p. 88). Many of its formerly robust production facilities have been written off, causing traumatic adjustments in the locations that house them.

The diminished status of steel production in the United States has hardly removed the industry as a significant player in the world economy. It may still be a leading industry in that economy, not to mention some other national economies. Various locations within the United States may still be power hubs for steel if they house corporate headquarters or research and /or planning facilities. They may perform such functions in concert with other hubs in other nations. What is true of steel may be true for the large multinational firms comprising various other industries.

If the impact of an industry upon the world economy can be measured through the use of employment or output data, then the force fields alluded to by Perroux can be identified. Speaking of steel, McKee writes, "Those fields are better understood when they are considered as emanating from an industry rather than from specific locations" (1991, p. 89). What is true of steel seems readily applicable to other industries. "[A]n abstract version of space that quantifies the components of firms or industries may add to the understanding of the role of the aggregated unit in the world, national, regional, or local economy concerned, depending upon which level the aggregation encompasses" (ibid).

IV

Edge Cities and Economic Linkages

HIDDEN IN THESE RELATIVELY RECENT CORPORATE industrial structures lie important economic impacts emanating from Edge Cities. By hosting corporate office and research facilities, Edge Cities are locations which support the corporate force fields alluded to above. Certainly such forces are apparent within corporations boasting Edge City facilities. If decisions are made in such facilities that impact a corporation's operations locally, regionally, nationally, or internationally, then definite linkages are being maintained between the Edge City and its exterior locations.

Beyond these intra-corporate linkages involving Edge Cities lie the force fields from the multinational corporate aggregates described earlier. Presumably Edge Cities share in these force fields as well. Insofar as Edge Cities in their capacities as hosts to corporate office functions are providing space and access to various facilitative functions to those corporate divisions, they are well integrated with major industrial players on the national and/or world scene. In this way, they may also be thought of as instrumental in maintaining ongoing linkages between the metropolitan areas to which they relate and national /global interests.

If Edge Cities are performing an integrative role involving their metropolitan hosts and wider economic forces, a major misconception involving services may be reduced. Thomas M. Stanback and his colleagues (1981) complained of an apparent spacelessness in service activity. In discussing this issue they suggest the need to reexamine how the physical landscape has been transformed, "the way the old landscape may have impeded the blooming of a new one, and the way the present physical structure may present a barrier to the future" (Stanback et al. 1981, p. 6).

It seems clear that Edge Cities have emerged on the periphery of existing metropolitan complexes in order to avoid the various diseconomies of central city locations, while at the same time availing themselves of what metropolitan complexes have to offer. In Stanback's terms the old landscape (the central city) may have been impeding the emergence of the activities that Edge Cities have come to contain. Unlike the physical structure of central city areas, that of the Edge City may not present barriers for the future to overcome. The corporate campuses of the Edge City appear to be capable of reasonably long run viability as office complexes. Unlike various defunct production facilities, they may be capable of attracting new enterprises should their current corporate tenants disappear from the scene.

In a word, the corporate office complexes and related services that have emerged in the Edge City format appear capable of a rather lengthy reign as viable additions to metropolitan economies. It would appear that while providing local employment opportunities, both of their own and of the induced variety, they are also insuring an ongoing place for their metropolitan hosts in the national and world economies. Indeed, this place may be more stable than that provided by corporate production facilities in the past.

It has been known for some time that "various service activities act to strengthen and facilitate the role of leading industrial operations" (McKee 1988, p. 21). By locating corporate headquarters in Edge Cities, companies are able to avail themselves of the various producer and other business-related services which major metropolitan complexes have to offer. Such services have been identified as aiding in setting up effective linkages between various stages of manufacturing processes, if not actually contributing directly to the efficiency of such processes. Of course the availability of such services may dictate which metropolitan areas may experience Edge City development. Corporate complexes in Edge Cities are themselves facilitators of the production role of their respective companies. They provide the planning and linkage functions which are designed to keep the operations of the multinational firms viable. In doing that they maintain links between their metropolitan hosts and the ever-changing national and international economies.

V

A Final Assessment

IT WOULD APPEAR AS THOUGH the corporate campuses of the Edge Cities are much more stable components of metropolitan economies than has been historically true in the case of production facilities. They should thus contribute some stability to the linkages with national and international economies which their metropolitan hosts enjoy. The firms that are present on those campuses need not be absolute leaders in the world economy. Provided that they are large and powerful enough to sustain profitable operations, actual leadership credentials are not the relevant concern.

Of course the impact of such firms on the metropolitan economy itself depends upon their size, their income-generating capacity, and their relative positioning. Old steel cities may not find corporate facilities in peripheral campus developments boasting as much employment potential as did the now depreciated plants. However, the new facilities may be much more stable elements in the metropolitan mix than most actual production facilities can hope to be. Their actual impact in the metropolitan mix is destination-specific and, of course, dependent upon their size and positioning relative to their metropolitan hosts.

The linkages that corporate operations in Edge Cities form with metropolitan service subsectors may be of special significance in strengthening and stabilizing the economic potential of urban complexes. The concentrations of business services which have developed in various metropolitan areas are facilitators of corporate activity. Such services have been recognized as "not industry or firm specific" (McKee 1988, p. 22). McKee suggests that "when a particular industry loses its leading position, engineering, financial and other business related services by their very nature help to sustain a climate conducive to the development of new growth poles" (1988, p. 22).

In the current context the issue is not so much whether or not service cadres housed in metropolitan complexes can attract successions of leading production-related industrial facilities. The multinational corporations have been closing older urban plants and relocating their production facilities to environments which they deem better suited to their current needs. The service cadres in question may even be assisting the corporations in such adjustments. In cases where a symbiosis has emerged between various service cadres and corporate planners housed in Edge Cities, the result should be a strengthening of the types of force fields envisioned by Perroux. The metropolitan settings where such symbiotics are in evidence should be well positioned in the era of the post-blue collar metropolis.

The importance of the functional relationship between corporate office units in Edge Cities and various sophisticated producer services housed in metropolitan areas seems clear. Office complexes in Edge Cities would appear to have a stronger potential for lasting economic impacts if they are of the corporate variety or are devoted to producer services. Offices purveying consumer services may be less significant, since demand for what they do is income-driven.

Garreau has acknowledged a retail role for the Edge City by relegating a minimum of six hundred thousand square feet to it. If retail and other consumer outlets emerge which are designed to service a clientele working rather than living in the Edge City, the result should represent an addition to the metropolitan complement of consumer related activity. If the facility in question represents a regional shopping center, its metropolitan impact is more likely to include subtractions from previously successful businesses. In any case, retailing and other consumer services appear to be much less significant as components of Edge Cities than is the office component. Generally their impacts will be local or regional in nature.

Edge Cities may be entrepreneurial as well—witness Route 128 in the Boston area and, of course, Silicon Valley. Innovation-driven Edge Cities will generate extra-metropolitan linkages as well as symbiotic relations to the metropolis that spawned them. In both respects they are developing linkage functions which resemble in some ways those ascribed to corporate Edge Cities. Beyond those functions, however, they may facilitate the expansion of various corporate activities in their metropolitan hosts and beyond, through what they come to produce. Both entrepreneurial and corporate Edge Cities may induce the growth of sophisticated retail, entertainment, and consumer service facilities, thus adding to local employment opportunities. Clearly, Edge Cities have impacts both within and beyond their host jurisdictions.

They seem well suited to an economy which has been identified as service-oriented; at the same time they are capable of major impacts in manufacturing subsectors. As important as their local impacts may be, their exterior linkage functions may be even more significant.

References

Garreau, Joel (1991). *Edge City: Life on the New Frontier.* New York: Anchor Books.
Hermansen, Tormod (1972). "Development Poles and Development Centers in National and Regional Development," in Antoni Kuklinski (ed.), *Growth Poles and Growth Centers in Regional Planning,* pp. 1–68. Paris: Mouton and Co.
Katouzian, M.A. (1970). "The Development of the Service Sector," *Oxford Economic Papers,* New Series. Vol. 22, No. 3, November, pp. 362–382.
McKee, David L. (1988). Growth, Development and the Service Economy in the Third World. New York: Praeger.
———. (1991). *Schumpeter and the Political Economy of Change.* Westport, CT: Praeger.
———. (1993). "Change and Innovation in a Post-Schumpeterian World Economy," in Libecap, Gary D. (ed.), *Advances in the Study of Entrepreneurship, Innovation, and Economic Growth,* Vol. 6, pp. 21–36. Greenwich, CT: JAI Press Inc.
———. (1994). "Some Observations on Physical Structure in Advanced Metropolitan Areas" in David L. McKee, *Urban Environments in Emerging Economies,* pp. 3–16. Westport, CT: Praeger.
Noyelle, Thierry J. and Thomas M. Stanback, Jr. (1984). *The Economic Transformation of American Cities.* Totowa, N. J.: Rowman & Allanheld Publishers.
Perroux, Francois. (1950). "Economic Space: Theory and Applications," *Quarterly Journal of Economics.* Vol. 64, No. 1, February, pp. 89–104.
———. (1964). *L'Economie du XXe Siecle, Deuxieme Edition Augmentee.* Paris: Presse universitaire de Paris.
———. (1970). "Note on the concept of Growth Poles," in David L. McKee, Robert D. Dean and William H. Leahy (eds.), *Regional Economics: Theory and Practice,* pp. 93–104. New York: The Free Press.
Stanback, Thomas M., Jr., Peter J. Bearse, Thierry J. Noyelle, and Robert A. Karasek (1981). *Services: The New Economy.* Totowa, N. J.: Allanheld, Osmun Publishers.

Manufacturing and Rural Economies in the United States

The Role of Nondurable Producers, Labor Costs and State Taxes

By MARK JELAVICH*

ABSTRACT. This paper investigates the preferences of manufacturers in deciding whether to locate in metropolitan or nonmetropolitan (rural) areas. Using 1997 state-level data and OLS regression estimation, it was determined that nondurable goods manufacturers prefer rural areas, while durable goods manufacturers are indifferent as to area. However, both sets of manufacturers prefer to locate in larger states. Wage rates are not significant in the regressions, while durable manufacturers appear sensitive to state taxes. Some policy conclusions for local economic developers are derived from these findings.

I

Introduction

SEVERAL RECENT STUDIES HAVE CONCLUDED THAT manufacturing activity has been increasing in rural areas of the United States since at least the mid-1980s (e.g., Gordon et al. 1998; Galston and Baehler 1995). One such example is meatpacking (Drabenstott et al. 1999). Various reasons have been given as to why rural locations are now relatively attractive to at least some manufacturers compared to metropolitan ones, such as lower wages, less unionization, better road transportation, and cheaper real estate (e.g., Levy 1994; Kaufman 1994; Galston and Baehler 1995). Firms looking to produce "green" (environment-friendly) products is yet another reason (Carlton 2000). An earlier study by this author (Jelavich forthcoming), using 1993 state-level

*The author is a full professor of Economics at Northwest Missouri State University. His research interests include regional economic development and multinational firm location decisions. His most recent publications have appeared in *Regional Science Perspectives* and the *Journal of Regional Analysis and Policy*.

American Journal of Economics and Sociology, Vol. 60, No. 1 (January, 2001).

data, concluded that manufacturers prefered to locate in less urbanized states.

At the same time, there is other evidence that manufacturing activity is still attracted to urban locations. For instance, two recent articles have come to opposite conclusions concerning the locational preferences of foreign-owned manufacturers producing in the United States: Luker (1998) found that these firms prefer rural locations, while Coughlin and Segev (2000) determined that they prefer urban locations.

More generally, regional economic development specialists have been looking at the process of *clustering* as a basis for local economic development policy. Porter (2000) defines a cluster as a "geographically proximate group of interconnected companies and associated institutions. . . linked by communalities and complementarities" (p. 16), which can occur in both urban and rural settings (p. 18). Thus the thrust of economic development policies focussing on clusters is not to attract just one particular industry, but rather that industry and other industries and economic activities that will support that first industry through linkages. For instance, Porter makes reference to the "California wine cluster," which includes vineyards, wineries, bottling, winemaking equipment, and tourism, as well as other endeavors (p. 17).

Kim, Barkley and Henry (2000) looked at manufacturing clustering in urban compared to rural locations. They found that labor-intensive industries are attracted to rural locations, as well as to rural sites with appropriate raw materials and other natural resources. Interestingly, for labor intensive industries, Kim et al. found that industries are attracted to rural areas that have low-skilled as well as high-skilled labor, but that rural areas with "medium-skilled" labor pools do not do as well. As a policy conclusion, they argue that clustering is not always necessary for successful rural economic development.

Theoretically, the recent book by Fujita, Krugman and Venables (1999) models regional economic growth partially in terms of urban vs. rural locations as well as manufacturing vs. agricultural activity, with labor as the only input. Purchases among manufacturers leads to a cluster-like outcome in their model of urban areas. Firms migrate from high- to low-wage urban areas. However, the Fujita et al. model assumes that manufacturing takes place only in "urban" areas, not rural ones. Their focus on labor costs does make sense, however: Anderson and Wassmer (2000) note that labor productivity, labor compensation, and labor relations are the three most important factors in firms' decisions to expand or relocate (p. 34).

This paper addresses several questions that arise from economic development issues related to attracting manufacturing to rural locations. These questions include (1) Are durable goods manufacturers or nondurable goods manufacturers more likely to locate in rural areas? (2) What is the significance of labor costs? and (3) What role do state taxation policies have in such locational choices?

The level of analysis in this paper is the state. Other studies, such as Kim et al., have used substate data. Miller (1998) suggests that state-level forecasts are more accurate than substate ones because of measurement errors.

II

Model

MANUFACTURING ACTIVITY IN A STATE is specified as being determined by the following function:

(1)   MANUF = f(GSP, MWAGE, RTW, STAXPC, RPIRAT)

where:

MANUF = 1997 manufacturing activity in a state, measured as the manufacturing component of that state product (GSP);

MWAGE = June 1997 average manufacturing wage in that state;

RTW = a binary number equal to 1 if the state is a "right-to-work" state;

STAXPC = 1997 state taxes per capita in that state; and

RPIRAT = 1997 ratio of total nonmetropolitan personal income to total personal income in that state.

Means and standard deviations for the variables are given in Table 1, while the data appendix discusses data sources. GSP is included in the specification to test whether manufacturing enterprises, *ceteris paribus*, prefer larger over smaller regions (states); one might presume that the larger the state, the greater the number of clusters. MWAGE attempts to measure labor cost; the hypothesis is that high-wage states

Table 1

Means and Standard Deviations of Variables

VARIABLE	MEAN	STD. DEVIATION
MANUF	$27.55600 billion	29.34613
DURMAN	$15.67000 billion	18.20479
NONDMAN	$11.88600 billion	12.38716
MWAGE	$ 12.83580	1.380098
GSP	$ 161.0180 billion	188.8114
RTW	0.420000	0.498569
STAXPC	1659.380	379.6330
RPIRAT	0.280370	0.193185

will not be attractive to manufacturers. RTW is an indirect measure of unionization as well as the ease with which plants can be organized; it is hypothesized that employers will prefer right-to-work states. States with high state taxation levels are presumed to be unattractive to manufacturers.

RPIRAT is used as a measure of the "ruralness" of any state; the higher the RPIRAT value, the less urbanized the state. If more rural states are attractive to manufacturers (compared to more urban states), then the coefficient of RPIRAT should be significantly positive.

To test the proposition that different manufacturing industries behave differently in choosing locations, Equation (1) was estimated using not only MANUF as the dependent variable, but also DURMAN, the durable manufacturing component of GSP, and NONDMAN, the nonmanufacturing component of GSP. The signs of the independent variable coefficients are hypothesized to be the same for the DURMAN and NONDMAN equations as for the MANUF equation.

III

Regression Results

REGRESSION ANALYSIS WAS DONE VIA ORDINARY LEAST SQUARES (OLS), using eViews. The estimations were done using the White correction process for heteroskedasticity. The variables (except for RTW) were regressed using their logarithmic values. The data set includes 49 states; the eViews program deleted one state, Rhode Island, that had an RPIRAT value of zero (i.e., no rural locations). The estimated equations are given in Table 2. All three equations have R-squared values exceeding 0.80.

For all three estimations (MANUF, DURMAN and NONDMAN), the coefficient of GSP was significantly positive. Since the logarithmic specifications mean that the coefficients can be interpreted as elasticities, the fact that all three GSP coefficients exceed 1 means that manufacturing activity in general, as well as both durable and nondurable activity, increases proportionally faster than the economic size of the state.

Table 2.

OLS Estimates of Manufacturing Location Equations (using White heteroskedasticity correction procedure)

Dependent variables Equation no.	ln(MANUF)	ln(DURMAN)	ln(NONDMAN)
Dependent variables			
constant	1.191549	6.030853	−4.506845
	(0.413697)	(1.386481)	(−1.531950)
ln(GSP)	1.304914	1.349452	1.353074
	(12.32520)**	(9.873482)**	(11.64994)**
ln(MWAGE)	0.152346	−0.491455	0.328882
	(0.162949)	(−0.319122)	(0.375780)
RTW	−0.205124	−0.449131	0.043016
	(−1.249640)	(−1.632229)	(0.268519)
ln(STAXPC)	−0.578309	−1.122947	−0.009731
	(−1.390437)	(−1.701939)*	(−0.032397)
ln(RPIRAT)	0.300468	0.247920	0.401108
	(2.297433)**	(1.539291)	(2.867025)**
R-squared	0.889924	0.802429	0.876082
F-statistic	69.52774**	34.92866**	60.80060**

*= significant at 10%; **= significant at 5%.

The state tax variable (STAXPC) has the anticipated (negative) sign in all three equations, but is only significant in the DURMAN equation. The MWAGE and RTW coefficients are all insignificant; in the case of the wage variable, this may reflect the oft-discussed issue that the wage rate per se does not control for labor productivity and thus unit labor costs.

The RPIRAT variable is significantly positive in the MANUF and NONDMAN equations, but not the DURMAN one. Thus nondurable goods producers appear to prefer more rural states, whereas durable goods producers appear to be indifferent between relatively urban and rural states.

Multicollinearity may be a problem in these equations. The correlation between ln(RPIRAT) and ln(GSP) is -0.700, while the correlation between RTW and ln(MWAGE) is -.587. The other correlation coefficients between the independent variables are considerably lower.

IV

Policy Conclusions

THE REGRESSION RESULTS PROVIDE BOTH GOOD AND BAD NEWS for rural economic development specialists. The good news is that nondurable manufacturers are attracted to nonmetropolitan locations. Furthermore, these firms seem insensitive to state tax policies (although they might be sensitive to local tax policies). High wages per se do not appear to be a deterent to attracting these firms, a finding that supports Kim et al.'s results on high-skilled labor.

The primary bad news is that large states (as measured by GSP) appear to attract a disproportionate share of manufacturing activity. This may make it difficult for small states, such as North Dakota or Wyoming, to attract such employers. Indeed, the correlations between ln(RPIRAT) and (respectively) the logarithmic values MANUF, DURMAN and NONDMAN suggest that manufacturing activity is associated with more urbanized states, as seen in Table 3.

If larger states contain more manufacturing clusters than do smaller states, this could explain the negative correlations. Thus the regressions results in Table 2 can be interpreted in part to mean that for the *same sized states* (measured by GSP), nondurable manufacturers pre-

Table 3.

Correlations between Rural Location and Manufacturing
Variables

Manufacturing variable	Correlation with ln(RPIRAT)
ln(MANUF)	−0.5317
ln(DURMAN)	−0.5123
ln(NONDMAN)	−0.4972

fer more rural states. However, as Kim et al. argue, clustering is not necessary for a successful rural economic development strategy.

Appendix

Data on 1997 GSP, DURMAN, and NONDMAN values came from the U.S. Bureau of Economic Analysis' web site (www.bea.doc.gov), while STAXPC came from the U.S. Bureau of the Census' web site (www.census.gov). June 1997 wage data came from *Employment and Earnings*, September 1997, Table B-18. Data on 1997 state nonmetropolitan and total personal income (used to compute RPIRAT) came from *Survey of Current Business*, May 1999 (and are also available at the BEA web site). RTW is based on information in Kaufman (1994).

References

Anderson, J.E., and R.W. Wassmer. (2000). *Bidding for Business*. Kalamazoo, MI: W. E. Upjohn Institute for Employment Research.

Coughlin, C. C., Eran Segev. (2000). Location Determinants of New Foreign-Owned Manufacturing Plants. *Journal of Regional Science*. Vol. 40, May, no. 2, pp. 323–351.

Carlton, Jim. (2000). Farm Community Gets Creative to Survive. *Wall Street Journal,* June 5, p. A2.

Drabenstott, Mark, Mark Henry, and Kristin Mitchell. (1999). Where Have All the Packing Plants Gone? The New Meat Geography in Rural America. *Economic Review,* Vol. 84, Third Quarter, no. 3, pp. 65–82.

Fujita, Masahisa, Paul Krugman, and A. J.Venables. (1999). *The Spatial Economy*. Cambridge, MA: The MIT Press.

Galston, W. A., and K. J. Baehler. (1995). *Rural Development in the United States*. Washington, DC: Island Press.

Gordon, Peter, H. W. Richardson, and Gang Yu. (1998). Metropolitan and Non-metropolitan Employment Trends in the US: Recent Evidence and Implications. *Urban Studies*. Vol. 35, June, no. 7, pp. 1037–1057.

Jelavich, Mark. (forthcoming). Manufacturing and Rural Economic Development in the US. *Southwestern Journal of Economics*.

Kaufman, Bruce. (1994). *The Economics of Labor Markets*, 4th ed. Ft. Worth, TX: Dryden.

Kim, Yunsoo, D. L. Barkley, and M. S. Henry. (2000). Industry Characteristics Linked to Establishment Concentrations in Nonmetropolitan Areas. *Journal of Regional Science*, Vol. 40, May, no. 2, pp. 231–259.

Levy, J. M. (1994). *Contemporary Urban Planning*, 3rd ed. Englewood Cliffs, NJ: Prentice Hall.

Luker, Bill. (1998). Foreign Investment in the Nonmetropolitan US South and Midwest: A Case of Mimetic Behavior? *International Regional Science Review*, Vol. 21, August, no. 2, pp. 163–184.

Miller, J. R. (1998). Spatial Aggregation and Regional Economic Forecasting. *Annals of Regional Science*, Vol. 32, no. 2, pp. 253–266.

PART III

Case Studies: Land Value Taxation and Real Estate Development

American Journal of Economics and Sociology, Vol. 60, No. 1 (January, 2001).

Value Capture as a Policy Tool in Transportation Economics

An Exploration in Public Finance in the Tradition of Henry George

By H. WILLIAM BATT*

ABSTRACT. Value capture is a means by which to finance capital infrastructure, particularly transportation services, in a way that allows for efficient economic performance, simple administration, financial justice, and social facility. Because American society needs to find new means to finance transportation capital investment, particularly public transit, value capture offers an essentially painless opportunity to achieve these goals. It has the ancillary benefit also of concentrating population densities in a way that makes public transit particularly viable. This study shows how value capture could have been used to finance a portion of the New York State Interstate Highway System, a nine-mile stretch of I-87 known as the Northway, from its southern terminus to the point where it crosses the Mohawk River in Albany County. This section is the most heavily traveled area of the Northway and has experienced the greatest contiguous development of any location along the Northway's 178 miles since its construction in the late 1950s. While the right of way and construction costs of this stretch were in the range of $128 million (current dollars), the additional land value that has been generated on its account within just two miles on

* H. William Batt, Ph.D., is the Executive Director of The Central Research Group, Inc., a non-profit grant-funded research organization specializing in public budgeting and finance in accord with sustainable development principles (Central Research Group, Inc. P.O. Box 4112, Patroon Station, Albany, New York 12204-0112). He is also a consultant to governments on property taxes, transportation finance, and land use. The GIS analysis was provided by Kathy Fisher of Applied GIS, Inc., in Schenectady, New York. The principle investigator wishes to express his appreciation also to officials of the New York State Transportation Department, especially Mr. Frank Mengel of the Office of Real Estate, and Mr. Pete Kelly of the Region One Design and Construction Unit. This paper was prepared with support from the Robert Schalkenbach Foundation, committed to disseminating the virtues of land-value taxation in all its forms.

American Journal of Economics and Sociology, Vol. 60, No. 1 (January, 2001).
© 2001 American Journal of Economics and Sociology, Inc.

either side has totaled $3.734 billion. This study shows that the capital finance of the Northway, at least in this area, could easily have been done by recapturing these windfall gains that fell to private landowners. One could argue that this added value, the direct result of public investment, should rightfully be returned to the public and should be recaptured to pay off the bonds that were issued to build the project, rather than left for opportunistic speculators to reap private gain. Value capture therefore offers a promising approach for funding future transportation development, leaving fees, that are presently used, to recover operating and environmental costs.

I

Introduction

THIS STUDY EXPLORES how a large infrastructure investment in the Capital Region of New York State might have been financed through value capture with greater effect and benefit than the method that was used. As with every bit of the Interstate Highway System, the chosen method was the Highway Trust Fund, established in the 1950s, which relies upon motor fuel revenues to support both capital and maintenance costs. The cost shifting and the diversion of burdens which this approach entails has resulted in a transportation system that has been expensive, inefficient, and unbalanced. An alternate approach would have been to employ a method known as value capture. This method would have better balanced costs and benefits and also discouraged the over-consumption of infrastructure and land that we have witnessed under the existing approach.

Although the interstate highway system is essentially complete and the only further costs involved for the most part are in its maintenance, value capture offers a convincing approach in ensuring that the highway systen will remain adequate to serve motor vehicle needs for the indefinite future. This can be done by the inducement it offers to capitalize on the land value created in the vicinity of the access and exit nodes, and the discouragement for speculators to continue holding their parcels off the market in expectation of future gains. Indeed, value capture can be an attractive means for the capital finance of future enterprises and infrastructure, particularly if the public elects to build transit projects to complement and redress our current over-reliance on private motor vehicle use. The record shows that the illustrations of value capture applied to date have been in the finance of public transit systems, not for highway service. But it can work for many infrastructure projects.

II

Motor Vehicle Ascendancy

IN THE POST WORLD WAR II ERA, the pent-up consumer demand of the American population was nowhere more manifest than in the acquisition of motor vehicles. At the war's end in 1946, new car sales added 2.14 million passenger cars to the 25.80 million already on the road; by 1965 total passenger car registrations had reached 75.26 million, with 9.3 million new vehicles sold just that year. Moreover, it was not only the number of cars that increased; the total number of miles driven more than doubled from 284,650 million vehicle miles in 1946 to 713,984 million in 1965. And this was just cars! All indications were that the auto trend showed no signs of leveling off, while congestion roads led to popular demand for ever more and wider roads.[1]

The New York State Thruway

Transportation planners, certainly dominated by highway interests—a coalition of auto-manufacturing, oil, rubber and construction industries—but in a larger sense by almost all Americans, were only too willing to mark up land maps with an ever-increasing number of lane miles of new highway. New York State was in the vanguard of those states outlining where new roads would expedite the flow of traffic, even before the passage of the National Defense Highway Act of 1956. New York State's Department of Public Works[2] had responsibility for about 14,000 miles of highway, with trunk lines carrying the overwhelming proportion of traffic even though they represented only about a seventh of all the roads in the state. Because the state government had the resources to finance further highway development through its power of taxation, it took the lead in proposing new projects, often bypassing more reticent local interests.

Several New York limited-access highways were long in use, even congested, by the time the 1956 highway bill was passed. Robert Moses, a towering political figure in New York for decades, had already pushed through a network of parkways in the downstate metropolitan area and Long Island well before the advent of World War II. Following the war, Governor Thomas Dewey promulgated and trumpeted the construction start of the New York State Thruway, which extends from Westchester County north to Albany before heading to Buffalo and on to the border of the state. Its first section opened in 1954, and by 1960 it was completed in its entirety. To this day, the 641-mile Thruway is the longest tollroad in the United States. It was regarded as a boon to economic development throughout the state, especially in the region of the Capital District, where it skirted the southern edge of Albany before turning west.

With the passage of the Federal Highway Act and all the new funding that went with it, a still larger network of limited access roads was laid out, nowhere more ambitious than in Albany where Governor Nelson Rockefeller had a reputation for large scale projects. In the four years immediately following the passage of the highway act, New York spent about $250 million of state money alone to complete improvements on 5,200 miles of road, approximately a third of the state highway-parkway system.[3] Figure 1 shows a map of interstate urban bypass roads in Albany that the State Department of Public Works envisioned in 1961.

One can see that only about half of those lane miles were ever constructed. (See Figure 2.) The north-south crosstown arterial that was planned to transect the city of Albany at its central point was met with strong neighborhood resistance, and those familiar with the city today know the points where the imposing strips of four-lane pavement awkwardly stop. But plans to bypass the city on the north side, with a spur cutting off downtown access to the Hudson River to expedite traffic along the eastern edge, and a third north-south corridor—what would become the Northway, extending the Thruway north to Montreal—were easily acquiesced to, especially since the Federal government put up 80 percent of the cost and the state government paid the remainder. Whatever local governments' views might have been, they were unlikely to change things. In fact, the

Figure 1.

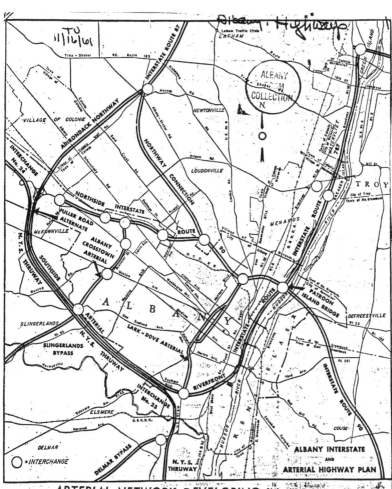

ARTERIAL NETWORK DEVELOPING IN ALBANY

This State Public Works Department map is the most comprehensive issued to date, showing how Albany will become the hub of interstate and arterial highways. Only arterial section now under construction is the Albany crosstown route. Bids on the first three miles of the Delmar bypass will be opened today.

Figure 2.

North

Figure 3.

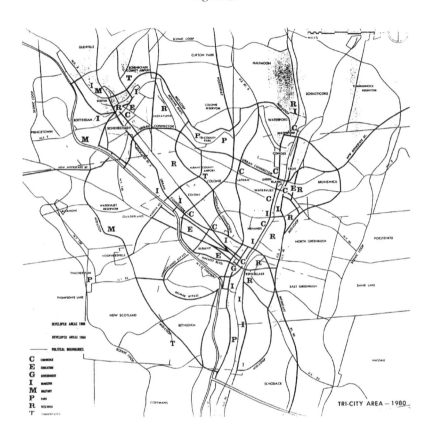

highway planners had visions far wider than even this. Figure 3, created in 1962, delineates a still wider design of limited access corridors envisioned for Capital District transportation by 1980. Ultimately
a fair number of these were constructed.

Influence of the Northway

The corridor for the Northway was a foregone conclusion even before
being put to paper. It was largely the work of federal and state planning offices, and it was not likely that the path of the highway could

have been much altered because the topography limited its options. It is likely, however, that knowledge of its layout and construction schedule was known to insiders well before the public, or even property owners in its path, had had opportunity to react. Local government was controlled by one of the most powerful political machines in the nation, and that machine was largely the province of one man. The mayor of Albany, Erastus Corning II, was the scion of an old WASP family, who relied upon a strongly Irish Catholic coterie for support and essential control of almost all decisions at both the city and county levels. He served as mayor from 1940 to 1982, a total of 42 years, longer than any other mayor in the nation. Dispensation of favors went to the small as well as to the mighty, and any decisions about land use planning were likely done in camera and difficult to trace. But the corridor path was set largely due to geographic limits outlined in the federal highway legislation of 1946.[4]

The one available place to link the New York State Thruway to an interstate north to Montreal was at the western edge of settled Albany where the area was largely farmland. The bulk of the land that would be taken was in the rural towns of Guilderland and Colonie, still part of Albany County which the mayor controlled. A sliver of Albany extended out further to the west, the locus of the earliest waterworks servicing the city, originally developed by the first Erastus Corning who was President of the New York Central Railroad and, not coincidentally, also mayor a century earlier. Since the water supply had now been replaced by a larger reservoir further away, this vacant land stood open to development. Washington Avenue, the middle of three corridors extending west of the city, would subsequently extend through the heart of this area, threatening an ecologically sensitive area of pine bush, dunes and even an endangered species of butterfly. No matter that other areas were available to settlement; Washington Avenue Extension is easily accessible to Northway and currently invites—almost demands—development on account of that very infrastructure investment, even though the Corning era passed nearly two decades ago.

In the 1950s the land on the western edge of the city of Albany was largely truck farms. In fact it was some of the best farmland in Albany County and even in the State of New York, because it was at the confluence of the Mohawk and Hudson Rivers, largely flat alluvial terrain.

But the construction of the New York State Thruway, finished in the early 1950s, had already influenced the pace of suburban development in the area, and post-war prosperity and the boom in families further spurred the growth of housing on what was, by city standards, cheap land. The Northway's construction would further influence the pace of development. Saratoga County to the north had receded in importance with the decline of rail service, despite its attractions of thoroughbred racing and gambling. But in the 1970s and 1980s it became the fastest growing county of the State, a suburban community servicing Albany, the seat of government, Schenectady, the home of General Electric, and Troy, the home of Rensselaer Polytechnic Institute. Saratoga County epitomized the development of residential sprawl, while the downtowns of Albany, Schenectady, and Troy across the Hudson River floundered. By the mid-1990s these three cities were suffering major financial problems due to their declining commerce and industry, while the suburbs flourished. Figure 4 shows the area of the Northway discussed in this paper, from its origin at the juncture of Route 20, the old westward post road, to the point where it crosses the Mohawk River/Erie Canal nine miles to the north.

The Northway was thus linked not just to the New York State Thruway but to the two major state highway corridors extending west as well. These were the earlier-mentioned Route 20 and the even more established Route 5 which led to the City of Schenectady. Centers of capital development and major areas of economic activity shifted to the lands close by these corridors, especially to areas accessible to the Northway. Enormous retail shopping centers and office parks soon lined up on either side. Parallel to the Northway was Wolf Road, formerly a farm road, and now Albany County's "million dollar mile." Exacerbating the suburban exodus further was the fact that it was located just outside Albany city limits in the unincorporated Town of Colonie, allowing businesses to take full advantage of lower taxes than the city exacted.

The development alongside the Northway has been robust but also haphazard. At this writing, in the year 2000, the Northway's third lane is far beyond capacity to serve traffic, especially during rush hour. Even Wolf Road has become so congested that some businesses as well as some state government agencies have elected to move elsewhere, pre-

Figure 4.

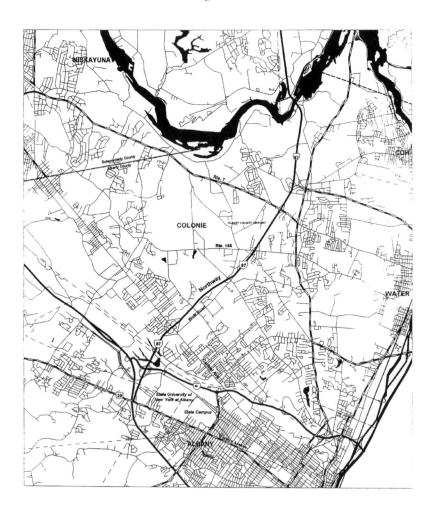

sumably to less expensive space. Ironically, in an effort now to retain
the value of this location, sidewalks will soon be constructed to encourage people to park their cars and walk from site to site as necessary. Meanwhile, titleholders to lands contiguous to the Northway access points have seen their properties soar in value. Sometimes the

luck fell fortuitously to farmers; others' fortunes were a result of speculative calculation. Adding to planners' challenges is the fact that the Albany County Airport, which serves the entire Capital Region, is less than a mile away and that local access roads are now being expanded and rerouted to respond to the traffic it generates. The airport terminal has just undergone major expansion; feeder traffic looms as a incipient problem. But as yet the region has not seen so much congestion that land values have been adversely affected, and the only alarms seem to be from environmentalists who note that the Capital Region is now identified by the EPA as a marginal non-attainment area for ozone.

Interstate Highway System: Costs and Benefits

The question is sometimes raised whether the costs of the interstate highway system are justified relative to its benefits. Defenders of highway development will always argue affirmatively, but this is not the point of this paper. It is in any case a moot question, because the nation was in a highway building mood in the 1950s and few could have foreseen the downside costs we are now experiencing, half a century later. The decision to build the interstate system under the National Defense Highway Act of 1956 was not a decision based on solid cost benefit analysis. As with most infrastructure projects in past American history, its promulgation grew out of a confluence of vested interests that could decidedly profit by the venture. Even today it is accepted conventional wisdom that highway development is an essential and integral piece of all economic development strategies. There are only a few studies that are equivocal.[5]

Articles and books now appear daily that consider the problems that general reliance upon motor vehicle transportation have brought about.[6] America faces a far greater problem because of how its landscape has been configured than most people today realize. One must first understand that an estimated 90 million Americans have been disenfranchised by not being able to drive, therefore lacking the essential mobility which this society requires for full participation. For many people, reliable cars are prohibitively expensive, and yet they are subject to the vicissitudes of auto dependability. One 1993 study concludes that "when the full range of costs of transportation are tallied, passenger ground transportation costs the American public a total of $1.2 to $1.6 trillion each year. This is equal to about one-quarter of the annual GNP and is greater than our total national annual expenditure on either education or health."[7] Conventional American land use configurations and the automobile dependent lifestyle that goes with it sap our resources and what efforts could be used for other ventures and activities. Since so much of this activity is consumption and not production, it weakens America's world economic position and precludes reinvestment in more productive areas. Because of the way in which we have encouraged development, people who need jobs are frequently too poor to own the cars necessary to get to them. Programs are now being implemented to help the urban poor travel to the suburbs to where the jobs have now moved.[8] It can be argued further that we have overbuilt an inefficient highway infrastructure that we now cannot afford to maintain.

Enormous environmental externalities also result from our over-dependence upon cars, especially in air pollution and in the emission of greenhouse gases. The consequences of SO_2, CO_2, and ozone are no longer a matter of debate; they are scientific fact. Despite frequent headlines about replacing the internal combustion engine, all the realistic substitutes also ultimately rely upon fossil fuel power; solar powered cars are far in the future, if at all, and also fail to deal with any transition. Even further, there are the costs of highway crashes. Public pleas for people to drive safely are not likely to change the reality that people are fallible, and that every person driving his or her own car simply multiplies the probabilities of accidents. Just the costs of crashes—nothing else—represents a figure equal to 8 percent of the American Gross Domestic Product.[9] Finally, driving is no longer regarded as fun. There was a time when most people drove cars for pleasure; today people resent their having to drive so much and often see driving as a burden.[10]

III

Mechanisms of Interstate Highway Finance

THE INTERSTATE HIGHWAY SYSTEM was from the beginning almost entirely financed by the imposition of an *ad valorem* tax on motor fuel. With the passage of that act, the tax (on both gasoline and diesel fuel) was raised from 2¢ to 3¢ per gallon, and would continue at that rate until 1978 when it was raised to 4¢.[11] In addition, a tax was levied on tires, initially at 8¢ a pound, gradually increasing further over the years. No distinction was made in the funding mechanism with regard to capital cost debt service or operating costs, and charges for negative externalities were never even considered. Over the years, there have been instances when the Highway Trust Fund was overflowing with money; other times, it has failed to cover even basic costs. In recent years, there has been a general recognition that maintenance has not been addressed in a timely way and has led to a general deterioration of the roads and bridges that are part of the system. This can be interpreted in one of two ways: either that the public has chosen to address more pressing priorities, or that the initial capital construction has overextended the nation's capacity to maintain it.

The local and state share amounted to a token contribution, as most state and local highway revenues, regardless whether they were dedicated or not, were directed to the non-interstate network of roads. The result of having funding provided by a government source distant from its application site was that it provided an incentive to bias projects in favor of highway construction. Had the financial arrangements for the project insisted upon a greater share for local and state authorities, there would have been less inclination for highway interests to override other local considerations. As it was, highway transportation advocates easily prevailed over competing claimants when public policy decisions were called for. This is well illustrated by the controversies that arose in areas where competing concerns were manifest.[12] The interstate network was completed first in areas where land could quickly and easily be acquired and where construction could proceed without difficulty. Although the network was pronounced as completed in the early 1980s, certain extensions still continue to be carried out to this day. Yet roads continue to be congested, and all the problems associated with motor vehicle transportation—the sprawl development, the pollution, the evisceration of the urban cores, and the inordinate expense of this mode of travel—have failed as yet to foster a full national debate about the wisdom of this half-century-old decision.

IV

Capital Cost Recovery through Value Capture:
An Alternative Approach

VALUE CAPTURE, most simply defined, is the means by which capital infrastructure investment is financed through means of "capturing" either some or all of the added value of real property that results directly from that investment. Value capture in transportation investments works in two ways:

1. Insofar as infrastructure investments are capitalized in land values in the vicinity of stations or gates by improved accessibility, those values can be recaptured as "rents" put at the service of debt, even perhaps for operating expenses, in support of the services provided.

2. The higher rents on land values in the proximity of the services serve further as an incentive to development density. This occurs because landowners seek to recover their investments, pressed by the immediacy of the rents, rather than holding them for speculative gain.[13]

Value capture is an old idea, given this new name by the US Department of Transportation which is exploring innovative approaches to infrastructure finance.[14] It can be traced in the theories of public finance to the work of the 18th century French physiocrats.[15] In the past century this approach compares closely to the thinking of Henry George and his followers.[16] There are now enough cases where value capture has been employed to finance infrastructure that there is no longer doubt about its merit.[17] As conventional approaches to capital finance are found to be wanting and are exhausted or discarded, value capture represents a tried and true method of both public infrastructure finance and an incentive to further sound growth. In a word, value capture becomes an effective engine to its own further development.

Using a tax on land values that benefit from particular capital investments satisfies all the virtues of sound taxation theory.[18] Unlike finance methods that rely directly or indirectly on income, sales, or franchise taxes, a levy on land correlates well with benefits received, and is likely to be stable, simple, administrable, progressive,[19] and, most of all, efficient. It is efficient because it is economically neutral; that is, it imposes no distortions on economic choices because land, particularly strategically located land, is limited in supply—in economic terms, inelastic. Whereas operating costs are frequently better financed from user fees that also employ the benefit approach, capital development costs are reflected in good part by location, and the resulting added value can be recaptured at the same rate that bond financing projects are amortized.

Experience in other nations shows that the extent to which land can sustain tax burdens is considerable, depending on the economic growth and development pressures of a region.[20] For example, within walking distance of commuter rail stations (typically about ¼ mile), the land values may increase as much as 25 percent as a direct result of public investment in transit. Rather than permitting this windfall resulting from public investment to redound to the private landowners, land taxes in the form of value capture instruments can easily recoup the typical debt of projects.[21] Depending upon the planned density of the land use for commercial or residential purposes, the return can even be higher.

Much of the projected return on investment necessarily relates to the demand for development in a region. In regions where projections show substantial in-migration, the demand for housing is typically reflected in increased land values. But increased housing development does not need to mean commensurate increased land use. The attractive ambience of "walkable" communities may engender still higher growth levels, precisely because they accommodate human beings rather than motor vehicles. Fixed guideway systems, for example, financed through the value capture approach can channel development pressures to narrowly contained areas, in contrast to conventional sprawl patterns typically found in motor vehicle commuting communities.[22]

Development along these lines can occur in one of two ways: either as joint development (wherein significant capital finance is likely to be required concurrently "up front") or by induced development through such mechanisms as incentive taxation and "value capture." Creating a heavier tax burden on landowners in a defined region exerts a downward pressure on price, inducing greater incentive for investment and opportunities for development. Many students of incentive taxation argue that the full limits to which such taxes can be imposed are unexplored and that they offer great promise for the economic enrichment of a region.[23]

Few studies if any outside the Georgist economic tradition have recognized the relationship between the automobile, land use, and taxation.[24] Had value capture been the approach by which to pay the capital costs of highway construction, it would have facilitated far more compact and efficient development at the nodes of highway access; there would have been fairer sharing of the burden of the capital costs; and there would have occurred development densities to facilitate the reliance upon a public transit system complementary to motor vehicle reliance. What follows is an examination of how much value might have been enjoyed to pay the capital costs of the Northway's construction had value capture been relied upon as the chosen approach to finance.

V

Methodology

THE MEANS BY WHICH to calculate the added increment of land value resulting from infrastructure investment is quite simple. It involves:

1. identifying the land parcels within service proximity of the infrastructure investment;
2. ascertaining the assessed and market value of those land parcels prior to the project's beginning;
3. obtaining the assessed and market value of those same land parcels when the bonds will be paid off;
4. converting both totals to constant dollars; and
5. establishing the debt service of the project, so that the proper level of value capture tax can be imposed.

Small costs should be apportioned to local service as opposed to thru-traffic, just as property taxes currently pay for local roads. These costs should be subtracted from the burden to be assigned to beneficiaries of the new investment. For this study the data for all this was available from the public records of New York State agencies.

Records of the purchase prices of the land parcels acquired by the State of New York for development of the Northway were acquired from old Department of Transportation files, noting particularly the parcel area in acres and whether or not the parcels had improvements. Since the State paid fair market value for each parcel, this provided a baseline for calculating what the land value was of all parcels—essentially farmland—in the area. New York State Real Property Tax Law requires assessment of all properties according to land value and total value,[25] but until recently assessments have not had a reputation for accuracy, so the sale price records of the State of New York provide a far more reliable indicator of land value. Therefore, only the total acreage and total purchase price of parcels that were unimproved (Figure 5) were used as an indicator of average value of market price per acre for 1958, the year they were acquired. Instead of computing land value differences for the whole distance of the Northway, a total of 178 miles to the Canadian border, the area close by its southern terminus (Route 20 at Western Avenue) to the Mohawk River was used as the basis of study, a distance of nine miles. It is the most commercially developed of any stretch along the road.

Establishing the values of parcels at various distances from the Northway was even easier, as the two major towns involved—Guilderland and Colonie—elected in 1995 to assess real property at full value. This data is available from both the towns and from the New York State Office of Real Property Services. The sliver of land running between the two parcels, less than a mile belonging to the City of Albany, has not had a comprehensive reassessment for over four decades, however. It is also probable that some of its transactions were not arm's length exchanges, and for both these reasons the few Albany parcels were excluded from the numbers used to establish current value per acre, although they are used later in the total calculation extrapolating from the data from the contiguous municipalities. Enough sample parcels from adjacent lands are available as data points that a reasonably accurate identification of their market value is possible.

Figure 5.

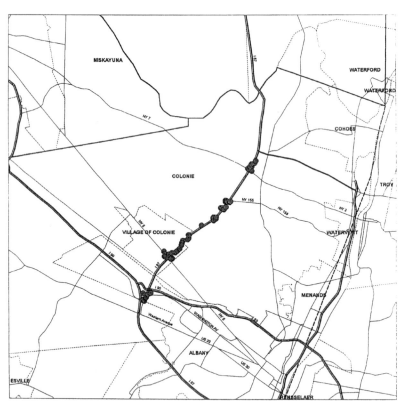

● Approximate Location of Properties Purchased by Fee

The next step was to average the current land values for all parcels at various distances from the present Northway. Reliance upon new geographic information system (GIS) computer technology makes such tasks simple, and averages were computed (Figure 6) for distances of up to ½ mile on either side, then from ½ mile to 1 mile away, and lastly for distances from 1 mile to 2 miles away. To be sure, the presence of the Northway and other components of the Interstate arterial system has influenced the value of land parcels at distances far

Figure 6.

◯ Study Area Boundaries (1/2 mile, 1 mile, 2 mile buffers around Northway)

greater than two miles—but the actual reach of this impact is ultimately a matter of speculation.[26] The principle of value capture is easily illustrated, however, by identifying values at distances within the
two-mile margin.

The last step is to ascertain the actual cost of construction of the Northway in the area being serviced. Using only a section involves trade-offs. Highway construction costs are not equally spread along all sections of a project, nor are the costs of acquiring the right of way corridor the same. Therefore selecting a short intensively developed strip has both advantages and disadvantages for study. It should be understood that the southernmost nine miles of the Northway are the most intensely developed, have the most interchanges, and may be atypical in any number of other ways. The costs involved in the area under review are far beyond that of straight open construction in the more rural areas. But of course so are the returns in increased land value.

VI

Findings

CALCULATING THE INCREASE in land value in defined areas contiguous to the southernmost nine miles of the Northway is relatively simple. Its economic value relative to that in urban and suburban areas was low since it was essentially farmland. It also had relatively uniform value because location was not a significant factor in its use for truck farming. Records show that parcels identified for purchase by the State of New York for use by the Department of Transportation were purchased at the time for an average $3,600 per acre, typical of the price of farmland generally at the time. A total of 307.4 acres of land were purchased in 1958 from the Route 20 (Western Avenue) southern terminus of the Northway to the point at which a bridge was to be built across the Mohawk River and Erie Canal. Figure 5 shows the centroid of several of the parcels that were then acquired by the State of New York.[27] Had there been no changes in land use, this land in 1995 dollars would be worth approximately $16,568 per acre.[28] In fact the land is now worth many times that amount. That change in use is due directly to the advent of the Northway and its connecting Interstate network.

To be sure, the Northway alone cannot explain the increase in land values along its borders; it is all the highways taken together that make the area the attractive locus that it is for commerce and industry.

That is to say, there is no reason to believe that the Northway's construction had an impact on aggregate land values greater or lesser than the other highways of the region, except by noting the relative proximity of various links in the system. The I-87 Northway has likely contributed as much to the increased land values of the I-90 east-west corridor as the latter has contributed to those of I-87. The strategic value of the site must be understood as a whole, by the fact that interchange is one of the major transportation hubs of Northeast United States.

The influence of the interstate system on land values of course extends far beyond the delimited area of two miles on either side that this study identifies. As a network serving the nation, its value and its impact is national. But identifying just the adjacent areas demonstrates how much additional land value the highway's presence has brought about. The land values most proximate to the corridors themselves, more at the entry/exit points, and most of all at the junctures of different routes of course have the greatest value. Identifying just the increase in land values close by one of the major junctions is easily demonstrable.

The lands bordering on the Northway from the Western Avenue terminus to the Mohawk River have been separately identified for their land value on either side for the first ½ mile, for from ½ to one mile, and from one to two miles. Figure 6 is a map of the three land areas and Table 1 shows the number of acres involved in each. The data show that the land closest to the Northway has an average value almost twice that of the land between one and two miles distance, and over 40 percent higher than the land in areas just the next half to one mile away.

The most compelling number of all is that which shows that the 30,516 acres of remaining private land that lie within two miles on each side of the first nine miles of the Northway's corridor has an average value today of $4.179 billion, representing an increase of $3.734 billion (using 1995 constant dollars) over what the land would have been worth had the Northway not been built. This figure does not include the value of any improvements; only the land value. This simple study does not include the added value that arose on feeder roads beyond the two-mile distance to the Northway.[29]

The cost of construction of part of the Northway, represented in 1995 dollars, are calculated by NYS Transportation officials in straight-

Table 1

Added Increment of Land Value Due to Northway Construction in Albany County

Distance	Acres	50s $acre adj to '95	95 $/Acre	95 Total Value	% Increase	$ Diff or $ Gain
		$3,603 to $18,605				
½ mile	5,928	$103,301,480	$211,008	$1,250,855,424	1274%	$1,212,331,432
½-1 mile	7,206	$119,389,008	$148,050	$1,066,848,300	894%	$947,462,116
1-2 miles	17,382	$287,984,976	$107,132	$1,862,168,424	647%	$1,574,184,420
Total	30,516	$510,675,464		$4,179,872,148	831%	$3,733,977,968

Table 2

Total Right-of-Way and Construction Costs ($1995)

Right of Way	Road Construction	Bridge Construction	Total Costs
307.4 Acres	54 Lane-Miles	34 Bridges	
$16,568 ea	$1m each	$175 / sq ft	
$5,093,003	$54,000,000	$69,000,000	$128,093,003

forward formulas. The acquisition of right-of-way are calculated separately, since they vary so widely. They then use a rough figure of $1 million/lane-mile as the cost for the highway (including interchanges) and $175 per square foot of deck for bridge structures.[30] The six-lane wide (three in each direction) Northway from Western Avenue (Route 20) to the Mohawk River is a distance of nine miles, a total of 54 lane-miles. This $54 million cost is supplemented by the further cost of 34 bridge structures. The working projections used for these costs are $175 per square foot of bridge deck.[31] The 34 bridges on, over, or servicing the Northway have a total of 394,470 square feet, representing a projected (1995) construction cost of slightly over $69 million. The cost of the 307.4 acres purchased as the right-of-way in 1958 is $5,093,003.[32] Together with the separate costs of the highway, the total projected cost is $128 million.

The added increment of land value identified earlier reflects a figure over eleven times that of the cost of construction. That is, the added increment of value that resulted from the construction of the section of the Northway under discussion was left to the titleholders of the parcels to receive rather than to the society which was responsible for the creation of that wealth. This reveals how great the potential is for financing the cost of transportation infrastructure by recapturing that increase.

VII

Discussion

LAND VALUE IS a function of the social and economic traffic that the land generates. Excluding resources that a parcel of land may contain (lumber, minerals, water, fish and game, etc.), it has economic value solely by virtue of its location. It is not what any lone individual does that makes a parcel of land valuable; rather it is through joint community effort that land acquires worth. This is the logic on which value capture rests. Traffic volume, whether by foot, bicycle, bus, rail, or car, all make for increases in land value, and that variable is social in nature. Because that value derives from social effort, society has a principled right to its claim. Yet what happens more often than not is that private individuals secure for themselves what should be rightfully a social gain. All the increases in land value that resulted from the social resources invested to build the Northway were left for private parties to enrich themselves, totaling at least $3.734 billion just within the small area under study.

On the other hand, government acting in the name of society undertook to secure bonds to finance the development of this costly infrastructure without any recognition of the fact that financial means were already available to be tapped under the appropriate system of finance. Value capture raises the taxes on impacted lands, thereby doing two things: 1) removing the invitation of title holders to speculate, and 2) raising the holding costs high enough that there is immediate reason for titleholders to seek a return on their investments. This facilitates more robust economic activity in the very region where the public has placed its investment. It fosters more concentrated development in contrast to the sprawling and slow-developing ventures that typically characterize land configurations using conventional policies.[33] Most of all, it reduces the opportunity to engage in an egregious practice well captured by George Washington Plunkett almost a century ago:

> There's an honest graft, and I'm an example of how it works. I might sum up the whole thing by sayin': "I seen my opportunities and I took 'em."
>
> Just let me explain by examples. My party's in power in the city, and it's goin' to undertake a lot of public improvements. Well, I'm tipped off, say, that they're going to lay out a new park in a certain place.
>
> I see my opportunity and I take it. I go to that place and I buy up all the land I can in the neighborhood. Then the board of this or that makes its plan public, and there is a rush to get my land, which nobody cared particularly for before.

Ain't it perfectly honest to charge a good price and make a profit on my investment and foresight? Of course, it is. Well, that's honest graft (Riordan 1963, p. 3).

VIII

Conclusion

URBAN ENVIRONMENTS have been largely taken away from people and become dominated by motorized traffic because urban and transportation planners have confused two core concepts: accessibility and mobility. These are explained particularly well in a recent text, *The Geography of Urban Transportation*:

> *Accessibility* refers to the number of opportunities, also called activity sites, available within a certain distance or travel time. *Mobility* refers to the ability to move between different activity sites (e.g., from home to a grocery store). (Hanson 1995, p. 5.)

Transportation planners have confused mobility with access, expending enormous sums to move people efficiently while neglecting the matter of access. Planners by and large accept the premise that people should be free to make their own locational decisions and that these decisions are rational and should be accommodated when devising transportation services. To this extent they often respect the market. But they typically fail to realize that market decisions grow out of a context and are premised largely upon perception of economic costs. Since it is through public policies that land and transportation use are priced, people are not aware of how much those prices are distorted by economic factors. And it is through pricing incentives, or rather by removing disincentives, that it becomes possible to facilitate the access that makes for a congenial and livable urban environment.

Policy makers have two modes of leverage by which to implement public will: 1) so-called "command and control" approaches that are typically enforced by what state and federal constitutions group under "police powers" and 2) fiscal approaches that typically involve a variety of taxes, fees, fines, and other charges that derive constitutionally from either "police powers" or "tax powers." When governments administer either of these powers they are legitimate and authoritative. Fiscal measures available to governments can come from either ground and differ from charges that the private sector usually imposes, which are usually responsive to market forces. Prices which are established by government, however, are not responsive to market forces, nor are they intended to be. Rather they are set in order to accomplish certain public policy goals.[34] They can be no less efficient, however, when responsibly instituted.

Governments face the challenge of knowing which of the tools at their disposal—"command and control" approaches versus "pricing" approaches—will satisfactorily serve effective and efficient completion of public policies. Only in recent years, however, has there been a renewed interest in fiscal levers to achieve the goals which policy makers seek. There is particular interest among students of welfare economics in incorporating costs earlier regarded as externalities. Moreover, use of pricing approaches to recover costs of government services which have a high level of private good about them can bring about more attractive and achievable goals than can reliance upon conventional police power approaches. User fees, environmental fees, and other such fiscal tools have become more fascinating—at least to students of public policy—than conventional taxes.

Because public fiscal policy today involves much more than simply collecting revenue to support the purposes of government, it is important to evaluate various alternatives in the light of the principles of sound tax theory that were enumerated early on. At times it is important that a revenue source be totally neutral—that is, it should be designed to distort the economic behavior of parties as little as possible. In other cases, since it is the behavior itself that has a social cost to the larger society, as externalities, it is important that government impose a charge on such behavior that will recover its costs and/or correct the behavior. Transportation policy has evolved in ways that distorts our economic choices in a highly destructive and costly manner. So have the methods that we have chosen to pay for such services. Value capture is an approach consistent with sound economic and tax principles, provides a means by which the ill effects of past decisions can begin to be corrected, and uses relatively painless methods to support the next generation of transportation services.

Notes

1. *Historical Statistics of the United States: Colonial Times to the Present, Bicentennial Edition, Vol. II,* U.S. Department of Commerce, Bureau of the Census, 1975, Table Series Q. As this century ends, the total passenger car sales in United States now approaches 20 million, and total travel is near three trillion vehicle miles annually. *Highway Statistics, 1998,* http://www.fhwa.dot.gov/ohim/hs98/hs98page.htm, Sections II and V. In one noteworthy article a mathematician, challenged by the dilemma of highway traffic growth, has shown that the construction of more roads leads inevitably to greater traffic problems. See Bass 1992.

2. Only much later was the New York State Department of Public Works given the much broader and more inclusive name of Department of Transportation, addressing multi-modal transportation services and not just roads.

3. Ellis 1967, p. 451.

4. Grondahl 1997.

5. See, for example: Munnell 1990, Munnell with Cook 1990, "Comment on Charles R Hulten and Robert M. Schwab, 'Is There Too Little Capital? Infrastructure and Economic Growth,'" *Infrastructure Needs and Policy Options for the 1990s,* Proceedings of the American Enterprise Institute Conference, Washington, D.C., February 4, 1991; and "Policy Watch: Infrastructure Investment and Economic Growth," *The Journal of Economic Perspectives,* Vol. 6, No. 4 , Fall 1992.

6. A few of the more popular ones are worthy of note: Goddard 1994; McShane 1994; and Kay 1997. One particularly compelling article was written by Hank Dittmar, until recently a high level administrator with the U.S. Department of Transportation. His article, appearing in *Enough,* the magazine of the Center for a New American Dream, is titled "Road to Nowhere: The Automobile, Sprawl, and the Illusory Suburban Dream," at www.newdream.org.

7. Miller and Moffet 1993, p. ii. Japan, by way of comparison, spends an estimated 10.4% to satisfy *all* its transportation requirements, although the figure might be somewhat low because not all externalities are included in the calculation. See Hook 1994, p. 28. See also The Conservation Law Foundation 1994; and MacKenzie et al. 1992.

8. President Clinton has recently taken actions to give low-income families better access to work opportunities by exempting ownership of automobile from eligibility requirements for food stamps. White House Press Release, February 23, 2000.

9. In 1988, a study by the Urban Institute calculated that $71 billion were borne in out-of-pocket costs, another $46 billion in lost wages and household production, and $217 billion in pain, suffering and lost quality of life. Translated into vernacular, the total of $334 billion in lost property, worktime, and injuries and deaths (Miller et al. 1991).

10. In a study done by the *Washington Post* in the early 1990s, 25 percent of

Americans are "road haters" who don't enjoy driving. Another 15 percent consider cars a necessary evil but take little interest in style, color or upkeep. Forty percent of drivers may be disenchanted, but except for those living in cities with good public transportation ,driving remains the only reasonable way to get around. Cited in Nadis and McKenzie 1993, p. ix.

11. As this is written, the federal excise tax per gallon is 18.4¢ on gasoline and 24.4¢ on diesel fuel. *Highway Statistics, 1998,* Table FE-21E, at http://www.fhwa.dot.gov/ohim/hs98/hs98page.htm.

12. The best book recounting how highway interests were able to overwhelm competing forces in local communities is Robert Caro (1975), *The Power Broker: Robert Moses and the Fall of New York,* Vintage Books, , and this documented an era even before the Highway Trust Fund was established.

13. Under current practices the selling price of land balloons immediately after projects are announced because future rents are expected to increase. Rent is the present value of expected future net rents; the land value is now a function of expected rental value in the future. If half the rent is taxed, then half the future rents are taxed, and the present value of the land will be half the pre-tax value. So a tax on the land value is still equivalent to the tax on the rent. The relationship between the amount of rent taxed and the tax rate on the land value is: $x = t/(i+t)$, where t is the tax rate on the price of land, x is the percentage of the rent that is taxed, and i is the real interest rate after deducting inflation.

14. Walther, Hoel, Pignataro and Bladikas 1991.

15. Spengler, pp. 443–445.

16. Henry George (1839–1897) was most famous for his book *Progress and Poverty,* which argued that taxing land according to its value instead of labor or capital would be both more just and more economically efficient. For an overview of Georgist approaches to taxation, see Lindholm and Lynn 1982.

17. The most comprehensive study of the value capture approach in Hagman and Misczinski 1978. Among other significant studies on the merits of value capture as an approach to infrastructure finance are the following: Allen 1987; Allen, Chang, Marchetti, and Pokalsky 1986; Callies 1979; Cervero, Hall, and Landis 1993; Monograph 42; Cervero 1994; Johnson, and Hoel 1985; Rybeck, assisted by Wade and Josephs 1981; Sharpe 1977.

18. Adam Smith's *Wealth of Nations* (1776) remains even today a starting point for students of tax design, for he captured, even at that early time, not just the sum of learning to that date but his own acute insights. *See,* for example, "Principles of Taxation, in Light of Modern Developments," *Federal Tax Policy Memo,* The Tax Foundation, Washington, DC. For further discussion of what students of tax policy regard as the principles which should guide their design, see, for example, Musgrave and Musgrave 1989; Break 1993; *Tax Notes* 1988; Davies, 1986; and *Unleashing America's Potential: a Pro-Growth, Pro-Family Tax System for the 21st Century.* Washington: Report of the National Commission on Economic Growth and Tax Reform (Kemp Commission), 1996.

19. See, for example, the discussion in the current leading graduate text in graduate public finance courses: Rosen *Public Finance*, 5th Edition. Homewood, IL: Irwin Press, 1999, pp. 486–495. See also Gaffney [1971] 1972; Heilbrun 1983; Aaron 1975; Geisler 1995; Reschovsky 1998; Wolff 1998; and Earthright:The Economics of Freedom, at http://www.geocities.com/RainForest/3046/

20. Andelson 1998.

21. A feasibility study of the Washington Metro in 1980 showed that conservative interpolation of the findings to all completed stations, as well as an accounting of the increments in value that were being recorded along much of the 101-mile system in advance of construction, made it evident that the growth in the Metro-induced land values easily exceeded $3.5 billion, compared with the $2.7 billion of federal funds invested in Metro up until that time. See Rybeck 1981, pp. 23–27.

22. A study proposing just such a project, intended primarily to respond to projected population increases over the next few decades, has been done under contract with Orange County, New York: *2020 Vision: A Transportation Plan for Orange County, New York*. See also Shinbein and. Adler 1995.

23. Cord 1986. See also Oates and Schwab 1995. A second and very recent study by Florenz Plassmann found that "on average, a one percentage point increase in the tax differential will yield an increase in the total value of construction of 17.8 percent"(Plassmann 1997, p. 122). This study can be found at http://scholar.lib.vt.edu/theses/public/etd-61097–13834/edt-title.html. Lists of publications on incentive taxation in its various forms are available from The Robert Schalkenbach Foundation in New York City, The Center for the Study of Economics in Columbia, Maryland, and The Lincoln Institute for Land Policy in Boston, Massachusetts.

24. Recognition of the relationship between land use policy and transportation policy is beginning, however, even though little attention is paid to tax policy. In 1995 a major conference was sponsored by The Brookings Institution and the Lincoln Institute of Land Policy, held in Washington, to explore alternatives to sprawl. See *Alternatives to Sprawl*, Conference Report published by the Lincoln Institute (Boston, 1995). A team of researchers at Rutgers has recently updated a 1974 study entitled *The Costs of Sprawl*, entitled *The Costs of Sprawl—Revisited*, TCRP Report 39 (1998), sponsored by the Federal Transit Administration, Transportation Research Board of the National Research Council.

25. NYS Real Property Tax Law § 502(3) states that "the assessment roll shall contain a column for the entry with respect to each separately assessed parcel of the assessed valuation of the land exclusive of any improvements, followed by a column for the entry of the total assessed valuation."

26. For this reason, the ideal approach to value capture would be to employ a tax on land value not locally but comprehensively, even nationally.

27. In calculating the average land price per acre which was paid by the

state to property owners, not all parcels were included. This is because many parcels had structures on them, and it is impossible to know how much value should be attributed to structures and how much to land. The parcels that consisted of land only were distributed sufficiently widely that no distortion on that account is apparent. However, the price per acre which the state paid to titleholders varied a great deal according to the negotiating skills and other variables that typically go into such sales. Whereas the average price was just over $3,600 per acre, they ranged far higher in a few cases. One landowner received $3,260 for a parcel of only .009 acres, and another $2,800 for .003 acres. This amounts to $362,222 per acre in the first case and $933,333 per acre in the second. It may just be that, in a few instances, some landowners really struck a bargain. In a few cases it may also be that the lands that they were left with after state purchase was so substantially lowered in value that the price had to reflect this factor as well.

28. The choice of which adjustment factor to employ to arrive at this figure is the result of a discussion with several land economists, and few indicators go back to 1958. Using a standard price deflator to calculate changes in land value raises problems, as no one factor is likely to apply in all regions of the country. The index employed here is the St. Louis Federal Reserve Board's Implicit Price Deflator at www.stls.frb.org/fred/data/gdp/gnpdef. Using 1996 as the base 100, the 1958 rate is roughly 21.50—it extends back only to the 1st Quarter of 1959. The 1995 (4th Quarter) is 98.85. If the GDP Price deflator is used, with the base year of 1982 as 100, the 1958 rate is 24.81, and for 1995 is 128.79. The latter index is a bit more generous, and was used in a prior draft of this paper. It leads to an adjusted 1995 value per acre of $18,700. The precise increase in land value is beside the point however; it is certainly a small fraction of what prices obtain for the same parcels in current circumstances.

29. Value capture studies can sometimes be exceedingly sophisticated. Indeed one major study was so complex that it required a Cray computer to do the analysis. See *Transit Access and Land Value: Modeling the Relationship in the New York Metropolitan Area*, U.S. Department of Transportation, Federal Transit Administration, (FTA-NY-06–0152–93–1), September, 1993.

30. Of course these figures vary widely depending upon the design engineering complexity. Cutting through mountain terrain or wetlands will involve far higher costs than laying a highway over open flatland. When interchanges were expanded for the new Exit 8 of the Northway in 1995, the costs per lane mile came out to be as follows:

Date Const	Proj ID Number	#Lane-Mile	Proj Cost	Cost/Ln-Mi
2/23/1995	I-90 Exit 8	10.8	$6,995,000	$647,685
12/14/1995	I-90 Exit 8	10.8	$8,848,752	$819,328
Average			$7,921,876	$733,507

31. Interestingly, the cost per square foot is relatively invariant regardless of the size of the bridge.
32. 307.4 acres x $16,568 = $5,093,003.
33. Nowhere is the ex-urban development resulting from automobile dependency better described than Joel Garreau's *Edge City: Life on the New Frontier*, New York: Doubleday, 1991.
34. One recent exploration of this is a chapter entitled "Catalytic Government: Steering Rather than Rowing," in David Osborne and Ted Gaebler, *Reinventing Government: How the Entrepreneurial Spirit is Transforming the Public Sector*, New York: Penguin Books, 1993.

References

Aaron, Henry J. (1975). *Who Pays the Property Tax: A New View.* Washington: The Brookings Institution.

Allen, B. (1987). "Value Capture in Transit," *Journal of the Transportation Research Forum*, Washington DC, 28: 50–57.

Allen, B., Chang, K., Marchetti, D., and J. Pokalsky (1986). *Value Capture in Transit: The Case of the Lindenwold High Speed Line*, Final Report # PA-11–0031–86–1, UMTA, US Department of Transportation and Philadelphia: University of Pennsylvania.

Andelson, Robert V. (ed.)(1998). Land-Value Taxation Around the World: Reports on Current and Historical Efforts to Apply the Principle of Collecting the Community-Created Value of Land for Community Benefit, New York: Robert Schalkenbach Foundation.

Anonymous, "Principles of a High Quality Revenue System," *Tax Notes*, March 21, 1988.

Bass, Thomas (1992). "Road to Ruin," *Discover:* May 1992.

Break, George (1993). "Taxation," *Encarta* Encyclopedia by Microsoft.

Callies, D. (1979). "A Hypothetical Case: Value Capture / Joint Development Techniques to Reduce the Public Costs of Public Improvements." In *Urban Law Annual.* St. Louis, Washington University School of Law. 16: 155–192.

Cervero, R. (1994). Rail Transit and Joint Development: Land Market Impacts in Washington, DC and Atlanta. Journal of the American Planning Association, 60, 1:83–94.

Cervero, R., Hall, P., and J. Landis. (1993). *Transit and Joint Development in the United States,* University of Calif. Berkeley, Institute of Urban and Regional Development.

Cord, Steven (1986). "How Much Revenue Would a Full Land Value Tax Yield?" *American Journal of Economics and Sociology*, 44, 3 (July): 279–294.

Davies, David G. (1986). *United States Taxes and Tax Policy.* New York: Cambridge University Press.

Dittmar, Hank (1999). "Road to Nowhere: The Automobile, Sprawl, and the Illusory Suburban Dream," *Enough*, The Center for a New American Dream, www.newdream.org.

Ellis, David (1967). *A History of New York State*, Rev. Edition, Ithaca: Cornell University Press.

Gaffney, Mason (1971). "The Property Tax is a Progressive Tax," *Proceedings*, National Tax Association, 64th Annual Conference, Kansas City. [Republished (1972) in *The Congressional Record*, March 16: E 2675–79. Resources for the Future, Inc., The Property Tax is a Progressive Tax, Reprint No. 104, October, 1972].

Geisler, Charles C. (1995). "Land and Poverty in the United States: Insights and Oversights," *Land Economics*, 71, 1 (February): 16–34.

Goddard, Stephen B. (1994). Getting There: The Epic Struggle between Road and Rail in the American Century, Chicago: University of Chicago Press.

Grondahl, Paul (1997). *Mayor Erastus Corning: Albany Icon, Albany Enigma*, Albany: Washington Park Press.

Hagman, Donald G. and Dean J. Misczinski (editors) (1978). *Windfalls for Wipeouts: Land Value Capture and Compensation*, Chicago: American Society of Planning Officials.

Hanson, Susan (Ed.) (1995). *The Geography of Urban Transportation*, Second Edition, New York: Guilford Press.

Heilbrun, James (1983). "Who Bears the Burden of the Property Tax?" in C. Lowell Harriss (ed.), *The Property Tax and Local Finance*. Proceedings of the American Academy of Political Science, 35, 1 New York.

Hook, Walter (1994). *Counting on Cars, Counting out People*, New York: Institute for Transportation Development Policy Paper, Winter.

Johnson, G. and L. A. Hoel (1985). *An Inventory of Value Capture Techniques for Transportation*. University of Virginia, Charlottesville, VA.

Kay, Jane Holtz (1997). Asphalt Nation: How the Automobile Took Over America and How We Can take It Back, New York: Crown Publishers.

Lindholm Richard W. and Arthur D. Lynn, Jr. (eds.) (1982). *Land Value Taxation: The Progress and Poverty Centenary*, Madison: University of Wisconsin Press.

MacKenzie, James J. et al. (1992). *The Going Rate: What it Really Costs to Drive*, Washington: World Resources Institute.

McShane, Clay (1994). *Down the Asphalt Path: The Automobile and the American City*, New York: Columbia University Press.

Miller, Peter and John Moffet (1993). *The Price of Mobility: Uncovering the Hidden Costs of Transportation*, New York: Natural Resources Defense Council, October.

Miller, T. et al (1991). *The Costs of Highway Crashes*, The Urban Institute, Washington, D.C., October.

Munnell, Alicia H. (Ed.) (1990). *Is There a Shortfall in Public Capital Investment?* proceedings of a conference sponsored by Federal Reserve Bank of Boston.

Munnell, Alicia H. with Leah H. Cook (1990). "How Does Public Infrastructure Affect Regional Economic Performance?" *New England Economic Review* (Federal Reserve Bank of Boston), September/October.

Munnell, Alicia H. and Leah H. Cook, "Comment on Charles R Hulten and Robert M. Schwab, 'Is There Too Little Capital? Infrastructure and Economic Growth,'" *Infrastructure Needs and Policy Options for the 1990s*, Proceedings of the American Enterprise Institute Conference, Washington, D.C., February 4, 1991.

Munnell, Alicia H., "Policy Watch: Infrastructure Investment and Economic Growth," *The Journal of Economic Perspectives*, Vol. 6, No. 4 , Fall 1992.

Musgrave, Richard and Peggy Musgrave (1989). *Public Finance: Theory and Practice*, Fifth Edition. New York: McGraw Hill, pp. 210–314.

Nadis, Steve and James J. McKenzie, (1993). *Car Trouble*, Boston: Beacon Press.

Oates, Wallace and Robert Schwab (1995). "The Impact of Urban Land Taxation: The Pittsburgh Experience." Cambridge, MA: Lincoln Institute of Land Policy, WP92W01.

Plassmann, Florenz (1997)."The Impact of Two-Rate Taxes on Construction in Pennsylvania." Doctoral Dissertation, Virginia Polytechnic Institute.

Reschovsky, Andrew (1998). "The Progressivity of State Tax Systems," *The Future of State Taxation*, David Brunori, (Editor), Washington: Urban Institute Press.

Riordan, William L. (1963). *Plunkett of Tammany Hall*. New York: Dutton.

Road Kill: How Solo Driving Runs Down the Economy, Boston: The Conservation Law Foundation (May, 1994).

Rosen, Harvey S. (1999). *Public Finance*, 5th Edition. Homewood, IL: Irwin Press.

Rybeck, W., assisted by Wade J., and R. Josephs (1981). *Metrorail Impacts on Washington Area Land Values*. Subcommittee on the City Committee on Banking, Finance and Urban Affairs US House of Representatives.

Rybeck, Walter (1981). "Transit-Induced Land Values: Development and Revenue Implications," *Economic Development Commentary* (National Council for Urban Economic Development), 5,. 1 (October): 23–27.

Sharpe, C. (1977). *Value Capture and Joint Development Applications: Chicago/ Louisville/ Los Angeles*. Rice Center for Community Design and Research. Report No. DOT-TST-77–72, US Department of Transportation. Houston, TX.

Shinbein, Phillip J. and Jeffrey L. Adler (1995). "Land Use and Rail Transit," *Transportation Quarterly*, 49, 3 (Summer): 83–92.

Spengler, Joseph, "Physiocratic Thought," *International Encyclopedia of Social Sciences*, 4: 443–445.

Unleashing America's Potential: a Pro-Growth, Pro-Family Tax System for the 21st Century. Washington: Report of the National Commission on Economic Growth and Tax Reform (Kemp Commission), 1996.

Walther, E, Hoel, L. A, Pignataro, L. J., A. Bladikas (1991). *Value Capture Tech-*

niques in Transportation: Final Report, Phase One. No. DOT-T-90–11, Washington DC: US Dept. of Transportation Program of University Research.

Wolff, Edward N. (1998). "Distributional Consequences of a National Land Value Tax on Real Property," in Dick Netzer (ed.) *Land Value Taxation: Can it Work Today?*, Cambridge: Lincoln Institute of Land Policy.

Coordinating Opposite Approaches to Managing Urban Growth and Curbing Sprawl

A Synthesis

By THOMAS L. DANIELS*

ABSTRACT. The purchase of development rights to farmland and open space has recently gained in popularity as a growth management tool. A purchase of development rights program pays the landowner for the unearned increment in exchange for strong deed restrictions, limiting the use of the property. On the other hand, land value taxation, a modification of Henry George's Single Tax, would tax land more heavily than improvements, thus encouraging the development of land. While land value taxation and the purchase of development rights appear to be opposing fiscal policies, they could be employed together as part of a regional planning strategy to encourage in-fill development within and near cities and to curb sprawl by retaining farm, forest, and ranch lands.

I

Henry George and the Evolution of Land Policy

IN A 1997 PUBLICATION OF THE LINCOLN INSTITUTE, several authors suggested that Henry George's ideas about land markets need to be refined and adapted to current situations of land use, taxation, and urban sprawl.[1] Writing in the Gilded Age of the nineteenth century, George felt that powerful financial interests threatened to create a monopoly in land ownership. The majority of people would not be able to afford land or would be forced to pay exorbitant prices for it. The result would be an inefficient underutilization of land resources. George's famous Single Tax was aimed at breaking the speculators' hold on land and improving the distribution of wealth in society. The Single Tax would apply to land only and would capture all or nearly all of the economic rent of land and eliminate all or much of the mo-

*Thomas L. Daniels is Professor in the Department of Geography and Planning, State University of New York at Albany.

American Journal of Economics and Sociology, Vol. 60, No. 1 (January, 2001).

nopoly rent, while providing governments with significant tax revenues. A further advantage of the Single Tax is that it could not be passed from landowners to land renters or buyers, because all pure rents would be collected from the landowner or seller.

Economists almost universally agree that unearned increments or economic rents to bare land can be taxed away without any disruption to economic efficiency[2] or diminution of the value or income of land improvements.[3] These are cogent arguments for the use of the Single Tax since the tax would fall only on unearned increments to land value and not on rising property values caused by improvements from labor and capital.[4] These unearned increments would accrue from nearby public improvements or improvements by one's neighbors that create a rise in the value of one's land.

Hence, the tax would tend to force a landowner to make additional investments in capital and labor to develop the property more intensively or else sell the property to someone who would make those investments.

Henry George envisioned the Single Tax as the only tax that would be needed nationwide. As yet, the Single Tax has not been implemented in America in its pure form. The closest example has been the split-rate land value tax that taxes land at a higher rate than buildings. Land value taxation embodies George's concept of differential tax rates on land and buildings. George's Single Tax—the extreme example of land value taxation—falls completely on land. Land value taxation levies a higher tax rate on land than on buildings, unlike the traditional property tax which applies the same tax rate to both land and buildings.

For example, since 1979, the City of Pittsburgh has taxed land for property tax purposes at a rate five times as high as that on buildings. In the decade after the introduction of this variation of the Single Tax, the value of new construction in Pittsburgh increased by 70 percent compared to 1960–1979. The higher land tax may have compelled the owners of open land to construct buildings and to move up the timing of construction. In 14 midwestern cities *not* utilizing higher land taxes over the same two time periods, only Columbus, Ohio experienced an increase in building activity. Nine of the cities saw building permits fall by more than 30 percent in the 1980s.[5]

Population, transportation, public sewer and water, development circumstances, land use regulations, and institutions affecting land use have changed dramatically since George's day. Before 1900, there were fewer than 75 million Americans, far below the nation's 1998 population of 270 million. Lack of access to urban land was the primary problem in the nineteenth century. Thanks in large part to the interstate highway system, unfettered access to the countryside in the second half of the twentieth century has yielded the sprawling pattern of development that has turned America from an urban nation to a suburban one.

Disinvestment in central cities has been coupled with the conversion of roughly one million acres of farmland each year as Americans further expand the reach of exurbia. George devised the Single Tax long before American cities and counties had adopted comprehensive land use planning and zoning for regulating land use. Even so, planning and zoning alone have not shown much success either at encouraging in-fill development or at curbing sprawl.

The missing ingredients in achieving these aims are effective land taxation policy and public spending. Wedded to meaningful land use planning and zoning, land value taxation could encourage in-fill development of open land within cities and older suburbs as well as the re-development of underutilized properties. But such a tax will only work if the option of escaping to the exurbs is discouraged.[6]

Because land value taxation is essentially a pro-development tool, it could promote sprawl in areas not appropriate for development if not limited geographically. This tendency is clearly explained by Backhaus (1997):

> Every expanse of land, of course, has its limits and there will be tracts of land still devoted to their original use, such as extensive farming or ranching. As a consequence of the improvements through the development efforts, the adjacent land has increased in value but not itself has been improved. The land rent has risen. This land rent is what George envisioned would be taxed away. It will therefore become increasingly expensive to use this land in its original extensive way as a farm or ranch land. Taxing away the land rent makes extensive ranching or farming less and less attractive. Due to the taxed land's proximity to development, the farm or ranch land needs to be re-allocated to more productive purposes, and the Henry George tax drives this process of re-allocation along.[7]

In the nineteenth century with limited transportation, public sewer and water facilities, the von Thunen model of land rents was convincing.[8] The highest land rents were found at the city center and gradually decreased with distance from the city. In this scenario, land value taxation—and especially the Single Tax—would make land farther from the city center less attractive for development, and land closer to the city center more attractive.

But the von Thunen model no longer applies. There are many suburbs with higher rents than parts of their central cities. Why? The suburbs have better access to amenities, transportation, and public investment in schools and sewer and water. Access is value. Land value taxation alone will not limit the spread of suburbs, because public investment in roads, schools, and sewer and water is causing the unearned increments on nearby land to rise. Land value taxation applies to those rising land values, thus creating an incentive for the land to be developed.

Some kind of demarcation line is therefore necessary to determine where the encouragement of development should stop, and the retention of farm, ranch, and forest lands continue.

There are two ways that this demarcation line can occur. One is by government fiat. For example, the State of Oregon in its 1973 land use act required each city and its adjacent county to agree upon the establishment of urban growth boundaries. Within each boundary is sufficient land to support population growth and development over a 20-year horizon. Public infrastructure that induces growth, such as public sewerage, water, and schools, must be located with the growth boundary. In this way, growth evolves in a more compact fashion that is cheaper to service and minimizes the loss of farm, ranch, and forest land to development. The growth boundaries are flexible, in that they can be expanded as population growth and development needs change. This way local governments have replaced unplanned sprawl with "phased growth."

The second method for creating the demarcation line is for governments to use financial incentives: to purchase development rights from the owners of farms, ranches, and forest lands on the outside edge of the growth boundaries. Development rights could be purchased around a city or village and thus limit the potential growth of that municipality. Alternatively, development rights could be acquired along a segment of the growth boundary and hence compel the boundary to expand only in certain directions. Such a strategy has been implemented in Lancaster County, Pennsylvania.[9]

II
The Purchase of Development Rights: Buying the Unearned Increment

THE PURCHASE OF DEVELOPMENT RIGHTS involves a voluntary exchange of money in return for strong deed restrictions on property. The rights to land are often compared to a bundle of sticks, with each stick representing one right. Three examples of rights include mineral rights, the right to sell property, and the right to develop the property. Like the sticks in the bundle, rights in land may be sold as a complete bundle in fee simple, or individual rights may be severed off and sold separately. For instance, it has been a common practice to sell off mineral rights.

Under the purchase of development rights approach, the landowner voluntarily sells to a government entity the right to develop the property while still retaining title to the property; however, the uses of the property are limited according to a legally-binding deed of easement. Development rights, also known as negative easements in gross, run with the land either for a specified period of time or in perpetuity. However, purchasing development rights in less than perpetuity may simply subsidize a landowner's holding costs while the land value ripens for development.

The payment for development rights is based upon an appraisal of value in which the appraiser estimates the value of the property before and after the development rights have been sold off. The difference between the two values is the development rights value, which can be thought of as the difference between what the property would be worth on the open market at its highest and best use, and the property's value in its current use in farming, ranching, or forestry. In essence, the value of the development rights is the unearned increment that would accrue to the landowner from selling the property on the open market.

Purchase of development rights programs began in the 1970s as a means of controlling growth and permanently preserving farmland

and open space on a local or regional basis. Especially on the East and West Coasts where these programs are popular, bare land is scarcer today than in the late nineteenth century. The amount of land devoted to development has mushroomed, thanks to the automobile, improved building technology, and greater affluence. And the real price of land, adjusted for inflation, has risen significantly, especially since the 1960s.

Thus, it would appear that owners of bare land in metropolitan areas would be able to earn windfall profits from the sale of land. Because land resources are scarce, open land is often at a premium both for development and as open space. While the private market demand is for building sites, the public demand is typically for the land to remain in agriculture or as open space.

In the past 20 years, the economic returns to farmland within 50 miles of major metropolitan areas have generally exceeded the returns to farm labor and capital. That is, public investments in roads, schools, and other infrastructure have been capitalized into private land values. Indeed, farmers commonly view their land as a pension account that will be cashed in at retirement. This practice often means selling the farm for development rather than agriculture to maximize net returns.

From a public perspective, agricultural land produces open space amenities as well as food and fiber. Recent studies on cost of community services have found that agricultural land tends to generate more income in property taxes than it uses in public services. Conversely, residential development typically costs more in public services than it pays in property taxes. Thus, farmland produces net revenue gains compared to residential development.[10]

Various farmland protection techniques have been employed to discourage or minimize development, especially in rural-urban fringe areas. Yet most of these techniques provide the farmer with scant compensation for the development restrictions placed on the farm. Property tax breaks are usually small in comparison to the sums offered by developers. And often property tax breaks merely subsidize farmers' holding costs until they decide to sell for development. Agricultural zoning frequently encourages the breakup of farms into large residential lots with little capacity for agricultural production. But even where agricultural zoning significantly restricts land use, this restriction is not permanent.

Rather, zoning in general is notoriously changeable as decisions on re-zonings are made by politically vulnerable local officials.

Farmers are thus left with two choices: either tough it out in farming and hope to sell the farm to the children or another farmer, or else sell out for development. An alternative to these choices is the sale of development rights to a state or local government.[11] In a purchase of development rights program, a landowner receives payment for the unearned increment in the land: the difference between the development value and the land value restricted to agricultural use. The payment is for one time only, and does not reflect the potential appreciation in the unearned increment over time. In return, the government is able to lock up land in agriculture or open space use in perpetuity (or for a time period specified in the easement document).

Critics charge that a purchase of development rights program is merely paying the landowner for the increase in property value that was caused by public investment in nearby roads, schools, and sewer and water lines. But the strong limitations on future development of the property make for a compelling quid pro quo arrangement. The value of the land for agricultural use may rise, which may indeed reflect the greater scarcity of land for farm use. But this increase in value is likely to occur much more slowly than the increase in recreation, residential, commercial, or industrial real estate values. Moreover, the purchase of development rights is less expensive than purchasing the land in fee simple.

Suffolk County on Long Island, New York pioneered the use of the purchase of development rights in the 1970s. The county has acquired easements on some 6,000 acres at a cost of about $31 million, or just over $5,000 an acre. Yet, many easements were purchased from land speculators rather than farmers.[12]

As of 1998, fifteen states and several counties and municipalities had adopted purchase of development rights programs (see Table 1 and Table 2). State and local governments have spent nearly $900 million to preserve more than 500,000 acres of farmland. In 1996, the United States Congress authorized $35 million in grants to state and local governments for the purchase of development rights to farmland.

A program of purchasing development rights in perpetuity must be sustained over a medium to long term (10 to 30 years) in order to min-

Table 1

Purchase of Development Programs by State, March 1998

STATE	ACRES/FARMS PRESERVED	FUNDS SPENT
California	460/3	$.84 million
Colorado	1,878/3	$.8 million
Connecticut	25,566/169	$74.83 million
Delaware	16,107/85	$20.0 million
Kentucky*	0/0	$0
Maine	540/3	$.5 million
Maryland	139,828/968	$140.6 million
Massachusetts	40,040/441	$96.1 million
Michigan	579/4	$1.97 million
New Hampshire	11,732/57	$10.49 million
New Jersey	43,972/278	$167.8 million
New York*	0/0	$0
Pennsylvania	111,752/861	$172.2 million
Rhode Island	2,429/31	$14.0 million
Vermont	69,693/202	$34.8 million
TOTAL	464,576/3,105	$734.93 million

*Both Kentucky and New York have authorized funding for the purchase of development rights, but neither state had completed a purchase as of March of 1998. *Source:* American Farmland Trust, PDR Fact Sheet, March 1998. *Farmland Preservation Report*, unpublished data.

imize speculation in development rights and to assemble a critical mass of farmland. The critical mass will enable agriculture to survive as an industry with farm service firms and agricultural processing companies. Critical mass varies according to the type of farming, but certainly thousands of acres would need to be preserved. In some suburban places, development rights are very expensive, averaging over $5,000 an acre. In other places, they average less than $2,000 an acre, and hence more land can be preserved for the money.

Some states have been half-hearted toward purchasing development rights. This has been the case in Maine, New Hampshire, and

Table 2

Sample of Local Purchase of Development Programs, March 1998

LOCALITY	ACRES/FARMS PRESERVED	FUNDS SPENT
Marin County, CA	25,504/38	$16.6 million
Sonoma County, CA	25,146/62	$38.8 million
Boulder, CO	1,092/6	$6.8 million
Peninsula Township, MI	955/15	$2.8 million
Suffolk County, NY	6,081/103	$31.1 million
Forsyth County, NC	1,236/20	$1.8 million
King County, WA	12,731/210	$53.9 million
Town of Dunn, WI	304/2	$.6 million
TOTAL	73,049/456	$152.4 million

Source: American Farmland Trust, PDR Fact Sheet, March 1998. *Farmland Preservation Report,* unpublished data.

Rhode Island where programs have gone unfunded for several years at a time. Timing is also important. King County, Washington had an aggressive purchase of development rights program in the 1980s, then let the program lie dormant until the mid-1990s. In the meantime, the cost of development rights steeply escalated as development pressures sharply increased. A purchase of development rights program should be employed together with agricultural zoning to discourage speculation on non-preserved adjacent properties. This will protect the preserved farms from being surrounded by development that could make farming the preserved farm difficult. Agricultural zoning can also hold down the cost of purchasing development rights as well as provide greater stability in the land base, and so encourage neighboring farmers to remain in farming.

Available figures on acreage preserved and cost do not provide sufficient information on the location of the land being preserved. Unless purchases of development rights are coordinated with local or regional planning efforts, they may result in the preservation of land either for agriculture or for open space that should be developed. For example, it makes little sense to purchase development rights on land adjacent to public sewer and water lines unless an urban growth boundary has been designated to separate the developed area from the farmland. Otherwise, there is a good chance the preserved land will eventually be surrounded by development, thus defeating the purpose of preservation. Finally, the preservation of land for the purpose of blocking the outward expansion of development needs to occur in large contiguous blocks.

III
Implications for Land Policy and Public Finance

THE OPPOSING RATIONALES OF LAND VALUE taxation and the purchase of development rights raise several issues about land policy and public finance. Both measures share the underlying assumption that the land market fails to perform in socially desirable ways, and that government intervention in the land market could improve the efficiency of land allocation among competing uses and hence overall social welfare. Although the existence of market failure is a necessary condition for government intervention, it is not a sufficient condition. That is, there is no a priori guarantee that in practice either the Single Tax or a purchase of development rights program will result in a more socially efficient use of land than the market mechanism.

Land value taxation and the purchase of development rights both embody the recognition that in a system of private property rights, a landowner does have a right to develop land. This right may, of course, be limited by local planning and zoning so long as there is no "taking" of private property under the Fifth Amendment. The purchase of development rights is a hybrid of the police power restrictions of government, permitted under the Tenth Amendment, and a payment as in an eminent domain action of government. Land value taxation, by comparison, effectively encourages a landowner to exercise the right to develop land.

From a public finance perspective, land value taxation may not generate revenues sufficient to meet all public needs, as George envisioned with the Single Tax. Nonetheless, land value taxation can raise revenues to be invested in cities and suburbs for parks, schools, etc., rather than for subsidizing sprawl into the hinterlands. Tax revenues could even be spent on a purchase of development rights program.

A purchase of development rights program can be expensive, especially in suburban areas. Both the costs and the voluntary nature of the program may result in the preservation of only a small fraction of all farmland in a county or region. But as more land is preserved, tax revenues from that land would tend to fall. This loss would likely be more than offset by the tax savings from avoiding new infrastructure if the land were developed into houses. Still, the loss of tax revenue suggests a need for state and even federal funding to help local governments purchase development rights.

IV

Equity Effects of Purchasing Development Rights and Land Value Taxation

A PURCHASE OF DEVELOPMENT RIGHTS PROGRAM is rarely equitable, either horizontally or vertically. Part of the reason is that the sale of development rights is voluntary and hence does not apply to all landowners or even all owners of farmland. Horizontally, a purchase of development rights benefits only owners of farmland and open space. Vertically, the largest payments go to those landowners with the greatest difference between market value and the deed restricted agricultural value, regardless of the landowner's financial condition. Moreover, because of limited public funds, not all landowners who are willing to sell development rights may be accommodated.

But a larger equity problem is that sellers of development rights are being allowed to capture an unearned increment in land value brought on largely by public investment in infrastructure. In essence, the public is paying both for infrastructure *and* the increase in land value that the infrastructure created. On the other hand, landowners who sell development rights are surrendering the potential to capture future unearned increments. Also, the public is likely to gain a tax savings in the long run, given that most residential development generates greater public costs than revenues.[13]

A purchase of development rights program may also shift part of the property tax burden away from owners of preserved land and onto owners of unpreserved land, such as residential, commercial, and industrial uses.

By contrast, land value taxation in general, and the Single Tax in particular, is very appealing in terms of vertical equity because it falls most heavily on those landowners with the greatest unearned increments, and thus with the greatest potential wealth or ability to pay. Georgists would add that people who own land tend to be wealthier than those who don't; thus, a tax on land values is generally progressive. In terms of horizontal equity, the land value tax falls more on owners of underdeveloped property, and less on improvements from capital or labor.

V

Land Value Taxation and the Purchase of Development Rights in a Regional Growth Management Program

LAND VALUE TAXATION AND THE purchase of development rights appear to emanate from diametrically opposed philosophies on the treatment of unearned increments. Land value taxation, like the traditional property tax, is a mandatory public program, whereas the purchase of development rights is a voluntary public-private partnership arrangement. Governments that use the land value tax must decide when and where enough development has occurred and when there is a need for open space. Some Georgists might contend that the Single Tax would solve this problem naturally and automatically.[14] Administrators of purchase of development rights programs must decide when and where enough open space and farmland have been preserved and when and where more development is needed. Yet the two techniques could be effectively combined in a regional growth management program. A typical metropolitan region in the United States consists of a central city of several hundred thousand residents plus sprawling suburbs. The central city has probably experienced some decline in population and economic vitality with the rise of the suburbs and would benefit from new development. Curbing sprawl would limit outward expansion and force more in-fill development.

But the simultaneous use of the purchase of development rights and land value taxation would have to be exercised carefully. This is particularly important in delineating where development is to be encouraged or discouraged. For instance, if the two approaches were to overlap, the purchase of development rights would tend to undercut land value taxation as a revenue source because the economic rents would be largely removed. There could still be some unearned return to farmland as farmland in expectation of higher future returns, but not for the higher valued development potential. Similarly, attempts to employ land value taxation in agricultural areas could lead to premature and even haphazard development.[15] And the purchase of development rights in densely settled areas could prove to be prohibitively expensive.

A potential drawback to both land value taxation and the purchase of development rights is that they could be difficult to administer. Land value taxation would require a computation of the land value and building value to be taxed every few years, or more often in a hot real estate market. A purchase of development rights program would involve annual monitoring and possible enforcement of the terms of the easement agreements.

VI

Conclusion

THE HEIGHTENED COMPETITION FOR LAND in the United States, particularly in the densely settled Northeast and West Coasts, has resulted in a public push to preserve privately held agricultural land and open space. Although Henry George would probably object to the use of public funds to pay off unearned increments, the benefit of permanent preservation of natural resource lands is attractive in areas with large and growing populations. Ideally, a comprehensive planning and public finance program that combines both land value taxation and the purchase of development rights could reduce sprawl by achieving both more compact urban/suburban development as well as the retention of farmland and open space.

Notes

1. Brown, H. James, ed., *Land Use and Taxation: Applying the Insights of Henry George.* Cambridge, MA: Lincoln Institute of Land Policy, 1997.

2. See Martin Feldstein, "The Surprising Incidence of a Tax on Pure Rent: A New Answer to an Old Question," *Journal of Political Economy*, Vol. 85 (1977), p. 357.

3. Barlowe, Raleigh. *Land Resource Economics* (3rd edition). Englewood Cliffs, NJ: Prentice-Hall, 1978, p. 642.

4. However, a problem in determining the land value increment may arise with the increase in the value of one's land caused by one's own improvements.

5. Cited in Harrison, Fred, "Rent-ability," in Nicholaus Tideman, ed. *Land and Taxation*. London: Shepheard-Walwyn, 1994, p. 12. See also Oates, Wallace and Robert Schwab.1992. "The Impact of Urban Land Taxation: The Pittsburgh Experience." Working Paper, Cambridge, MA: The Lincoln Institute.

6. Georgists believe that the Single Tax by itself would effectively limit sprawl. But public investment drives much of the increase in the unearned increment of land value on nearby properties. This causes the tax on land to rise and encourages development of the land. A mechanism to limit the extension of public infrastructure is thus necessary. See note 14 below.

7. Backhaus, Jurgen G. 1997. "Henry George's Ingenious Tax: A Contemporary Restatement." *American Journal of Economics and Sociology*, Vol. 56, No. 4, pp. 456–7.

8. See Peter Hall, ed. *Von Thunen's Isolated State*. London: Pergamon Press, 1966.

9. See Daniels, Tom and Deborah Bowers, 1997. *Holding Our Ground: Protecting America's Farms and Farmland*, p. 142 and Chapter 13.

10. See Daniels and Bowers, p. 55.

11. A landowner may sell or donate development rights to a private, non-profit land trust. But because most land trusts do not have substantial financial resources, this article will discuss only the purchase of development rights by state and local governments.

12. Lyons, William. "Suffolk County, New York: Pioneering the Purchase of Development Rights Method to Protect Farmland," in Hiemstra and Bushwick, eds. *Plowing the Urban Fringe: An Assessment of Alternative Approaches to Farmland Preservation*. Fort Lauderdale, FL: Florida Atlantic University and Florida International University, 1989.

13. See Daniels and Bowers, p. 308, "According to Bucks County [PA] P[urchase of] D[evelopment] R[ights] administrator Rich Harvey, 'The underlying theme is it costs more to build a school than preserve the land.'"

14. See Gihring, Thomas A. 1999. "Incentive Property Taxation: A Potential Tool for Urban Growth Management." *Journal of the American Planning Association*, Vol. 65, No. 1, pp. 64–79. Gihring ran a series of hypothetical two-rate tax calculations on different classes of land use at different levels of land value taxation (55% land value and 45% buildings value to 95% land

value to 5% buildings value), using the properties within the urban growth boundary of Clark County, Washington. Gihring concluded, "It does seem apparent that certain legal mechanisms would be needed to prevent premature land conversion in outlying areas. The dilemma of using incentive taxation for fringe land sites is that the greater the margin between use value and market value, the greater is the impact of the tax. Because a high tax on resource lands and open space works against their preservation, a means of reducing market values to use value levels is needed" (p. 76).

15. For example, Gihring calculated that the tax burden on farmland, forestland, and open space would more than double with a 95% land value tax (p. 71).

Leapfrogging, Urban Sprawl, and Growth Management

Phoenix, 1950–2000

By Carol E. Heim*

ABSTRACT. Through a case study of Phoenix, Arizona, this paper examines how urban sprawl is linked to opportunities for capital gains. It focuses on "leapfrogging," in which developers skip over properties to obtain land at a lower price further out despite the existence of utilities and other infrastructure that could serve the bypassed parcels. The paper examines patterns of growth since 1950 and planners' efforts to structure that growth. It discusses two programs that addressed consequences of leapfrogging: development impact fees to help pay for infrastructure costs of new development and an Infill Housing Program to encourage residential development on vacant land. It concludes with a brief discussion of the future of growth management in Phoenix.

I

Introduction

CHANGES IN THE BOUNDARIES BETWEEN CITY AND COUNTRY often occur in discontinuous leaps, rather than through a smooth and steady process of outward expansion. Developers may skip over properties to obtain land further out, leaving vacant tracts behind. This process, called leapfrogging, is one manifestation of the broader phenomenon of urban sprawl. Bradford Luckingham noted in his book *Phoenix: The His-*

*Carol E. Heim is a Professor of Economics at the University of Massachusetts, Amherst. Her address is Department of Economics, University of Massachusetts, Amherst, MA 01003; telephone is (413) 545–0854; e-mail address is cheim@econs.umass.edu. She is an economic historian who has written on regional economic decline and currently is studying the history of urban growth, property development, and planning in Phoenix and neighboring cities. Her most recent publication is "Structural Changes: Regional and Urban," in *The Cambridge Economic History of the United States*, vol. 3, *The Twentieth Century*, eds. Stanley L. Engerman and Robert E. Gallman (Cambridge: Cambridge University Press, 2000).

American Journal of Economics and Sociology, Vol. 60, No. 1 (January, 2001).
© 2001 American Journal of Economics and Sociology, Inc.

tory of a Southwestern Metropolis (1989, p. 193) that 40 percent of the land within the city of Phoenix was vacant in 1980. In part this reflected the city's aggressive annexation policy which increased the size of the city from 17 square miles in 1950 to 330.59 square miles by 1980 (and further to 473.215 square miles by 2000) (Wenum 1970, p. iv; Maricopa Association of Governments 1993, p. 5; City of Phoenix 2000a). Leapfrogging occurred beyond the city limits into other parts of Maricopa County as well.

As cities have expanded, urban sprawl has evoked concerns about environmental degradation and loss of open space and farmland. A vast literature on urban sprawl seeks to identify its causes and to assess its costs and benefits.[1] Leapfrogging is identified as one form of urban sprawl, which also includes scattered development, strip or ribbon development, and continuous low-density development.[2] A primary motivation for leapfrog development is lower land costs in outlying areas. Capital gains are a crucial component of a developer's return.

> His success depends on buying land cheap, and selling it dear. Everything else that he buys is purchased in a national market and at price levels over which he has little influence. But he can leapfrog, buy and develop cheap land, mount an adequate advertising campaign and persuade prospective home-buyers to share with him in the anticipated capital gain. His marketing and management skills are focused on land value appreciation. He succeeds only if he can suburbanize the countryside (Raup 1975, p. 374).

While outlying areas are not the only places developers can succeed, such areas often have clear advantages. Land prices for vacant parcels closer in may be driven up by expectations of price appreciation and hopes of speculative gains to be made when the parcel ultimately is developed (Clawson 1962; Harvey and Clark 1965; Sargent 1976a).[3] Large parcels of land are more likely to exist in outlying areas or to be easier to assemble. Other complications of infill development are less likely to be present, such as contaminated sites, poor perceptions of inner-city neighborhoods, or the need to negotiate with neighborhood groups, although surrounding property owners do in some cases mobilize against leapfrog development. "Developers say it is far easier to work with a vast tract of empty land at the city's periphery than to weave new homes into older neighborhoods" (Pitzl 1996a).

In addition to economic forces such as rising incomes and technological changes affecting industrial location, government programs and subsidies contribute to urban sprawl. Low-density suburban growth has been promoted by the operation of federal home mortgage loan programs, transportation subsidies favoring the private automobile, subsidization of infrastructure such as waste treatment systems, and federal and local tax policies (Raup 1975; Jackson 1985; Ewing 1994; Burchell et al. 1998). In many cases developer and homebuyer participants in the land market are not confronted with the full social costs and benefits of their decisions, which can lead to inefficient use of urban-fringe land (Archer 1973). In the specific case of leapfrog development, local government's role is perhaps most visible in rezoning decisions to allow residential, commercial, or industrial development on previously agricultural or undeveloped land and in decisions to extend infrastructure to outlying areas.

Section II below examines growth patterns in Phoenix from 1950 to the present with particular emphasis on the phenomenon of leapfrogging. It includes discussion of how planners have sought to structure the city's growth. Sections III and IV examine the two programs set up by the city of Phoenix that most directly addressed consequences of leapfrog development. In 1987 an ordinance was adopted to institute development impact fees requiring developers to pay some of the costs of providing infrastructure in areas of new development. The Infill Housing Program created in 1995 sought to encourage residential development in vacant areas within the city that had been bypassed. Section V concludes the paper and briefly describes recent legislative action in Arizona and the citizens' initiative that could affect the future of growth management in Phoenix and the rest of Arizona.

II

Growth Patterns in Phoenix

PHOENIX PROVIDES AN INTERESTING AND IMPORTANT CASE for studying the phenomenon of leapfrogging.[4] Now the sixth largest city in the United States, it has grown very rapidly in recent decades. The population of Phoenix increased from 106,818 in 1950 to 439,170 in 1960, 584,303 in 1970, 789,704 in 1980, and 983,403 in 1990 (U.S. Bureau of the Census

1993, p. 593). By 1999 it stood at 1,240,775 people, more than a ten-fold increase since 1950 (Maricopa Association of Governments 1999). Maricopa County's population grew from 331,770 in 1950 to 2,122,101 in 1990 and it had the largest net increase of population between 1990 and 1997 of any county in the United States (U.S. Bureau of the Census 1993, p. 82; Maricopa Association of Governments 1998, p. 1). By 1999 Maricopa County had 2,913,475 residents (Maricopa Association of Governments 1999).

Observers of Phoenix's urban development began commenting on its discontinuous character soon after the wartime growth of the 1940s accelerated in the 1950s. Listed third among the major findings of a 1959 study was the following:

> The Phoenix Urban Area contains an unusual amount of undeveloped land, about 43,385 acres. Intermittent vacant parcels exert adverse economic effects on developed property and have disrupted the continuity of streets and utilities making public service more expensive and less efficient (Advance Planning Task Force 1959, p. i).

The Task Force argued that leapfrogging had resulted in unstable property values and called for positive land development policies to prevent continued scatteration of urban development throughout the Valley (Advance Planning Task Force 1959, pp. 4, i, 17, 28, 11, 14).

A 1965 study pointed out the large amount of developable land available in its Greater Phoenix study area, including "startling large acreage figures" for small parcels in particular sub-areas.

> By-passed land in small parcels of 40 acres or less is very much in evidence. Such parcels are widely distributed throughout the urbanized area and often exist in the midst of highly developed adjacent land. The comparatively small size of these by-passed parcels makes them both a problem and an asset to the community—an asset because they provide land for "filling-in" developments which may be sorely needed; and a problem because, by their very nature, they become a source of interminable requests for zoning changes and they are almost immune to public influence under present subdivision regulations (Western Management Consultants, Inc. 1965, p. 231).

The small parcels often had qualitative features making them difficult to develop, such as irregular shapes, narrow frontage, shallow depths, and unfavorable juxtaposition to other development. However, the study pointed out that a considerable amount of infilling did occur during 1960–1964 after a period of more extensive growth from 1956–1960. Strip development along major trafficways connected "isolated islands of low-level development"—presumably the outcome of previous leapfrogging—with the main body of urban development (ibid., pp. 234–236).

Although discontinuous development already had been occurring, a change appeared around 1970. The City of Phoenix Planning Department described 1970–1990 as a phase in which "residential growth . . . began to rapidly leap out into what had been more remote parts of the valley" (City of Phoenix Planning Department 2000). Growth was no longer largely a Phoenix experience; it went over the North and South Mountain and out to the east and west valley (City of Phoenix Planning Commission 1994, p. 4). Planned communities in outlying areas began to proliferate. By 1972 Greater Phoenix had sixteen major planned communities ranging in size from 640 to over 10,000 acres in various stages of development. Only seven had existed or been in process before 1970. New developments included Fountain Hills, 19 miles northeast of Scottsdale; Rio Verde, some 26 miles northeast of Scottsdale and 10 miles east of Reata Pass; Sun Lakes, seven miles from Chandler, as well as others. Only four, including Dobson Ranch and McCormick Ranch, were less than five miles from the edge of metropolitan Phoenix. Most of the sixteen communities were in the jurisdiction of Maricopa County although subject to later annexation (Sargent 1973, pp. 2, 7–8, 57–90).

The planned communities were themselves examples of leapfrog development, but also could contribute to two other forms of urban sprawl—strip or ribbon development along major transportation routes and continuous low-density development—by serving as foci of growth corridors. Moreover, while they offered many amenities and might be very well-planned internally, the early planned communities were not part of larger plans for the region as a whole and their existence could complicate later planning efforts (Sargent 1973, pp. 39–41). A key issue in terms of their implications for ribbon development and environmental damage from automobiles was whether the planned communities would be self-contained with a balance of jobs and housing (i.e., genuine "new towns") or would entail long journeys to work. Few of the early planned communities appeared to have the potential to be self-contained.

In later decades these questions surfaced in controversial development cases such as the Belmont case in 1991. Belmont's Development Master Plan proposed placing approximately 150,000 people at a site about 35 miles west of the incorporated boundary of Phoenix. A large number of jobs on-site and a high degree of self-containment were projected, although the proposal also called for several freeway interchanges and several connections with the Sun Valley Parkway, which might be expected to lead to increased dependence on the automobile and on Phoenix. County Supervisor Carole Carpenter voted against approval of the Development Master Plan on the grounds that

> This is not leap frog development; I think it's leap frog olympics, and I frankly believe that this will not be a self-contained community. I have not seen a community, any community, in this valley which is self-contained in the sense that the jobs are provided on-site, and that the jobs are such a good match for housing and employment interests that people stay on-site. I believe there will be, if this actually is built, long commutes. I believe if there are long commutes that clearly will impact air quality in this valley, and I have very strong concerns about the air quality in the valley already (Maricopa County Board of Supervisors 1991).

Supervisor Carpenter and others also were concerned about depletion of the aquifer in that area. Supervisor Bayless and Chairman Freestone, however, voted in favor of the plan, which passed 2–1. The Belmont development, however, was not built.

Anthem, another planned community about 35 miles north of downtown Phoenix, has begun development. Its master plan for a community of 50,000 people also was approved by the Maricopa County Board of Supervisors (in 1995) despite considerable opposition. Editorials in the *Arizona Republic* and *Phoenix Gazette* endorsed the proposal, arguing that growth was inevitable and that the intensity of the development would allow the developer, Del Webb, to contribute to infrastructure and services in ways that would not be possible with a continuation of the "one-lot-per-acre" pattern which aggravated the problem of urban sprawl (*Arizona Republic* 1995; *Phoenix Gazette*

1995). The editorial in the *Gazette* added, however, that "Frankly, we are concerned that the development 12 miles north of Phoenix boundaries, so far beyond existing residential developments, might undermine the city's plans to encourage infill in mature urban areas." The first 1,300 of 14,000 planned homes began to be occupied in the summer of 1999. Demand for the houses was strong; at the grand opening 7,000 people showed up in a day and about 1,000 lots were sold in a week. The aim is for a retail center, offices, and a hospital to provide employment for residents but toward the end of its first year most people were commuting (Morrison 2000). The I-17 corridor connecting Anthem to Phoenix has been identified by Phoenix city planners as an area into which growth is to be channeled, which distinguishes Anthem from some other planned community developments. Sierra Club spokespeople and other critics remain worried about environmental and other consequences of growth in outlying areas.

Passage of the Arizona Groundwater Management Act in 1980 made leapfrogging to remote areas more difficult although not impossible. The legislation required developments in Active Management Areas to demonstrate that they had a 100-year assured supply of water without contributing to decline in groundwater tables. Developers could no longer simply drill a well and service their remote development with a private water company since this would not demonstrate a 100-year supply. In most cases they would need to rely on municipal infrastructure to obtain access to an assured supply. The Anthem case was an exception. Del Webb, a very large developer, arranged to lease water rights from the Ak-Chin Indian Community which had rights to Central Arizona Project water and to build a pipe system to get the water.

Other large scale developments, not all of which were planned communities, began or continued to build as growth picked up in the mid-1990s after the real estate slump of the late 1980s and the recession of the early 1990s. By 1997 21 large scale developments, each with more than 1,000 acres of land, were under construction and another 10 proposed in the Phoenix urban area. As in earlier years, they were found primarily on the urban periphery. Developments under construction included The Foothills to the south, Estrella to the southwest, Sun City Grand to the northwest, and Desert Ridge to the northeast (Maricopa Association of Governments 1998, p. 20).

Phoenix city planners described a third phase of growth after 1990 in which development went out into new territories. Desert Ridge was viewed as one of the keystones (City of Phoenix Planning Commission 1994, p. 4). Residential growth from the mid-1990s continued at the edge of the valley's urban area but was more compact than in the past. It was anticipated at the end of the 1990s that as construction reduced the number of vacant sites with streets and water, new residential growth would move into outlying areas lacking this infrastructure. This growth also would be located beyond the traditional commute shed for employment in the central valley (City of Phoenix Planning Department 2000).

While many criticized Phoenix's leapfrog development into farmland or desert and were alarmed at the urban sprawl which, according to a series in the *Arizona Republic*, was eating up "an acre an hour" of Valley land (Ingley 1994), not all saw these phenomena as a major problem. Gammage (1998, p. 61) argued that Phoenix had little of "the classically derided 'leapfrog' phenomenon" and stated that "metropolitan Phoenix has a cleaner edge than most American cities" (Gammage 1999, p. 68). Rex (1998, p. 55) pointed out that "a certain amount of leapfrog development is a natural feature of development" and argued that in rapidly growing western cities such as Phoenix, unlike slow-growing eastern or midwestern cities, bypassed land usually is developed fairly quickly and newly growing areas do not lack services for long.[5] Phoenix has always had a very strong pro-growth orientation and even in the mid-1970s when anti-growth forces were growing in other cities its citizens remained relatively unconcerned (Gottschalk 1974). Sargent (1976b) characterized the situation as a conflict between "frontier values" and effective land-use control.

Recent polls indicate much greater citizen dissatisfaction with consequences of leapfrog growth and urban sprawl and there is a growing concern with the question of who should bear the costs of growth (Morrison Institute for Public Policy 1999; Guillory 1998). The development impact fees discussed in section III below were one response to this question, although as Gammage (1999, pp. 128–136) indicated, they are complex and not a panacea. Moreover, there remains a problem of the gap in timing between when infrastructure is needed and when tax and impact fee revenues are generated.

Concerns about leapfrog development and efforts to structure Phoenix's rapid growth are reflected in planning documents produced by the City of Phoenix, Maricopa County, the Maricopa Association of Governments, and other individual communities within the region. Among the themes which emerged clearly were "orderly and appropriately timed development" outward from a core, "efficient use of infrastructure," and "economy in the provision of municipal services." Jobs/housing balance, frequently not present in leapfrog developments, became an important goal. By the 1990s the preservation of desert open space also was a priority.

The current General Plan for Phoenix (now under revision) was adopted in 1985. It was based upon the urban village concept adopted in 1979 in the *Phoenix Concept Plan 2000*. Urban villages, each with a core, gradient, and periphery, were to contain a variety of housing, jobs, stores, and recreational and educational facilities and to be identifiable communities within the larger city. Nine villages and four Peripheral Areas (A, B, C, and D) were defined (see Figure 1). Peripheral Area A was west of I-17, between Maryvale and South Mountain Villages; Peripheral Area B was west of I-10, south of South Mountain Village; Peripheral Area C was northeast of Deer Valley and Paradise Valley Villages; and Peripheral Area D, added later, was north of Area C and Deer Valley Village. Peripheral Areas C and D often were described as the land above the Central Arizona Project Canal. These four Peripheral Areas included a considerable amount of land outside the city limits. They were areas in which the city sought to influence patterns of growth and where the issue of financing new infrastructure would be important (City of Phoenix 1985). In later years the Peripheral Areas were included in urban villages as additional villages were designated and some existing villages redefined.

The 1979 *Concept Plan* had been based upon the work of eight Urban Form Directions Committees. One was a Land Use Committee that identified "structuring future growth" as an important goal.

> . . . as opposed to allowing spontaneous growth and continued sprawl, new growth will be encouraged to take place within the existing city fabric at planned locations or nodes and will be strongly discouraged in other locations. New development not located within the existing fabric of city ser-

Figure 1.

Phoenix Urban Villages and Peripheral Areas, 1989

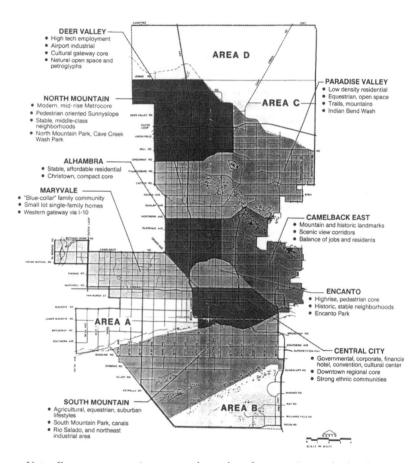

Note: For a more precise eastern boundary for Area D see the land use map in City of Phoenix (1989).

Source: City of Phoenix (1989).

vices will be discouraged, and this fabric will not be extended until development of the desired intensity within the existing fabric has been obtained (Urban Form Directions Committees, 1975, p. 11).

The *General Plan for Phoenix, 1985–2000* called specifically for the development of existing zoned and vacant land before granting additional rezoning and stated that rezoning should occur only when the proposed land use could be developed "within the capacities of existing infrastructure and public facilities and services" (City of Phoenix 1985, pp. 8, 67). General plan elements subsequently were developed for each of the four peripheral planning areas. Their goals included providing supporting capital facilities in an orderly and efficient manner (Quay 1993). The plan for Peripheral Areas C and D stated that "remote (leap frog) patterns are discouraged" (City of Phoenix Planning Department 1987, p. 5).

In developing its Comprehensive Plan Maricopa County explicitly addressed the problem of leapfrogging. Existing Area Land Use Plans for individual areas within the county contained goals and policies intended to discourage leapfrog development and urban sprawl. An early version of the Comprehensive Plan's Goals and Policies stated that "new urban zoning shall be within one mile of existing urban development." According to Commissioner Jones, this policy was intended to prevent leapfrog development, especially with urban densities. The proposed policy proved to be controversial, however. At a public hearing on the Goals and Policies Ms. Jackie Guthrie of Cornoyer Hendrick Associates requested that the phrase above be expanded to state "unless within an approved Development Master Plan." Commissioner Hawks noted that there was concern that the policy as originally proposed might prohibit a relatively large self-sustaining project (satellite community) (Maricopa County Planning Commission 1992).

The policy subsequently was modified with additional goals and policies specifically to address development master plans (for planned communities to be built in the county) to be developed for later inclusion in the Comprehensive Plan (Maricopa County Planning Commission 1992; Maricopa County Department of Planning and Development 1993a). The growth guidance policy language ultimately approved stated that "New urban zoning shall be in close proximity to existing urban development or be consistent with the goals and policies of approved Development Master Plans" (Maricopa County Department of Planning and Development 1993b). In 1993 a Large-Scale Development Working Group was formed to develop goals and policies relating to large-scale developments in rural areas.

Infill development also has been an explicit objective of county and regional planning. The land use element of Maricopa County's Comprehensive Plan ultimately adopted by the county listed "Promote infill development" first among its objectives (Maricopa County 1997, pp. 26–29). The *Desert Spaces* plan of the Maricopa Association of Governments (MAG) included infill development as the last of its eight objectives (Design Workshop Inc. 1995, p. 8). MAG's *Valley Vision 2025* stated, "We envision a future where the edges of the developed area reflect regional and local goals to promote infill, support revitalization of center city and downtown districts, spend government funds efficiently, and protect existing public and private investment in civic infrastructure" (Maricopa Association of Governments 2000, pp. 164–165). Under its "place" theme it included as part of its vision a move from "sprawling, undifferentiated development" to "high quality, distinctive development" and "preserving landscapes, open space, culture" (Maricopa Association of Governments 2000, p. 173). MAG's 1995 Urban Form study did not recommend a preferred urban form for the region but it did point out that infrastructure costs would be lower if new development could be located near existing facilities with unused capacity and it concluded that "leap frog development, if allowed should be required to pay for the extra cost of extending infrastructure" (BRW, Inc. et al. 1995, pp. 16, 14, 2).

The aim of orderly expansion within the fabric of existing city services was not easy to attain. As described above, rezonings were not limited to cases where existing infrastructure already was in place. As growth continues to extend into new areas, current planning efforts are focusing on channeling it into defined locations. In 1994 Phoenix began to implement a set of growth concepts called the Strategic View of Growth. Six emerging growth areas were identified to absorb new population: Central Corridor, Estrella, Laveen, Baseline, Desert Ridge/Paradise Ridge, and the North Black Canyon Corridor (City Council Report 1998; City of Phoenix Planning Department 2000). The

North Black Canyon Corridor Concept Plan, adopted in 1997, included a new planning tool: an infrastructure limit line. Water and sewer infrastructure would be extended and development encouraged only within the limit line. The limit line would be reviewed by the City Council after either the development of 65 percent of the growth area or the passage of ten years. Employment growth within the Corridor would be encouraged to promote jobs/housing balance and reduce commute trips (City of Phoenix Planning Commission and Planning Department 1997, pp. 19–20; City of Phoenix Planning Department 1999). The Baseline Area Master Plan, approved in 1996, highlighted the Baseline Road corridor near South Mountain Park as a "skipped over" area that could be a key location for infill and an alternative to further extension into outlying areas. The hope was that residential development in the Baseline area would promote job locations in the central city near the airport and the inner-city freeway system, although concerns about crime and schools were noted (City of Phoenix Planning Department [c. 1997]; City of Phoenix Planning Commission and Planning Department 1996, p. 4).

Although planning documents had sought to address problems of leapfrogging and urban sprawl since the 1960s, specific policies and programs were much slower to emerge. Luckingham (1989, p. 193) noted that in the late 1970s "[Mayor] Hance and other city officials discussed offering incentives to developers to build on leapfrogged vacant land, but little was accomplished." In the 1980s and 1990s Phoenix did create two programs relating to consequences of leapfrog growth: development impact fees and an Infill Housing Program. These programs are discussed in sections III and IV below.

III

Development Impact Fees

The Development Fee Ordinance (G 3040) was adopted by the Phoenix City Council on July 22, 1987. It provided for development fees to help finance public facilities, stating that "new development should pay for itself by assuming its fair share of the cost of providing necessary capital facilities" (City of Phoenix 1987). Fees would be applied in areas for which specific infrastructure financing plans (SIFPs) had been prepared to project future infrastructure needs in eleven categories: equipment repair, fire, libraries, major streets, storm sewers, parks, police, solid waste, storm drainage, wastewater, and water. These areas were to include the Peripheral Areas and potentially other planning areas in the city. A schedule for adoption of SIFPs, first for Peripheral Areas C and D and then for A and B, and a methodology for calculation of the development fees were included in the ordinance (City of Phoenix Planning Commission and Planning Department 1986, 1987).

Much more limited fee ordinances had been adopted in 1981 and 1982 for sewer and water projects, respectively. In each case a residential development occupational fee and a commercial and industrial development occupational fee were estblished to recover part of the capital cost from customers receiving service. Fiscal difficulties faced by the city during the mid-1980s were one of a number of economic and political factors that contributed to the adoption of development impact fees. The immediate trigger was a proposal for a large master planned development (Tatum Ranch, originally Continental Foothills) north of the city in an area lacking infrastructure. The arrangements worked out for the Tatum Ranch case formed the basis for the subsequent development impact fee program although they differed in certain respects.[6]

In March 1986 the City Council created a Fiscal Impact Subcommittee to estimate public costs of new development on vacant lands and in peripheral areas and to determine techniques of financing them. In July the Subcommittee endorsed the conceptual approach to infrastructure financing presented in a consultant's report and proposed that staff proceed to prepare an infrastructure financing plan for selected portions of Areas C and D, specifically including the Continental Foothills development (Burke, Bosselman & Weaver 1986; City Council Report 1986). At Mayor Goddard's recommendation a 15 member ad hoc citizen's task force was established to assist and advise the Fiscal Impact Subcommittee.

The task force specifically addressed leapfrog developments in its January 1987 report, criticizing them for the "inordinate fiscal burden" they placed on the city and for the way such projects "interfere with the development of the City in an orderly, planned way by producing undesirable and unmanageable urban sprawl" (Fiscal Impact Advisory Task Force 1987). It cited the Tatum Ranch project as an example and proposed the idea of a leapfrog cost premium to discourage such developments in the future. The methodology ultimately developed for calculating development impact fees did incorporate an amount for any extraordinary costs necessary to extend infrastructure to new development from the developed portion of the city.[7]

By April 1987 the Subcommittee had produced recommendations which included a proposed phase-in of the development impact fees over six years "to soften the impact of the new system on developers" (City Council Report 1987a). Comments had been received from the Home Builders Association of Central Arizona and from SunCor (the developer of Tatum Ranch after 1986 when it purchased the property from the Amcor Investment Corporation associated with Charles Keating) and city staff had prepared responses to their concerns. In May the City Council adopted the concept establishing a methodology for determining development fees. Further analysis by staff and discussions with the Homebuilders Association, SunCor, Steve Earl, and Mountain West produced amendments to the draft ordinance, one of which altered the language defining "extraordinary costs" from "those costs of providing capital facilities to a particular development project that are additional to the ordinary average cost of those capital facilities because of the distant location of the development project from existing capital facilities" to "those additional costs of providing capital facilities to a particular development that are incurred sooner than shown in the specific infrastructure financing plan because of the distant location of the development project from existing capital facilities" (City Council Report 1987b). After adoption of the ordinance in July work proceeded on the SIFPs, which were adopted for Peripheral Areas C and D in March 1988, for Peripheral Area A in October 1988, and for Peripheral Area B in May 1993 (City of Phoenix Planning Commission and Planning Department 1988, 1993).

In September 1993 the idea of suspending development impact fees in Peripheral Area A (the southwest peripheral area) was raised. Planning Department staff requested the Planning Commission to initiate an amendment to the Area's SIFP, which would allow an opportunity to examine the area's recent growth patterns and to assess the impact of the program on the area during the past five years (Quay 1993). The conclusion was that in Area A the program was not working. There had been little to no interest in residential development in Area A, in or out of the city; residential projects were further west. Commercial and industrial properties had paid the fees but were becoming resistant to doing so and it had cost more to administer the fee than had been collected (Subcommittee on the Economy 1994). Concern was expressed that "desired growth and development might in fact be stifled by the imposition of the development impact fees" (City of Phoenix Planning Department 1994).

Not all agreed that growth in Area A was desirable. One citizen argued that impact fees originally had two purposes—financing infrastructure and discouraging leapfrog development—and was concerned about the message that would be sent if fees were suspended. Councilman Rimsza, however, viewed Area A as an infill area rather than an area in which growth should be discouraged (Subcommittee on the Economy 1994). The collection of fees was suspended in Area A although they later were reintroduced in the western portion of Estrella, the Phoenix urban village that approximately coincided with the former Area A, after substantial residential development had been approved.

Beginning in 1994 a major review of the development impact fee program was undertaken which resulted in refinement of several aspects of the program and an increase in fees. The existing fees for Areas C and D had not been reviewed and updated since their establishment in 1988 because of the lack of development in those Areas. But as growth picked up in the early 1990s a more systematic approach to the development impact fee program was felt to be necessary. Work was undertaken to review the equivalent dwelling unit (EDU) factors used to calculate the fees and a more complex structure was adopted. The EDU factors take into account the different demands that different types of facilities (e.g., single family homes vs. multifamily vs. nonresidential uses) place on infrastructure. Other enhancements were related to (1) socioeconomic projections used to estimate future infrastructure needs, (2) offsets for alternative revenue sources used to pay for infrastructure, (3) estimates of unit costs of capital facilities, (4) calculations of service levels, and (5) preparation of long range capital facility plans. Progress was made toward developing a system that was both fair and administratively manageable (Mee 1997).

Development impact fees were increased in 1995 and 1996 with the substantially higher fees to be phased in over a period of several years. Strong opposition to the fee increases was voiced by the Home Builders Association of Central Arizona when they were proposed in 1995 on the grounds that they would drive up prices and hurt the homebuilding industry, and the City Council decided not to implement the full fee schedule immediately (Jarman 1995). Amendments to the Development Fee Ordinance were passed in 1996 and specific infrastructure financing plans were updated or drafted for various areas in the late 1990s.

As of May 31, 2000 development impact fees were being assessed in Deer Valley, North Gateway, Desert View, Estrella, Laveen, and Ahwatukee Foothills Villages. In some villages fees were assessed in only part of the village and a given village could include several different fee levels. Single family residential impact fees ranged from $2,112 (plus a $136 administration charge) in Ahwatukee east of 19th Avenue to $9,471 (plus a $372 administration charge) in North Gateway inside Black Canyon Corridor. These fees assumed standard density, 5/8" or 1" water meter, 4" building sewer, and payment of $600 Water and $600 Sewer Development Occupational Fees (City of Phoenix Development Services Department 2000).

As the process of determining and administering development impact fees in Phoenix becomes more refined, three larger questions remain. First, how effective are the fees in deterring leapfrog development and promoting infill? To be sure, this was not the only—or perhaps even the primary—reason for their adoption and some commentators warn that the objectives of paying for costs of growth and discouraging growth are distinct objectives, perhaps not best met through the same governmental policies (Worden and de Kok 1998, pp. 188–189). As Gammage put it:

> In devising mechanisms to pay for growth, we should not be disguising an effort to discourage growth, or to change its shape, density, or form. If we want to do any of those things, we need to honestly and fairly debate whether we want higher density, less commercial, slower development, or more open space, and reach a conclusion (Gammage 1999, p. 136).

The probability that fees will deter leapfrog development obviously increases as the fees themselves increase, other things being equal. After the fee increases that began in 1995 fees in Phoenix came closer to covering the full costs of new development. However, higher fees raise two other issues that have been the subject of public debate in Phoenix and elsewhere (Arizona Town Hall 1996, p. x).

The first issue is affordable housing. Developers have argued that the development impact fees will be passed on to homebuyers, raising the price of homes they seek to buy and perhaps putting them out of the reach of many. The Fiscal Impact Advisory Task Force addressed this issue explicitly in its January 1987 report and concluded that a more likely outcome was that the effect would be shared between lowered land costs and somewhat higher house prices. It calculated a worst-case scenario in which the fees were doubled and added to home prices (the prediction of one homebuilder). With a $3,000 fee the increase in the monthly mortgage payment for a 30-year level payments loan at 10 percent would be $52.70 (Fiscal Impact Advisory Task Force 1987). Current fees in many areas of Phoenix are much higher and worry affordable-housing advocates (McKinnon 2000a).

The likelihood that fees will be passed on to homebuyers depends on a number of demand and supply factors including the sensitivity of demand to housing prices, market conditions and barriers to developers' entry, and landowners' behavior. In some situations housing prices could increase with homebuyers paying the largest share of the fees. Impact fees also could have a negative impact on lower-income families in multifamily housing projects by raising rents or delaying their construction (Worden and de Kok 1996, pp. 189–90). However, even in these cases there may well be better approaches to housing affordability than seeking to ensure it through the level of development impact fees.

The second issue raised by higher development impact fees is that of competition from nearby jurisdictions. Will desired development go elsewhere if it is required to pay more of the costs of infrastructure development in some locations but not in others? The Phoenix area has a long history of rivalry among its municipalities, reflected in the annexation wars in which they sought increases in territory to ensure their sales tax revenue bases. The Fiscal Impact Advisory Task Force alluded to this issue of competition, asserting that "to the extent that Phoenix's new fees may exceed those of other Valley cities, we believe the disparity will be of relatively-short duration" (Fiscal Impact Advisory Task Force 1987). Other Valley municipalities did not immediately follow suit. After 1994 as the costs of growth became increasingly apparent, many did institute and later increased fees, although fees in Phoenix remained higher than in most. Some municipalities such as Queen Creek deliberately sought higher fees as a way to limit development and retain a rural character. But in 1999 Peoria exempted seven commercial developers from hundreds of thousands of dollars in impact fees that were scheduled to rise dramatically out of fear that projects would be withdrawn and future tax revenues lost (McGavin 1999; McKinnon 1999). Similar concerns about losing two supermarket chains' distribution warehouses to Tolleson had been part of what led Phoenix to suspend impact fees in the southwestern part of the city in 1994 (Kwok 1994a).

IV

The Infill Housing Program

ON MARCH 8, 1995, THE CITY COUNCIL APPROVED ESTABLISHMENT of an Infill Housing Program for single-family housing on vacant land in the central part of the city and authorized $100,000 in contingency funds for the program. The funds were to be used to reimburse city departments for lost revenues for fee waivers granted to applicants. The fee waivers included building plan review and permit fees and water and sewer development occupational fees. In addition, infill projects would be eligible for an expedited development process. The designated infill area lay between Cactus Road on the north and South Mountain. The program was intended to encourage development of additional quality owner-occupied housing, of a variety of styles, types, and price ranges, within this area. Housing design standards had been an important part of the discussions leading up to the program's creation and its focus on owner-occupied housing was intended "to help deter blight and decay and to promote neighborhood stability through residents' financial commitment and long term residency" (City Council Report 1995).

Earlier efforts to encourage infill had included density incentives and fee waivers but these efforts were relatively unsuccessful. Among its programs were two the city initiated in 1981: the High-Rise Incentive District (allowing greater residential building height and density within the Central Corridor to stimulate residential and mixed commercial/residential projects) and the Residential Infill R-1 District (allowing greater densities to encourage new multi-family development within central Phoenix). Fee waivers were granted for items such as building permits, rezoning, zoning adjustment, abandonments, and certain water and wastewater fees. A small portion of south Phoenix that was regarded as needing development stimulation was also eligible for fee waivers. However, the High-Rise Incentive District did not produce any mixed use or residential projects and only two commercial projects had been completed by 1990. The incentives available for the Residential Infill R-1 District initially did not attract large developers; small-scale builders constructed low-quality buildings, some of which quickly fell into disrepair. By 1990 two large downtown projects had been constructed by major developers: St. Croix Villas and Renaissance Park. Discussion of possible infill strategies for Phoenix at that time noted several factors limiting its potential for infill, including a high housing vacancy rate, dispersed employment centers, lower land prices in outlying areas, and the lack of growth controls (City Council Report 1990; Real Estate Research Corporation 1982, pp. 61, 87).

As the city's economy recovered in the 1990s from the recent economic downturn, the prospects for infill came to look more promising. Infill was viewed as an alternative to costly peripheral growth. In 1994 Councilman Skip Rimsza wrote to the City Manager:

> While it is exciting to see an upswing in our economy, we must be careful in how we plan for future growth. Even with fiscal impact fees, development on the outskirts of the City is taxing on our budget. It is imperative for the City of Phoenix to encourage infill projects where the infrastructure and services are already at a high service level recognized worldwide (Rimsza 1994).

An Infill Housing Task Force reported to the City Council in March 1994 and presented a list of concepts and possible incentives including fee reductions, expedited reviews, and code waivers, while pointing out that the proposed program would be costly and that funding sources would need to be found to compensate for lost fee revenues (City Council Report 1994a).

Concern about the potential revenue losses (as much as $1.3 million to $1.9 million a year) delayed City Council action on the recommendations but the Council was receptive to a more limited approach (Jarman 1994).[8] Staff evaluated a pilot infill project of 27 homes in the fall of 1994 and recommended that it be funded. Seeking to emphasize potential cost savings if an existing or new resident chose a home in the infill area rather than on the fringe, the staff report pointed out that the current infrastructure cost to the city for each new home on the fringe was about $6,000 after deducting payment of developer impact fees (City Council Report 1994b). Infill became "the defining issue" in the special mayoral election in October 1994. The election was won by Rimsza, who had promoted the idea of infill for many years but differed from other candidates in being unwilling to penalize owners who held vacant land for speculation by taxing them more highly (Kwok 1994b).

Stage I of the Infill Housing Program was approved by the City Council on January 17, 1995 subject to modifications by the Housing and Neighborhoods Subcommittee; the program received final approval in March. A 1995 Planning Department staff report outlined some of the challenges the program would face. The report took the view that "the large number of vacant parcels in Phoenix that have either been skipped over by earlier development or have been cleared of older structures but not yet reused is both a problem and an opportunity" (City of Phoenix Planning Department 1995, p. 2). Based on a survey of over 60 people including builders and developers, professionals associated with property development, neighborhood activists, City Council and Planning Commission members, and City staff in several departments, the report listed sixteen barriers to infill. The top five in the order in which they were ranked in the survey were crime and perception of crime, perception of schools as inadequate and/or unsafe, difficulty in finding and acquiring land suitable for development (due to multiple owners, unrealistic expectations and speculation that inflated land prices, and property not being on the market), perception of declining property values, and a variety of reasons for higher development costs including in some cases the cost of retrofitting infrastructure.

Interviews with developers identified availability of financing as a major problem for some potential infill projects. Profit margins also could be an issue. One builder provided a cost assessment for a 1,500 square foot, $80,000 infill house with a 4 percent profit margin (considered on the low end of the spectrum by home builder standards). Waiving city fees or reducing land acquisition costs by $2,500 could increase the profit margin to as much as 7 percent, a profit margin easily obtained by a home builder on the periphery.

Bankers pointed out that "the infill market is 'totally separate' from the peripheral market. Developers who are building residential subdivisions on the periphery do not get involved with infill projects" (City of Phoenix Planning Department 1995, p. 16). Smaller companies within the Home Builders Association of Central Arizona supported the establishment of the Infill Housing Program but the Association's assistant director predicted that large builders would not be affected (Padgett 1995). This division largely has persisted up to the present. The Infill Housing Program has not primarily operated by inducing large builders to switch from peripheral to infill locations. Instead, its incentives went heavily to smaller nonprofits and/or homebuilders and to individuals.[9] Some builders and developers specialize in infill projects as their niche.

By August 31, 1995, 49 applications had been reviewed. Thirty-two building permits had been issued, 5 applications had been rejected, and 12 applications were in the plan review process or awaiting issuance of building permits. The estimated construction value of the permits issued was $3,718,785 and the average fee waiver per unit was $1,975. As the program moved into its second year, the volume of applications exceeded expectations. Early in 1996 the City Council approved limits on the amount of the fee waiver for the building permit and the building plan review and on the number of houses within a project which could receive fee waivers. These actions were intended to maximize the use of the city's resources (City Council Report 1996). Throughout its operation the program has sought to target its efforts on projects that the market would be unlikely to produce without incentives. This, as well as concern about the program's costs, led to a desire to de-emphasize subdivisions in favor of individual units, although in 1999 subdivisions still constituted approximately 64 percent of all permits issued (City Council Report 1997; City Council Report 1999).

At that point the program had permitted 1,081 projects with an estimated construction value in excess of $130 million. The average fee waiver was approximately $1,700 although higher waivers could be granted. Modifications had been made and pilot projects were underway to address three categories of barriers to infill: regulatory requirements pertaining to public health, safety, and welfare, plan review times, and costs associated with city review (City Council Report 1999). For many applicants expedited building plan review and personalized service in the development process, rather than the financial incentives, had been the most important benefits (City Council Policy Session 1999).

During the life of the program larger tracts of vacant land in the central city were becoming more scarce and by the spring of 2000 the program's coordinator noted a migration south toward Laveen where vacant land was more readily available. A majority of the projects in what was by then an approximately 175 square mile designated infill area were located south of the Salt River (Doefler 1997; McKinnon 2000b; Fimea 2000). Preparation of an inventory of vacant parcels within the designated infill area to help developers locate eligible parcels had been envisioned as part of the program from its inception. There also was interest in identifying underutilized land. Dr. Elizabeth Burns of Arizona State University and her students have contributed to work on a database including the inventory and other information available through the city's Geographic Information Systems (GIS) Program (City of Phoenix Planning Commission and Planning Department 1995, 1996, 1997, 1998).

A total of 1,699 projects had been permitted by early 2000 and current fiscal year 1999–2000 funding for the program was $530,000. An additional $44,000 was requested for the remainder of the fiscal year (City Council Report [2000]) The maximum waivers available at that point were $2,250 per house ($1,000 for building plan review and building permit fees, $1,200 for water and sewer development occupational fees, and $50 for a fence permit if applicable) plus an additional $500 per house/subdivision for development processing fees for zoning variance, abandonments, subdivision/lot splits, dedication of easements and rights-of-way, pavement cut surcharges, and building code modifications. The number of houses that could receive fee waivers was limited to 12 units per subdivision (City of Phoenix 2000b).

The Infill Housing Program appears to be succeeding in many respects although it is difficult to know how much of the development associated with it would have occurred in any case without its incentives.[10] But at its best the program could be only a partial solution to problems of leapfrogging and urban sprawl. Realistic advocates of the program recognized its limits from the beginning. From 1990 to 1994, more than 5,200 homes had been built each year outside central Phoenix (Pitzl 1996a).[11] Mayor Rimzsa warned against banking on central-city development to prevent sprawl. "'In my wildest dreams, we wouldn't build 5,000 infill homes in a year,' he said. 'It's too difficult to do.'" (Pitzl 1996b). Instead, he thought 50 homes would be a "good year" and 300 would be a "home run" (Fischer 1996). Councilman Craig Tribken, Chair of the Housing and Neighborhoods Subcommittee, set a higher goal for the program which he believed had "major public benefits." But even that goal was only 500 homes per year (Housing and Neighborhood Subcommittee 1994).

As noted above, the Infill Housing Program's objectives were by no means confined to countering leapfrog development and urban sprawl. Promoting owner-occupancy and better quality housing in the central city also were important goals. Unlike some other infill programs, such as the widely-praised one in neighboring Tempe, Phoenix's program did not have a strong commercial or mixed-use component nor did it attempt to stress higher-density development. Such efforts might not have succeeded. Robert Franciosi, a research associate with the Goldwater Institute, argued that "no one moves to Arizona to live in a twenty-story apartment building" (Franciosi 1997). Twenty-story apartment buildings are, of course, not the only possible form of higher-density development, although he is right that there are strong preferences in Phoenix for low-density forms. Unfortunately, even if new residential development were 50 percent denser than in nearby neighborhoods, developing all vacant residential land in the 1990 Phoenix urban area could accommodate only 9 years of population growth if it continued at the rapid 1990–1995 rate (as opposed to 6 years of population growth if existing densities were maintained) (Ellman 1997, p. 10).[12]

V

Conclusion

Concern about leapfrogging and urban sprawl in Phoenix appeared along with the extraordinarily rapid growth of the 1950s and continued in later decades. That concern coexisted with a strong commitment to growth and to individual property rights and "frontier values" that made land-use controls difficult to implement. Competition among jurisdictions within the region also undermined effective growth management (Berman 1998). Planners sought to structure the city's growth and to ensure that orderly expansion and efficient use of infrastructure would occur, but it was not within their power fully to realize these goals. Effective growth management also was hampered by difficulties, not discussed in this paper, of integrating transportation planning and land use planning. Two programs were created that addressed consequences of leapfrog growth although each had other objectives as well. Development impact fees alleviated some of the fiscal strain caused by the costs of providing infrastructure in outlying areas. They also addressed the growing sentiment that new development should pay its own way. The Infill Housing Program sought to encourage development on vacant parcels that had been bypassed by leapfrog growth.

One of the lessons to be drawn from the history of leapfrog development in the Phoenix area concerns the difficulty of controlling such development (or urban sprawl more generally) with the planning and growth management tools available to the city of Phoenix during most of the period discussed in this paper. As discussed above, intentions embodied in land use plans were not always realized and rezoning decisions could contribute to leapfrog development and sprawl. The Arizona state legislature opposed other measures used by cities in other states such as schemes to tax vacant land. There also were limitations on what Maricopa County could do. The county, unlike the city of Phoenix, was not permitted to adopt development impact fees until very recently.

However, it is not clear to what extent responsibility for Phoenix's growth patterns lay with inadequate tools as opposed to a lack of political will. Clearly some features associated with leapfrog development and low-density growth were desired by many Phoenix residents and builders opposed restrictions on these development patterns. Single-family homes were in demand although, as critics have pointed out, a desire for single-family homes is not necessarily identical to a desire for low-density sprawl development and single-family homes can be provided in other configurations. Relatively few types of housing options have been available in the Phoenix area, in part because builders are reluctant to take chances on types of development for which there is not a proven market.

It also is not clear to what extent leapfrog development per se has entailed or will entail negative long-run consequences for Phoenix, particularly if low-density development is a desired outcome. As noted above some of the negative consequences of leapfrog development diminish if vacant lands ultimately are filled in. At that point the question becomes one of the pros and cons of continuous low-density development (if the infill has been low-density) rather than of leapfrog development. Infill development may be at a higher density than development that would have occurred on those parcels without leapfrogging and some would consider this a desirable outcome. Phoenix's Infill Housing Program did not strongly encourage higher-density development, in part because of its emphasis on owner-occupied residential development. Also, in some cases higher-density infill development has been opposed by local residents. There has, nonetheless, been some increase in the overall density of Phoenix. It would be interesting to know more about the extent to which this resulted from higher-density development of previously skipped-over parcels, higher-density development in new subdivisions in more outlying areas, or both.

Certain undesired consequences of Phoenix's growth patterns have become increasingly evident, however, and changes in political will may result in significant changes in available planning and growth management tools. The Phoenix case provides several illustrations of the negative externalities that can be associated with urban growth. Air pollution is perhaps the most striking example. Phoenix has attracted national attention for its "brown cloud" and has been rated as having serious air quality deficiencies by the Environmental Protection Agency. Widespread dissatisfaction with traffic congestion, air pollution, loss of desert open space, and other consequences of urban growth in Phoenix and other Arizona cities led to the introduction of a Citizens' Growth Management Initiative (CGMI) by the Arizona Center for Law in the Public Interest, the Sierra Club, and other environmental and community groups.

There is disagreement in the literature as to what extent the problems mentioned above are exacerbated by sprawl as opposed to more compact forms of growth. Various factors including the location of employment opportunities and the provision of transportation infrastructure play an important role, particularly for traffic congestion. Sufficient evidence exists, however, to convince many that urban sprawl is a serious problem and limiting sprawl is an explicit goal of the CGMI. Problems resulting from low-density, automobile-dependent urban forms also could be addressed by producing more energy-efficient vehicles and by requiring drivers to pay the full social costs associated with the types of vehicles, distances, and times of day that they drive, thereby internalizing externalities.

The CGMI did not initially obtain enough signatures to be put on the ballot, but another effort is under way at this time (July 2000) to get the CGMI passed in November 2000. One of its most controversial provisions is a call for ten-year urban growth boundaries around Arizona's cities and towns. It also stipulates that developers must pay full impact fees to cover the costs of public facilities for new projects except in infill incentive areas, requires that voters approve growth plans and major amendments, and includes an enforcement provision allowing any person to file a civil action alleging violations and seeking injunctive and other relief.

The CGMI evoked strong opposition and legislative action. Governor Jane Hull already had been interested in growth proposals and some segments of the business community put a high priority on blocking the CGMI. In 1998 a proposal by the Governor and legislators called "Growing Smarter" was passed, followed by "Growing Smarter Plus" in February 2000. This legislation takes a much less aggressive approach to urban growth and does not satisfy the proponents of the CGMI although it does address some similar issues. For example, the Growing Smarter Act required that cities and towns' plans have a cost of development element to identify policies and strategies regarding how development would pay its fair share of the costs it generated. Growing Smarter Plus required that the land use element of plans identify programs and policies to promote infill and allowed the designation of infill incentive districts where fees for the cost of additional public facilities could be reduced. There also were legislative and ballot measures pertaining to the acquisition and preservation of open space and the management of state trust lands. In the process of emergence of Growing Smarter more players entered the growth debate and the terms of that debate shifted (Melnick 1998). If the CGMI passes in November 2000, the actual practice of growth management in Phoenix will be dramatically altered as well.

Notes

    I would like to thank Marvin A. Andrews (Phoenix City Manager, 1976–1990), Corey Cox (Regional Development Manager, Maricopa Association of Governments), Janine Hatmaker (Planner II, City of Phoenix Planning Department), Renée Guillory (Campaign Coordinator, Citizens for Growth Management), Mitchell A. Hayden (Business Assistance Coordinator, City Manager's Office, Phoenix), Matthew Holm (Senior Planner, Maricopa County Planning and Development Department), William R. Mee, Jr. (Infrastructure Financing Coordinator, City of Phoenix Planning Department), and Rita Walton (Information Services Manager, Maricopa Association of Governments) for helpful discussion of topics addressed in this paper. None of them is responsible for any errors or omissions. I also would like to thank the numerous other people in Phoenix and Tempe who took time to talk with me and to help me locate research materials. The Department of Economics, University of Massachusetts, Amherst provided financial support for this research.
    1. See Ewing (1994) and Burchell et al. (1998) for surveys of this literature. Burchell et al. (1998) included a critical assessment of the widely-cited but flawed 1974 report by the Real Estate Research Corporation, *The Costs of Sprawl*, and brief summaries of many subsequent contributions. There is no universally accepted or scientifically precise definition of urban sprawl. The term often is applied as a negative normative judgment. Views differ widely, however, as to whether urban sprawl constitutes a serious problem. See Burchell et al. (1998) for discussion of positive impacts that have been argued to result from sprawl in the areas of public/private capital and operating costs, transportation and travel costs, land/natural habitat preservation, quality of life, and social issues.
    2. Leapfrog and scattered development result in a checkerboard pattern of land use in which vacant land alternates with developed land. Strip or ribbon development refers to linear spread, particularly of commercial land uses, along major transportation corridors. Critics argue that it results in longer

travel distances and greater automobile use, with negative environmental consequences. Continuous low-density development is most often associated with residential development of single-family homes on lots that opponents of sprawl regard as too large and as consuming too much land. Many writers treat leapfrogging and scattered development as synonymous; some distinguish leapfrogging as involving greater distance from existing urban development. Ewing (1994) defined leapfrogging as a type of scattered development that assumes a monocentric city. Since Phoenix is not a monocentric city, presumably he would use the term scattered development to describe the activity in the Phoenix area that others have called leapfrogging. Leapfrogging and scattered development frequently are regarded as inefficient in terms of travel requirements and the provision of infrastructure and public services. However, if discontinuous development is concentrated in new centers, the resulting polycentric form can be more efficient for large metropolitan areas by reducing trip lengths without producing excessive congestion (Haines 1986). Although Phoenix planners have attempted to encourage a polycentric form by the designation of urban villages and measures to promote jobs-housing balance (described below), Phoenix is not generally regarded as having fully attained the benefits of that form. Leapfrogging also is defended by some writers on the grounds that it preserves flexibility for future development and that if higher densities are allowed on infill parcels, leapfrogging may result in higher overall density than would have occurred if discontinuous development were prevented (Lessinger 1962; Ohls and Pines 1975; Ottensmann 1977; Peiser 1989; Altshuler and Gómez-Ibáñez 1993). For more complete and detailed discussion of negative impacts that have been argued to result from the various forms of urban sprawl see Ewing (1994) and Burchell et al. (1998).

3. These expectations may be unrealistic and the hopes disappointed. Moreover, if the growth rate of land values slows and speculators wait too long—i.e., if they wait until the rate of growth of their land's value is less than the interest rate—they will lose some or all of their gains (Fischel 1985, p. 265).

4. In this paper I focus primarily on leapfrog development, a type of sprawl that was especially important in contributing to the emergence of development impact fees and the Infill Housing Program. I also concentrate on the city of Phoenix and its programs although the phenomenon of leapfrog development occurred on a wider scale, affecting unincorporated territory and many of the other 23 incorporated cities and towns in Maricopa County. Some of these municipalities also have developed development impact fee and infill programs. This paper is an initial exploration and forms part of a larger research project on the history of urban growth and planning in Phoenix and neighboring cities.

5. Rex (1998) also provided an interesting analysis of the costs and benefits of growth to different groups, arguing (p. 53) that "the divergence of con-

tinued net benefits to the private sector and to certain individuals while the net benefits to the other groups are disappearing results in the growth of an area beyond the size desired by a majority of its residents."

6. The question of why development impact fees were adopted in 1987 and not earlier is an interesting one that I am investigating as part of my ongoing research.

7. Some, although not all, infrastructure costs vary with distance and can be expected to be greater for leapfrog developments. In the case of water and sewer services, one of three components of costs—the costs associated with the delivery of services such as sanitary sewer lines—generally increase proportionally as distance increases. The capital costs of producing the service (in facilities with economies of scale and declining average costs) and the short-term costs of actually producing the good, or the maintenance and operation costs (e.g., the costs of processing sewage once it has been collected) generally are independent of distance (Nicholas et al. 1991, p. 50). Using data from a case study of a subdivision near Lexington, Kentucky, Archer (1973) found that leapfrog development two miles from the edge of the built-up area entailed large additional capital costs ($234,681) for water, gas, telephone, electricity, and sanitary sewage, although he pointed out (p. 368) that "much of this was only a temporary additional cost because it was excess capacity in the utility network which would be used when the intervening land was developed." Downing and Gustely (1977) estimated that for a 1,000 unit neighborhood the annual capital and/or operating cost of providing public services (police, fire, sanitation, schools, water supply, storm drainage, and sanitary sewers) per mile of distance from public facility site was $68,498. Their data suggested that "for a subdivision located five miles from each of these facilities, annual incremental costs per household would be in excess of $300" (p. 84). Altshuler and Gómez-Ibáñez argued that Downing and Gustely's estimates for capital costs for water, sewage, and storm drainage overstated the effects of distance because they did not take into account economies of scale in central treatment plants. There also may be economies of scale in pipe sizes: "a community can economize in serving more distant neighborhoods if it has the foresight to install larger trunk lines when the close-in neighborhoods are developed" (Altshuler and Gómez-Ibáñez 1993, p. 73). Frank (1989) reanalyzed a number of earlier studies and found that ten miles of distance from central facilities and the major concentration of employment increased total capital costs of development for streets, sewers, water, storm drainage, and schools by almost $15,000 per unit in a development with three dwelling units per acre. He also provided estimates of additional leapfrog costs associated with arterial roads and sometimes trunk utility lines needed to traverse vacant land within a community (as opposed to linking that community to distant central facilities).

8. The City Council appears to have focused quite heavily on the cost side

of the program at this point. Unless the fee waivers went only to builders who would have built in the infill area even without the incentives, the program would result in additional revenues as well as additional costs. Moreover, to the extent that the program succeeded in its goal of deterring blight and decay it might also reduce some costs resulting from blight that the city would have incurred in the absence of the program. There were, nonetheless, grounds for caution. First, some waivers might be granted for projects that would have been built anyway. Second, as noted above even in cases where new development ultimately pays its own way there is a problem of the gap in timing between costs associated with the development (including incentives necessary to induce it) and the revenues it generates. Finally, while conditions vary greatly depending on specific local circumstances, in many cases "development does not cover new public costs; that is, it brings in less revenue for local governments than the price of servicing it" (Altshuler and Gómez-Ibáñez 1993, pp. 77).

9. According to Mitchell Hayden, the Business Assistance Coordinator in the City Manager's Office in Phoenix, "over 70% of our projects are affiliated with subdivision developments while only 30% are individual owner/building type projects. We classify subdivisions as any project consisting of more than 12 lots. Within this 70%, many are smaller non-profits and/or homebuilders. Major home builders generally are developing in areas outside the infill boundary" (personal communication, June 23, 2000).

10. Ideally one would like to be able to compare what would have happened in the absence of the incentives with what did happen with the incentives in place. One approach would be to construct a model for this purpose. However, the data requirements for adequate models are considerable and the infill area is not one for which economic data generally are collected. Some similar issues arise in the evaluation of urban enterprise zones. See Rubin and Wilder (1989) for a discussion of these issues and an evaluation of the Evansville, Indiana enterprise zone based on an unusual availability of micro-level data from annual surveys of zone firms from 1983 to 1986. There is a large body of studies using economic models and other approaches to examine the effects of various economic development incentives (or disincentives, such as taxes) offered to business firms by states and local governments. The studies have produced contradictory results and the results are very sensitive to the assumptions incorporated in the models. See Bartik (1991) and Fisher and Peters (1998) for discussions of this literature.

11. The numbers are likely to have been higher in the later as opposed to earlier years of this period, as the economy recovered from recession and the single-family housing market rebounded from a 1990 trough. Single-family new housing units authorized in the Phoenix Metropolitan Area as a whole were 10,909 in 1990, 13,840 in 1991, 18,809 in 1992, 23,196 in 1993, and 28,224 in 1994 (AzStats 1996, p. 46).

12. Cities in the Valley differed in the 1990s in the extent to which development involved converting land to urban uses as opposed to being more of a filling-in process. In some communities such as Gilbert, Glendale, Scottsdale, and Surprise development entailed a significant amount of conversion of previously rural land to urban uses. Phoenix, Avondale, Chandler, Fountain Hills, Mesa, Paradise Valley, Peoria, and Tempe had lower land absorption coefficients, indicating more of a process of funneling additional population into existing urban land (Gober et al. 1998).

References

Advance Planning Task Force. 1959. *Land Use of the Phoenix Urban Area: A Study Basic to Long Range Planning.* [Phoenix]: Advance Planning Task Force, City of Phoenix and Maricopa County, Arizona.

Altshuler, Alan A. and José A. Gómez-Ibáñez, with Arnold M. Howitt. 1993. *Regulation for Revenue: The Political Economy of Land Use Exactions.* Washington, D.C. and Cambridge, MA: The Brookings Institution and the Lincoln Institute of Land Policy.

Archer, R. W. 1973. "Land Speculation and Scattered Development; Failures in the Urban-Fringe Land Market." *Urban Studies* 10(3), pp. 367–372.

Arizona Republic. 1995. "New River Development; Approve the Plan." Editorial/Opinion, April 4, p. B4.

Arizona Town Hall. 1996. *Arizona's Growth and the Environment—A World of Difficult Choices.* Sixty-Eighth Arizona Town Hall, May 5–8, 1996. Phoenix: Arizona Town Hall.

AzStats. 1996. *Arizona Statistical Review.* Phoenix: Arizona Public Service Company, Economic Development Department.

Bartik, Timothy J. 1991. *Who Benefits from State and Local Economic Development Policies?* Kalamazoo, MI.: W. E. Upjohn Institute for Employment Research.

Berman, David R. 1998. "The Growth Management Challenge in Arizona." In *Growth in Arizona: The Machine in the Garden,* pp. 113–119. Tempe, AZ: Morrison Institute for Public Policy, Arizona State University.

BRW, Inc., GIS Southwest, and Hammer Siler George Associates. 1995. *Maricopa Association of Governments Urban Form Study: Final Report.* [Phoenix]: Maricopa Association of Governments.

Burchell, Robert W., Naveed A. Shad, David Listokin, Hilary Phillips, Anthony Downs, Samuel Seskin, Judy S. Davis, Terry Moore, David Helton, and Michelle Gall. 1998. *The Costs of Sprawl—Revisited.* Transit Cooperative Research Program Report 39. Washington, D.C.: National Academy Press.

Burke, Bosselman & Weaver. 1986. "Consultant's Report to the Fiscal Impact Subcommittee," 7/18/86. Blue Ring Binder, "Development Fees," William Mee, City of Phoenix Planning Department.

City Council Policy Session 1999. Tuesday, May 11, 1999 - 2:30 p.m. Office of the City Clerk, Phoenix.

City Council Report. 1986. Ray Bladine (Community and Economic Development Manager) to Peter Starrett (Acting City Manager), "Staff Follow-Up to Fiscal Impact Report," July 25, 1986. Office of the City Clerk, Phoenix.

————. 1987a. Councilman Dr. Bill Parks, Chair, Councilman Calvin Goode, Councilwoman Mary Rose Wilcox, City Council Ad Hoc Subcommittee on Fiscal Impact to Mayor and City Council, "Recommendations for Peripheral Areas Development Impact Fee Methodology," April 30, 1987. Office of the City Clerk, Phoenix.

————. 1987b. Robert J. Cafarella (Planner III) to Raymond F. Bladine (Community & Economic Development Manager), "Proposed Changes to Development Fee Ordinance," July 21, 1987. File: "Development Fee Ordinance 1987," William Mee, City of Phoenix Planning Department.

————. 1990. Ronald N. Short (Planning Director) to Denny Maus (Acting Deputy City Manager), "Infill Plans/Inner City Request for Information by Councilman Goode" and attached material, October 4, 1990. Office of the City Clerk, Phoenix.

————. 1994a. Frank Dolasinski (Infill Housing Task Force Chairman) to David Garcia (Deputy City Manager), "Infill Housing Recommendations" and attached report, March 4, 1994. Office of the City Clerk, Phoenix.

————. 1994b. Frank Dolasinski (Business Assistance Administrator) to Raymond Bladine (Deputy City Manager), "Infill Housing Program," October 28, 1994. Office of the City Clerk, Phoenix.

————. 1995. Frank Dolasinski (Business Assistance Administrator) to Raymond Bladine (Deputy City Manager), "Infill Housing Program - Stage I: Fee Waivers - Detailed Report," January 11, 1995. Office of the City Clerk, Phoenix.

————. 1996. Frank Dolasinski (Business Assistance Adminstrator) to Raymond F. Bladine (Deputy City Manager), "Infill Housing Program - Status Report," May 15, 1996. Office of the City Clerk, Phoenix.

————. 1997. Frank Dolasinski (Business Assistance Adminstrator) to George Britton (Deputy City Manager), "Status Report and Modifications to the Infill Housing Program," October 14, 1997. Office of the City Clerk, Phoenix.

————. 1998. David Richert (Planning Director) to Jack Tevlin (Deputy City Manager), "Phoenix at a Crossroads - A Strategic View of Growth," February 11, 1998. Office of the City Clerk, Phoenix.

————. 1999. Mitchell Hayden (Acting Business Assistance Administrator) to George W. Britton (Deputy City Manager), "Infill Housing Program - Status Report and Potential Barriers to Infill Development," March 4, 1999. Office of the City Clerk, Phoenix.

————. [2000]. Mitchell Hayden (Acting Business Assistance Administrator) to

George W. Britton (Deputy City Manager), "Request for Contingency Funds for the Infill Housing Program." Consent Agenda. Agenda Date: Add on March 1, 2000. Office of the City Clerk, Phoenix.

City of Phoenix. 1985. *General Plan for Phoenix, 1985–2000.* Adopted by the City Council October 2, 1985.

———. 1987. Ordinances of the Council, Ordinance No. G 3040, adopted July 22, 1987. Office of the City Clerk, Phoenix.

———. 1989. *General Plan for Phoenix, 1985–2000: General Plan Summary and Land Use Map.* Adopted by the City Council October 2, 1985; July 1989 revision.

———. 2000a. City Statistics. At http://www.ci.phoenix.az.us/CITYGOV/stats.html.

———. 2000b. Infill Housing Program Incentives. At http://www.ci.phoenix.az.us/BUSINESS/inflinct.html.

City of Phoenix Development Services Department. 2000. "Phoenix Development Impact Fee Program." Development Services Department, City of Phoenix.

City of Phoenix Planning Commission. 1994. Planning Commission Notes, 4:00 p.m. Briefing Session, July 13, 1994. Office of the City Clerk, Phoenix.

City of Phoenix Planning Commission and Planning Department. 1986, 1987, 1988, 1993, 1995, 1996, 1997, 1998. *Annual Report.* Phoenix: City of Phoenix Planning Commission and Planning Department.

City of Phoenix Planning Department. 1987. *General Plan: Peripheral Areas C and D.* Phoenix: City of Phoenix Planning Department.

———. 1994. "Planning Department Staff Report for Planning Commission Hearing of March 23, 1994," n.d. Filed with "Notice of Public Meeting of the City of Phoenix Planning Commission [on March 23, 1994]," February 18, 1994. Office of the City Clerk, Phoenix.

———. 1995. "Urban Infill Strategies, Phase I: Opportunities, Barriers, Process." March.

———. [c. 1997]. *Baseline Area Master Plan.* Phoenix: City of Phoenix Planning Department.

———. 1999. *North Black Canyon Corridor Plan.* Phoenix: City of Phoenix Planning Department.

———. 2000. "Strategic View of Growth," in Phoenix Preservation, Growth, and Redevelopment, Version 3. CD-ROM. Revised March 2000 (originally prepared March 1998).

Clawson, Marion. 1962. "Urban Sprawl and Speculation in Suburban Land." *Land Economics* 38(2), pp. 99–111.

Design Workshop, Inc. 1995. *Desert Spaces: An Open Space Plan for the Maricopa Association of Governments.* Final report prepared for the Maricopa Association of Governments by Design Workshop, Inc. in association with Cornoyer-Hedrick, SWCA Environmental Consultants, BBC

Research & Consulting, Research Advisory Services, and Streich Lang. Tempe, AZ.: Maricopa Association of Governments.

Doerfler, Sue. 1997. "Filling in the Blanks; as Land Becomes Scarce, Infill Builders Look for Alternatives." *Arizona Republic*, November 8, p. AH1.

Downing, Paul B. and Richard D. Gustely. 1977. "The Public Service Costs of Alternative Development Patterns: A Review of the Evidence." In *Local Service Pricing Policies and Their Effect on Urban Spatial Structure*, ed. Paul B. Downing, pp. 63–86. Vancouver: University of British Columbia Press for the British Columbia Institute for Economic Policy Analysis.

Ellman, Tara. 1997. "Infill: The Cure for Sprawl?" Arizona Issue Analysis No. 146, Goldwater Institute, Phoenix. August.

Ewing, Reid H. 1994. "Characteristics, Causes, and Effects of Sprawl: A Literature Review." *Environmental and Urban Issues* 21(2), pp. 1–15.

Fimea, Mike. 2000. "Grassroots for Infill Involvement Essential to Project's Success." *Arizona Business Gazette*, April 13, p. 1.

Fiscal Impact Advisory Task Force. 1987. "Report and Recommendations of the Fiscal Impact Advisory Task Force," January 14, 1987. File: "Tatum Ranch," William Mee, City of Phoenix Planning Department.

Fischel, William A. 1985. *The Economics of Zoning Laws: A Property Rights Approach to American Land Use Controls*. Baltimore, MD: Johns Hopkins University Press.

Fischer, Howard. 1996. "Senate Kills Infill Incentives Plan State Will Pay More Later, Says Phoenix Mayor." *Arizona Business Gazette*, March 14, p. 9.

Fisher, Peter S. and Alan H. Peters. 1998. *Industrial Incentives: Competition among American States and Cities*. Kalamazoo, MI: W. E. Upjohn Institute for Employment Research.

Franciosi, Robert. 1997. "Can Infill Stop the City from Moving Out?" Perspectives on Public Policy No. 97–18, Goldwater Institute, Phoenix. August 14.

Frank, James E. 1989. *The Costs of Alternative Development Patterns: A Review of the Literature*. Washington, D.C.: Urban Land Institute.

Gammage, Grady, Jr. 1998. "Phoenix and the Vision Thing." In *Growth in Arizona: The Machine in the Garden*, pp. 61–66. Tempe, AZ: Morrison Institute for Public Policy, Arizona State University.

———. 1999. *Phoenix in Perspective: Reflections on Developing the Desert*. Tempe, AZ: Herberger Center for Design Excellence, College of Architecture and Environmental Design, Arizona State University.

Gober, Patricia, Elizabeth K. Burns, Kim Knowles-Yanez, and Jeffrey James. 1998. "Rural to Urban Land Conversion in Metropolitan Phoenix." In *Growth in Arizona: The Machine in the Garden*, pp. 40–45. Tempe, AZ: Morrison Institute for Public Policy, Arizona State University.

Gottschalk, Earl C., Jr. 1974. "Boom Town: Phoenix Area's Sprawl Worries City Planners But Not Its Citizenry." *Wall Street Journal*, June 18, p. 1.

Guillory, Renée. 1998. *Sprawl Costs Us All: A Citizens' Guide to the Hidden Costs of Sprawl and What We Can Do To Grow Responsibly.* Phoenix: Sierra Club Grand Canyon Chapter and Southwest Office.

Haines, Valerie A. 1986. "Energy and Urban Form: A Human Ecological Critique." *Urban Affairs Quarterly* 21(3), pp. 337–353.

Harvey, Robert O. and W. A. V. Clark. 1965. "The Nature and Economics of Urban Sprawl." *Land Economics* 41(1), pp. 1–9.

Housing and Neighborhoods Subcommittee, Phoenix City Council. 1994. Summary Minutes, November 2, 1994. Office of the City Clerk, Phoenix.

Ingley, Kathleen. 1994. "Growing Pains; Relentless Expansion Cuts Quality of Valley Life." *Arizona Republic*, September 25, p. A1.

Jackson, Kenneth T. 1985. *Crabgrass Frontier: The Suburbanization of the United States.* New York: Oxford University Press.

Jarman, Max. 1994. "Phoenix Weighs Infill Home Push But City Council Wary of Incentive Costs." *Arizona Business Gazette*, September 29, p. 1.

———. 1995. "Rethinking Development Fees Phoenix Considering Hikes for Assessments on Growth to North." *Arizona Business Gazette*, October 5, p. 12.

Kwok, Abraham. 1994a. "Council May Scrap Development Fees in Southwest Phoenix." *Arizona Republic*, May 3, p. B3.

———. 1994b. "Urban Planning Runs in Mayor Race." *Arizona Republic*, October 9, p. B1.

Lessinger, Jack. 1962. "The Case for Scatteration: Some Reflections on the National Capital Region *Plan for the Year 2000.*" *Journal of the American Institute of Planners* 28(3), pp. 159–169.

Luckingham, Bradford. 1989. *Phoenix: The History of a Southwestern Metropolis.* Tucson: University of Arizona Press.

Maricopa Association of Governments. 1993. *Update of the Population and Socioeconomic Database for Maricopa County, Arizona.* Phoenix: Maricopa Association of Governments.

———. 1998. *Urban Atlas: Phoenix Metropolitan Area.* Phoenix: Maricopa Association of Governments.

———. 1999. Summary Table 1-A, "October 27, 1995. Special Census Data and July 1, 1999 Resident Population and Housing Update." Prepared by Maricopa Association of Governments, November 2, 1999.

———. 2000. *Valley Vision 2025: Alternatives, Choices, Solutions.* Phoenix: Maricopa Association of Governments.

Maricopa County. 1997. *Maricopa County 2020, Eye to the Future.* Comprehensive Plan adopted October 20, 1997. Maricopa County, Arizona.

Maricopa County Board of Supervisors. 1991. Minute Book, Minutes for Formal Session, April 15, 1991, Formal Session, May 20, 1991, and Informal Session, May 23, 1991. Office of the Clerk of the Board, Maricopa County Board of Supervisors, Phoenix.

Maricopa County Department of Planning and Development. 1993a. Report to the Planning and Zoning Commission and Board of Supervisors, "County-wide Comprehensive Plan," for Planning and Zoning Commission Meeting Date: January 21, 1993, Agenda Item No: 1. File A 3420, "Comprehensive Plan County-wide." Office of the Clerk of the Board, Maricopa County Board of Supervisors, Phoenix.

Maricopa County Department of Planning and Development. 1993b. Report to the Planning and Zoning Commission and Board of Supervisors, for Planning and Zoning Commmission Meeting Date: June 3, 1993, Agenda Item No: 14, and attachments. File: "Large Scale Group." Maricopa County Department of Planning and Development, Phoenix.

Maricopa County Planning Commission. 1992. Extract of October 1, 1992, Planning Commission Minutes; Extract of October 15, 1992, Planning Commission Minutes. File A 3420, "Comprehensive Plan County-wide." Office of the Clerk of the Board, Maricopa County Board of Supervisors, Phoenix.

McGavin, Gregor. 1999. "Municipalities Trying to Limit Development." *Arizona Republic*, July 25, p. EV1.

McKinnon, Shaun. 1999. "Peoria Skips Developers' Fees as Quid Pro Quo, Businesses Commit to Build Projects." *Arizona Republic*, November 16, p. 7.

———. 2000a. "Rising Impact Fees West Valley Norm; Developers, New Homes at Issue." *Arizona Republic*, May 27, p. 9 (Chandler Community section).

———. 2000b. "Development Looking Inward; Incentives Used to Revitalize City Centers." *Arizona Republic*, May 31, p. 1 (Sun Cities/Surprise Community section).

Mee, Bill. 1997. "Phoenix Updates its Development Impact Fee Program." *Arizona Planner*, September/October, pp. 1, 5, 8.

Melnick, Rob. 1998. "Growing Smarter and the Citizens Growth Management Initiative: Early Lessons." In *Growth in Arizona: The Machine in the Garden*, pp. 199–200. Tempe, AZ: Morrison Institute for Public Policy, Arizona State University.

Morrison, Melissa. 2000. "A Sudden Oasis, or Just Sprawl?" *Washington Post*, June 5, p. A3.

Morrison Institute for Public Policy. 1999. *What Matters in Greater Phoenix: Indicators of Our Quality of Life*. Tempe, AZ: Morrison Institute for Public Policy, Arizona State University.

Nicholas, James C., Arthur C. Nelson, and Julian Conrad Juergensmeyer. 1991. *A Practitioner's Guide to Development Impact Fees*. Chicago: American Planning Association.

Ohls, James C. and David Pines. 1975. "Discontinuous Urban Development and Economic Efficiency." *Land Economics* 51(3), pp. 224–234.

Ottensmann, John R. 1977. "Urban Sprawl, Land Values and the Density of Development." *Land Economics* 53(4), pp. 389–400.

Padgett, Mike. 1995. "Home Builders Attracted to Infill Projects." *Arizona Republic*, March 15, p. 5.

Peiser, Richard B. 1989. "Density and Urban Sprawl." *Land Economics* 65(3), pp. 193–204.

Phoenix Gazette. 1995. "A Strong Endorsement for Planned Growth." Editorial/Opinion, April 6, p. B4.

Pitzl, Mary Jo. 1996a. "Urban Pioneers Discover City's Benefits." *Arizona Republic*, April 28, p. A1.

———. 1996b. "Ex-Mayor: Infill Could Make Phoenix a True City." *Arizona Republic*, April 28, p. A21.

Quay, Ray. 1993. Ray Quay (Assistant Planning Director) to Planning Commisssion, "Initiation of Infrastructure Plan Amendment," September 1, 1993. Office of the City Clerk, Phoenix.

Raup, Philip M. 1975. "Urban Threats to Rural Lands: Background and Beginnings." *Journal of the American Institute of Planners* 41(6), pp. 371–378.

Real Estate Research Corporation. 1982. *Infill Development Strategies.* Washington, D.C.: Urban Land Institute and American Planning Association.

Rex, Tom. 1998. "Growth Brings Uneven Benefits for Arizonans." In *Growth in Arizona: The Machine in the Garden*, pp. 49–58. Tempe, AZ: Morrison Institute for Public Policy, Arizona State University.

Rimsza, Skip. 1994. Councilman Skip Rimsza (Chair, Subcommittee on the Economy) to Frank Fairbanks (City Manager), "Update on Infill Incentives," February 11, 1994. Office of the City Clerk, Phoenix.

Rubin, Barry M. and Margaret G. Wilder. 1989. "Urban Enterprise Zones: Employment Impacts and Fiscal Incentives." *Journal of the American Planning Association* 55(4), pp. 418–431.

Sargent, Charles S., Jr. 1973. *Planned Communities in Greater Phoenix: Origins, Functions and Control.* Papers in Public Administration No. 25. Tempe, AZ: Institute of Public Administration, Arizona State University.

———. 1976a. "Land Speculation and Urban Morphology." In *Urban Policymaking and Metropolitan Dynamics: A Comparative Geographical Analysis*, ed. John S. Adams, pp. 21–57. Cambridge, MA: Ballinger.

———. 1976b. "Arizona's Urban Frontier: Myths and Realities." In *The Conflict Between Frontier Values and Land-Use Control in Greater Phoenix*, ed. Charles S. Sargent, pp. 4–23. Phoenix: Arizona Council on the Humanities and Public Policy.

Subcommittee on the Economy, Phoenix City Council. 1994. Summary Minutes, March 8, 1994. Office of the City Clerk, Phoenix.

Urban Form Directions Committees. 1975. *Urban Form Directions: Committee Reports.* Phoenix: Phoenix Planning Commission.

U.S. Bureau of the Census. 1993. *1990 Census of Population and Housing: Population and Housing Unit Counts, United States*, 1990 CPH-2-1. Washington, D.C.: U.S. Government Printing Office.

Wenum, John D. 1970. *Annexation as a Technique for Metropolitan Growth:*

The Case of Phoenix, Arizona. Tempe, AZ: Institute of Public Administration, Arizona State University.

Western Management Consultants, Inc. 1965. *The Economy of Maricopa County, 1965 to 1980.* Phoenix: Western Management Consultants, Inc.

Worden, Marshall A. and David A. de Kok. 1996. "Agents, Strategies and Proposals for Managing the Impacts of Growth." In *Arizona's Growth and the Environment—A World of Difficult Choices*, pp. 181–203. Sixty-Eighth Arizona Town Hall, May 5–8, 1996. Phoenix: Arizona Town Hall.

A City without Slums

Urban Renewal, Public Housing, and Downtown Revitalization in Kansas City, Missouri

By KEVIN FOX GOTHAM*

ABSTRACT. Most scholarly efforts to understand the political economy of postwar urban redevelopment have typically viewed urban renewal and public housing as "housing" programs that originated with the "federal" government. Yet this view is problematic for two reasons. First, it fails to specify the key actors and organized interests, especially real estate officials and downtown business elites, in the programmatic design and implementation of urban renewal and public housing. Second, this view does not fully acknowledge the dislocating and segregative effects of urban renewal and public housing on central city neighborhoods and the role these private-public initiatives played in shaping demographic and population patterns in the postwar era. I draw upon archival data and newspaper articles, real estate industry documents, government reports, and interviews to examine the origin, local implementation, and segregative effects of urban renewal and public housing in Kansas City, Missouri. I explore the role of the ideology of privatism—the underlying commitment by the public sector to enhancing the growth and prosperity of private institutions—in shaping the postwar "system" of urban economic development in which urban renewal and public housing were formulated and implemented. Focusing on the interlocking nature of race and class, I identify the critical links between urban renewal and public housing, and the long-term impact of these programs on metropolitan development in the decades after World War II.

* Kevin Fox Gotham is an assistant professor of sociology at Tulane University in New Orleans. His research interests include the political economy of real estate, housing policy and housing finance, and the redevelopment of public housing. He is currently investigating the impact of city revitalization efforts and pro-growth strategies on metropolitan development, gentrification, and neighborhood socio-economic stability.

American Journal of Economics and Sociology, Vol. 60, No. 1 (January, 2001).

I

Introduction

THIS PAPER EXAMINES THE ORIGIN, LOCAL IMPLEMENTATION, AND segregative effects of post-World War II urban renewal and public housing, using a case study of Kansas City, Missouri. During the 1930s and later, many American cities began to experience increasing physical deterioration of their core neighborhoods and commercial districts, forced concentration of inner city blacks into crowded areas, and loss of population and industry (Banfield and Wilson 1963; Silver 1984; Mollenkopf 1983; Teaford 1990). In the middle 1930s, urban leaders and real estate industry spokespersons, especially those affiliated with the National Association of Real Estate Boards (NAREB), began calling for the federal government to curb the ruinous effects of urban decay, revitalize the central city, and protect downtown real estate investments. Much of the real estate industry's lobbying efforts from the 1930s through the 1950s included the development of a series of policy proposals that could facilitate public acquisition of slum land in blighted areas for clearance and resale to private builders (Davies 1958, pp. 182–185). These proposals included state acts empowering municipalities to redevelop blighted areas, close public-private coordination of urban land-use and control, long-term federal loans to cities at low interest rates, and generous tax subsidies and write-offs for local redevelopers—proposals that in time would become a hallmark of urban revitalization schemes throughout the nation and profoundly affect population and demographic trends and the spatial transformation of central cities in the postwar era (Barnekov, Boyle, and Rich 1989, pp. 38–39; Gelfand 1975, pp. 151–156, 275–276; Hays 1985, chapter 5; Kleniewski 1984; Weiss 1980; see Wilson 1966 for an overview).

Up to now, most scholarly efforts to understand the political economy of postwar urban redevelopment have typically viewed urban renewal and public housing as "housing" programs that originated with the "federal" government (Hays 1985; Teaford 1990; Anderson 1964). In many accounts, scholars argue that federal officials and policy makers designed urban renewal and public housing to improve the living conditions of the poor and that the programs "failed" to meet their objectives (Bauman 1987; Von Hoffman 2000; Teaford 2000, 1990). I argue that this view is problematic for two reasons. First, it neglects to identify the key private actors and organized interests, especially real estate officials and downtown business elites, in the formulation and implementation of urban renewal and their opposition to public housing. As I show in this paper, the NAREB was a key lobbying force behind the development and passage of the urban renewal legislation, and a powerful opponent of public housing. The 1949 and 1954 Housing Acts provided federal funds for local redevelopment authorities to designate "blighted" areas, acquire and clear land, and then sell the land to private developers or local housing authorities for public housing. The Housing Act of 1954 changed the name of the program from "urban redevelopment" to "urban renewal," empowered municipalities to redevelop blighted areas, and drastically reduced the funds to build public housing. As I show, the major outlines of the 1949 and 1954 Acts appeared at least as early as 1941 in the NAREB's plans and reports for developing the means of teaming state action and private enterprise to carry out large-scale clearance of slum areas (Davies 1958, pp. 182–185; Weiss 1980). By the time the bills that were to become the Housing Acts of 1949 and 1954 had reached Congress, leading officials within the real estate industry had already set the basic agenda and legislation. There were disagreements over administrative issues but not basic policy goals.

Second, while researchers have investigated the failure of urban renewal and redevelopment programs to revitalize cities and urban neighborhoods, they have yet to examine the impact of urban renewal and public housing in concentrating the poor in the central city while allowing the middle class to escape to the suburbs. Using a case study of Kansas City, Missouri, I explore the impact of urban renewal and public housing on central city neighborhoods and the role these private-public initiatives played in transforming demographic, socioeconomic, and population patterns in the postwar era. In 1940, Kansas City contained approximately 430,000 residents living within 60 miles. The city was a clearly bounded spatial form that dominated, in both an emotional and economic sense, the areas surrounding it. Two decades later, urbanized development extended over 100 miles around the central city and contained a mix of independent cities, decentralized housing and business patterns, sprawling suburbs, and the emergence of outlying centers of metropolitan dominance not controlled by the central city. By this time, more parts of the Kansas City area were losing population than were gaining, thus hollowing out the urban core and expanding what planners call the "hole in the donut." For Kansas City, the two decades after World War II represented the beginnings of a long-term demise of the downtown as the economic nucleus of the city and the gradual eclipse of the central city by the suburbs. Today, its suburbs are no longer extensions of the central city but are autonomous and self-sufficient political entities that provide many of the educational and employment resources, shopping facilities, professional services, and entertainment amenities that once drew residents into downtown. My goal is to link the process of metropolitan transformation in Kansas City in part to the local implementation of the urban renewal and public housing programs. I identify the critical links between urban renewal and public housing and their impact on metropolitan development.

In the following section I discuss my theoretical orientation. I then examine the mobilization of real estate officials, central city businessmen, and the lobbying efforts of the NAREB for government assistance in remedying physical deterioration and reclaiming blighted land for private development. As I show, postwar urban renewal and redevelopment rested upon an ideology of *privatism* that assumed giving generous public subsidies to the private sector to designate, acquire, and clear residential land for redevelopment could reverse urban obsolescence. It was during the 1940s and 1950s that the term "downtown redevelopment" entered the glossary of city planning and implied an amalgam of land-use control techniques aimed at restoring economic vitality to the core city. Local real estate elites and city officials advanced the proposition that the Central Business District (CBD) is the heart of the metropolitan area and based all planning decisions on the need to preserve and enhance its development and prosperity (City Plan Commission 1956; Cookingham 1954, p. 144). By the early 1950s, it was fashionable for major urban elites and powerful private investors to champion government largess and call for federal intervention to revitalize central city property values. I then discuss the local implementation and segregative effects of urban renewal and public housing in Kansas City. Drawing upon archival data and newspaper articles, real estate industry documents, planning reports, and interviews, I examine the key actors, important decisions, and political struggles surrounding urban renewal displacement and public housing site selection in the 1950s and 1960s.[1] Finally, I discuss the impact of urban renewal and public housing in contributing to the class and racial segmentation of U.S. society in the decades after World War II.

II

Privatism and the Political Economy of Postwar Urban Redevelopment

THROUGHOUT THE POSTWAR ERA, government officials and policy makers designed public policy to stimulate and bolster private investment. Their objectives were congruent with an ideology of privatism that views the private sector as the most effective mechanism for the delivery of public services, the creation of stable and growing "markets," and the stimulation of local economic development. As discussed by Antonio and Bonanno (1997), Barnekov, Boyle, and Rich (1989), Squires (1994), and other sociologists, privatism is the underlying commitment by government to helping the private sector grow and prosper. It is an entrenched and deep-rooted belief in the supremacy of the private sector in nurturing societal development, with the public sector adopting a "hands-off" (laissez faire) strategy whose principal obligation is to encourage private profit. R. Allen Hays (1985, pp. 16–18) and Gregory Squires (1993; 1991, p. 197) identify three major assumptions that have historically been central to the ideology of privatism. First, because the desire for material well-being drives human productivity, the market must encourage and reward acquisitiveness and competitiveness. Second, "the free market is the most effective and least coercive mechanism for allocating goods and services since it harmonizes individual self interest with society's collective development." Third, "government's role is to reinforce and supplement the market in regulating exchange in a manner that maximizes individual freedom and choice" (Squires 1993, p. 136).

As the notion of privatism implies, government policy making may be narrowed by a biasing or filtering process whereby the state selects against some policy initiatives (e.g., market-centered public subsidies, tax breaks, and so on) while others are systematically ignored and never considered (e.g., direct state intervention and socialization of specific industries) (Hays 1985, p. 8). As Glasberg and Skidmore (1997, p. 21) recognize, the state and its policy making process are not neutral but "responsive to particular strategies and resources rather than to others; few of the possible policies and organizations surrounding a given issue receive serious political consideration." Over time, this "strategic selectivity" (Jessop 1990, p. 333) perpetuates biases that have asymmetical effects on the organization of state power, the unity and effectiveness of class segments, and the dominance of business elites (Glasberg and Skidmore 1997, p. 18; Barnekov and Rich 1977). Both local and national level governments and the ideology of privatism play a critical role in setting the rules and "greasing the skids" for business profitability (Feagin 1988, chapter 2). According to Barnekov and Rich (1989, p. 223), the ideology of privatism effectively depoliticizes policy making by systematically excluding all those voices and interests who reject the sanctity of the "free-market" and the desire to maximize private profits through the use of public policy and government subsidies. The effect is to insulate the government policy making process from public influence and scrutiny, stymie groups supporting alternative strategies, and promote policies that favor private actors and corporations rather than the public good.

As an ideology and political strategy, privatism has been the mechanism through which public policy and planning has traditionally reinforced social inequalities by dispensing public resources unequally (Gotham 2000; Squires 1994). In his historical account of urban development in the United States, Sam Bass Warner argues that "[w]hat the private market could do well, American cities have done well; what the private market did badly, or neglected, our cities have been unable to overcome" (1968, p. x). Evan McKenzie argues in *Privatopia: Homeowner Associations and the Rise of Residential Private Government* that "private developers and businessmen, rather than government, have long been the dominant forces in American urban planning" (1994, p. 7). The most activist public policies on housing, land-use regulation, and suburban development have historically involved insuring real estate firms and developers "against the consequences of their own mistakes so that profits remained in private hands while losses were socialized" (p. 104). Similarly, Dennis Judd (1984, pp. 412–413) maintains that "American urban growth has always been dictated by private institutions and not by public policies," because public policy "follows rather than precedes the activities of the entrepreneurs who have changed the urban landscape." Sociologists John Logan and Harvey Molotch (1987) observe that urban "growth machines" are composed mainly of private real estate interests, with local government officials playing a subservient role, operating as facilitators of private economic growth and development. Extensive research by Joe Feagin (1988) in his case study of growth politics in Houston suggests that while government officials are important actors in the land development process, the role of government is largely promotional rather than regulatory or directive.

Until now, few scholars have specified the role of the ideology of privatism in determining the programmatic shape and local implementation of urban renewal or have examined the impact of the program on metropolitan development. A number of historical studies have documented the role of powerful actors, such as urban mayors (Teaford 1990), federal officials and "political entrepreneurs" (Mollenkopf 1983), and real estate officials, in the development of postwar urban renewal and redevelopment (Weiss 1980; see Hirsch 1993 and Mohl 1993 for overviews). However, these studies have failed to theorize the relationship between the actions of powerful political and economic actors and the broader political economy of urban redevelopment, as well as the impact of privatism in shaping the urban redevelopment policy making process. A number of neo-Marxian scholars have attempted to develop a theoretical understanding of the role of urban renewal and public housing in the process of capital accumulation and labor control (Sawyers 1984; Cummings 1988). While these scholars have highlighted the unequal effects of the "capitalist" context of public policy, their accounts have been reductionistic—overemphasizing the power of class at the exclusion of other salient factors (race, gender, politics, culture, and ideology, among others), and homogenizing and totalizing the interests of "capital" by stressing its "need" for public coordination to maximize profits. Marxian scholars have made impressive contributions to the study of the land development process, the economic context of public policy, and the capitalist dynamics of urban credit markets (Gordon 1984; Storper 1984; Storper and Walker 1983; Castells 1977, 1983; Harvey 1973, 1976; Scott 1988). However, Marxian accounts have little to say about the political context of urban redevelopment and the ideology of privatism because these are not particularly relevant to the capitalist production process per se.

Although privatism draws inspiration from Marxian urban theory and analyses of capitalist dynamics, its pervasive influence as an ideology and "cultural tradition" (Warner 1987; Barnekov and Rich 1989) extends beyond Marxian categories and assumptions. Following Antonio and Bonanno (1997), Warner (1987), and Barnekov and Rich (1989), I view privatism as a set of cultural assumptions and social expectations that have shaped and constrained policy making and private and public actions within the political economy of urban redevelopment. It is the task of this paper to illustrate the impact of privatism in shaping the postwar "system" of urban economic development in which federal slum clearance programs—urban renewal and public housing—were formulated and implemented.

III

Urban Blight, Decentralization, and the Real Estate Industry

BEGINNING IN THE 1930S, URBAN LEADERS BEGAN devising strategies to curb the ruinous effects of decentralization and blight that were endangering the economic stability and fiscal status of the central city. In New York, Chicago, Cincinnati, Philadelphia, Buffalo, and Atlanta, among other cities, real estate elites and planners recited the same litany of ills—declining population, dilapidated neighborhoods, declining property values and declining revenues from commercial and industrial sites, snarled traffic, and an increasingly "drab appearance" (see Teaford 1990 for an overview). The approach in Kansas City, Missouri reflected a national tendency to view deterioration of the CBD as symptomatic of a general urban malaise. The decay of the downtown was evident in figures showing that in the ten-year period after 1935 there had been a loss of 6% in assessed valuation in the CBD compared with a 0.5% loss in the entire city (City Plan Commission, October 1947; Anderson 1957, p. 128). Prominent real estate official J. C. Nichols argued that the CBD represented the "life-blood sections of the city,"[2] while City Manager L. Perry Cookingham believed that the CBD "is the core of operations—the nerve center —of the city and the metropolitan area" (Cookingham 1954, p. 142). For Cookingham, "blight" represented one of the most "difficult problems facing American cities today" that, if not arrested, would have corrosive effects "upon the value of the central business district in the city of the future" (ibid., p. 140). Throughout the 1930s and later, the official publication of the Kansas City, Missouri Real Estate Board, the *Kansas City Realtor*, published many articles and editorials lamenting the spread of blight and corrosive effect of slums on property values within the CBD. In many of its articles, the paper assailed blighted neighborhoods as physical threats to the financial viability of the CBD, an impediment to future growth and progress, and a cumbersome burden to the public treasury ("Campaign Against Decentralization," 2/15/40, p. 3; "Factors in Decentralization," 10/31/40, p. 4; "Remove Blight," 3/11/43; "Rebuilding of Blighted Areas," 6/17/43; "Real Slum Clearance," 1/27/44; "New Plan for Slum Clearance," 3/2/44).

On the national level, representatives of the NAREB bemoaned declining central city property values and recommended a vigorous attack on the problem of slum housing, obsolete building codes, pernicious tax policies, and oppressive state and local land-use regulations (Davies 1958, pp. 181–185). The future of central cities focused on two major fears: the decentralization of people and industry, and the social, economic, and political deterioration of the historic downtown. As early as 1932, the NAREB and its affiliated organizations called for government assistance to simplify and coordinate local building codes to promote new building and urban revitalization. In 1936, the NAREB's Committee on Housing recommended that local government acquire land, undertake demolition, and "sell or lease it back to private enterprise for the construction of housing or business facilities. In no case would it be wise for local government to erect housing structures of any kind, either residential or business, and to attempt to operate them." As the NAREB saw it, "if municipalities need financial help in carrying forward demolition and land clearance of slum areas, we suggest that Federal loans or grants be available for such purposes" ("New Low-Cost Housing Plan Is Proposed," 1936, p. 2).

In 1939, the NAREB formed a research agency, the Urban Land Institute (ULI), to study and research the causes and consequences of urban blight and to identify the policy and financial tools needed to curb the ruinous effects of decentralization (Weiss 1980). The ULI undertook as its first major research project a study of blight and decentralization in 221 cities (Urban Land Institute 1940a). During the next two years the ULI published case studies on Boston, Cincinnati, Detroit, Louisville, Milwaukee, New York, and Philadelphia, recommending a plan whereby cities could condemn land in the blighted areas near the CBD and then sell or lease the land to private developers for replanning and rebuilding (Urban Land Institute 1940b; 1941a; 1941b; 1941c; 1941d; 1942a; 1942b). Government aid and subsidies, the ULI maintained, would be necessary to revitalize the central city, eliminate blight, and maintain profitable land sales and real estate markets. According a 1940 report by the ULI,

> [e]stablished business districts are affected adversely and severely when decentralization within a city takes place at an overrapid rate. But the causes of their loss of business volume may lie largely in the decay of residential areas whose former residents have moved farther out. Action with sufficient scope to ease the transition and present huge and unnecessary losses will require co-ordinated effort of business groups, owners of property, and governmental bodies ("Urban Land Institute Formed," 1940, p. 4).

By the early 1940s, local and national real estate elites openly called for federal and local government assistance in revitalizing downtown business districts and eliminating blighted areas ("Plan To Rebuild City Blighted Areas," 1941). In 1941, the Federal Housing Administration (FHA) released a report, *A Handbook for Urban Redevelopment for Cities in the United States*, proposing the use of federal subsidies and granting the power of eminent domain to local agencies to acquire and clear blighted land and sell it for reuse (Rowe 1995, pp. 177–178). A year later, at the January-February meeting of the ULI in Chicago, real estate industry officials recommended a "concerted onslaught on eliminating blighted districts in the nation's cities" through the creation of a "federal urban land commission" that would have the powers and funds "for the purpose of acquiring land in blighted areas for redevelopment by private enterprise" ("Land Institute Proposes Huge Replanning Program,"1942, p. 2). In 1944, the NAREB proposed that state governments create "Municipal Redevelopment Authorities" which would have power of eminent domain and the right to issue re-development bonds ("New Plan for Slum Clearance," 1944, p. 2). NAREB representatives at the congressional hearings on the General Housing Act of 1945 testified that federal financial assistance and sub-sidies should in the form of outright grants with no stipulations or conditions attached (Bauman 1981, p. 7).

During the 1930s and 1940s, members of the NAREB and down-town business elites agreed that state action—through eminent do-main and public subsidies for private revitalization—was necessary to counter the specter of urban blight and obsolescence. Yet a number of problems forestalled private efforts to harness the legal and financial power of the local state to undertake slum clearance. First, private in-terests proved incapable of acquiring land in large enough parcels to permit large-scale revitalization. Second, the most desirable inner city land sought by downtown businesses tended to be residential land-use. Hence, private business did not have the organizational ca-pacity or legal right to acquire such properties. Financing also proved to be a major problem since few private firms and redevelopers pos-sessed the huge cash reserve necessary to pay for clearance and revi-talization (Davies 1958, pp. 183–184). Thus, while real estate elites wholeheartedly supported public-private action for urban revitaliza-tion, the existing political structure in many local areas of the country did not possess the legal or fiscal capacity to undertake large-scale slum clearance and redevelopment during the 1930s and 1940s (Hirsch 1993, pp. 87–88; Gelfand 1975, pp. 151–156, 275–276; Hays 1985, chapter 5; Kleniewski 1984; Weiss 1980; Wilson 1966).

In many cities, public housing provided a partial answer to the prob-lem of freeing inner city land for private development. The Housing Act of 1937 empowered local communities to create local housing au-thorities with the legal power of eminent domain to acquire pri-vately-owned land for slum clearance and rehousing (McDonnell 1957; Bauman 1987, pp. 40–42). By the mid-1940s, a number of cities and states had passed legislation to enable local governments to designate, acquire, and clear "slum" areas and sell the land to private developers.

Yet early on there were opposing views over whether public housing legislation was supposed to be "housing" legislation or whether it was "slum clearance" legislation (Hoffman 1996, p. 425; Marcuse 1986; Jackson 1985, chapter 12). Proponents of public housing, including progressive housing advocates, social workers, and union officials, argued for the federal government's building low-rent housing for the working and middle class (Bauman 1987, 1981). On the other hand, real estate industry and home building officials rejected a strong federal role and embraced a privatist vision of slum clearance with no government regulations on private redevelopment. The NAREB favored a trickle down model of housing distribution, where excess production of suburban housing would free up dwelling units at the lower end of the housing market for low-income families displaced by slum clearance (Keith 1973, pp. 28–39; Davies 1958, pp. 180–182; Gelfand 1975, pp. 184–204; Checkoway 1984).

Throughout and after the 1930s the NAREB and real estate elites attacked the view of public housing shared by labor unions, social workers, and housing activists as "creeping socialism" and opposed any federal building of low-income housing on the grounds that it would put the government in competition with private housing construction and real estate (Keith 1973, pp. 30–38, 94–95; Bratt 1986, pp. 336–337; Bauman 1981, p. 8). Seward H. Mott, head of the ULI, argued before Congress in 1945 that public housing is "a failure . . . It has not taken care of the people it should have, it is building political constituencies founded on shelter, it puts a premium on dependency . . . We don't believe in it . . . and we challenge it as a social policy" (U.S. Senate 1945, p. 1603; Bauman 1981, p. 8). In January 1947, Herbert U. Nelson, Executive Vice-President of the NAREB, proposed that "no further funds should be appropriated for public housing" because "public housing is European socialism in its most insidious form" ("Nelson Proposes Eight-Point Plan to Beat Shortage," 1947). The philosophy of the NAREB was that the private sector should dictate and control government aid. As Nelson put it in 1950, "I do not oppose government intervention in housing. I only believe that the powers of government should be used to assist private enterprise" (quoted in Abrams 1971, p. 154). By the early 1950s, the NAREB and its affiliate organizations had succeeded in defining the problem of urban blight and decentralization as a "slum clearance" and urban redevelopment problem. Advocates for low-income housing for working class and poor families were relegated the margins of policy debates and organized labor, housing reformers, civil rights activists, and interracial housing advocates had little input on the development of subsequent housing legislation (Bauman 1981, 1987).

The Housing Acts of 1949 and 1954 represented the culmination of real estate industry lobbying efforts to curtail the production of public housing, create local redevelopment authorities with broad powers of eminent domain, and provide generous public subsidies for private redevelopment. Title I of the 1949 Act financed slum clearance. Title II raised by $500 million the amount the Federal Housing Administration (FHA) was allowed to offer as mortgage insurance. Title III authorized the federal government to build 810,000 new public housing units over the next ten years and required local public housing authorities to demolish or renovate one slum dwelling for every public housing unit they built. Title IV provided for funds to conduct research into the economics of housing construction, markets, and financing. Title V reorganized and expanded the loan program initiated under the Farm Tenant Act of 1937 which allowed farmers to purchase and improve loans. The Housing Act of 1954 broadened the urban renewal program, increased funding for federal home financing activities, and established the first specific housing for elderly citizens through the public housing program. Due to opposition from the real estate industry, public housing never came close to the construction levels provided in the 1949 Act (810,000 units). By 1960, only 250,000 units had been made available (Mitchell, 1985, pp. 9–11). While the stated goal of Housing Acts of 1949 and 1954 was "[t]o provide a decent home and suitable environment for every American family," urban leaders and real estate elites considered the Acts less as a "housing" program and more of urban "redevelopment" program.

IV

Implementation and Dislocating Effects

IN 1953, THE STATE OF MISSOURI CREATED THE Land Clearance for Redevelopment Authority (LCRA) for planning and administering local urban renewal activities including slum clearance of blighted neighborhoods according to the Housing Acts of 1949 and 1954. While the preamble to the Housing Act of 1949 called for a "decent home" as the official goal of federal policy, local real estate officials and downtown business elites looked to the Act as a policy mechanism for eliminating blighted land-uses surrounding the CBD and using federal subsidies to engineer downtown growth ("Slum Law Legal," 1954). The city government established the LCRA as a separate legal entity not directly responsible to City Hall or the city manager but to its own board, composed of leaders from the private sector (Land Clearance for Redevelopment Authority 1969). While the federal government provided the bulk of the funding, important decisions about site selection and size and project cost and duration were left to LCRA officials working with closely with downtown business interests, including the Downtown Committee (renamed the Downtown Redevelopment Corporation [DRC] in 1952), the Building Owners and Managers Association, the Citizens Regional Planning Council, the Hotel Association, the Chamber of Commerce, and the Merchants Association (Bohanon 1971, pp. 66–67, 88–94, 100–109). The federal government supplied two-thirds of the $80 million to finance Kansas City's urban renewal activities from 1953 through the end of the 1960s. However, federal officials played a decidedly subordinate role, leaving key decision making to the LCRA while supplying vast financial resources for urban redevelopment.

The initiation of large-scale slum clearance and public housing building in the early 1950s represented the beginning of a dramatic socio-spatial transformation of the urban core that would continue over the next two and a half decades. In March 1950, a journalist for *Holiday* observed that "Kansas City is marked by sharp physical contrasts. There are tenements only a few blocks from skyscrapers, the landscaped lands of elaborate homes face vacant lots cluttered with billboards, and there are area shanties only a short distance outside the business district" (quoted in Brown and Dorsett 1978, p. 258). A few short years later urban renewal was reshaping the downtown core as residential neighborhoods were cleared to make way for new commercial and industrial land use (Cookingham 1958). Very early, urban renewal received unabashed support from the *Kansas City Times* and

Kansas City Star with such celebratory headlines as "A Dream City Without Slums" (12/19/52), "Out of the Rubble a New Kansas City Rises"(6/1/58), "Kansas City's Battle on Blight is a Major Feat" (1/3/60), "To Redeem the Whole West Side" (7/6/53), "Praise Kansas City Renewal Projects"(5/2/59), "City Faces Great Era" (10/1/58), "Slums on the Retreat" (3/7/56), and "Slum War is On" (7/3/55) (Bohanon 1971, pp. 66–67, 88–94, 100–109). As one 1958 editorial proclaimed,

> You see it everywhere around you, the building drama of the dynamic city. The earth vibrates with the great machines of progress. A wrecker's weight smashes a wall. A few weeks later a new structure rises . . . A few men of vision believed that blight could be stopped. Today we can see the promise for the future. Civic enterprise is on the move. Before our eyes, a great city is being remade for the 20th century ("Out of the Rubble a New Kansas City Rises," 1958).

So impressive were Kansas City's slum clearance efforts that in 1958 *Look* magazine awarded the city the Community Home Achievement Award for reclamation and redevelopment of slum areas ("City Honored for Face Lift," 1958; "Award for a Program that is Rebuilding a City," 1958). In 1959, the American Institute of Architects (AIA) awarded the Kansas City AIA chapter the Citation of Honor Award, an honor given only fifteen times in the previous 102 years, for its comprehensive plan for downtown revitalization ("Architects Group Given High Honor," 1959). During the 1950s Kansas City's renewal efforts equally impressed federal and municipal leaders from around the country, including mayors, planners, and other elites from Lincoln, Tulsa, Milwaukee, Akron, New York, Omaha, Minneapolis, Louisville, Dallas, Indianapolis, Chicago, Denver, St. Louis, and Memphis ("Vitality in City Growth," 1957; "City Impresses Urban Leaders," 1959; "Praise Kansas City Renewal Projects," 1959; "Hail Vital City Pride," 1957; "Writers Laud City Renewal Action," 1957; "Urban Plan as Model," 1958).

Despite the fanfare and publicity, large-scale slum clearance did not benefit everyone living in the city. From the middle 1950s through the late 1960s, urban renewal uprooted thousands of residents living in the downtown core, transforming their residential neighborhoods into industrial and commercial land-uses. Table 1 lists individual urban re-

Table 1

Urban Renewal Projects in Kansas City, Missouri, 1954-1969

	Project Duration	Acreage	Displacement			Total Businesses
			Blacks	Whites	Total	
Northside	1953-60	6.6	88	432	520	71
Attucks	1955-65	54.2	478	0	478	85
South Humbolt	1956-65	27.6	28	203	231	66
Eastside	1958-65	58.3	88	582	670	95
Woodland	1963-65	46.3	58	162	220	23
Garfield	1963-65	206.6	0	131	131	0
Hospital Hill	1965-67	36.8	46	47	93	29
W. Main	1964-66	3.3	0	27	27	58
Trinity-St. Mary's	1966-72	22.5	1	159	160	48
Manual	1966-72	86.5	320	4	324	113
Town Fork Creek	1967-72	654.8	NA	NA	62	2
Independence Plaza	1968-72	259.8	NA	NA	387	47

Columbus Park	1968-72	146.5	0	59	59	18
Attucks East	1968-72	103.8	367	129	496	33
CBD	1968-72	284.7	0	6	6	14
East 23rd	1968-72	857.8	NA	NA	218	4
Oak Park	1968-72	2241.1	NA	NA	5	0
12th and Vine	1969-72	33.1	309	19	328	49
Total		5130.3	1783	1960	4415	755

Sources: Bohanon. 1971, p. 175; Land Clearance for Redevelopment Authority. Report on Urban Renewal Activities, 1955-72. LCRA to HUD, 2/12/73. "Status of Real Estate and Rehabilitation Activities in Kansas City's Uncompleted Urban Renewal Projects." Mid-America Urban Observatory, 2/74; Memorandum from A. J. Harmon, Executive Director and Council, LCRA, to Honorable Charles Hazley, Chairman, Plans and Zoning Committee. 2/12/73. X2814. Box 210. KC 250. Arthur A. Benson, II. Legal Papers. WHMC-KC; X353G. Comparison of Households Relocated by LCRA of Kansas City, Missouri From Clearance Urban Renewal Projects and Households Living in Area Prior to Clearance. Exhibit prepared by Yale Rabin. Sources: LCRA and Central Relocation Agency Annual Reports, Census of Population 1950, 1960, 1970, and Census Block Data. Box 201. KC 250. Arthur A. Benson, II. Legal Papers. WHMC-KC. In 1966, all on-going urban renewal projects were converted into the Neighborhood Development Program (NDP), a comprehensive program of neighborhood redevelopment where planning and budgetary priority was shifted away from financing and redeveloping slum clearance projects toward rehabilitation and conservation of housing.

newal projects launched in the 1950s through the late 1960s, showing the total acres of each individual project, and the number of blacks, whites, and businesses displaced in each urban renewal area.

As Table 1 shows, the LCRA launched eighteen urban renewal projects from 1953 to 1969. The first area designated for slum clearance was the Northside area, with the Attucks, South Humbolt, and Eastside urban renewal projects following consecutively during the 1950s (Land Clearance for Redevelopment Authority 1954). The purpose of the 54.2 acre Attucks project was to clear predominantly black neighborhoods adjacent to the downtown. The 6.6 acre Northside area was cleared to provide parking lots near the downtown while the 85.9 acres cleared for the South Humbolt and Eastside renewal projects were to expedite construction of the downtown freeway loop (Land Clearance for Redevelopment Authority 1969; Anderson 1957; "A Northside OK," 1953; "Old Northside Gone," 1954; "Attucks Ordinance In," 1954; "East Side Renewal Project Gets OK," 1956; "Old North Side Gone," 1954; "Start Near on Huge City Job," 1956; "Modern Look for Northside Horizon," 1957).

Besides the Attucks, Northside, South Humbolt, and Eastside urban renewal projects, the LCRA initiated fourteen more major redevelopment projects in the 1960s. These included the Woodland (46.3 acres), Garfield (206.6 acres), Hospital Hill (36.8 acres), West Main (3.3 acres), Trinity-St. Mary's (22.5 acres), Manual (86.5 acres), Town Fork Creek (654.8 acres), Independence Plaza (259.8 acres), Columbus Park (146.5 acres), Attucks East (103.8 acres), the CBD itself (284.7 acres), East 23rd Street (857.8 acres), Oak Park (2241.1 acres), and 12th and Vine (33.1 acres) (Land Clearance for Redevelopment Authority 1969). As Table 1 shows, urban renewal displaced thousands of individuals and businesses, including 1783 blacks, 1960 whites, and 755 businesses. Of those urban renewal projects reporting data on numbers of displaced blacks and whites, 48 percent of those displaced were blacks while whites made up 52 percent of displacees.

To qualify for federal urban renewal subsidies through the Housing Acts of 1949 and 1954, municipalities had to insure that a sufficient supply of replacement housing would be available to families displaced by slum clearance (Gelfand 1975, chapter 6; Hirsch 1993, pp. 85–86; Pynoos, Schafer, and Hartman 1973). Throughout the 1950s and up to 1964, the Housing Authority of Kansas City, Missouri (HAKC) segregated its public housing residents by race. By 1954, the HAKC had three major public housing projects—Guinotte Manor (454 units) and Riverview (232 units) built in 1954 and 1952 "for whites" and T. B Watkins Homes (462 units) built in 1953 for "Negro families." Projects in planning or under construction during this time included Wayne Miner Court (738 units) for blacks and Chouteau Court (140 units), West Bluff (139 units), and Pennway Plaza (250 units) for whites and minorities other than blacks (Housing Authority of Kansas City, Missouri 1953, 1956, 1957; "Three Public Housing Sites on Fringe of Downtown Area," 1957).

The question of where to build public housing was a source of bitter controversy during the 1950s and 1960s. While middle class whites opposed predominantly black public housing in their neighborhoods, in many cases middle class blacks objected to the same public housing in their own neighborhoods, revealing that class as well as racial conflicts were central to the public housing controversy. In response, the HAKC built all of its housing developments within six miles of each other, thus concentrating public housing in the city. During this time, the Greater Kansas City Urban League and the local African American newspaper, the *Kansas City Call*, repeatedly voiced opposition to the HAKC's segregative public housing site selections and demanded that housing authority officials build public housing on vacant land outside the city ("Interracial Housing Project in Order," 1953; "Speaking the Public Mind," 1952; "Oppose a Housing Sit," 1950). In 1953, the *Kansas City Call* castigated the "rigid pattern of segregation which the Housing Authority has adopted in the operation of Kansas City's low rent housing projects." It is "unfair and unrealistic," as the *Call* lamented, for the HAKC to expect the Watkins project "to take care of the housing needs all over the city." A year later, the *Call* expressed outrage at the HAKC's policy that black families displaced by urban renewal and public housing construction "will be housed in the Watkins project which means that some of the families in the central Negro area which would normally have secured housing there will not be accepted because there will not be enough units to take care of all" ("Segregation in Housing Must Go," 1954, p. 22).

Like other cities, Kansas City's urban renewal clearance activities frequently did low-income residents and racial minorities substantial harm, forcing them to sever neighborhood ties, and channeling them into inferior and substandard housing and segregated neighborhoods. During the late 1960s through the 1970s, the Missouri Commission on Human Relations, the City's Temporary Advisory Commission on Housing (TACH), the City's Model Cities agency, and the Department of Housing and Urban Development (HUD) cited the LCRA for numerous and repeated violations of federal regulations and civil rights statutes in its relocation program.[3] Based on a series of investigations, in June 1973, HUD found that the LCRA was violating the 1964 and 1968 Civil Rights Acts for engaging in discriminatory relocation activities. HUD concluded that the "LCRA's urban renewal program has contributed to the development and perpetuation of racial housing patterns [and] has and will concentrate large segments of the population by racial . . . characteristics."[4]

A number of residents I interviewed recalled the destablizing effect of urban renewal on city neighborhoods. For example, a former assistant city manager and lifelong resident remembered that "urban renewal became the synonym for 'black removal' and it broke the back of black stable neighborhoods" (Alvin Brooks [pseud.], interview by author). Other residents remembered how urban renewal clearance destroyed many thriving black businesses and neighborhood convenience stores in the southeast fringes of the CBD. As the following black residents recalled:

> There had been semi-economic centers for black businesses that were around 12th Street, 18th Street, coming up Vine, say to 25th Street because I remember Barker's Market, Johnson's Drug Store, and a cab company and a bunch of stuff like that. And all of the clientele was in walking distance, mainly because in the 1940s and early 1950s . . . people lived closer together. With urban renewal and people moving out, they lost their clientele (Mary Jacqueline [pseud.], interview by author).

> All up and down Vine, which is two blocks away from here, there were thriving black businesses. There was a cab company, matter of fact there were two cab companies. One near 25th and Vine, the other at 24th and Vine. There was a thriving grocery store, a drive-in drug store, there were thriving businesses along here. But no more, they are just not here. The matter of urban renewal has not always served well the black community (Brian Charles [pseud.], interview by author).

> I remember many people called the urban renewal years urban removal years, because what occurred was large-scale removal of neighborhoods that were abolished under the guise of economic development and the core fabric of those communities was forever changed. . . . I remember very vividly those years because I was a product of the 1960s and was very active in the activities of those days, where there were dramatic demonstrations and protests regarding persons displeased with the plight of blacks living in the inner city. And so, when urban renewal, compounded with the introduction of the freeway system, came about little did many people realize the resulting impact and effect it would have on the destruction of core communities (Martin Fletch [pseud.], interview by author).

As these excerpts show, residents were familiar with the dislocating effects of urban renewal, the devastating impact of the program on inner city neighborhoods, and efforts of local groups and activists to halt the disruption of neighborhoods. In addition to the displacement of residential neighborhoods, a number of residents remembered how small business owners were forced to move to make way for parking lots and redevelopment for larger, nationally-based businesses. For some residents, the loss of small businesses and neighborhood grocery stores was equally traumatic as the displacement of people and houses was. Urban renewal not only dislocated residents but disrupted entire neighborhoods as residents were now forced to travel outside their neighborhoods to obtain groceries, clothes, and other services.

In Kansas City and other cities, urban renewal and public housing worked at cross-purposes with one another. The former displaced poor residents from their housing while the later concentrated them into crowded and deteriorating neighborhoods. No matter how much government officials proclaimed the Housing Act of 1949 to be a policy for a "decent home in a suitable living environment," the consequences of urban renewal were the removal of housing and the concentration of the poor in the central city. Different groups of actors had different motivations in attacking the problems of urban blight and obsolescence but effect was the same. Urban renewal officials and private real estate interests were motivated by profits and economic gain and public housing administrators segregated displaced residents in a racially unequal fashion. In many cities, including San Francisco, Chicago, and New York, blacks bore the burden of the dislocating effects of urban renewal, as local authorities converted slum clearance into "Negro clearance" along the very lines black leaders had feared (Gelfand 1975, p. 212; Hirsch 1983, 2000). Other ethnic groups suffered as well, including predominantly Italian-American residents in Boston's West End (Gans 1962) and Mexican-Americans in the Bunker Hill neighborhood in Los Angeles (Hines 1982). Although racial discrimination and segregation undoubtedly played a major role in shaping the experience of blacks and other ethnic and racial minorities, they remained closely intertwined with class. The urban poor of all races and ethnic groups were more likely to be displaced than those blacks and other minority groups living in affluent and upscale neighborhoods. Racial motivations on the part of government officials and profit motivations on the part of private developers combined to transform the central city and cement patterns of racial and class segregation in the postwar metropolis.

V

Discussion and Conclusion

IN SUM, THE TWO DECADES AFTER 1950 REPRESENTED AN ERA of slum clearance and public housing that dramatically transformed Kansas City's urban core, clearing away thousands of dwellings and converting low-income neighborhoods into industrial and commercial land-use. As this paper shows, in the 1950s and 1960s the city experienced a series of unprecedented socio-spatial changes, including a reorientation of downtown land-uses, large-scale slum clearance, and a restructuring of city government activities. In 1951, the City Council revised the 1923 zoning ordinance and enacted a minimum housing code. Land annexations in 1947 and 1950 extended the city's geographical size from 59.64 to 81.62 square miles, the first sizable additions to the city's area since 1909. A huge 1947 bond program passed, the first since 1930, to expedite the construction of new parks and recreation areas, zoning, public buildings, and slum clearance. Redevelopment bonds approved by voters in 1952 and 1954, in addition to federal urban renewal money, helped pay for land clearance in slum areas. By the 1960s, the Missouri Department of Highways and Transportation (MDHT) was building Interstates 70, 29, and 35 and the South Midtown Freeway (the Bruce R. Watkins Drive) to reach beyond the city's hinterland to facilitate suburban access to the downtown. In the three-year period from 1947 to 1950, the city resurfaced more than 228 miles of streets and by 1957 had removed all street cars to make way for the dominance of automobile transportation and the creation of an automobile-dependent populace (Cookingham 1956, 1957).

Moreover, by 1970 it was painfully clear that the optimism and promises of urban redevelopment touted by central city businessmen and real estate elites during the 1950s and 1960s had not been fulfilled. Urban renewal was supposed to reverse central city decline, counteract decentralization trends, revitalize blighted neighborhoods, and create a "city without slums," as the *Kansas City Star* proclaimed in a February 1953 editorial ("For a City Without Slums," 1953). Yet by 1970, population and settlement patterns graphically illustrated the steadily decreasing supply of affordable inner city housing, widespread displacement, and flight of people and business. In 1970, over a half million city residents lived in 316 square miles sprawling more than three counties. Two decades earlier in 1950, 457,000 residents had been living in 20 percent of the 1970 area. Employment trends in the CBD told a similar story: from 1963 to 1976, total employment in the CBD dropped 19 percent, from 61,144 in 1963 to 49,585 by 1976.[5] Obviously, urban renewal had not halted decentralization trends but reinforced the exodus of people and industry, creating more urban blight and exacerbating the urban housing problem.

While specific renewal programs differed from city to city, the types of activities and dislocating effects were remarkably consistent. Herbert Gans's (1962) case study of the "urban villagers" in Boston's West End, Arnold Hirsch's (1983) study of Chicago, and Ronald Bayor's (1988) analysis of Atlanta show that the urban renewal program contributed greatly to clearing vast areas of slum housing in many CBDs, replacing low-rent residential housing with high rise-office towers and luxury apartments. In New York City, as Robert Caro (1975) points out in *The Power Broker*, Robert Moses eagerly exploited the power of eminent domain in the Housing Act of 1949 to launch a series of slum clearance programs that dislocated thousands of people and, in turn, produced new pockets of deterioration and blight. Although urban leaders used urban renewal to attack substandard housing conditions, very few resources went to improve deteriorated or dilapidated housing or "renew" slum neighborhoods (Greer 1965, p. 3; Jacobs 1961; Hartman 1966; Hartman and Kessler 1978; National Commission on

308   *American Journal of Economics and Sociology*

Urban Problems 1969, p. 153). Nationally, the program destroyed thousands more units than it replaced and dislocated tens of thousands of small businesses and residents (Friedland 1982, pp. 81, 85, 195; Weiss 1980; Kleniewski 1984).

In the 1960s and later, the character of urban redevelopment underwent a change in emphasis from large-scale clearance to neighborhood conservation and preservation. Critics such as Jane Jacobs (1961) and Herbert Gans (1962) attacked urban renewal for destroying neighborhoods while Martin Anderson (1964) blasted the principle that government could take away one person's property and give it to another for private gain. In Boston (Gans 1962), San Francisco (Hartman and Kessler 1978), and other cities, resident dissatisfaction with displacement helped spawn combative coalitions of housing activists, civil rights organizations, and historical preservationist groups dedicated to halting slum clearance. In 1974, the federal government discontinued the urban renewal program amid widespread urban protest and neighborhood discontent surrounding the destabilizing effects of the program on inner city communities (Von Hoffman 2000; Teaford 2000; Hirsch 1983; Weiss 1980). In the 1970s, the public housing program survived but other programs—especially Section 8—became the core components of low-income housing policy (Gotham and Wright 2000). In the 1980s and 1990s, federal resources for local economic development were reduced and local governments have been encouraged to be more self-reliant in forming strategic partnerships with the private sector and to compete with other cities to attract capital and jobs (Feagin 1988; Barnedov and Rich 1989; Anderson and Wassner 2000; Fisher and Peters 2000). At the beginning of the twenty-first century there is increasing interest among planners, policy makers, and government officials for developing new methods to revitalize cities and a search for new frameworks to guide economic growth and remedy the problems of uneven development.

Notes

1. I use data from four major sources to examine the redevelopment of Kansas City, Missouri and the implementation of postwar urban renewal and public housing. First, I examined public documents and planning reports issued by Kansas City, Missouri's City Plan Commission, the Housing Authority

of Kansas City (HAKC), the Land Clearance for Redevelopment Authority (LCRA), and the City Development Department, among other agencies. Second, I searched three local newspapers (the *Kansas City Times, Kansas City Star,* and the *Kansas City Call*) and a number of local archives for material about public housing and urban renewal. Third, I accessed every weekly issue of the *Kansas City Realtor,* the official publication of the Kansas City Real Estate Board, from 1925 to 1985 (the last year published) for data on the local real estate industry and the role of business elites in redevelopment efforts. Finally, this study draws on data from 21 in-depth interviews conducted in 1996 with local residents who had first-hand knowledge and experience with the dislocating effects of urban renewal upon city neighborhoods and local businesses. I gathered these interviews through a snowball sample that included seven white males, three white females, seven black males, and four black females. Most of these interviewees were either former or current real estate agents, civil rights activists, neighborhood coalition leaders, city planners, church leaders, block club heads, and the like. To protect the confidentiality of interviewees I use pseudonyms for nonpublic persons quoted in the paper.

2. Nichols, J. C. 1948. "Planning for Permanence." Speech before the National Association of Real Estate Boards. New York City, November 18, 1948. J. C. Nichols Company Records. KC 106. folder 42. Western Historical Manuscript Collection - Kansas City, Missouri (WHMC-KC).

3. Commission on Human Relations 1974; Metropolitan Planning Commission 1971; Department of Housing and Urban Development. 1972. Final Investigative Report. Region VII, Kansas City, Missouri. 07–72–11–024–300. Complaint filed by United Citizens City-Wide PAC Organization on 11/22/71. HUD complaint investigation of LCRA from 12/15/71 - 3/15/72. X2659. Box 209; *Hospital Hill Conservation Program, et al., Plaintiffs, vs. City of Kansas City, Missouri, et al., Defendants.* Filed on June 19, 1972. RE: Administrative Complaint, Workable Program Recertification. X649C. Box 202; Memorandum from William R. Southerland, Area Director, HUD, to Al Harmon, Executive Director, LCRA. RE: Relocation Deficiencies. 12/27/72. X2813. Box 210; Memorandum from A. J. Harmon, Executive Director and Council, LCRA, to Honorable Charles Hazley, Chairman, Plans and Zoning Committee. 2/12/73. X2814. Box 210; Model Cities Field Review of Kansas City, Missouri. 9/13/71 (survey). Thomas F. Brinton, Assistant Director, Planning and Relocation Branch, HUD. X2819A. Box 210; KC 250, Arthur A. Benson, II. Legal Papers. WHMC-KC;

4. Memorandum from Walter Cade, Jr., Equal Opportunity Division, HUD, to William Southerland, Area Director. 6/11/73. Re: NDP Application (10532 Determination). X2817. Box 210. KC 250, Arthur A. Benson, II. Legal Papers. WHMC-KC.

5. Table F-2. "Changes in CBD Employment 1963, 1976." Box 334. KC 250. Arthur A. Benson, II. Legal Papers. WHMC-KC.

310   *American Journal of Economics and Sociology*

References

Abrams, Charles. 1971. *The City is the Frontier.* New York: Harper and Row.
Anderson, John E., and Robert W. Wassner. 2000. *Bidding for Business: The Efficacy of Local Economic Development Incentives in a Metropolitan Area.* Kalamazoo, MI: W. E. Upjohn Institute.
Anderson, Annette. 1957. *Relocation of Site Occupants in Urban Renewal Activities.* Masters Thesis. Kansas City, MI: University of Missouri, Kansas City.
Anderson, Martin. 1964. The Federal Bulldozer: A Critical Analysis of Urban Renewal, 1949–1962. Cambridge: MIT Press.
Antonio, Robert J., and Alessandro Bonanno.1997. "Post-Fordism in the United States: The Poverty of Market-Centered Democracy." Pp. 3–32 in *Current Perspectives in Social Theory.* Vol. 16. JAI Press.
Banfield, Edward C., and James Q. Wilson. 1963. *City Politics.* New York: Random House.
Barnekov, Timothy, and Daniel Rich. 1977. "Privatism and Urban Development: An Analysis of the Organized Influence of Local Business Elites." *Urban Affairs Quarterly.* 12(4):431–460.
———. 1989. "Privativism and the Limits of Local Economic Policy." *Urban Affairs Quarterly.* 25 (2): 212–238.
Barnekov, Timothy, Robin Boyle, and Daniel Rich. 1989. *Privatism and Urban Policy in Britain and the United States.* New York: Oxford University Press.
Bauman, John F. 1981. "Visions of a Postwar City: A Perspective on Urban Planning in Philadelphia and the Nation, 1942–1945." *Urbanism Past and Present.* Vol. 6, Issue 11, No. 6, pp. 1–11..
———. 1987. Public Housing, Race, and Renewal: Urban Planning in Philadelphia, 1920–1974. Philadelphia, PA: Temple University Press.
Bayor, Ronald H. 1989. "Urban Renewal, Public Housing, and the Racial Shaping of Atlanta." *Journal of Policy History.* 1 (4): 419–439.
Bohanon, Jack Roy. 1971. *A History and Economic Analysis of the Kansas City, Missouri Federal Urban Renewal Program.* Masters Thesis. Department of Economics. University of Missouri, Kansas City.
Bratt, Rachel G. 1986. "Public Housing: The Controversy and Contribution." Pp. 362–377 in Rachel G. Bratt, Chester Hartman, and Ann Meyerson, eds., *Critical Perspectives on Housing.* Philadelphia, PA: Temple University Press.
Brown, A. Theodore, and Lyle W. Dorsett. 1978. *K. C.: A History of Kansas City, Missouri.* Boulder, CO: Pruett Publishing Company.
Caro, Robert A. 1975. *The Power Broker: Robert Moses and the Fall of New York.* New York: Vintage Books.
Castells, Manuel. 1977. *The Urban Question.* Cambridge: MIT Press.

————. 1983. *The City and the Grass Roots*. Berkeley and Los Angeles: University of California Press.

Checkoway, Barry. 1984. "Large Builders, Federal Housing Programs and Postwar Suburbanization." Pp. 152–173 in William K. Tabb and Larry Sawyers, eds., *Marxism and the Metropolis: New Perspectives in Urban Political Economy*. Second Edition. New York: Oxford University Press.

City Plan Commission. October 1947. *Kansas City Metropolitan Area. City Plan Commission, Kansas City, Missouri*. Kansas City, Missouri: City Plan Commission.

————. 1956. *Central Business District: Kansas City, Missouri Study*. Kansas City, Missouri: City Plan Commission.

Commission on Human Relations. 1974. *Report on the Relocations Practices of the Land Clearance for Redevelopment Authority*. Kansas City, Missouri: Commission on Human Relations.

Cookingham, L. P. 1954. "Expressways and the Central Business District." Pp. 140–146 in *American Planning and Civic Annual*.

————. 1956. Blueprint for the Future: Today's Challenge, Tomorrow's Achievement. City Manager's Annual Report, 1956–7. Kansas City, Missouri.

————. 1957. "Urban Renewal and Your City's Arterial Route Planning Job." *Street Engineering*. Feb. 1957: 16–18.

————. 1958. "The Kansas City Story." Pp. 170–174 in *The American City*. September.

Cummings, Scott, ed. 1988. *Business Elites and Urban Development: Case Studies and Critical Perspectives*. Albany: State University of New York Press.

Davies, Pearl Janet. 1958. *Real Estate in American History*. Washington, DC: Public Affairs Press.

Feagin, Joe R. 1988. *Free-Enterprise City: Houston in Political-Economic Perspective*. New Brunswick: Rutgers University Press.

Fisher, Peter S., and Alan H. Peters. 2000. *Industrial Incentives: Competing Among American States and Cities*. Kalamazoo, MI: W. E. Upjohn Institute.

Friedland, Roger. 1982. *Power and Crisis in the City*. London: Macmillan.

Gans, Herbert J. 1962. The Urban Villagers: Group and Class in the Life of Italian-Americans. New York: Free Press.

Gelfand, Mark I. 1975. *A Nation of Cities: The Federal Government and Urban America, 1933–1965*. New York: Oxford University Press.

Glasberg, Davita Silfen, and Dan Skidmore. 1997. *Corporate Welfare and the Welfare State: Bank Deregulation and the Savings and Loan Bailout*. New York: Aldine de Gruyter.

Gordon, David. 1984. "Capitalist Development and the History of American Cities." Pp. 21–53 in William K. Tabb and Larry Sawyers, eds., *Marxism and the Metropolis: New Perspectives in Urban Political Economy.* Second Edition. New York: Oxford University Press.

Gotham, Kevin Fox. 2000. "Racialization and the State: The Housing Act of 1934 and the Origins of the Federal Housing Administration (FHA)." *Sociological Perspectives* (43).

Gotham, Kevin Fox, and James D. Wright. 2000. "Housing Policy." Chapter 15 in James Midgley, Martin Tracy, and Michelle Livermore, eds., *Handbook of Social Policy.* Oak Grove, CA: Sage Publications.

Greer, Scott. 1965. *Urban Renewal and American Cities: The Dilemma of Democratic Intervention.* New York: Bobbs-Merril.

Hartman, Chester. 1966. "Housing of Relocated Families." Pp. 293–335 in James Q. Wilson, ed., *Urban Renewal: The Record and the Controversy.* Cambridge: MIT Press.

Hartman, Chester, and Rob Kessler. 1978. "The Illusion and Reality of Urban Renewal: San Francisco's Yerba Buena Center." Pp. 153–78 in William K. Tabb and Larry Sawyers, eds., *Marxism and the Metropolis: New Perspectives in Urban Political Economy.* First Edition. New York: Oxford University Press.

Harvey, D. 1973. *Social Justice and the City.* Baltimore, MD: Johns Hopkins University Press.

———. 1976. "Labor, Capital, and Class Struggle Around the Built Environment," *Politics and Society.* 6: 265–95.

Hays, R. Allen. 1985. *Federal Government and Urban Housing: Ideology and Change in Public Policy.* New York: State University of New York Press.

Hines, Thomas. 1982. "Housing, Baseball, and Creeping Socialism: The Battle of Chavez Ravine, Los Angeles, 1949–1959," *Journal of Urban History.* 8(12):123–144.

Hirsch, Arnold R. 1983. Making the Second Ghetto: Race and Housing in Chicago, 1940–1960. Cambridge: Cambridge University Press.

———. 1993. "With or Without Jim Crow: Black Residential Segregation in the United States." Arnold Hirsch and Raymond H. Mohl, eds., *Urban Policy in Twentieth Century America.* Rutgers, NY: Rutgers University Press.

———. 2000. "Searching for a 'Sound Negro Policy': A Racial Agenda for the Housing Acts of 1949 and 1954." *Housing Policy Debate.* 11(2): 393–442.

Housing Authority of Kansas City, Missouri. 1953. *Sixth Annual Report.* Kansas City, MI: Housing Authority of Kansas City, Missouri.

———. 1956. *Tenth Annual Report.* Kansas City, MI: Housing Authority of Kansas City, Missouri.

———. 1957. *Eleventh Annual Report.* Kansas City, MI: Housing Authority of Kansas City, Missouri.

Jackson, Kenneth T. 1985. *Crabgrass Frontier: The Suburbanization of the United States.* New York: Oxford University Press.

Jacobs, Jane. 1961. *The Death and Life of Great American Cities.* New York: Random House.

Jessop, Bob. 1990. *State Theory: Putting the Capitalist State in its Place*. Pennsylvania State University Press.

Judd, Dennis. 1984. *The Politics of American Cities: Private Power and Public Policy*. Second Edition. Boston, MA: Little Brown.

Keith, Nathaniel S. 1973. *Politics and the Housing Crisis Since 1930*. New York: Universe Books.

Kleniewski, Nancy. 1984. "From Industrial to Corporate City: The Role of Urban Renewal." Pp. 205–222 in William K. Tabb and Larry Sawyers, eds., *Marxism and the Metropolis: New Perspectives in Urban Political Economy*. Second Edition. New York: Oxford University Press.

Land Clearance for Redevelopment Authority. 1954. *First Annual Report*. Kansas City, MI: Land Clearance for Redevelopment Authority.

———. 1969. *Urban Renewal Kansas City, Missouri. 16 Year Progress Report, 1953–1969*. Kansas City, MI: Land Clearance for Redevelopment Authority.

Logan, J. and Harvey Molotch. 1987. *Urban Fortunes: The Political Economy of Place*. Berkeley, CA: University of California Press.

Marcuse, Peter. 1986. "Housing Policy and the Myth of the Benevolent State." Pp. 248–63 in Rachel Brat, Chester Hartman, and Ann Meyerson, eds., *Critical Perspectives on Housing*. Philadelphia, PA: Temple University Press.

McDonnell, Timothy. 1957. *The Wagner Housing Act: A Case Study of the Legislative Process*. Chicago: Loyola University Press.

McKenzie, Evan. 1994. Privatopia: Homeowner Associations and the Rise of Residential Private Government. New Haven, CT: Yale University Press.

Metropolitan Planning Commission. 1971. *A Decent Home For All: Housing Action in the Kansas City Metropolitan Region*. Kansas City, MI: Metropolitan Planning Commission, Kansas City Region.

Mitchell, J. Paul, ed. 1985. *Federal Housing Programs: Past and Present*. Rutgers, NJ: State University of New Jersey Press.

Mohl, Raymond. 1993. Shifting Patterns of American Urban Policy Since 1900. In Arnold Hirsch and Raymond H. Mohl, eds., *Urban Policy in Twentieth Century America*. New Brunswick, NJ: Rutgers University Press.

Mollenkopf, John H. 1983. *The Contested City*. Princeton, NJ: Princeton University Press.

National Commission on Urban Problems. 1969. *Building the American City. Report of the National Commission on Urban Problems*. New York: Frederick A. Praedger Publishers.

Pynoos, Jon, Robert Schafer, and Chester W. Hartman. 1973. *Housing Urban America*. Chicago: Aldine Publishing Company.

Rowe, Peter G. 1995. *Modernity and Housing*. Cambridge: MIT Press.

Sawers, Larry. 1984. "New Perspectives on Urban Political Economy." Pp. 3–20 in William K. Tabb and Larry Sawyers, eds., *Marxism and the Metropolis: New Perspectives in Urban Political Economy*. Second Edition. New York: Oxford University Press.

Scott, A. 1988. *Metropolis: From the Division of Labor to Urban Form.* Berkeley and Los Angeles: University of California Press.

Silver, Christopher. 1984. *Twentieth Century Richmond: Planning, Politics, and Race.* Knoxville: University of Tennessee Press.

Squires, Gregory D. 1991. "Partnership and Pursuit of the Private City." Pp. 196–211 in M. Gottdiener and Chris Pickvance, eds., *Urban Life in Transition.* Vol. 39. Urban Affairs Annual Reviews. Newbury Park: Sage Publications.

———. 1993. "The Political Economy of Housing: All the Discomforts of Home," *Urban Sociology in Transition.* Research in Urban Sociology. 3:129–157.

———. 1994. *Capital and Communities in Black and White: The Intersections of Race, Class, and Uneven Development.* State University of New York Press.

Storper, M. 1984. "The Spatial Division of Labor: Labor and the Location of Industries." In L. Sawyers and W. Tabb, eds., *Sunbelt/Snowbelt.* New York: Oxford University Press.

Storper, M., and R. Walker. 1983. "The Theory of Labor and the Theory of Location." *International Journal of Urban and Regional Research.* 7:1–41.

Teaford, Jon. C. 1990. The Rough Road to Renaissance: Urban Revitalization in America, 1940–1985. Baltimore, MD: Johns Hopkins University Press.

———. 2000. "Urban Renewal and its Aftermath." *Housing Policy Debate.* 11(2):443–466.

U.S. Senate. 1945. "Statement of Seward H. Mott." *Hearings Before the Subcommittee on Housing and Urban Redevelopment, Special Committee on Post-War Economic Policy and Planning.* US Senate. 79th Congress, 1st session. Washington, DC: Government Printing Office.

Urban Land Institute. 1940a. Decentralization: What is it Doing to Our Cities? New York: Urban Land Institute.

———. 1940b. *Proposals for Downtown Boston.* New York: Urban Land Institute.

———. 1941a. *Proposals for Downtown Cincinnati.* New York: Urban Land Institute.

———. 1941b. *Proposals for Downtown Milwaukee.* New York: Urban Land Institute.

———. 1941c. *Proposals for Downtown Philadelphia.* New York: Urban Land Institute.

———. 1941d. *Proposals for Downtown Detroit.* New York: Urban Land Institute.

———. 1942a. *Proposals for Downtown Louisville.* New York: Urban Land Institute.

———. 1942b. *Proposals for Downtown New York City.* New York: Urban
    Land Institute.
Von Hoffman, Alexander. 1996. "High Ambitions: The Past and Future of
    American Low-Income Housing Policy." *Housing Policy Debate.* 7(3):
    423–446.
———. 2000. "A Study in Contradictions: The Origins and Legacy of the
    Housing Act of 1949," *Housing Policy Debate.* 11(2):299–326.
Warner, Sam Bass, Jr. 1987 (1968). *The Private City: Philadelphia in Three Pe-
    riods of Its Growth.* Philadelphia: University of Pennsylvania Press.
Weiss, Marc A. 1980. "The Origins and Legacy of Urban Renewal." Pp. 53–79
    in Pierre Clavel, John Forester, and William W. Goldsmith, eds., *Urban
    and Regional Planning in an Age of Austerity.* New York: Pergamon
    Press.
Wilson, James Q, ed. 1966. *Urban Renewal: The Record and the Controversy.*
    Cambridge: M.I.T. Press.

Newspaper Articles

"A Northside OK," 1953. In *Kansas City Times.* August 22.
"A Dream City Without Slums," 1952. In *Kansas City Star,* December 19, p.
    D-4
"Architects Group Given High Honor," 1959. In *Kansas City Star.* June 14, p. 4.
"Attucks Ordinance In,"1954. In *Kansas City Times.* August 18
"Award for a Program that is Rebuilding a City," 1958. In *Kansas City Times.*
    April 10, p. 32.
"Campaign Against Decentralization," 1940. In *Kansas City Realtor,* February
    15, p. 3
"City Honored for Face Lift," 1958. In *Kansas City Times.* April 9, p. 1.
"City Faces Great Era," 1958. In *Kansas City Star.* October 1.
"City Impresses Urban Leaders," 1959. In *Kansas City Times,* April 28, p. 1.
"East Side Renewal Project Gets OK," In *Kansas City Times.* June 14.
"Factors in Decentralization,"1940. In *Kansas City Realtor,* October 31.
"For a City Without Slums," 1953. In *Kansas City Star.* February 24.
"Hail Vital City Pride," 1957. In *Kansas City Star,* October 7, p. 1
"Interracial Housing Project in Order," 1953. In *Kansas City Call.* February 13,
    p. 22.
"Kansas City's Battle on Blight is a Major Feat," 1960. In *Kansas City Star.* Janu-
    ary 3
"Land Institute Proposes Huge Replanning Program," 1942. In *Kansas City
    Realtor.* February 5, p. 2.
"Modern Look for Northside Horizon," 1957. In *Kansas City Star.* January 6
"Nelson Proposes Eight-Point Plan to Beat Shortage," 1947. In *Kansas City
    Realtor.* January 9.

"New Low-Cost Housing Plan Is Proposed," 1936. In *Kansas City Realtor*, December 9, p. 2.

"New Plan for Slum Clearance," 1944. In *Kansas City Realtor*, March 2.

"New Plan for Slum Clearance," 1944. In *Kansas City Realtor*, March 2, p. 2.

"Old Northside Gone," 1954. In *Kansas City Times*. July 25.

"Old North Side Gone," 1954. In *Kansas City Star*. July 25.

"Oppose a Housing Site," 1950. In *Kansas City Times*, June 20, p. 6.

"Out of the Rubble a New Kansas City Rises," 1958. In *Kansas City Star*. June 1.

"Plan To Rebuild City Blighted Area," 1941. In *Kansas City Realtor*. September 11.

"Praise Kansas City Renewal Projects," 1959. In *Kansas City Times*. May 2, p. 4A

"Praise Kansas City Renewal Projects,"In *Kansas City Times*, May 2, p. 4A.

"Real Slum Clearance," 1944. In *Kansas City Realtor*, January 27.

"Rebuilding of Blighted Areas," 1943. In *Kansas City Realtor*, June 17.

"Remove Blight," 1943 In *Kansas City Realtor*, February 11.

"Segregation in Housing Must Go," 1954. In *Kansas City Call*. April 2, p. 22;

"Slum Law Legal, 1954. In *Kansas City Times*. July 13.

"Slum War is On," 1955. In *Kansas City Star*. July 3, p. 7E

"Slums on the Retreat," 1956. In *Kansas City Star*. March 7

"Speaking the Public Mind," 1952. In *Kansas City Star*. July 24.

"Start Near on Huge City Job," 1956. In *Kansas City Star*. November 18.

"Three Public Housing Sites on Fringe of Downtown Area,"1957. In *Kansas City Times*. December 7, p. 21.

"To Redeem the Whole West Side," 1953. In *Kansas City Times*. July 6, p. 24

"Urban Land Institute Formed," 1940. In *Kansas City Realtor*. May 2, p. 4

"Urban Plan as Model," 1958. In *Kansas City Star,* September 24, p. 1.

"Vitality in City Growth," 1957. In *Kansas City Times*. October 8, p. 1;

"Writers Laud City Renewal Action," 1957. In *Kansas City Star*, October 12, p. 15.

A City Divided by Political Philosophies

Residential Development in a Bi-Provincial City in Canada

By GURA BHARGAVA[*]

ABSTRACT. This paper examines the impact of two distinct political ideologies on the development of residential dwellings, particularly single-family residences, in Lloydminster, a bi-provincial city in Canada. Lloydminster is a city of about 22,000 which straddles the provinces of Alberta and Saskatchewan. The two provinces are recognized for the dissimilarities in their political orientations. These dissimilarities are reflected in different taxation policies, different Medicare and health insurance policies and different auto insurance policies, which have given rise to a quantitative and qualitative split in the market for single-family residences in Lloydminster. This duality of the housing market is manifested in Saskatchewan's "affordability" and Alberta's "desirability." Alberta's tax policies have attracted "place entrepreneurs" to build upscale residences on its side for homeowners in high income brackets, who benefit from its tax policies. Saskatchewan's health care and auto insurance advantages have attracted those with such priorities and with moderate incomes. It is contended here that while distinct policies may have contributed to an uneven bi-provincial housing market, the disparity between the markets has been sustained and reinforced by all players who construct the housing reality through myths and perceptions as well as interpretations of policies and their underlying ideologies.

*Gura Bhargava is an Assistant Professor of Sociology at the University of Saskatchewan, Saskatoon, Canada. Her current research interests include urban and rural communities, deviance, cultural components of housing, and ethnicity. This is a revised version of a paper presented at the Fourteenth World Congress of the International Sociological Association (Montreal, Quebec, July 1998). The author would like to thank the Lloydminster Real Estate Board and the City of Lloydminster (especially Bob Germann and Tom Lysyk) for providing the data; Anami Bhargava of McMaster University for helping in statistical computation; Roberta Lee of the University of New Brunswick, Saint John, for proofreading; and Sarah DeVarenne, also of UNBSJ, for typing the manuscript, and the University of Saskatchewan for the research grant..

American Journal of Economics and Sociology, Vol. 60, No. 1 (January, 2000).

I

Introduction

SINCE THE SECOND WORLD WAR, Canada has witnessed a steady rise in urban settlements, places defined as cities. Cities vary in size, history, topography, centrality, major occupations, economic texture, cultural diversity, and other attributes. Despite these differences, a city may also be viewed as a physical and social construction shaped by prevailing political philosophies and ideologies. This social construction may be reflected in a city's built environments of which residential arrangements constitute a vital part. Residential development, particularly the growth of single-family residences in a city, is often seen as indicating its good health and prosperity. Smaller cities with less population density tend to have a greater proportion of single-family dwellings–more detached than semi-detached–than alternative varieties (Bourne and Bunting 1993) and reportedly higher home ownership rates than are evident in larger urban areas (Ley and Bourne 1993). Research on Canadian cities and various aspects of their residential development abounds. However, larger cities have generally been the beneficiary of such endeavours (Harris 1986; Hertzog and Lewis 1986; Che-Alford 1990; Balakrishnan and Selvanthan 1990; Ray and Moore 1991, among others) with some exceptions (Qadeer and Chinnery 1981; Dahms 1986; Everitt and Gill 1993).

An exploration into the relationship between political ideology and the development of space has generally escaped the attention it deserves. The present study addresses this relatively unexplored area by focusing on an almost one-hundred-year-old settlement which was divided into two separate municipalities by a boundary established to divide the provinces of Alberta and Saskatchewan when they were created in 1905. Lloydminster, this bi-provincial city of approximately 22,000[1], has its Saskatchewan section located on the eastern side and its Alberta complement situated on the western side.

Unlike municipalities of even five times its size, Lloydminster presents a unique set of possibilities to its residents: it offers them the option of choosing one province over the other as a place of residence, while still allowing them residence under one municipal jurisdiction.

This paper contends that the housing market on each side of the border reflects the philosophy, the ideology, and the economic status of the corresponding province more than it does a commonly shared municipal identity. The disparity between the age, size, structure, and value of the single-family houses on both sides of the border relates to the political and economic history of each province and specifically to the differences between their tax policies, auto insurance policies, and home improvement policies. Perceptions and myths surrounding these policies and their interpretation by "speculator-developers" (Harvey 1975a) and other "place entrepreneurs" (Logan and Molotch 1987) are equally important. These interpretations, which revolve around the "use value" and "exchange value" of the houses (Harvey 1975b; Logan and Molotch 1987) have shaped the housing market; previous research has demonstrated the impact of public policies on decisions regarding residential location (Rossi and Shlay 1982; Turner and Struyk 1989). The discussion of public policies in such research has referred to zoning regulations, homeowners' income tax deductions, government subsidized loans, and amortization rates. The present research focuses instead on provincial policies that are not directly related to home ownership, but which nevertheless have had a profound effect on the development and ownership of homes in Lloydminster. It also addresses another issue. One such policy which may have promoted an uneven development of single family residences in Lloydminster is the policy of different personal income tax rates in both provinces. Seemingly, Alberta's policy of a lower personal income tax rate has contributed to the popularity of this location among homeowners, builders, and developers in Lloydminster. Evidently, the balance of the rate of production of single family residences in Lloydminster tilted towards Alberta in the mid-1970s when Alberta's statutory personal income tax rate was phenomenally lower than that of Saskatchewan. However, once this pattern began, it has continued despite diminishing differences between the statutory personal income tax rates of both provinces. An answer to this paradox is sought in the embeddedness of economic behavior (Granovetter 1985) and in the role of dominant ideology in shaping decisions to choose an area for purchasing a house and making an investment.

II

Lloydminster: Two Provinces in One City

As EARLY AS 1964, Lloydminster obtained the reputation of being the only bi-provincial city in Canada:

> The city of Lloydminster is unique in North America because it in effect exists legally in two provinces at the same time. There are many examples of twin cities...but in those cases two corporate bodies exist. What is unique about Lloydminster is that there is only one and it is recognized by both provinces. (Atlas of Alberta, p. 129)

Lloydminster remains the only bi-provincial city. It became bi-provincial in 1930 and received city status in 1958. Lloydminster started as a colony of British settlers who were called the Barr Colonists. Originally, this group consisted of 2,684 people and was led by Reverend Isaac Barr and his English Missionary Society. The group split up in Saskatoon, with 500 members following Anglican minster Reverend George Exton Lloyd to the site of Lloydminster (Atlas of Alberta 1964). An interesting account of their journey to this promised land is presented by a historian whose grandfather was a Barr colonist (Bowen 1992). The area was originally called Britannia Settlement, but in order to honour Reverend Lloyd, who later became the Anglican Bishop of the diocese of Saskatchewan, its name was changed to Lloydminster in 1903. In 1905, when the provinces of Alberta and Saskatchewan were formed with the fourth meridian as the boundary, Lloydminster as a townsite found itself divided between two provinces. It became a village in the Province of Alberta in July 1906 and a town in the Province of Saskatchewan in April 1907. The two had separate elections for mayor and councillors and separate police and fire departments with no jurisdiction outside municipal boundaries. This situation created a condition of municipal confusion and unnecessary duplication of expenses. These factors gave rise to the amalgamation of the village and town of Lloydminster on May 20, 1930, by Order of Council in both provinces. On January 1, 1958, Lloydminster obtained its Charter as a city. The city is governed by a city council consisting of six aldermen and a mayor under a special charter agreed upon by the two provinces. The Lloydminster Charter, a combination of provincial statutes from both provinces, sets out instructions for the municipal government. The city qualifies for grants in both provinces on the basis of per capita population on each side, but not on the basis of per capita population of the city as a whole.

In the following, I provide glimpses of the differences in the political philosophies of the provinces of Alberta and Saskatchewan and a brief review of the ideologically encouraged asymmetrical spatial development of infrastructure in both Lloydminsters which have had a significant bearing on its residential development: retail businesses, schools, medical clinics, hospitals, and open spaces. This discussion will be followed by identification of the bi-provincial differences in the market of single-family residences. Finally an attempt will be made to explain these differences and draw some broad conclusions from this case study.

III

Alberta and Saskatchewan: Twins with Divergent Political Philosophies

THE PROVINCES OF ALBERTA AND SASKATCHEWAN were born on September 1, 1905, following an agreement by Prime Minister Laurier's cabinet that the territories should be divided into two provinces. Laurier chose the fourth meridian (Highway 17) as the dividing line, explaining that it would give roughly the same area and population to each province. According to Brennan (1992), the terms of the Alberta and Saskatchewan Act of July, 1905 consisted of two unique and controversial clauses:

1. The rights of a minority to separate schools to safeguard the educational rights of Roman Catholics in these new provinces.
2. The control of the land and its resources to the federal government, apparently to benefit Central Canada.

The contention that prairie farms were quasi-colonies created to serve the interests of Central Canada (Macpherson 1962) derives from the second clause. Prairie farmers were placed in a disadvantaged position engendered by discriminatory freight rules, unfair tariff barriers, high marketing costs, and unreasonably high interest rates controlled by banks in Central Canada. This situation generated intense discontent and an agrarian revolt against Central Canada, which in 1930 resulted in an amendment to the British North America Act. This amendment granted Alberta and Saskatchewan the right to exercise control over the land, natural resources, and royalties derived from their exploitation.

Alberta: Right-Wing Political Philosophy

Initially, the protest movements in both Saskatchewan and Alberta seemed to have shared a left-wing philosophy. In the early 1920s, the United Farmers of Alberta (UFA), which replaced the Liberal party—seemingly adopted a left-leaning egalitarian philosophy[2] similar to the one espoused by the Co-Operative Commonwealth Federation (CCF) of Saskatchewan, which was a populist party that formed a provincial governement in Saskatchewan in 1944. However, the UFA res\presented and Amercan style populism whereas the CCF espoused socialist ideology (Wiseman 1992). Describing Alberta as the American Midwest on the Prairies[3], Nelson Wiseman reasons that although settlers in Alberta arrived from Ontario, Britain, and Continental Europe, the cultural wave of Anglo-Saxon settlers from the United States was predominant. He contends that the dominant ideology of the American wave was that of:

> a radical "populist" liberalism that stressed the individual rather than the community or the state as a Tory or Socialist would. This wave's greatest impact was in rural Alberta, the continent's last agricultural frontier. Populist liberalism expressed itself in an unconventional farmers movement/government of Alberta known as the United Farmers of Alberta and in the long tenure of Social Credit (1992, p. 642).

The Social Credit party remained in power in Alberta for 36 years (1935–1971). This right-wing party was an outgrowth of the reform wing of the UFA, which stressed monetary reform and was much influenced by anti-statist ideology imported from the USA. Its leader, Premier William Aberhart, was referred to by his supporters as Alberta's Abraham Lincoln.[4] In 1935, Premier Aberhart introduced the Ultimate Purchases Tax to fight the depression. This tax was short lived, making Alberta the only province to discontinue a tax so started. The earlier years of the Social Credit regime witnessed a pro-business orientation[5] and fiscal conservatism; the later years saw a rise in moral and social conservatism as well.

The Conservatives under Peter Lougheed's leadership achieved electoral success in 1971 and have maintained their governing prerogative since. Thus, Alberta politics has been characterized by one-party dominance and right-wing orientation. The Liberals, once defeated and displaced, have not been able to regain ruling status. Even Peter Lougheed's brand of conservatism, which had liberal leanings, was called Crypto Socialist by Western Canada Concept, a party that echoed Aberhart's social credit philosophy. The province-building, the consequent proliferation of small rural hospitals, and the spending on other social programmes during the Lougheed era was made possible due to the unprecedented and fortuitous rise in world oil prices in the 1970s, which benefitted Alberta substantially since it owned about 80% of Canada's oil. Interestingly, during this period the relationship between business and government became even closer than during the Social Credit regime (Richard and Pratt 1979). Referring to this relationship, Claude Denis noted:

> the elements of the welfare state that were developed directly by the provincial government...were not connected to a corresponding state oriented ideology and were not financed with taxpayers' money but rather with oil royalties (1995, p.90).

Pro-business policies, self-reliance discourse, right wing corporatism with public support (Harrison 1995, p. 119), and free market ideology have been the trademarks of Alberta's political philosophy. Alberta's provincial motto "Strong and Free" reflects this philosophy. Lougheed was succeeded by Don Getty's Conservative government in 1985. During the Getty years Alberta faced a devastating downturn in the economy. The price of oil was drastically reduced and Alberta, like the states of Texas and Louisiana in the United States, faced an oil bust. Getty's government ran deficit budgets and accumulated a large debt in order to balance the budget. Getty did not dare to balance the budget through raising taxes, because it was unAlbertan, incongruent with the then and still prevailing myth and image which defines Alberta. He did reduce public spending on non-business programmes but incurred large expenditures on subsidies to businesses and risky investments, all of which caused a series of financial scandals. Getty resigned in

1992, both as a Tory leader and as Premier of Alberta. Ralph Klein, who won the Tory leadership in December 1992 and the provincial election in June 1993, has been Premier since. Klein's government has reduced the deficit and debt, balanced the budget, and created a surplus through downsizing and privatization of public services (Laxer 1995). Some privatized services have also been subsidized, as was the case with private liquor stores.[6] This conservative government is seen as pushing for an American-style for-profit type of health care, a two-tier health care system, and a greater role for private sector medicine through its controversial Bill 11[7] which was passed in May, 2000 despite protests. Klein's government has also been noted for giving concessions to various business organizations.[8] The province of Alberta levies the lowest personal income tax in Canada; this tax will be reduced even further in 2001, when this province will implement a flat tax system. It may also be noted that Alberta is forecasted to lead other provinces in economic growth in 2000.[9]

Saskatchewan: Left-Wing Political Philosophy

Unlike Alberta's motto that emphasizes individualism, the provincial motto of Saskatchewan, "From Many People's Strength," reflects the ideology of egalitarianism. As in Alberta, settlers in Saskatchewan originated from Ontario, Continental Europe, Britain, and the United States. However, the British rural presence was greater in Saskatchewan than in Alberta. According to Wiseman, the British brought over:

> . . . a socialist, labourist and agrarian heritage which stressed the abolition of a competitive system and the substitution of a cooperative system of manufacturing, transportation and distribution (Wiseman 1992, p. 651).

Following the pattern of British Labourism, the cooperative movement became the central core of the CCF constituency in Saskatchewan. Moreover, there were fewer Anglo-Saxon Americans in Saskatchewan than in Alberta, and the European and American Scandinavians in Saskatchewan were accepting of socialism. The Continental Europeans brought Roman Catholicism with them, making Saskatchewan the strongest Catholic centre in the prairie provinces. Catholics supported the Liberal party, which governed Saskatchewan for 39 years, from 1905 to 1944. In the early 1940s, the Catholic church rendered its support to cooperative movements and social welfare programs. This support further legitimated and reinforced the left-wing cooperative movement in Saskatchewan. Saskatchewan is reported to have the highest number of cooperative members of any Canadian province (Brym 1986). In 1998 the Centre for the Study of Co-operatives in Saskatchewan released a report indicating that Saskatchewan co-operatives were contributing significantly to the province's social and economic growth and thus maintaining the tradition of community building within the province. Medicare, the sacred trust in Canada, was born in Saskatchewan in 1962 during Tommy Douglas's regime. The CCF in Saskatchewan had been transformed into the New Democratic Party (NDP) in 1961. Saskatchewan was the first province to have the NDP as a governing party, and has had an NDP government for a longer period than any other province in Canada. It is still referred to as a socialist heartland.[10]

In 1964 the Liberal party, under the leadership of Ross Thatcher, won the provincial election and remained in power until 1971. This liberal leadership was followed by 11 years (1971–1982) of NDP regime under the leadership of Premier Alan Blakeney. In 1982, a Progressive Conservative government was elected for the first time in Saskatchewan. Premier Devine, leader of this PC government, who was operating in a province used to social democratic ideas, acted in a manner highly inconsistent with the conservative philosophy, particularly in his second term. He did not alter the existing tax structure in a significant way, but went on an irresponsible spending spree. Devine's government created an alarming increase in Saskatchewan's debt and deficit. During the late eighties, Saskatchewan's debt became the highest per capita debt of any province in the country. The NDP government of Roy Romanow, who won the provincial election in 1991, has proven to be far more conservative in its fiscal and economic policies than the Tory government of Grant Devine. Romanow's government has been able to reduce the deficit and balance the budget continuously for the last six years. However, until 1996, this goal was achieved primarily through increases in the retail sales tax,[11] utility tax, and fuel tax, as well as a debt reduction surcharge on personal income tax. Since 1996, the Saskatchewan government has cut taxes and has recently announced further cuts in the personal income tax for 2001 "to remain competitive with its rich neighbour Alberta."[12]

Unlike Alberta, Saskatchewan has maintained a restructured but relatively effective Medicare available to all citizens, regardless of income and social status, and without any health care premiums. Like Alberta Health, Saskatchewan Health is owned by the Crown. However, public ownership in Saskatchewan is not confined to health, but extends to power (SaskPower), energy (SaskEnergy), telephone (SaskTel), and auto insurance (SGI). The Saskatchewan Government Insurance (SGI) is a unique feature of the Saskatchewan government. SGI has recently increased the value of deductible by $200; it has also raised premiums, but compared to Alberta, it still offers a less expensive coverage for drivers under 25 years of age and for families with young drivers. Reportedly, SGI statistics claim that "the average 30-year-old Saskatchewan male pays CDN $572 on a 1992 Taurus. By contrast, the same person would pay CDN $1,087 in Alberta and CDN $923 in British Columbia."[13]

Some of Saskatchewan's crown corporations, such as the Potash Corporation of Saskatchewan Inc. (PCS) and the Saskatchewan Wheat Pool, have been privatized. The NDP government, which philosophically favours public ownership, is encountering increasing pressure to privatize from right-wing forces and globalization. Such pressure seems to be changing the monopolistic nature of these crown corporations, as is evident from the fact that SaskTel now allows its customers the option of choosing an alternative service. However, Saskatchewan defends its socialistic thrust by maintaining that crown corporations serve society better than privatized operations, and that advancing technology and international competition have not made crown corporations obsolete.[14]

The socialist government of Saskatchewan has been constantly criticized for creating a high tax burden by the opposition,[15] by Saskatchewan and Canadian Taxpayer's Associations,[16] as well as by concerned citizens and corporate citizens. In fact, a study by the Canadian Association of Petroleum Producers has indicated that Saskatchewan is the only province that levies a corporate capital tax on oil and gas companies and that the energy companies in Saskatchewan pay more than do their competitors in Alberta, Manitoba, or North Dakota.[17] In response to these voices, Romanow's socialist government has willingly redefined its philosophy and in its 1998 budget provided for a lowering of the amount of royalties required from energy companies and a return of their oil and gas rights to the unexplored depths of crown leases. Such provisions are indicative of the dynamic nature of political ideologies which allows political players to move right and centre of their political spectrum.

A continuing economic recovery and an ability to be current and pragmatic have created a favourable perception of Saskatchewan among Lloydminster's residents. Its housing market has picked up since 1996. Yet, the merchants in Lloydminster still tend to perceive Saskatchewan in Lloydminster as a growth-resistant and less business-friendly than Alberta.[18]

IV

Lloydminster: Selective Glimpses of Ideologically Stimulated Asymmetries

Political philosophies create perceptions and interpretations, not to mention policies, which affect various aspects of a city's built environment. The perception of Alberta as pro-business and pro-privatization, as well as its policy of no retail sales tax, have indeed contributed to the uneven development of business facilities, particularly retail businesses on the Alberta side in Lloydminster. The oral accounts of senior citizens, specifically merchants, indicate that earlier in the 1940s and 1950s, Saskatchewan surpassed Alberta in overall development, including business development. For example, the Lloydminster and District Co-operative Ltd., known as the Lloydminster Co-operative, was built on the Saskatchewan side in 1914. This co-operative developed into a comprehensive retail facility, serving community needs with complete home and farm services. However, over time, merchants began to prefer Alberta locations to those in Saskatchewan because they perceived the Alberta government as less bureaucratic, easier to deal with, and more supportive. A pro-conservative and anti-liberal attitude is said to have surfaced in the mid 1960s, when Thatcher's Liberal government tried rather unsuccessfully to collect retail sales tax from businesses in Lloydminster, Saskatchewan.[19] As a rule of thumb, merchants on the Saskatchewan side did not charge the retail sales tax if customers were not willing to pay it. Such occurrences were few and far between, but still perceived as common enough to create a politically favourable economic climate for Alberta and an unfavourable one for Saskatchewan. During this period, some businesses even moved to Lloydminster's Alberta side. It may be of note that Saskatchewan's retail sales tax, called the Education and Health Tax, existed in law until 1993. On August 10,1993, Roy Romanow's NDP government formally passed an Order in Council, providing:

> an exemption from liability for paying the tax imposed by the Education and Health Tax Act on tangible personal property and taxable services purchased in Lloydminster, Saskatchewan by an individual for non-business consumption or use in Lloydminster.[20]

The difference in the labour standards of Saskatchewan and Alberta, arising from their very different political philosophies, may also have had some bearing on the preference among Lloydminster merchants for Alberta locations. Saskatchewan laws concerning trade unions and labour standards have included mandatory benefits to part time employees, shortened qualifying periods for parental leave, and longer notice periods or pay in lieu to laid-off workers. The provincial minimum wage is higher in Saskatchewan than that in Alberta.

Almost all major retail shopping centres in Lloydminster–Lloyd Mall (the main shopping mall), the Real Canadian Superstore, Sears, Staples, WalMart, Canadian Tire, Home Hardware–are located on the Alberta side. The Lloydminster Trade Area Report, conducted in 1995 by the Lloydminster Economic Development Authority, indicates that the trade area population in Lloydminster is estimated to be 85,000; and that the retail stores situated on the Alberta side on the Yellowhead Highway (also called Highway 16) and the Meridian (Highway 17) draw more consumers than their counterparts on the Saskatchewan side. The reasons for this difference may include the highway location, parking facilities, competitive prices, and availability of a wide variety of goods. Nearly 60% of the shoppers in both locations come from Saskatchewan–east, south, and north–presumably to procure the sales tax advantage, often referred to as the "Alberta Advantage."

The differential perception of the two provinces has contributed to an uneven development in yet another way. Lloydminster is referred to as the Heavy Oil Capital of Canada because it is located in the middle of the heavy crude pools.[21] It is this resource that resulted in the establishment of Husky Oil Operations and the Bi-Provincial Upgrader (BPU) which originated as a joint venture between Husky Oil and the Govertments of Canada, Alberta, and Saskatchewan. The BPU is now exclusively owned by Husky. The BPU is located in Lloydminster on the Saskatchewan side. This corporate citizen, the BPU has contributed equally to industrial/commercial development in both provinces in Lloydminster. Nevertheless, it has stimulated an increasing demand for single family residences on the Alberta side, because a good majority of its employees have chosen the Alberta side.

Just as Lloydminster's Alberta side has attracted businesses, Lloydminster's Saskatchewan location has been preferred for primary health care. Since 1908, and despite changing its locations in 1917 and 1988 due to the need for expansion, Lloydminster Hospital has always been on the Saskatchewan side. The hospital is a not-for-profit enterprise: the Provincial Governments of Alberta and Saskatchewan share the majority of the costs of the hospital; some is borne by the community. This is not to imply that all health care facilities are concentrated in Saskatchewan. An auxiliary hospital is located on Alberta side and medical clinics and long term care facilities are evenly distributed in both provinces. Residents of either province may choose to patronize any clinic in either province and be covered by their provincial health plans. Thus, in matters of health, Saskatchewan seems to occupy a special position in Lloydminster. This may well signify the continuity of the historical role this province has played in introducing Medicare to Canada. According to *Plan LLoydminster 1985*, prepared by Makale & Kyllo Planning Associates, a broad division of labour exists between three governments–federal, Alberta, and Saskatchewan–for services provided by the City of Lloydminster. The Department of Health in general is serviced by the Saskatchewan government. In a personal communication, the then city clerk, Tom Lysyk, clarified:

> Lloydminster Charter does not direct the role either province should play in health matters. Nonetheless, conventionally, health is well ingrained into

Table 1

Population of Lloydminster Bi-Provincial Distribution
(1948-1996)

Year	ALTA	%	SASK	%	TOTAL
1948	1398	41.79	1947	58.21	3345
1949	1411	41.83	1962	58.17	3373
1950	1535	44.08	1947	55.92	3482
1951	1756	45.16	2132	54.84	3888
1952	1791	44.99	2190	55.01	3981
1953	2175	47.57	2397	52.43	4572
1954	2495	51.04	2393	48.96	4888
1955	2503	50.40	2463	49.60	4966
1956	2615	51.13	2499	48.87	5114
1957	2737	50.81	2650	4919	5387
1958	2783	52.06	2563	47.94	5346
1959	2806	52.15	2575	47.85	5381
1960	2886	53.43	2515	46.57	5401
1961	3052	53.17	2688	46.83	5740
1962	3108	52.51	2811	47.49	5919
1963	3344	54.39	2804	45.61	6148
1964	3344	52.47	3029	47.53	6373
1965	3622	54.62	3009	45.38	6631
1966	3710	54.26	3128	45.74	6838
1967	4303	55.42	3461	44.58	7764
1968	4306	55.38	3469	44.62	7775

the Saskatchewan system. It is natural to assign a special role to Saskatchewan in this regard.

The city's educational system is governed by the Saskatchewan School Act, but the majority of schools, high schools and junior high schools both public and separate (Catholic) are located in Alberta. Lloydminster Comprehensive High School was originally located on the Saskatchewan side but was moved later on to the Alberta side, as popu-

Table 1 *(continued)*

Year	ALTA	%	SASK	%	TOTAL
1969	4306	55.24	3489	44.76	7795
1970	4318	55.17	3509	44.83	7827
1971	4738	54.52	3953	45.48	8691
1972	4904	54.52	4091	45.48	8995
1973	5076	54.52	4234	45.48	9310
1974	5241	54.96	4295	45.04	9536
1975	5994	54.64	4975	45.36	10969
1976	5818	56.43	4493	43.57	10311
1977	6137	55.09	5003	44.91	11140
1978	6866	58.14	4944	41.86	11810
1979	7532	58.12	5428	41.88	12960
1980	8423	59.77	5670	40.23	14093
1981	9029	60.07	6003	39.93	15032
1982	9029	60.07	6003	39.93	15032
1983	9226	60.57	6005	39.43	15231
1984	9226	60.57	6005	39.43	15231
1985	10557	61.10	6721	38.90	17278
1986	10201	58.78	7155	41.22	17356
1987	10201	58.78	7155	41.22	17356
1988	10201	58.78	7155	41.22	17356
1989	9457	58.18	6797	41.82	16254
*1991	10042	58.10	7241	41.90	17283
*1996	11317	59.71	7636	40.29	18953

Source: The City of Lloydminster *Statistics Canada, 1991 and 1996 Census

lation on this side out-proportioned the population on the Saskatchewan side.

As Table 1 shows, in 1948 58.2% of the population lived on the Saskatchewan side; in 1996 the situation reversed itself with 59.71% residing on the Alberta side. The city's residential areas can be divided into four quarters; north-east or north-Saskatchewan; north-west or

Figure 1.

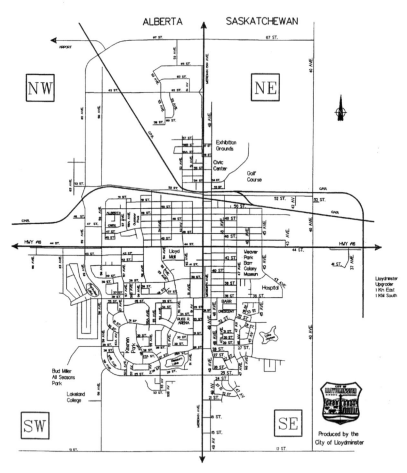

THE CITY OF LLOYDMINSTER

north-Alberta; south-east or south-Saskatchewan; and south-west or south-Alberta.

The Yellowhead Highway divides north and south; the Meridian draws the boundary between east and west. Whereas east and west represent the provincial divide, the north and south represent the divide between old and new, with the exception of a section of the south-east area which is quite old.

It appears from oral accounts of senior citizens that the earliest residential development took place in the north-Saskatchewan area and the northern part of the south-east quarter. Residential development then moved westward to the north-Alberta side, where then-prestigious neighbourhoods, such as Alberta Crescent, were developed. The status of this area declined as new residential subdivisions developed south of the Yellowhead Highway and as affluent, educated, skilled professionals and young households migrating to Lloydminster started settling in that new area. The north-south disparity in the development and marketing of single-family residences invokes an old-new dimension, the new being more desirable and expensive than the old. The relatively lower status and lower value of the single-family residences in the north-east and north-west quarters of Lloydminster arises out of the age of residences and proximity of this location to the industrial area. The aging population of those who inhabit these residences is also an important factor as there is some evidence that the status of an area is affected by the age of those inhabiting it (Choldin and Hanson 1982). In general, Lloydminster is provided with well-built open space. Yet the development plan prepared by Makale & Kyllo Planning Associates Ltd. for the city of Lloydminster notes:

> There are some neighbourhoods and districts which are not nearly as well served as others. For example, the Northwest District has one small district part, the Northeast District has none, while the Southwest has 67 acres (1985, p. 67).

It is also observed in the above-stated plan, that the Southeast District has only 41 acres. *Plan Lloydminster 1985* attributes this disparity to the timing of development and reserve dedication policies. However, these factors do not fully explain the difference between the south Alberta and south Saskatchewan districts in Lloydminster.[22] Lloydminster has two regional parks. Weaver Park, situated on the Saskatchewan side and created in the early 1960s, is less attractive than Bud Miller All Season Park, which opened in 1986 at the south Alberta location. The latter presents an aesthetically appealing unique facility with bicycle and hiking trails, playgrounds, a leisure pool with a sloping beach, waves, mushroom water fountain, tot area, and a water slide. The recent growth of various residential subdivisions with relatively expensive and bigger houses around this park is hardly a coincidence.[23]

All in all, Alberta and Saskatchewan have experienced differential patterns and rates of growth in Lloydminster. The development plan prepared by Makale & Kyllo Planning Associates confirms these differences.

> While historically the urban growth was approximately equal on both sides on the provincial boundary, the growth on the Alberta side accelerated in the early seventies with the result that a major portion of residential development (approximately 65%) and commercial and industrial development (approximately 70%) is located in the Province of Alberta (1985, p. 4).

V

Single-Family Residences: Dual, Bi-Provincial Market

A SINGLE-FAMILY RESIDENCE IS UNLIKE any other commodity sold in the marketplace. It is immobile, durable, expensive, and constitutes a major investment decision for most buyers. It can be seen as an economic, physical, and social good (Carroll 1990) which possesses both a use value and an exchange value. The market for single-family residences expands and shrinks with "booms and busts" in the economy. It is created and sustained by the growth of the population, by a sense of financial security, and by economic growth or the perception of its possibilities among consumers and developers. It is also affected by government-initiated assistance programmes, low interest rates for mortgage loans, and favourable conditions of tenure offered by lending institutions, such as commercial banks, trust companies, and credit unions. Other influences on this market are the non-availability of suitable rental accommodation, life cycle factors, and last but not least, real estate agencies.

Homeownership is viewed as a Canadian tradition which started from a basic desire to homestead (Wragge and Bartel 1981). As a matter of fact, the West, including areas surrounding Lloydminster, was originally settled by homesteaders and farmers. Homeownership symbolizes status and stability. In the 1979 elections, the federal Progressive Conservatives contended that a society in which a major proportion of the population owns its own home is likely to be a more stable, settled, and productive society. Because capital gains on the sale of a principal residence are not taxed in Canada, homeownership allows one to accumulate wealth. Besides, a home is a form of stored wealth which allows its owner to maintain equity (Harvey 1975b).

In the 1980s the province of Saskatchewan, with its profound emphasis on socialist tradition, initiated various programmes to assist homeownership, even under Devine's progressive conservative regime. These programmes included "Build a Home," which allowed a $3,000 grant to a resident building a home. This incentive, opened unconditionally to all, was introduced on December 1, 1982 and terminated on May 1, 1983. The "First Time New Home Buyers Programme," which was started on March 26, 1986, provided a $3000 grant for a downpayment and up to $10,000 in loans at 6% interest. This scheme was abandoned on December 31, 1986. Beginning on September 1, 1986, the "Home Improvement Grant Programme," providing for a loan of up to $10,000 at 6% interest, was introduced and continued up until March 15, 1990.[24] The loan was allowed for subsidizing home renovation expenses up to a maximum of $1,500; thus, homeowners would qualify for this grant if they had incurred $3,000 on house repairs. On September 1, 1988, the Province of Saskatchewan introduced the "Mortgage Shielding Programme," which provided for protection at a rate of 9.75% for mortgages up to $50,000.

The Province of Alberta also supported homeownership in the 1980s. However, its programme of support was in line with its philosophy of individualism and self-reliance. Thus, beginning in the late 1980s and up until early February 1991, the Province of Alberta provided grant and mortgage shielding up to 12% for first home buyers: a grant consisted of a $4,000 interest-free loan to be repaid over a period of five years. This policy differed from Saskatchewan's in that no give-away grants were offered. The Saskatchewan-Alberta polarization in the development and marketing of single-family residences in Lloydminster can be seen as constituting a "scale as well as boundaries of spatial variations" (Duncan and Savage 1989). In this case, the scale addresses the range of affordability and desirability; the boundaries entail socially constructed processes which impute meaning and definition to an existing physical and political border. These processes include consumer preference, developers' selective investment into a space they assess as worth investing in, builders' and contractors' preferences for undertaking a construction project in one area over another and the selective attention given to some sites for the creation of sought-after facilities by city planners and politicians. The latter particularly refers to the future market exchange value of the property (Harvey 1975b).

The residential growth in Lloydminster had been affected phenomenally by the rise and fall of the agriculture and oil markets. The 1970s were the years of resource boom in both Alberta and Saskatchewan. During this period, the City of Lloydminster was perceived as prospering limitlessly; the investment in heavy oil drilling in the Lloydminster-Kindersley area was high (Laxer 1984) and there was a remarkable increase in the world price for oil. The construction industry grew by leaps and bounds during this period, providing an unprecedented opportunity to contractors, as well as to builders and developers such as Nelson Lumber and Musgrave Agencies. These speculator-developers participated actively in the development of residential areas and the building of single-family residences; they also invested disproportionately in Alberta. Their investment on the Saskatchewan side was relatively less and characterized by a tendency to create a market for those with modest budgets.

The rate of production of single-family residences, as measured by building permits issued by the City of Lloydminster for such construction in both provinces, elucidates the pattern of bi-provincial differences (Table 2). Until 1972, the rate of production was greater in Saskatchewan than in Alberta. However, this changed in 1973, when the balance tilted towards Alberta, and has continued to date. Exceptions occurred in 1980 and 1986. In 1980, but much more significantly in 1986, the construction activity on the Saskatchewan side outpaced considerably its Alberta counterpart, presumably due to programmes introduced by the government to invigorate the sagging housing market in the province of Saskatchewan.[25] This externally-stimulated market declined continuously in the following years. In 1991, however, when Lloydminster faced a vacancy rate of nearly zero percent,[26] almost 99% of the new construction occurred on the Alberta side, thus polarizing

Table 2

Number of Single Family Residence Permits Bi-Provincial Comparison (1970–1999)

| Year | ALTA | | SASK | | TOTAL |
	number	%	number	%	number
1970	15	41	22	59	37
1971	39	46	46	54	85
1972	37	41	54	59	91
1973	71	66	36	34	107
1974	76	66	40	34	116
1975	104	63	61	37	165
1976	79	61	50	39	129
1977	147	63	87	37	234
1978	136	70	59	30	195
1979	152	78	42	22	194
1980	104	49	108	51	212
1981	29	69	13	31	42
1982	23	59	16	41	39
1982	71	63	42	37	113
1984	108	57	81	43	189
1985	119	51	116	49	235
1986	50	33	103	67	153
1987	54	75	18	25	72
1988	57	81	13	19	70
1989	24	89	3	11	27
1990	50	96	2	4	52
1991	74	99	1	1	75
1992	36	92	3	8	39
1993	44	94	3	6	47
1994	44	96	2	4	46
1995	11	79	3	21	14
1996	77	73	29	27	106
1997	141	73	52	27	193
1998	98	79	26	21	124
1999	82	76	26	24	108

Percentages are rounded to whole numbers.Source: Planning and Development Department, The City of Lloydminster the city's residential growth in an unprecedented way. Apparently, this situation of scarcity of accommodation corresponded with the construction of the Bi-Provincial Upgrader (BPU),[27] which accounted for the huge influx of construction workers in the city. The BPU also created a sizable permanent workforce, some of whom originated from, and preferred to live in, Alberta. Approximately 85% of those employed at the BPU have chosen their residence on the Alberta side,[28] despite the fact that BPU is situated in Saskatchewan. Furthermore, addressing the disparity in the bi-provincial demand for the construction of single-family residences in 1991, an area newspaper[29] noted a City of Lloydminster official observing that the city has divided more land into lots on the Alberta side than it has on the Saskatchewan side. In 1997, the phenomenal boom in the agriculture and energy industry coincided with a zero vacancy rate and an invigorated construction of single-family residences.[30] The construction activity on the Saskatchewan side picked up at this time, although Alberta still enjoyed a high 73% of this activity. This improvement in the demand for the construction of single-family residences in Saskatchewan uncannily coincides with an image-lifting experienced by that province since 1997.[31] The spatial disparity in the single-family residences is not only indicated in magnitude, but also in quality, as reflected in the value of permits used for such construction. The values are based on the estimates of the construction costs, which imply the same cost for contracting, labour, hardware, and other material. The variation is accounted for by the lot size, design, number of bedrooms and bathrooms, double/triple garage, jacuzzi, ensuite and walk-in closets, and fireplace.

Table 3 presents the average value of permits issued by the City of Lloydminster for single-family residences from 1970 to 1999. On average, the value of these residences has been consistently higher in Alberta than in Saskatchewan for each year since 1971. Even in 1986, when 67% of permits were issued for Saskatchewan locations, the average value of a permit was $18,000 less than its Alberta equivalent. This difference has increased over time; in 1999, the average value of the permits issued for Alberta was $44,940 higher than those in Saskatchewan. An average single-family residence in Lloydminster, Saskatchewan is built on a smaller lot and seems to have been designed to serve basic needs and the goal of affordability. In contrast, an aver-

Table 3

Average Estimated Value of Single Family Residence Permits Bi-Provincial Comparison (1970–1999)

Year	Lloydminster Alberta	Lloydminster Saskatchewan
1970	$15,226.66	$16,295.45
1971	$17,112.82	$14,515.22
1972	$20,209.38	$15,725.93
1973	$23,360.85	$17,338.88
1974	$26,065.79	$22,170.00
1975	$32,364.76	$27,898.36
1976	$41,879.74	$31,406.00
1977	$44,416.33	$35,463.22
1978	$53,991.17	$45,440.67
1979	$62,296.05	$46,071.43
1980	$69,503.03	$51,374.30
1981	$57,655.17	$55,500.00
1982	$62,897.39	$50,543.43
1983	$56,569.71	$47,996.43
1984	$58,457.31	$54,045.86
1985	$70,205.29	$50,578.42
1986	$65,575.00	$47,504.85
1987	$65,846.29	$47,055.55
1988	$77,580.70	$48,346.15
1989	$76,166.66	$51,100.00
1990	$82,810.00	$46,000.00
1991	$86,378.38	$63,000.00
1992	$91,097.22	$47,333.33
1993	$86,704.55	$74,666.66
1994	$95,022.73	$75,000.00
1995	$95,818.18	$77,666.66
1996	$96,117.16	$77,344.83
1997	$105,703.19	$71,804.81
1998	$121,485.21	$82,100.00
1999	$128,286.59	$83,346.15

Source: Planning and Development Department, The City of Lloydminster

age single-family residence in Alberta is built on a relatively large lot, increasingly by those or for those who are moving up, with a view to realizing their consumption dreams and to building equity by allocating large income shares to homes.

The *east-west*, or *Saskatchewan-Alberta, duality* in the single-family residential market is further affirmed by the data on the sale/resale of such residences in Lloydminster and outlying areas. Prior to July 1987, the Lloydminster Real Estate Board did not record the sale information separately for each province. Hence, sale/resale data is only available for the years 1988–1999; the information for 1987 is excluded from the analysis because it provided data for only six months. The volume of sales of single-family residences in Alberta has been consistently higher than that of Saskatchewan for each year since 1988, the year when such data became available systematically (Table 4). This share

Table 4

Market Share of Single Family Residences
Bi-Provincial Comparison (1988–1999)

Year	Units Sold Alberta	Units Sold Saskatchewan	Total Sold	Market Share %	
				ALTA	**SASK**
1988	122	93	215	57	43
1989	137	81	218	63	37
1990	184	107	291	63	37
1991	253	108	361	70	30
1992	214	127	341	63	37
1993	198	91	289	69	31
1994	187	113	300	62	38
1995	206	131	337	61	39
1996	213	139	352	61	39
1997	269	186	456	59	41
1998	247	135	382	65	35
1999	230	137	367	63	37

Percentages are rounded to whole numbers. Source: Lloydminster Real Estate Board and Canadian Real Estate Association, Ottawa was highest (70%) in 1991. As indicated earlier, the vacancy rate in Lloydminster was very low, and BPU was creating permanent positions that were filled by Albertans as well as by others who preferred to live in Alberta. The Saskatchewan market witnessed a recovery in 1997, which presumably was due, at least in part, to the non-availability of suitable residences in Alberta. Saskatchewan did receive a note of positive endorsement by real estate professionals in Lloydminster.[32] Yet its market share was only 41%, much less than Alberta's.

The average value of the single-family residences sold by MLS in both provinces in Lloydminster is presented in Table 5. This evidence further ratifies the pattern of difference indicated earlier, viz, the persistence of lower (than Alberta) average prices in the single residence market in Saskatchewan.

The dual-provincial nature of the housing market is further documented by the proportion of the sale/resale of single-family residences according to price categories (Table 6). In order to compre-

Table 5

Average Price of Single-Family Residences
Bi-Provincial Comparison (1988–1999)

	Alberta$	Saskatchewan$	Difference$
1988	75,000	62,520	12,480
1989	77,800	62,454	15,346
1990	78,000	59,263	18,737
1991	84,800	61,757	23,043
1992	90,942	62,994	27,948
1993	99,900	70,322	29,578
1994	97,924	72,401	25,523
1995	99,882	70,848	29,034
1996	100,138	69,996	30,142
1997	106,719	77,649	29,070
1998	117,450	89,982	27,468
1999	114,845	90,189	24,656

Source: Lloydminster Real Estate Board and Canadian Real Estate Association, Ottawa

Table 6

Single-Family Residences Sold According to Price Categories
Bi-Provincial Comparison (1988-1999)

| | Price Categories | | | | |
	Under $70,000	$70,000–$89,999	$90,000–$119,999	$120,000 &Above	Total
Total Units Sold	1178	1011	976	754	3919
Alberta					
% within Price Categories	46	52	70	93	63
% within Province	22	22	28	29	100
Units Sold	546	529	681	704	2460
Saskatchewan					
% within Price Categories	54	48	30	7	37
% within Province	43	33	20	3	100
Units Sold	632	482	295	50	1459

Percentages are rounded to whole numbers, thus "Within Province" percentages may not add to 100. Chi-Square = 505.700 with 3 df., significant and 0.001 level.
Source: Lloydminster Real Estate Board and Canadian Real Estate Association Ottawa

hend the nature and extent of duality and to apply the Chi Square test, the data for twelve years, 1988 to 1999, were cumulated to have adequate frequencies in each price category.[33] The data reveal that Saskatchewan, as compared to Alberta, has a higher proportion of sales in the most affordable category and a lower proportion in the most expensive category; this proportion decreases with the progression from the lowest to the highest price category. An opposite pattern is indicated for Alberta. Compared to Saskatchewan, Alberta has a smaller proportion of sales in the lowest price category and a larger proportion in the highest price category. This corroborates the fact that single-family residences, under different price categories, are not independent of the provincial locations. The hypothesis of no difference was rejected at 0.001 level of significance.

The data in Table 6 also disclose another interesting difference:

within Saskatchewan, the highest proportion of sales occurs in the most affordable category and this proportion declines as the price increases. On the other hand, the sales within Alberta are rather evenly distributed between various price categories. This pattern elucidates the fact that Alberta offers its consumers a wide spectrum of single-family residences, old-new, small-big, basic-luxurious, ranging from highly affordable to highly desirable. The affordable variety is likely to be located in the north-Alberta area, which consists of older homes. Aside from their role as residences, these houses can also be bought as investment properties by those residing elsewhere.

The newly built single-family residences in south-Alberta, near Bud Miller All Seasons Park, constitute the category of the most sought after alternative, signifying a move-up market and a lifestyle of conspicuous consumption. South-Saskatchewan also has such residences, but they are fewer in number and are sold for less. According to real estate appraisers and real estate sales professionals, the interprovincial difference between the value of a single-family residence may be negligible for those priced under $75,000. Such a difference, however, increases with the value of the house. Thus, the Alberta equivalent of a house that sells for CDN $100,000 in Saskatchewan is likely to be $130,000. The highest selling price for a single-family detached residence in Alberta has been consistently and considerably higher than its Saskatchewan counterpart for each year since 1992, when such data became available (see Table 7). The difference between the price of both locations during these eight years (1992–1999) has ranged from CDN $44,000 to $110,000.

Responding to the demand for single detached residences, the City of Lloydminster in 1997 announced the possibility of opening 150 lots in Alberta and 50 lots in Saskatchewan.[34] According to officials at the City of Lloydminster, this disparity relates to consumer demand. The lots in the subdivisions created on the Alberta side since 1994 have sold steadily and at a much faster rate than the ones that were available in the Saskatchewan subdivision created in 1985. In order to attract customers, the prices of lots in Saskatchewan were reduced from the asking price.[35] Even after adjusting for the difference in size, the price of these lots is approximately $18,000 less than the price of their Alberta counterparts.

Table 7

Highest Selling Price for Detached Single-Family Residences
Bi-Provincial Comparison (1992-1999)

Year	Provinces Alberta$	Saskatchewan$	Difference$
1992	161,000	116,000	45,000
1993	185,000	108,000	77,000
1994	180,000	123,000	57,000
1995	183,000	116,000	67,000
1996	235,000	124,500	110,500
1997	183,900	139,900	44,000
1998	261,000	155,000	106,000
1999	249,900	141,000	108,900

Source: Lloydminster Real Estate Board

The above pattern corresponds with the bi-provincial construction and sale/resale market for single-family residences in Lloydminster. Saskatchewan and Alberta do present dual housing realities in Lloydminster. The idea of affordability is so ingrained in the social democratic philosophy that in 1994, during a news conference in Lloydminster, Roy Romanow, the Premier of Saskatchewan, is reported to have said that if Lloydminster residents weigh all the advantages of living in Saskatchewan, they would find it is cheaper to live in Saskatchewan than Alberta.[36] This seems to be a valid claim but one which raises the question of a choice between affordability and desirability. The latter seems to have been chosen by a majority in Lloydminster, presumably for the reasons discussed below.

VI

Explaining Bi-Provincial Disparity

IN 1996, A STUDY BY University of Saskatchewan students identified Lloydminster as a young city with about 30 percent of its population between 20–35 years of age, and with the level of its average personal income ($16,000) higher than that of Saskatoon ($15,000), a city more than ten times its size.[37] In 1998, this perception of the city's population was endorsed when several wealthy Lloydminster citizens, all from oil patch and cattle businesses, joined an investors' group to buy the Edmonton Oilers from Peter Pocklington and his bank.[38] All the same, the median income within Lloydminster varies according to province: Albertans in Lloydminster enjoy a higher median income than their Saskatchewan counterparts.

Table 8 presents the bi-provincial distribution of family income as well as bi-provincial differences in the median family income for the census years 1981, 1986, 1991, and 1996.[39] The data on family income have only been available since 1981 as no such data were reported in the 1970 and 1976 censuses for the City of Lloydminster. The hypothesis of no difference in the family income of residents in two Lloydminsters for census years 1981, 1986, 1991, and 1996 respectively was rejected at 0.001 level of significance. Indeed, families in each province progressively experienced an increase in median income for each census year. Whereas the highest family income reported in 1981 was $40,000 and above, it rose to $50,000 and above in 1986, to $70,000 and above in 1991, and to $100,000 and above in 1996. However, significantly more Albertan than Saskatchewan families have been located in "nearly highest" and "highest income" categories in each census year. In 1981, this range of "nearly highest" and "highest" categories included $30,000 to $40,000 and above; in 1986, it included $40,000 to $50,000 and above; in 1991, it included $50,000 to $70,000 and above; and in 1996, it included $60,000 to $100,000 and above. The difference between the median income of both provinces in Lloydminster has also increased successively in each census year. In 1996, the magnitude of this difference ($12,220) was the largest of all the previous years. The tendency toward increasing differences in median income indicates the growing polarisation of the two Lloydminsters. This may indeed be due to the remarkable growth and development of businesses on the Alberta side generated by this province's pro-business policies. This growth may partially account for an increasing proportion of high income families on this side of the border. It also indicates that the majority of those in high income brackets, even while working on the Saskatchewan side, have chosen and are choosing Alberta as their residence.

Table 8

Distribution of Family Income in Lloydminster
Bi -Provincial Comparison (1981-1996)

Annual Income	1981			1986			1991			1996		
	Alberta N=2210	Sask. N=1455	Total N=3665	Alberta N=2610	Sask. N=1825	Total N=4435	Alberta N=2605	Sask. N=1860	Total N=4465	Alberta N=3085	Sask. N=2000	Total N=5085
	%	%	%	%	%	%	%	%	%	%	%	%
Less than $10,000	8 (51)	11 (49)	9 (100)	7 (61)	6 (39)	6 (100)	4 (50)	6 (50)	5 (100)	4 (35)	10 (65)	6 (100)
$10,000-$19,999	17 (53)	22 (47)	19 (100)	13 (58)	14 (42)	14 (100)	10 (53)	12 (47)	11 (100)	7 (51)	11 (49)	9 (100)
$20,000-$29,999	28 (56)	34 (44)	30 (100)	12 (41)	24 (59)	17 (100)	12 (53)	15 (47)	13 (100)	11 (57)	13 (43)	12 (100)
$30,000-$39,999	24 (67)	18 (33)	21 (100)	18 (55)	21 (45)	20 (100)	13 (48)	20 (52)	16 (100)	13 (56)	16 (44)	14 (100)
$40,000-$49,999	24 (72)	14 (28)	20** (100)	18 (62)	16 (38)	17 (100)	17 (53)	20 (47)	18 (100)	12 (53)	17 (47)	14 (100)
$50,000-$59,999				32 (70)	19 (30)	27** (100)	16 (63)	13 (37)	14 (100)	12 (58)	13 (42)	12 (100)

Percent of Families Within Province (Within Income Group)

Income bracket	1986		1991		1996	
	Alberta	Sask.	Alberta	Sask.	Alberta	Sask.
$60,000-$69,999	9 (63)	8 (37)	9 (100)		10 (67)	8 (33)
$70,000-$79,999	20 (80)	7 (20)	7 (100)		10 (78)	4 (22)
$80,000-$89,999	8 (100)		5 (100)		6 (73)	4 (27)
$90,000-$99,999			4 (100)		5 (76)	2 (24)
$100,000 & Above	15** (100)		7** (100)		10 (89)	2 (11)

** Open ended Categories. Percentages are rounded to whole numbers, thus "Within Province" percentages may not add to 100.

Source: Statistics Canada, reconstructed and computed from 1981 - 1996, Census of Canada.

	1981		1986		1991		1996	
Chi-Squares	93.279		163.158		201.853		340.080	
DF	4		5		7		10	
Significant at	0.001		0.001		0.001		0.001	
Family Income	Alberta	Sask.	Alberta	Sask.	Alberta	Sask.	Alberta	Sask.
Median	$29,184	$23,858	$39,718	$33,341	$47,641	$39,326	$52,160	$39,940

This choice of Alberta among high income home owners has indeed been affected by the availability of a variety of quality houses, accessibility to socially desirable resources such as shopping centres, schools, and parks, and well-built roads in this area. However, the most important contributing factor appears to be the lower provincial personal income tax rates on this side of the border. The lower the income, the less the effect of this difference in tax policies on incumbents. On the other hand, the higher the income, the greater and more substantial the impact of such a difference on individuals and families. Apparently, those in the high income category do benefit appreciably by choosing to live in Alberta.

Table 9 presents a comparison of the statutory personal income tax rates of the provinces of Alberta and Saskatchewan from 1970 to 1999. Until 1972, the interprovincial difference was negligible. Since 1973 and particularly from 1975 until 1983, the difference in statutory personal income tax rate assumed a substantial magnitude. In the year 1977, the difference peaked to the phenomenal extent of at least -20%. Incidentally, 1973 was also the year when the preference for the construction for single-family residences in Lloydminster tilted towards Alberta (see Table 2). In the mid 1970s and early 1980s, when Alberta's statutory personal income tax rate was significantly lower than that in Saskatchewan, an Alberta advantage was instituted in Lloydminster's housing market. Comparing Alberta and Saskatchewan in terms of their tax policies, an article in *Macleans,* a popular Canadian weekly, describes a Rotary Club luncheon in Lloydminster:

> When the local president asked members who live in Saskatchewan to stand, only 9 of the 58 people present rose. Then, he asked members who used to live in Saskatchewan, but have since moved to Alberta, to rise—more than 20 stood up. The underlying reason for the emigration, residents say, is the lower tax rates on the Alberta side of the border (February 13, 1995, p. 21).

The Rotary membership in Lloydminster as elsewhere is more or less class-specific; it does not represent citizens at large. It is this group which specifically prefers Alberta locations, thus reinforcing the duality and solidifying the philosophical divide.

Alberta's provincial personal income tax advantage is seemingly counteracted by Saskatchewan's advantage of no health care premium

Table 9

Statutory Personal Income Tax Rates Bi-Provincial Comparison (1970–1999)

Year	Statutory Provincial Income Tax Rate (% of Basic Federal Tax)		Difference
	Alberta	Saskatchewan	
1970	33.0	34.0	−1.0
1971	33.0	34.0	−1.0
1972	36.0	37.0	−1.0
1973	36.0	40.0	−4.0
1974	36.0	40.0	−4.0
1975	26.0	40.0 + surtax	at least −14.0
1976	26.0	40.0 + surtax	at least −14.0
1977	38.5	58.5 + surtax	at least −20.0
1978	38.5	53.0 + surtax	at least −14.5
1979	38.5	53.0 + surtax	at least −14.5
1980	38.5	53.0 + surtax	at least −14.5
1981	38.5	52.0 + surtax	at least −13.5
1982	38.5	51.0 + surtax	at least −13.5
1983	38.5	51.0 + surtax	at least −13.5
1984	43.5	51.0 + surtax	at least−7.5
1985	43.5	51.0 + surtax and flat tax	at least–6.0
1986	43.5	50.0 + surtax and flat tax	at least–6.0
1987	46.5 + surtax and flat tax	50.0 + surtax and flat tax	about −3.5
1988	46.5 + surtax and flat tax	50.0 + surtax and flat tax	about −3.5
1989	46.5 + surtax and flat tax	50.0 + surtax and flat tax	about −3.5
1990	46.5 + flat tax	50.0 + surtax	about −3.5
1991	46.5 + flat tax	50.0 + surtax	about −3.5
1992	46.0 + flat tax	50.0 + surtax	about −4.0
1993	45.5 + flat tax	50.0 + surtax	about −4.5
1994	45.5 + flat tax	50.0 + surtax	about −4.5
1995	45.5 + flat tax	50.0 + surtax	about −4.5
1996	45.5 + flat tax	50.0 + surtax	about −4.5
1997	45.5 + flat tax	50.0 + surtax	about −4.5
1998	44.0 + flat tax	49.0 + surtax	about −4.5
1999	44.0 + flat tax	48.0 + surtax	about −4.0

Source: Revenue Canada

and state auto insurance. As noted earlier, Saskatchewan is the birthplace of Medicare in Canada. The idea of one state health scheme available to all, regardless of income, was introduced by Tommy Douglas, the Premier of Saskatchewan from 1944 to 1961. Woodrow Lloyd, Douglas's successor as Premier of Saskatchewan, introduced Medicare legislation which survived despite the immediate opposition of doctors and politicians (Avakumovic 1978) and changes in political regimes. In the seventies, during Alan Blakeney's NDP era—the period of resource boom and resource royalties—Medicare was expanded to include 100% coverage of prescription drugs and a children's dental programme which even provided coverage for orthodontal treatment, as well as medical services including those of chiropractors, chiropodists, and physiotherapists. With some modifications, the state's commitment to health care continued even under Conservative Premier Devine's leadership from 1982–1990. In the 1990s, the hegemony of the discourse of fiscal restraint has pushed every political party in Canada, including the NDP in Saskatchewan, to the right of centre of their political spectrum. Consequently, Saskatchewan has encountered severe cutbacks in the area of health services. Nevertheless, as compared to Albertans, Saskatchewan residents, regardless of their income, receive health care without any premiums and can avail themselves of the services of chiropractors and chiropodists for a nominal fee.

Usually employers such as Husky, Lakeland College, public schools, separate schools, and other work organizations provide medical benefits to their permanent employees. High income professionals, such as physicians, lawyers, real estate professionals, investors, and entrepreneurs, stand to benefit more from the Alberta personal income tax advantage than from the Saskatchewan health advantage. The health care advantage offered by Saskatchewan is most meaningful to those who are unemployed, underemployed, without any medical benefit from the workplace, and for those who have moderate incomes. The preponderance of affordable houses built on smaller lots in Saskatchewan may have some bearing on this province's philosophy to serve most the interest of lower and moderate income groups.

Auto insurance in Alberta is privatized. Consequently, premiums vary with the model and age of the vehicle as well as with the age and gender of the driver. Saskatchewan Government Insurance (SGI), on the other hand, is owned by the state. Premiums vary with the age and gender of the driver; a male under 25 particularly benefits by residing in the Saskatchewan area. Moreover, a moderate income family with one car but with more than one driver does not have to pay extra insurance for an additional driver, regardless of age. In contrast, extra insurance has to be bought in Alberta if the auto is frequently driven by anyone other than the principal driver. In case of an auto accident, it is very expensive for a moderate income family to get the young driver re-licenced in Alberta. Additionally, drivers of any age with a history of accidents and violations pay less in insurance in Saskatchewan than Alberta. Families and individuals with these concerns tend to choose a Saskatchewan location for their residence, as interviews with families revealed. Other families had stayed in Saskatchewan despite a desire to move to Alberta; while still others were residing in Alberta but were trying to sell their houses to buy ones in Saskatchewan for the same reason. In addition to these reasons, Saskatchewan locations were chosen by some in-migrants to maintain property rights on family farms located in the province and to qualify for subsidies if and when needed.

In Lloydminster, as well as elsewhere in Canada, the province of Alberta is perceived as prosperous, growing, and inviting.[40] Whereas Saskatchewan in Lloydminster tends to attract a good majority of in-migrants from the province of Saskatchewan, Alberta in Lloydminster attracts a sizable proportion from other provinces as well. This pattern has particularly been exhibited in the census years 1971, 1976, 1981, and 1986. In 1991, the percentage of in-migrants from the province of Alberta was greater than in previous years, presumably due to the creation of the Bi-Provincial Upgrader; the same was true of 1996, when various business organizations absorbed migrants from across the province of Alberta. Nevertheless, in both 1991 and 1996, as in previous years, Lloydminster, Alberta had a greater share of in-migrants from other provinces than did Lloydminster, Saskatchewan. Athough, the proportion of in-migrants from other provinces to the Lloydminster Saskatchewan area was greater in 1996 than it was in previous years, in-migrants entering high-income bracket positions were likely to locate in Lloydminster Alberta.

Table 10

In-Migrants in Lloydminster From the Same Province and
From Different Provinces
Bi-Provincial Comparison for Various Years

Years	From the Same Province		From Different Provinces	
	Alberta%	Saskatchewan%	Alberta%	Saskatchewan%
1971 AB.N = 1105 SK.N = 1170	46	73	54	27
1976 AB.N = 2000 SK.N = 1370	49	73	51	27
1981 AB.N = 4055 SK.N = 2405	41	58	60	42
1986 AB.N = 3190 SK.N = 2170	50	64	50	36
1991 AB.N = 2495 SK.N = 2120	54	74	46	26
1996 AB.N = 3315 SK.N = 1695	51	56	49	44

Percentages are rounded to whole numbers. Source: Statistics Canada, Censuses of Canada, various years. The categories of in-migrants from "outside Canada" and "Province not stated" are excluded from this analysis.

The Alberta edge in Lloydminster may have begun in the mid to late 1960s, when the province of Saskatchewan became unpopular in business circles for attempting to collect provincial sales tax from merchants in Lloydminster, Saskatchewan. This provincial sales tax ruling was almost never enforced, and is clearly a non-issue now. The only exceptions would be sales tax on items such as automobiles or similar consumer goods which require licensing and registration. Nevertheless, the myth of Saskatchewan as a tax-grabber has persisted over time through the daily streams of talks. This perception has boosted Alberta's status as a preferred location among home-owners in Lloydminster.

From the mid-1970s to mid-1980s, when the gap between the personal income tax rates of the two provinces was indeed immense, the popularity of Alberta locations soared among local builders, contractors, and developers. Some local entrepreneur-developers have played a vital role in boosting the growth of the city in myriad ways.[41] They have also shaped neighbourhoods that created an Alberta edge in Lloydminster's housing markets. Ray Nelson from Frontier Saskatchewan, owner of Nelson Lumber Company,[42] is a retailer, manufacturer, builder, and developer. Nelson's construction division has built homes and apartments, as well as some commercial buildings. Nelson owns parcels of land in Lloydminster, mostly in Alberta; some of these have been developed and some are still being developed into homes targeted to affluent consumers. His latest development was Parkview on the Lake, situated in a south Alberta area, just north of the Bud Miller All Seasons Park. For this group of architecturally controlled residential lots, it was required that homeowners, designers, or builders follow given guidelines for building forms and details. These highly desirable lots were not affordable for home seekers in general, but have indeed added excellence in design and lifestyle to this particular residential subdivision. In 1998, Nelson Homes announced its plan to develop 50' or wider lots on the Saskatchewan side (Figure2). Lots in the Saskatchewan location were portrayed as "Affordable Family Building Sites," whereas lots in Parkview on the Lake on the Alberta side were portrayed as "Custom Home Building Sites."

Since 1977, Bill Musgrave from Shaunavon, Saskatchewan, founder of Musgrave Agencies, has also shaped the development of residential

Figure 2.

Building Sites to Match all Budgets

Alberta Location

Custom Home Building Sites
Let us design & build the house you want!

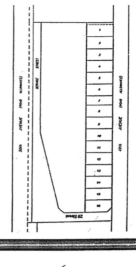

Parkview on the lake!
Just 11 of 19 lots are still available!

Saskatchewan Location

Affordable Family Building Sites
Lots are 50' or wider!

49 Avenue, Easy Access!
Ready for spring building!

Nelson Homes Delivers Dreams

Lloydminster Meridian Booster
May 31, 1998:A15

subdivisions in Lloydminster. In the late 1970s and early 1980s, Lloydminster was experiencing a boom; there was a scarcity of residential lots in the city. This agency was able to capture the market by developing sites, residential subdivisions, and neighbourhoods. Although Musgrave Agencies provide other services such as insurance, property management, and real estate, they have been a leader in land development and particularly in designing and building housing for affluent adult consumers. In 1981 the City of Lloydminster built a retention lake, called the Messum Lake, in a south-Alberta area, which was to be surrounded by open space, playgrounds, and an architecturally controlled subdivision designed to attract wealthy citizens. Although most of the area surrounding this lake was developed by the City of Lloydminster itself, some was developed by Musgrave Agencies. The majority of the land developed by this organization has been, and still is, in the south-Alberta area in Lloydminster. Musgrave has also built some residences on the Saskatchewan side, but its development in Saskatchewan was less extensive and more affordable "to fit the high 70,000 market.[43] In contrast, expensive homes have been built on south Alberta locations. Bill Musgrave is cited as describing homes as a reflection of the area in which they are situated.[44]

The gap between the personal income tax rates of both provinces has narrowed over time. Nevertheless, the prevailing myth of Alberta as a tax haven has accentuated the differences and fostered a preference for Alberta among home-owners. Almost all of the interviewees who chose to own homes on the Alberta side indicated that Alberta's tax advantage was a key reason for choosing this location for their homes.

Some home owners viewed moving between two Lloydminsters as career movements—up and down. One interviewee put it this way: "This is the way it is. You buy your first house in Saskatchewan and then move up, on the Alberta side, as you are a little more settled." Another confirmed this, when describing her move from Alberta to Saskatchewan as "moving down" from a large, expensive house to a relatively affordable and smaller house. She said, "We owned a big house on the Alberta side, but when my husband and I separated, I preferred to buy one in Saskatchewan; it was reasonably priced and smaller but enough for my boyfriend and myself. Also, my boyfriend had to pay less for auto insurance on this side of the border." The oral accounts of various citizens indicate that Alberta and Saskatchewan in Lloydminster evoke dissimilar class and status attributions. According to a real estate appraiser, "Saskatchewan with the majority of 900 square feet houses and lower land value is a haven for blue collar workers. Also, Saskatchewan's health advantage is most advantageous to low income groups." The same contention is echoed in the responses of six families who have moved from provinces such as Manitoba, Ontario, and Nova Scotia to accept employment with the Bi-Provincial Upgrader. They did not even look at houses in the Saskatchewan area because information gathered informally had convinced them that south-Alberta neighbourhoods were highly preferable and desirable: unlike Saskatchewan neighbourhoods, these neighbourhoods offered quality products, pleasant surroundings, and an opportunity for worthwhile investment.

Those moving from Calgary, St. Albert, or other Albertan cities tended to choose an Alberta residence; the same pattern existed for Saskatchewan residents. However, some Saskatchewan residents, after moving to Saskatchewan in Lloydminster, tended to change their location for reasons other than the tax difference. Thus, one of the interviewees who moved to Alberta from Saskatchewan commented, "We lived in Saskatchewan before moving to Lloydminster. However, while residing on the Saskatchewan side of the border, we felt as if we were living on the wrong side of the track." This response indicates that an Alberta location offers an "identity value" (Warde 1992) to its inhabitants which is more desirable than the identity offered by Saskatchewan. Harris and Pratt allude to this dimension when they observe,

> The home conveys messages about status and identity. Ownership is clearly one aspect of status message, but so too is neighbourhood, house style and interior and exterior decoration. It may be that home has become a more significant status object in recent times. (1993, p. 283).

Some homeowners, particularly in-migrants from other provinces who have chosen an Alberta location, referred to Alberta's marketability, potentiality of good resale value, or what has been termed as "exchange value" (Harvey 1975b; Logan and Molotch 1987; Warde 1992). This was reflected in comments such as, "We do not know how long we will live in Lloydminster. We bought a house on the Alberta side, because if we have to, it will be easy to sell it, and if we are lucky, we may get good returns as well."

Last but not least, there was an indication that residents also preferred a location for philosophical reasons—for their commitment to a way of life. An Alberta born and bred expressed his sentiments this way: "I would never choose to live on the Saskatchewan side, just for the sake of my belief in self reliance and individualism." Similar sentiments were echoed in the response of a family who moved to Lloydminster after selling their farm in Saskatchewan. This family chose a residence in Lloydminster Saskatchewan. They explained their choice this way: "We have always lived in Saskatchewan and believe in the communitarian-Saskatchewan way of life. Why should we pay $20,000 more for a similar house in Alberta? We are not that crazy."

The dual housing market in Lloydminster relates a great deal to the political philosophy of each province and its interpretations by all the players in the game: planners, developers, contractors, and builders who produce the product, as well as consumers who consume it. Clearly, a political philosophy favouring equality, compassion, and public ownership is outvoted in Lloydminster by the one that favours free market ideology, growth and individualism.

VII

Discussion and Conclusion

THE OPPOSING IDEOLOGICAL ORIENTATIONS of the provinces of Alberta and Saskatchewan which the city of Lloydminster straddles are well acknowledged (Brym 1978; Wiseman 1992). These dissimilar political ideologies have created a bi-provincial disparity-duality in Lloydminsters housing market. This duality manifests itself in Saskatchewan's "affordability" and Alberta's "desirability," sustained over time through planners, speculator-developers, and consumers. This binary character emerged in 1973, when the production of relatively expensive and desirable single-family residences in Alberta increased disproportionately, presumably because speculator-developers perceived this location as market-friendly, appealing to upperly mobile, high-income, and wealthy consumers and thus profit generating. The profitability was to derive from the perceived business-friendly climate, exemption from provincial sales tax, and liberal personal income tax policies of the province of Alberta: the former, likely to favour entrepreneurs as well as consumers in general, and the latter, homeowners in high income brackets. Although the difference between the personal income tax rates of these two provinces was nominal in the early 1970s, it became phenomenal in the mid-1970s and early 1980s (Table 10). It was during this period that the philosophical divide between these two provinces became wider and the Alberta advantage developed deeper roots in the Lloydminster housing market. The Alberta edge has continued to date despite a decline in the difference between the personal income tax rates of these two provinces. This continuation of difference has been problematized here.

If the rising difference between provincial personal income tax rates triggered an Alberta edge in the bi-provincial housing market in Lloydminster, why did it not decline with the reduction in tax differences? The answer seems to be provided by the observation that economic behavior, like "most behavior is closely embedded in networks of interpersonal relations" (Granovetter 1985, p. 504). This embeddedness allows for "trends to follow trends" which according to Bill Musgrave, a well established local real estate entrepreneur, explains the continuity of Alberta's edge in the housing market in Lloydminster.[45] Moreover, the development of a dominant ideology deserves a mention in this context. A dominant ideology perpetuates and proliferates through circulation of myths, tales, and day to day conversations on the streets, in gatherings - both formal and informal. An ideology, as Kemeny observes:

> may be said to be dominant when definitions of reality associated with a particular ideology are widely accepted. (1992, p. 102).

He also states:

> The term dominant ideology refers to widely accepted ideology that affects the setting of social, economic and political agenda. (1992, p. 97).

The prevailing dominant ideologies as revealed through conversations with retired merchants, city officials, real estate appraisers, real estate professionals, developers, and homeowners have portrayed Alberta as rich, prosperous, and a tax haven. It is also seen as less bureaucratic, more supportive of free markets, and a promoter of self-reliance. This discourse has tended to paint Saskatchewan as resistant to growth, bureaucratic, and a creator of tax burdens, despite also being recognized as compassionate and egalitarian. Undeniably, such discourses do refer to differences in policies which are real, not imaginary; differences in the personal income tax rates have lessened, but not disappeared. Besides the provincial personal income tax rates of these two provinces are not likely to be equal in the near future. Moreover, the above characterizations of Alberta and Saskatchewan have been rooted in some historical events, the interpretation of which has tended to reinforce the prevailing dominant ideology. This was indicated in a conversation with the late Blaire Bowsfield, who held a responsible position in the City of Lloydminster and later established himself as a reputable real estate entrepreneur. He explicitly stated,

> Progressive Conservatives have what it takes for growth and development of any area . . . If the political boundary of Alberta in Lloydminster was extended to cover its Saskatchewan complement and even beyond, that area will grow too. I used to be a Liberal, but not any more; ever since Liberals brought in National Energy Policy to the detriment of Western Canada and particularly of Alberta, I have become a strong supporter of the Progressive Conservative party.[46]

Such voices abound; those from the business community and in the fifty-plus age bracket were more likely than others to re-live the early 1980s, when the federal Liberal government introduced the National Energy Policy, which was viewed by Albertans as a gesture to undermine Alberta. This perception generated anti-Liberal sentiments which were generalized and extended to the New Democratic party as well: the NDP was seen as being ideologically closer to Liberals than Progressive Conservatives. Such discourses set a tone for a pro-conservative stance, which seems to have become a part of the dominant ideology among the entrepreneur class in Lloydminster.

While dominant ideology provided a context, developers, planners, and builders gave it a specific shape. They chose to acquire and develop land in the Lloydminster Alberta area which was perceived as profit-friendly and having a potential for generating "class-monopoly rent" (Harvey 1975a). The land in Lloydminster Saskatchewan is primarily owned by the City. On the other hand, a majority of the land on the Alberta side is owned by local entrepreneurs. These entrepreneurs have developed residential subdivisions in Alberta to deliver the consumption dreams and lifestyles of those in high income brackets. Even the City created such subdivisions exclusively in Alberta: as discussed earlier, a residential subdivision near Messum Lake was developed by the City to attract wealthy citizens in 1980, when oil prices peaked and Lloydminster was booming. The local entrepreneurs also developed some areas in Saskatchewan. In doing so, they developed and built a qualitatively different product, one that would be affordable enough to accommodate homeowners with modest incomes (Figure 2). Thus the dual—bifurcated — housing market was well sustained. Referring to the level of "class-monopoly rent" realized by speculator developers, Harvey stated:

> If the speculator-developer can persuade upper-income groups of the virtues of a certain kind of housing in a particular neighbourhood, gain...control over the political process and so on, then the advantage lies with the speculator-developer (1975a, p. 150).

Such has, indeed, been the case in Lloydminster. Given the availability of unique options, Lloydminster residents as consumers tended to choose a location which they perceive as beneficial and rewarding at a given time. The Alberta tax advantage, availability of quality upscale residences, and an opportunity to validate and enhance their identity and status claims have pulled high income groups to the Alberta side. On the other hand, Saskatchewan's advantages of health care without any premiums and cheaper auto insurance coverage have attracted those with such priorities to the Saskatchewan side. This group is also likely to prefer a moderately-priced, affordable home. Such a pattern of choice is congruent with the environmental-opportunity theory (Michelson 1973), which contends that people choose a particular place to live to match their preferred lifestyle. This pattern is also consistent with the claim of rational choice theorists that people choose after comparing the benefits or payoffs of alternative courses of actions (Wallace and Wolf 1998). This type of choice-making alludes to Max Weber's concept of "practical rationality," which "exists as a manifestation of man's capacity for means-end rational action" (Kalberg 1980, p. 1152).

Practical rationality implies that:

pragmatic action in terms of everyday interests is ascendent, and given practical ends are attained by careful weighing and increasingly precise calculation of the most adequate means (Kalberg,1980, p. 1152).

However, sometimes provincial locations have been chosen for sentimental reasons: those from Saskatchewan frequently settle in Saskatchewan locations, and those from Alberta almost exclusively settle in Alberta locations. Their choices have been primarily guided by a combination of practical rationality and substantive rationality. "Substantive rationality," a concept originating from Max Weber, refers to value orientation and regulation of actions and choices "from within" (Kalberg 1980). In the present case, it refers to a sense of pride, provincial identification and provincial loyalty.

Thus, the dual housing market in the provincially divided city of Lloydminster has emerged in response to various policies of both provinces. Until 1973, Saskatchewan dominated the housing market; since 1973, the balance has tilted towards Alberta. This duality has not only been perpetuated but has also proliferated over time through an ongoing favourable interpretation of Alberta's provincial policies by all players who construct this reality.

VIII

Data and Method

THE DATA IN THIS PAPER ARE DRAWN from the 1971, 1976, 1981, 1986, 1991, and 1996 censuses of Canada and municipal censuses collected by the city of Lloydminster until 1989. Other sources have also been used. These include information obtained from the Canadian Real Estate Association, Ottawa, and the Lloydminster Real Estate Board regarding the sale of single-family residential units in both provinces in Lloydminster according to price categories. The data regarding the construction of single-family residences, as reflected in the specifics of permits issued, were gathered from the city of Lloydminster. I have chosen to concentrate only on single-family residences because according to the 1996 census, 74.45% of all residential dwellings in Lloydminster are single houses; 95% of these are detached and 5% are semi-detached. Hence, this form of residence provides a sharper focus for the comparison of home ownership between the two locations. There is some indication that other forms of residences, such as tri-plexes and townhouses, tend to become rental units over time.

The indicators of the housing market in this study include:

a. The number of single-family units sold (or resold) on each pro-vincial side of Lloydminster as reported by the Lloydminster Real Estate Board.

b. The average value of a single-family residential unit sold (or re-sold) on each provincial side of Lloydminster as reported by the Multiple Listing Service (MLS) and obtained from the Lloyd-minster Real Estate Board.

c. Production of single-family residences as indicated through building permits issued by the city of Lloydminster for such con-struction on each provincial side.

d. The average value of the permits issued for the construction of single-family residences on each provincial side, calculated on the basis of details provided by the city of Lloydminster.

The information derived from various censuses of Canada which has explanatory value includes bi-provincial distribution of family in-come in Lloydminster, bi-provincial differences in some characteristics of occupied residences, and the proportion of in-migrants from other provinces in each provincial location in Lloydminster. The personal income tax rates for the provinces of Alberta and Saskatchewan, ob-tained from Revenue Canada, are examined to make sense of the dis-parity in the distribution of family income between residents of Al-berta and Saskatchewan in Lloydminster. This information is supplemented by the responses of thirty homeowners–fifteen each from Alberta and Saskatchewan–to a single open question: "Why did you choose the given location of your residence?" This probe into homeowners' reasons for choosing a particular location provides an invaluable insight into the nature of provincial housing markets in Lloydminster and helps to develop a comprehensive and balanced un-derstanding of the issue.

Further insight into the uneven residential development is gleaned from local developers' stories published in area newspapers and from their own accounts of the situation as gathered in formal and informal conversations. Also interviewed regarding their perception of the causes of uneven development of the two provincial locations in Lloydminster were real estate appraisers, city councillors, the mayor of the city, and some prominent senior citizens. These senior citizens with their reservoir of collective memory have witnessed the development of the city for more than fifty years. Snowball sampling was used to interview homeowners and senior citizens. This sampling entails "purposely selecting the starting point, then asking the starting point to recommend other suitable respondents" (Hessler 1992, p. 131). The oral accounts of these sources offer qualitative details valuable for understanding the dual character of spatial development, particularly that of the residential space in the city of Lloydminster.

Notes

1. The Lloydminster Meridian Booster, August 13, 2000, p. A10.

2·. The left leanings of the UFA in the pre-Depression period and a change in this orientation later on is elucidated by Brym (1978, p. 345) as follows:

Before the Depression, the UFA had rigorously excluded from its ranks small town merchants and other middle class townspeople since it regarded them as the exploiter of the farmer. But the years following 1929 brought about a marked change in this antagonistic relationship. Jean Burnet notes in a report on the fieldwork conducted in the area around Hanna, Alberta that during the Depression "farmers and merchants became more aware of their interdependence through the business failures which marked years of little rain and low prices" and agrees with one local businessman's observation that the drought "brought the farmers and townspeople closer … the store would give the farmer credit when the banks wouldn't give him a loan" (Burnet 1947, p. 403).

3. The American influence on Alberta is noted by other observers as well. Aside from Alberta's historical endorsement of American style individualism, Joanne Helmer (1995, p. 71) points to the strong economic and social connection between Alberta and the United States. She calls attention to a commonly observed practice in the town of Mcgrath: flying an American flag along with the Canadian and Albertan flag. Harrison and Laxer (1995, p. 10–11) allude to the current process of Americanizing from within, referring to Alberta's move towards the American model of two tiers of access for health and education.

4. Such analogies are still prevalent. In the mid 1990s, Barron's magazine compared Ralph Klein to the high-profile Republican in the United States House of Representatives, calling Klein Canada's Newt; Klein would have preferred "Newt North" (*The Edmonton Journal*, February 18, 1995:C1). Harrison

and Laxer (1995, p. XV) refer to the February 23, 1995 issue of the *Wall Street Journal* "dubbing Ralph Klein as Canada's Reagan."

5. Pro-business orientation implies the building of a political and economic climate which is conducive to the growth of business. This is usually reflected in granting concessions: tax exemptions to businesses, subsidizing businesses, accepting cuts in royalties, encouraging privatization, creating a less bureaucratic regulatory system, not to mention a provision of "no sales tax" for consumers. Such an orientation seems to have been an integral part of Alberta's political ideology since the rise of the Social Credit Party in 1935.

6. *The Lloydminster Daily Times*, June 30, 1997, p. 2A.

7. *Maclean's*, April 3, 2000, p. 42–45; *The Globe and Mail*, May 12, 2000, pp. A1, A9.

8. Klein's Progressive Conservative government wrote off more than $200 million in debt owed by the Miller Western pulp mill in Slave Lake; it waived $130 million worth of interest that Alberta Pacific pulp near Athabasca owes the province; it cut oil and gas royalties in late 1992 by an estimated $250 million a year (*Edmonton Journal*, January 6, 1998, p. A1). This government's loan losses during the past few years amount to $2.35 billion (*Edmonton Journal*, March 4, 1998, p. A1).

9. *The Globe and Mail*, March 29, 2000, p. B1.

10 Saskatchewan's socialist model has received recognition overseas as well. In a recent workshop sponsored by the Canadian International Development Agency in Havana, Cuban officials were impressed by the social democratic model of Saskatchewan (*Edmonton Journal*, April 29, 1998, p. A4).

11. The Saskatchewan government introduced the Education Tax Act in 1937, which allowed the levying of 2% tax on various commodities. This was the beginning of the retail sales tax in Saskatchewan. The tax was introduced to cope with the economic hardship caused by the Depression and adverse agricultural conditions. The Saskatchewan Education tax, renamed later on as Education and Health tax, still exists. It rose from 2% in 1937 to 9% in 1993; it was reduced to 7% in March 1997 and to 6% in March 2000.

12. Eric Cline, Saskatchewan's Finance Minister, is reported to have said that "income tax cuts are necessary if Saskatchewan is to stay competitive with its rich neighbour, Alberta" (*The Globe and Mail*, March 29, 2000, p. A5).

13. *The Lloydminster Meridian Booster*, March 8, 1998, p. A2.

14 *The Lloydminster Meridian Booster*, February 25, 1998, p. A15; The Lloydminster Meridian Booster, March 8, 1998, p. A2.

15. The Saskatchewan Party, the voice of opposition, emerged in August 1997 as a result of provincial Liberals and provincial Conservatives joining forces to form a united front. Presumably, the reason for this joint stance was that both the Conservatives and the Liberals, the opposition parties, were in grave disarray. Twenty Conservatives from the Devine regime were charged in a Saskatchewan corruption scandal, resulting in the ever declining credibil-

ity of the party. The Liberals in Saskatchewan were encountering internal battles and lacked an effective impact. With a new name and restructured identity, the opposition in Saskatchewan has come to describe itself as a right of centre, free enterprise alternative to the NDP.

16. *The Lloydminster Meridian Booster*, January 4, 1995, p. A4; *The Edmonton Journal*, December 28, 1997, p. A9.

17. *Red Deer Advocate*, December 13, 1996, p. C7.

18. Perception of growth-resistance relates to policies which indeed are less business-friendly than Alberta. Thus, although goods and services for personal consumptions are exempted from provincial sales tax in Lloydminster, Saskatchewan, commercial transactions are not. Recently, the Saskatchewan government announced its intention to extend tax on items such as real estate fees, lawyers fees, and accountant fees. This announcement created a deep concern in Saskatchewan's business community. To deal with this concern, the Lloydminster Chamber of Commerce invited Saskatchewan's Finance Minister, Eric Cline, to a closed door roundtable discussion with local business people, including many who deal on the Saskatchewan side. Arguing that the Saskatchewan government has an opportunity to share in the growth of this community, the President of the Lloydminster Chamber of Commerce stated, "If the government does something about the Provincial Sales Tax (PST), business will start up, they will stay, and they will renovate." (The Lloydminster Meridian Booster, June 25, 2000, p. A1). The meeting with the Finance Minister did result in an announcement of the granting of exemption from the new provincial sales tax measures by the Saskatchewan government. He announced that:

"The current exemption for business expenses will include the goods and services that were added to the tax base on March 30, 2000 as well as legal services, advertising services, and commercial cleaning services which will be added July 1, 2000." Additionally, the Finance Minister is reported to have pledged to undertake a review of the taxation of commercial construction and business assets in Lloydminster. (The Lloydminster Meridian Booster, "Finance Minister Grants PST Exemption", June 28, 2000, p. A1).

19. A story which had a profound impact on the business community's perception of Saskatchewan vis-vis Alberta was told by the late Ron Harris, a businessman and well-respected citizen of Lloydminster. His tale had it that during the mid sixties, the Saskatchewan Premier, annoyed in general with Lloydminster's merchants for not collecting sales tax and specifically with a particular merchant for actively protesting against this tax, went with an assistant to the merchant's residence with the intention of "punching" him, but was persuaded by his assistant not to do it!

20. The Order of Council passed by the Government of Saskatchewan. August 10, 1993, p. 2.

21. A geological survey conducted by G. S. Hume and C. O. Hage in 1940

observed: The fact...that gas and oil occur in the Lloydminster area...is not only decidedly important in itself, but even of greater importance as an indication of what may be eventually expected from the large area included within central eastern Alberta and western Saskatchewan (1940, p. 20).

22. The Jaycee park area surrounding Jaycee Lake–a retention lake–in south Saskatchewan was built earlier than any other area around a retention lake in Lloydminster. This area still remains underdeveloped. On the other hand, open space surrounding Messum Lake–another retention lake–in south-Alberta is aesthetically developed. The reason might be that Messum Lake is ringed by an opulent, wealthy residential neighbourhood and has come to acquire a prestigious status. On the other hand, the Jaycee park area serves residents residing in relatively modest homes, who supposedly have modest incomes and occupy a modest status; therefore, it has not received equal attention. Also, the City presumably collects substantial property taxes from those residing in the Messum Lake area.

23. The incoming president of the Lloydminster Chamber of Commerce is reported to have said that "people are inclined to move to the area in part because of amenities like Bud Miller All Seasons Park or because of a more rural setting than the big cities, but with all the services available" (*Lloydminster Daily Times*, March 2, 1998, p. 1A).

24. This programme came into effect almost simultaneously with the start of the election campaign, and thus was seen as a ploy to win re-election. This programme was reported to have assisted the homeowners with improvements, such as installing swimming pools (*The Globe and Mail*, September 4, 1986).

25. The reason for the sagging housing market was the downturn in the economy, which began with the drastic decline in oil prices in 1982. Although both Alberta and Saskatchewan encountered this situation, the Province of Saskatchewan was affected much more negatively than Alberta. It started losing its population: In 1986, there were 1,009,613 people in Saskatchewan; in 1991, there were 988,928, a loss of 20,685 people. It was increasingly perceived as a poor have-not province.

26. *The Lloydminster Meridian Booster*, January 20, 1991; *The Lloydminster Meridian Booster*, April 3, 1991, p. A1.

27. According to a market analyst for the Canada Mortgage and Housing Corporation, the growth in housing starts in Lloydminster reflected the good feeling about the construction of the BPU (*The Lloydminster Meridian Booster*, February 3, 1991, p. A2). Addressing the lopsided development of residential construction in Lloydminster, the then chair of the City's Planning and Development Committee observed, "It is free enterprise and investments will go on whatever side...if it is an Alberta company, that has a subsidiary office here, they are not going to particularly go into Saskatchewan because of all the implications of one government to the other" (*The Lloydminster Meridian Booster*, August 14, 1991, p. A1).

28. This information was gathered through informal sources and, as such, is an approximation. Husky Oil Operations in Lloydminster was unable to provide the information.

29. *The Lloydminster Times*, December 11, 1993, p. 3.

30. Canada Mortgage and Housing Corporation's Annual Rental Market Survey indicated that rental vacancy rates in Lloydminster were the lowest in Canada at 0.1% (*Border Business*, Fourth Quarter 1997, p. 3).

31. The population of Saskatchewan has increased since the 1991 Census. The increase is slight: in 1991, the population was 988,928; in 1996, it was 990,237. However, there are indications that few people are leaving the province as new jobs are being created in service industries, communications, construction, and manufacturing. In 1997, the social assistance case load also declined in Saskatchewan (*Lloydminster Sunday Sun*, July 6, 1997, p. 2). The province appears to have made a turnaround from being a have-not province to one with hope and possibilities of growth.

32. *The Lloydminster Regional Times,* January 14, 1998, p. 3A; *The Lloydminster Meridian Booster,* January 18, 1998, p. A8.

33. The price category of $120,000 and above had zero frequency for Saskatchewan for three years (1990, 1992, and 1993) and only one for four years (1988, 1989, 1991, 1995). However, the Lloydminster Saskatchewan housing market has witnessed a change since 1995. It had 17 single family residences sold in the above price category in 1997; 11 in 1998, and 13 in 1999. The corresponding numbers for its Alberta counterpart were 115 in 1997, 113 in 1998, and 115 in 1999.

34. *The Lloydminster Meridian Booster*, December 14, 1997, p. A18.

35. *The Lloydminster Meridian Booster,* March 20, 1996, p. A8.

36. *The Lloydminster Times*, October 23, 1994, p. A8.

37. *The Lloydminster Meridian Booster,* January 24, 1996, p. A1.

38. *The Edmonton Journal*, April 26, 1998, p. A1.

39. For the Census years 1981 and 1986, the lowest income category consisted of an annual family income under $5000. In these censuses an interval of $5000 was used between various categories. The lowest income categories for the 1991 and 1996 censuses have been changed to under $10,000, and an interval of $10,000 has been used between various categories. Hence, the tables for 1981 and 1986 have been constructed to make these compatible with 1991 and 1996 censuses, but no data are lost. The value of the median family income for each census year is the same as provided in the corresponding censuses.

40. On the other hand, Saskatchewan is seen as the stagnant poor-old country. In fact, Saskatchewan lost its sizable population to Alberta. According to figures quoted in *Maclean's*, Almost 211,000 of Alberta's 2.6 million inhabitants came from Saskatchewan, making the single biggest contributor of people to Alberta (February 24, 1997, p. 2).

41. The booster mentality of urban entrepreneurial elites on the prairies in

Canada has been noticed and studied (Artibise 1981; Voisey 1981; Thomas 1981). Such examples exist in Lloydminster as well. The entrepreneurial genius of Neilson gave birth to Husky Oil Operations, which has boosted the economic and socio-cultural growth of the city since 1947. Ray Nelson, another entrepreneur-booster, has contributed to this city's growth in many different ways. He has been instrumental in establishing the auxiliary hospital, the Dr. Cooke Nursing Home, the wave pool at the Leisure Centre, and the Barr Colony Heritage Centre. He is also credited with persuading the Great Canadian Superstore to open a branch in Lloydminster—a city of barely 20,000 people in 1990. According to a local area newspaper, in 1990 Nelson was the largest employer in Lloydminster, creating $300,000 in tax revenues for the city. Nelson asked the city for a tax concession, which was denied on the grounds that it would set a problematic precedent. There were anxious moments, and the concern that Nelson Lumber and the manufacturing jobs might move elsewhere in Western Canada. However, it all settled down, with the City of Lloydminster agreeing to a proposed $9 million redevelopment plan on Nelson Lumber property. The re-development plan entailed partially closing off two streets and re-zoning some of the property. In return, Nelson offered to strike a deal with Westfair, the Calgary-based wholesale and retail giant, to have the Real Canadian Superstore lease a 92,000 square foot building on Nelson property. The Superstore was expected to create up to 350 jobs and restore Lloydminster's status as a regional trade centre. Nelson also promised to keep its manufacturing plant and its 150 jobs in the city (*The Lloydminster Meridian Booster*: Special Section, August 5, 1990, p.D4-D7).

42. In 1997, this company was inducted into the Saskatchewan Business Hall of Fame for being a leading producer in the lumber and home building area for more than forty years.

43. Progress '95: A Supplement to the *Lloydminster Meridian Booster*, June 28, 1995, p. A29.

44. *The Lloydminster Meridian Booster*, November 1, 1995, p. A13.

45. Personal communication, May 1991.

46. In 1980, the federal Liberal government introduced the National Energy Policy. This policy was perceived by the Western oil and gas producing provinces as undermining their interests while serving the interests of Central Canada. The reason for this discontent was that the National Energy Policy had restricted the upward movement of Canadian oil and gas prices. Consequently, Canadian prices fell far below the rising world oil and gas prices. This situation benefitted the Canadian consumer at the cost of revenues to the Western oil and gas producers. Additionally, the Liberal government imposed the Petroleum and Gas Revenue Tax (PGRT) on oil producers; this tax further reduced their revenues. The National Energy Policy did indeed have a drastic impact on the oil and gas industry in Western Canada. Most importantly, it created a wedge between Western and Eastern Canada: energy-producing Western Canada was seen as the bearer of the burden of cost and Eastern

Canada as the consuming region—the beneficiary. This situation also reinforced an anti-Liberal and pro-Conservative stance in Alberta, the major oil and gas producing area in Canada.

References

Artibise, A. F. J. 1981. "Boosterism and the Development of Prairie Cities, 1871-1913" in Alan F. J. Artibise, ed., *Town and City: Aspects of Western Canadian Urban Development*, pp. 209-235. Canadian Plains Studies 10. University of Regina: Canadian Plains Research Centre.

The Atlas of Alberta: A Special Project of Alberta Report "Lloydminster." 1984. P. 129. Edmonton: Interwest Publications Ltd.

Avakumovic, I. 1978. Socialism in Canada: A Study of CCF-NDP in Federal and Provincial Politics. Toronto: McClelland and Stewart Ltd.

Balakrishnan, T. R. and K. Selvanathan. 1990. "Ethnic Residential Segregation in Metropolitan Canada" in S. S. Halli, Frank Trovato and Leo Driedger, eds., *Ethnic Demography: Canadian Immigrants Racial and Cultural Variations*, pp. 399-413. Ottawa: Carleton University Press.

Border Business, Fourth Quarter, 1997; p. 3.

Bourne, L. S., and T. Bunting. 1993. "Housing Markets, Community Development and Neighbourhood Change" in Larry S. Bourne and David F. Ley, eds., *The Changing Social Geography of Canadian Cities*, pp. 175-195. Montreal: McGill-Queen's University Press.

Bowen, L. 1992. *Muddling Through*. Vancouver: Graystone Books.

Bowsfield, Blaire. May 1991. Owner, Bowsfield Realty (a franchise of Royal Lepage). Lloydminster, AB/SK. Personal Communication.

Brennan, W. L. 1992. "The Autonomy Question and the Creation of Alberta and Saskatchewan, 1905" in R. Douglas Francis and H. Palmer, eds., *The Prairie West*, pp. 378-396. Edmonton: Pica Pica Press.

Brym, R. 1978. "Regional Social Structure and Agrarian Radicalism in Canada: Alberta, Saskatchewan and New Brunswick." *The Canadian Review of Sociology and Anthropology* 15:339-351.

———. 1986 "An Introduction to the Regional Question in Canada" in R. Brym, ed., *Regionalism in Canada*, pp. 1-45. Toronto: Irving Publishing.

Burnet, J. 1947. "Town-Country Relations and the Problem of Rural Leadership." *Canadian Journal of Economics and Political Science* 13:395-409.

Carroll, B. 1990. "Housing" in R. A. Loreto and T. Price, eds., *Urban Policy Issues*, pp. 86-106. Toronto: McClelland and Stewart Inc.

Centre for the Study of Cooperatives. 1998. The Social and Economic Importance of the Cooperatives Sector in Saskatchewan. Saskatchewan, May.

Che-Alford, J. 1990. "Home Ownership," *Canadian Social Trends,* Statistics Canada, Spring:2-5.

Choldin, H. M. and C. Hanson. 1982. "Status Shifts Within the City," *American Sociological Review,* 47:129-141.

Dahms, F. A. 1986. "Diversity, Complexity and Change: Characteristics of Some Ontario Towns and Villages." *Canadian Geographer* 30:158-166.

Denis, C. 1995. "The New Normal: Capitalist Discipline in Alberta in the 1990s" in Trevor Harrison and Gordon Laxer, eds., *The Trojan Horse: Alberta and the Future of Canada* , pp. 86-100. Montreal: Black Rose Books.

Duncan, S. and M. Savage. 1989. "Space Scale and Locality." *Antipode* 21:179-206.

Edmonton Journal. 1997. December 28:A9.

————. 1998. January 6:A1.

————. 1998. April 26:A1.

————. 1998. April 29:A4.

Everitt, J. C. and A. M. Gill. 1993. "The Social Geography of Small Towns" in Larry S. Bourne and David F. Ley, eds., *The Changing Social Geography of Canadian Cities,* pp. 252-264. (Montreal: McGill-Queen's University Press.

Globe and Mail. 1986. September 4.

————. 2000. March 29:A5,B1.

————. 2000. May 12:A1,A9.

Granovetter, M. 1985. "Economic Action and Social Structure. The Problem of Embeddedness." *American Journal of Sociology* 91:481-510.

Harris, R. 1986. "Boom and Bust: The Effects of House Price Inflation on Homeownership Patterns in Montreal, Toronto and Vancouver." *The Canadian Geographer* 30:302-315.

Harris, R. and G. J. Pratt. 1993. "The Meaning of Home, Homeownership and Public Policy" in Larry S. Bourne and David F. Ley, eds., *The Changing Social Geography of Canadian Cities,* pp .281-297. Montreal: McGill-Queen's University Press.

Harrison, T. 1995. "Making the Trains Run on Time: Corporalism in Alberta" in Trevor Harrison and Gordon Laxer, eds., *The Trojan Horse: Alberta and the Future of Canada,* pp.118-131. Montreal: Black Rose Books.

Harrison, T. and G. Laxer. 1995. "Introduction" in T. Harrison and G. Laxer, eds., *The Trojan Horse: Alberta and the Future of Canada, pp. 1-19.* Montreal: Black Rose Books.

Harvey, D. 1975a. "Class-Monopoly Rent, Finance Capital and the Urban Revolution" in Stephen Gale and Eric G. Moore, eds., *The Manipulated City: Perspectives on Spatial Structure and Social Issues in Urban America,* pp. 145-167. Chicago: Maaroufa Press.

————. 1975b. "The Nature of Housing" in Stephen Gale and Eric G. Moore, eds., *The Manipulated City: Perspectives on Spatial Structure and Social Issues in Urban America,* pp. 132-134. Chicago: Maaroufa Press.

Helmer, J. 1995. "Redefining Normal: Life in the New Alberta" in Trevor Harrison and Gordon Laxer, eds., *The Trojan Horse: Alberta and the Future of Canada,* pp. 70-85. Montreal: Black Rose Books.

Hertzog, S. and R. D. Lewis. 1986. "A City of Tenants: Homeownership and Social Class in Montreal, 1847-1881." *The Canadian Geographer* 30:316-323.

Hessler, R. M. 1992. Social Research Methods. New York:West Publishing Company.

Hume, G. S. and Hage, C. O. 1940. *The Lloydminster Gas and Oil Area, Alberta and Saskatchewan.* Geological Survey Paper 40-11. Ottawa: J. O. Patenaude, I. S. O.

Kalberg, Stephen. 1980. "Max Weber's Types of Rationality: Cornerstones for the Analysis of Rationalization Processes in History." *American Journal of Sociology* 85:1145-1179.

Kemeny, J. 1992. *Housing and Social Theory.* London: Routledge.

Laxer, G. 1995. "The Privatization of Public Life" in Trevor Harrison and Gordon Laxer, eds., *The Trojan Horse: Alberta and the Future of Canada*, pp. 101-117. Montreal: Black Rose Books.

Laxer, J. 1984. Oil and Gas: Ottawa, the Provinces and the Petroleum Industry. Toronto: James Lorimer and Company.

Ley, D. F. and L. S. Bourne. 1993. "The Social Context and Diversity of Urban Canada" in Larry S. Bourne and David F. Ley, eds., *The Changing Social Geography of Canadian Cities*, pp. 3-30. Montreal: McGill-Queen's University Press.

Lloydminster Daily Times. 1997. June 30:2A.

———. 1998. March 2:1A.

Lloydminster Economic Development Authority. 1995. *Trade Area Study: Lloydminster.* The City of Lloydminster.

Lloydminster Meridian Booster. 1990. August 5:D4-D7.

———. 1991. January 20:A2.

———. 1991. February 3:A2.

———. 1991. April 3:A1.

———. 1991. August 14:A1.

———. 1995. January 4:A4.

———. 1995. November 1:A13.

———. 1995. Progress '95: A Supplement. June 28:A29.

———. 1996. January 24:A1.

———. 1996. March 20:A8.

———. 1997. December 14:A18.

———. 1998. February 25:A15.

———. 1998. March 8:A2.

———. 2000. June 25:A1.

———. 2000. June 28:A1.

———. 2000. August 13:A10.

Lloydminster Regional Times. 1998. January 4:3A.

Lloydminster Sunday Sun. 1997. July 6:2.

Lloydminster Times. 1993. December 11:3.

————. 1994. October 23:A8.

Logan, J. R. and Harvey L. Molotch. 1987. *Urban Fortunes: The Political Economy of Place*. Los Angeles: University of California Press.

Lysyk, Tom. May 1998. City Clerk, The City of Lloydminster, Lloydminster, AB/SK. Personal Communication.

Maclean's. 1995. "To Tax or Not to Tax." February 13:16-22.

Maclean's. 1997. "Prairie Cousins." February 24:22.

Maclean's. 2000. "Health: The Alberta Test." April 3:42-45.

Makale & Kyllo Planning Associates Ltd. 1985. *Plan Lloydminster, 1985: Development Plan*. The City of Lloydminster.

Macpherson, C. B. 1962. *Democracy in Alberta: Social Credit and the Party System*. Toronto: University of Toronto Press.

Michelson, W. D. 1973. *Environmental Change* Research Paper No. 60. Centre for Urban and Community Studies, University of Toronto.

Musgrave, Bill. May 1991. Owner, Musgrave Agencies, Lloydminster, AB/SK. Personal Communication.

Qadeer, M. and K. Chinnery. 1981. *Canadian Towns and Villages: A Economic Profile*. Research and Working Papers 14. Institute of Urban Studies, University of Winnipeg.

Ray, B. K. and E. Moore. 1991. "Access to Homeownership among Immigrant Groups in Canada." *The Canadian Review of Sociology and Anthropology* 28:1-29.

Red Deer Advocate. 1996. "Tax Royalties Hurt Saskatchewan Patch" December 13:C7.

Richard, J. and L. Pratt. 1979. *Prairie Capitalism: Power and Influence in the New West*. Toronto: McClelland and Stewart Ltd.

Rossi, P. H. and A .B. Shlay. 1982. "Residential Mobility and Public Policy Issues: Why Families Move Revisited." *Journal of Social Issues* 38:21-34.

Saskatchewan Cabinet. August 10, 1993. "Saskatchewan order-in-council: Education and Health Tax." 622/93.

Thomas, L. H. 1981. "Saskatoon, 1883-1920: The Formative Years" in Alan F.J. Artibise, ed., *Town and City: Aspects of Western Canadian Urban Development*, pp. 237-258. Canadian Plains Studies 10, University of Regina: Canadian Plains Research Centre.

Turner, M. and R. J. Struyk. 1989. *Urban Housing in the 1980s: Markets and Policies*. Washington D.C.: The Urban Institute Press.

Voisey, P. 1981. "Boosting the Small Prairie Town 1904-1931: An Example from Southern Alberta" in Alan F.J. Artibise, ed., *Town and City: Aspects of Western Canadian Urban Development*, pp.147-176. Canadian Plains Studies 10. University of Regina: Canadian Plains Research Centre.

Wallace, R. A. and A. Wolf. 1998. Contemporary Sociological Theory: Expanding the Classical Tradition. New Jersey: Prentice Hall.

Warde, A. 1992. "Notes on the Relationship Between Production and Consumption" in R. Burrows and C. Marsh, eds., *Consumption and Class: Divisions and Change*, pp. 15-31. London: MacMillan.

Wiseman, N. 1992. "The Pattern of Prairie Politics" in R. Douglas Francis and H. Palmer, eds., *The Prairie West*, pp. 640-660. Edmonton: Pica Pica Press.

Wragge, P. and H. Bartel. 1981. An Evaluation of the Registered Home-ownership Savings Plan. Ottawa: CMHC.

PART IV

The Transformation of the City in the 21st Century

American Journal of Economics and Sociology, Vol. 60, No. 1 (January, 2001).
© 2001 American Journal of Economics and Sociology, Inc.

International Sister-Cities

Bridging the Global-Local Divide

By Rolf D. Cremer, Anne de Bruin and Ann Dupuis[*]

Abstract. With the demise of the sharp urban-rural divide as a framework for urban analyses, debates have arisen regarding the utility of the city as a theoretically significant construct. Recently however, the growing emphasis on globalization has brought the analysis of global cities into sharp focus. The countervailing trend emphasizes the significance of "the local." International sister-cities provide a site of analysis which illustrates the global-local interface and yet delves deeper. Initially conceived as a post-war means of developing friendships and cultural ties, sister-cities were based on similarities such as name or economic function. More recently, greater recognition has been given to the economic foundations and benefits of these connections. Providing an extension to an integrated approach to the study of sister-cities based on the multifold relationship between culture and commerce, this paper adds a further dimension by focusing on simultaneously operating multi-level entrepreneurial partnerships necessary to sustain active sister-city relationships. Drawing on New Zealand examples of twinning arrangements, it is demonstrated that the emergence and development of embedded partnership ties is vital to deriving sustainable economic and social benefits. While the global outreach of the sister-cities phenomenon appears to transcend the geographic confines of cities, strong locality considerations and local activism nevertheless predominate. A novel feature of this paper is the conceptualization of a hybrid form of entrepreneurialism, "municipal-community entrepreneurship," which is argued as a valuable facilitator of the economic and social vibrancy of cities.

* Rolf Cremer Ph.D. and Anne de Bruin Ph.D. are in the College of Business and Ann Dupuis Ph.D. is in the College of Humanities and Social Sciences, Massey University, New Zealand.

American Journal of Economics and Sociology, Vol. 60, No. 1 (January, 2001).

I

Introduction

WITH THE DEMISE OF THE URBAN-RURAL DIVIDE as a framework for urban analyses, debates arose regarding the utility of the city as a theoretically significant category of analysis (Castells 1977, 1978, 1983; Saunders 1986). Of late however, analyses of the city and the urban condition have emerged with renewed vigor (Dear 2000; Zukin 1995). A particular current focus has been one on the global processes that that have shaped the role of such major global cities as London, Tokyo and New York in a new global economy (Sassen 1996). A countervailing trend has been one that focuses on the significance of the local, tracing "urban diversity to internal force and the tactics used by local actors" (Fainstein 1996, p. 170). International sister-cities, the topic of this paper, illustrate the global-local interface. Yet the intricate workings of each sister-city relationship belie the superficiality of a simple, global-local divide. In fact, one purpose of this paper is to show through the sister-city example that the global-local dichotomy is a nebulous one requiring in-depth analysis of contextual uniqueness.

An examination of sister-cities must begin with the politics of locality and a recognition of the individualized operations of specific cities, then move on to an examination of how these particularities are used as a basis for forging city to city links across the globe. Specific to the phenomenon of sister-cities is that these links are made for a range of identifiable purposes and largely outside the auspices of any central government involvement.

A common trend in local government in developed countries, particularly since the 1980s, has been greater activism in promoting local economic development and employment growth. New Zealand has not been an exception (Lancaster 1993). This shift from "managerialism to entrepreneurialism" (Harvey 1989a) has increasingly resulted in local government being involved in enterprise initiatives and the searching out of other proactive means of promoting their particular sites or cities as desirable locations for economic and social activity. An important feature of this new entrepreneurialism is the element of "public-private partnership" that works "to lure highly mobile and flexible production, financial and consumption flows into its space" (Harvey 1989b, p. 11). Such features are clearly discernible in the workings of sister-city relationships. In order to better capture and elaborate on both this partnership focus and local government entrepreneurialism, in Section IV of this paper we develop the hybrid concept of "municipal-community entrepreneurship." Section IV also includes a discussion of agglomeration economies, which are argued as the "source of urban efficiency" and a key to "dynamic cities as engines of growth" (The World Bank 2000, pp. 125, 126).

This article is organized as follows. In the next section we describe the phenomenon of sister-cities, a topic on which there is a paucity of academic literature, despite the fact that thousands of such relationships exist between cities across the world and a significant proportion of the world's people live in cities that have formally entered into some form of twinning agreement. Section III sets out the integrative framework to examine the operation of sister-cities, based on the multifold relationship between culture and commerce. The extension we develop, which overlays this integrated approach with a focus on the simultaneously operating multi-level entrepreneurial partnerships necessary to sustain active sister-city relationships, follows in the next section. In order to accomplish this, we formulate the concept of "municipal-community entrepreneurship" which pivots on multi-level entrepreneurial partnerships, and argue for the necessity of such entrepreneurship when setting up and sustaining successful sister-city relationships. Section V is given over to a description of a successful sister-city relationship, that between Hastings in New Zealand and Guilin in China. This particular relationship was selected in order to highlight salient features of the extended integrated approach to the analysis of sister-cities and to demonstrate that when these features are present, sister-city relationships are likely to succeed. In the penultimate section, benefits of sister-city relationships are commented on. We end the paper with a concluding observation on the role that the sister-city movement plays in the global-local dynamic that characterizes the emerging landscape of the twenty-first century. The general applicability of municipal-community entrepreneurship and its potential for enhancing the sustainability of cities is also stressed.

II

The Sister-Cities Phenomenon

THE POPULAR LITERATURE ON SISTER-CITIES largely credits the development of the phenomenon of sister-cities to former US President Dwight D. Eisenhower's support (Hepler 1994, p. 22) at a White House conference in 1956 of a national initiative proposing a people-to-people program. It is claimed that President Eisenhower's intention was to "involve individuals and organized groups at all levels of society in citizen diplomacy, with the hope that personal relationships, fostered through sister city, county and state affiliations, would lessen the chance of future world conflicts" (Sister Cities International 1999). The initial aim of the broad movement was "to increase international understanding and foster world peace by furthering international communication and exchange at the person-to-person level through city-to-city affiliations" (Sister Cities New Zealand Inc. undated).

However, the roots of the sister-cities phenomenon can be traced back more directly to the aftermath of the Second World War and the help British cities gave European cities devastated by the conflict.[1] In 1944, even before the end of the War, Coventry formed a link with Stalingrad on the basis of their shared experiences of devastating German bombing. At the end of the War, Reading established a link with Zaandem in the Netherlands and Oxford, England's old established and famous university town, set up a relationship with its Dutch counterpart Leiden (Brown 1998, p. 3). The first city to help an ex-enemy town however was Bristol, which under the urging of Professor August Closs, the German-born head of the German Department at Bristol University, made the decision in August 1947 to twin with the city of Hanover. Sacks of food and clothes were sent as relief goods from Bristol to Hanover. A "music for old shoes" scheme began which comprised sending thousands of pairs of shoes to Hanover schoolchildren in return for performances by Hanoverian singers and musicians. "Operation scholar" was a reciprocal exchange of schoolchildren that had become established between the two cities by 1951. The scheme has continued uninterrupted since then and has involved the exchange of over 20,000 young people since its inception. Other early city to city links that have also survived for more than half a century include the Reading–Dusseldorf and the Oxford–Bonn connections (Brown 1998).

There are a number of key features unique to sister-city relationships. The first of these is that the relationship is cemented by the signing of a formal agreement, which is almost always done by city mayors (or corresponding local officials). Second, agreements are signed with the intention that they last indefinitely.[2] Third, because the relationship is an ongoing one, it is not limited to one single project, but covers a range of shared activities. The literature from the City Council of the city of Christchurch, New Zealand, lists some of the projects of its sister-cities program as school art exchanges; penpals; student exchanges; letter exchanges through the Internet; friendship visits between the sister-cities; reciprocal council staff visits; local cultural celebrations; and helping the exchange of trade, research and technology between Christchurch and its sister-cities (Christchurch City Council undated). While most of these activities are fairly typical of sister-city interactions, there is no one formula adhered to within sister-city relationships generally, but each relationship develops its own set of activities which best suit the needs and resources of both partners. Other possible activities include the extension of aid when one of the partners is struck by disaster, and assistance by way of advice, information, equipment and other help when the pairing involves a developed with a less developed community. Fourth, although city officials are crucial in setting up and supporting a sister-city relationship, the great majority of people involved in sister-city activities are unpaid volunteers. Fifth, these relationships are carried out largely at a grassroots and local body level and do not rely on the support or patronage of national governments. Finally, there is a tacit understanding that sister-city relationships should be characterized by "genuine reciprocity of effort and benefit, with neither community profiting at the expense of the other" (Zelinsky 1991, p. 3).

Zelinsky (1991, p. 1) claims that the choice of a sister-city is not a random process but is based on any number of criteria including "historical connections, shared economic, cultural, recreational and ideological concerns, similar or identical place names,[3] and, to a certain extent, the friction of distance." Just as importantly however, and not necessarily separate from the criteria Zelinsky outlines, are the individual contacts and private initiatives that go into establishing and sustaining city connections. An examination of the beginnings of many sister-city relationships will unearth the importance of these early individual connections, as is demonstrated in the example of the Hastings–Guilin sister-city relationship described in Section V of this paper.

In the United States, the implementation of sister-cities programmes has been seen as a support for democratic principles. For example, it is argued by Ward (1995, p. 68) that with the end of the Cold War and the rise of young democracies in Eastern Europe, the American organization Sister Cities International (SCI)[4] has used some of its resources to help train elected foreign officials. It has also been suggested (*The Economist* 1989; Zelinsky 1990) that some American cities have adopted sister-city partnerships as a way of expressing disapproval of and resistance to official American policies, which explains the very high number of twinnings (91 in 1990) with Nicaraguan communities. Increasingly, the sister-city relationship is being taken up as a model for other criteria-specific organizations, the members of which wish to contact and support one another. One such organization is Sister Cities Of Size Acceptance, made up of social, support and activist groups from New Zealand, Sweden and American cities and states including Philadelphia, South Carolina, South Jersey, Austin and Los Angeles "fighting for the rights of fat people and their supporters" (International Size Acceptance Association undated). A further use of sister-city relationships is the linking of groups and agencies to these relationships for specific purposes. An example of this is the link forged between the United States Department of Health and Human Services' Aging section with Sister Cities International, aimed at joining American aging programmes with those of other countries through the exchange of professionals, volunteers and technical assistance in the field of aging with the aim of strengthening aging services (Administration on Aging 1996).

III

The Integrated Approach

THE INTEGRATED APPROACH TO THE ANALYSIS OF SISTER-CITIES has been developed in New Zealand research on sister-cities by Cremer et al. (1996)

and Ramasamy and Cremer (1998). Basic to the approach is the idea that through formal sister-city arrangements "cities rediscover one of their original roles as meeting places between different people and cultures, and thus create a (market) place for economic and business activities (Ramasamy and Cremer 1998, p. 449). In their explanation of sister-city relationships the same authors note that the earlier phase of the sister-city movement was dominated by the idea of international friendship through the understanding of the culture of others. O'Toole (1999, p. 2) terms this phase of sister-city relationship "the associative phase," where the primary objectives of these types of twinning relations are based on notions of international friendship, cultural exchange and a general international awareness. More recently issues of commerce and economic development have become more important. This fits with O'Toole's third phase of sister-city relationships, the commercial phase. O'Toole (ibid) comments that in the Australian context the increasing pressure for local governments to act as economic developers has forced some cities to redefine their sister-city relationship in a commercial direction.[5] This does not necessarily mean abandoning the earlier phases, but rather is an attempt to take advantage of the relationship to further local economic aims. It is increasingly believed, however, that a two-way relationship exists between commerce and culture and that it is necessary that the two facets of the sister-city relationship remain closely interwoven. Understanding another culture contributes to trade and investment while engaging in business provides cultural understandings with a reliable and lasting base (Ramasamy and Cremer 1998, pp. 449–450). An overemphasis on either the cultural aspect of the relationship, as in the early days when friendship and understanding were so strongly the focus, or on the economic aspect of the relationship, which appears to be the current trend, are not likely to result in successful sister-city relationships, nor in the benefits that can accrue from these to the individual and the locality.

The integrated approach however, focuses on more than just the melding together of culture and economics. Cremer et al. (1996, p. 12) describe the integrated approach to sister-city relationships as one which "strives for a balance of cultural, political, social, and economic development for both cities, and insists on tangible results in all of those priority areas." Elsewhere Cremer is quoted as describing the integrated approach as one which "combines trade and cultural initiatives, strategic planning, leadership from the top, the involvement of community and the media and committing resources rather than "relying on the efforts of a few individuals"' (Sister Cities New Zealand 1999, p. 5).

Central to the integrated approach are implicit assumptions about the "nature of human nature" which together form a critique of the suppositions of the nature of individuals that underpin neoclassical economics. The successful operation of sister-city programs will not occur when the individuals involved act with nothing more than economic self interest, in terms of what England (1993) calls the "separative self" or what Granovetter (1985) views as atomization. The integrated approach recognizes a concern with sociability as an important supplement to the profit motive. It also acknowledges the frequent demonstration of altruism and trust and the intertwining of non-economic goals with economic goals.

Moving from the nature of the individuals involved to that of the relationship itself, Cremer et al. (1996, p. 12) argue that to pay insufficient attention to, or to not take account of, the economic dimension of sister-city relationships and the contribution that commerce can make to the sustainability of relationships is "expensive romanticism." Such a perspective pays little heed to the centrality of economic activity in people's lives. In addition, they claim that in the long run, the most reliable and strongest drivers for international understanding and exchange are economic and business links and work opportunities. They are not, however, arguing that a sister-city relationship driven solely by economic interests will be successful. Cultural exchanges and the development of greater cross-cultural understandings are the prime motivations for the grassroots involvement necessary to sustain sister-city relationships. In turn, along with a supportive administration, it is the cultural understandings that are built up over time that provide the positive environment which can reduce risks and uncertainties involved in economic enterprises such as trade, tourism and investment. The authors then go on to comment that "a trade mission to a country which includes visits to a sister-city is almost certainly a winner, whereas a one-off trade mission to any country will be almost certainly a failure" (ibid.).

The integrated approach to sister-city analysis developed from research into these relationships in which New Zealand cities are involved. Major findings from the research showed that while all cities responding to a survey attached a high importance to culture, international understandings and educational objectives, they were sharply divided over the importance of economic objectives, with almost one in three placing low priority on economic objectives. This suggested to the researchers a low likelihood of a sustainable sister-city relationship in the long term and a significant loss of financial support and possible benefits for the respective New Zealand cities. The data also showed that the strongest motivation for pursuing sister-city relationships came from non-commercial areas. This is explained by the gains from such facets of the relationship as increased international understandings and cultural and educational exchanges being open to large numbers of people. The researchers commented here, however, that although economic benefits might appear to assist only a small number of people, economic activities do advantage the wider community in terms of employment creation and income and tax generation. This realization, they argue, is important for the success of sister-city relationships (Cremer et al. 1996).

An examination of New Zealand's sister-city relationships reveals that choice of city with which to twin has shown an interesting shift over time. Not surprisingly, New Zealand cities had more sister-city affiliations with Australian cities than with any other individual country (as of 1998). However, of the 38 New Zealand–Australia affiliations, only one had been established since 1990. Although 14 New Zealand—European sister-city affiliations existed in 1998, all were formed prior to 1990 and of the 31 New Zealand–North America sister-city affiliations, only 1 was formed since 1990. However, 20 New Zealand city–Asian city affiliations were formed after 1990. The majority of these were with Japanese cities, but currently Chinese cities are making a concerted push to intensify their links with New Zealand cities and formal relationships with China are steadily increasing.[6] Attempts by China to free up its economy and open up the country to tourism have coincided with Chinese efforts to establish sister-city links not just in New Zealand but many other countries as well.

The opportunity to analyse the China-New Zealand sister-city relationships adds support for the integrated approach. Initially it is important to ask the question: Why are Chinese city officials so keen to develop such relationships? At a pragmatic level it is clear that among other things, the Chinese seek investment in their economy and proficiency in English language skills. To focus only on these components of the Chinese motivation, however, is limited. We know that any sister-city links that are formed with China must be accompanied by motives other than sheer economic profit and understood by both parties as multi-faceted. It is here that we turn to an intertwining of the cultural with the economic in order to understand how best to establish and sustain links between cities in the two nations. It is understood that China takes a very long term view of its international relationships and takes time to develop friendships. Of major importance too is an understanding of the controlled nature of Chinese life. This demands that any contacts, other than those of individuals, must be made through official channels, and for this reason a lot of formality and procedural issues have to be accommodated (Cross 2000, p. 2).

The integrated approach to sister-cities is particularly necessary in the early phases of establishing a sister-city relationship with a Chinese city, when the formal, protocol based input of the mayor and councillors cannot be underestimated. Without visible and active support from the mayor and city councillors and other leading local personalities, initiatives and activities in China lack credibility and clout. Building a good relationship between the two respective city mayors is, on a very practical level, seen as a signal that administrative and bureaucratic procedures and obstacles can be overcome smoothly, a perception equally appropriate to business ventures and the involvement of chief executive officers. The cultural background to this is that the Chinese tend to emphasize individual authority, integrity and linkages more than procedures, contracts and organisations. The Chinese concept of "face" and "giving face to somebody" is also a good reason why city officials should be involved in sister-city activities whenever possible, especially at the beginning (Cremer et al. 1996).[7]

The integrated approach as developed by Cremer et al. (1996) and outlined above is based on a multifold relationship between culture and commerce. In the following section we advocate an extension to this approach with a focus on simultaneously operating, multi-level entrepreneurial partnerships which we conceive as municipal-community entrepreneurship.

IV

Municipal-Community Entrepreneurship

AT THE OUTSET OF THIS PAPER, in the Introduction, we alerted the reader to the new entrepreneurialism of local governments. Describing this as "municipal entrepreneurship" we note here that there are several variants ranging from "alternative" revenue-raising ventures such as advertising on public property or the sale of the city imprimatur as in the case of Atlanta to VISA USA so it could offer the "official credit card" of the city of the 1996 Summer Olympics (Myers 1995), to the wooing of domestic and foreign investors with offers of incentives. At the more international end of the spectrum, there are growing attempts by local governments to act as a catalyst in capitalizing on new opportunities for innovation and cooperation presented by globalization-localization forces. Posing the question, "Can city governments become strategic brokers that influence their city's . . . position in the global urban hierarchy?", the latest *World Development Report* answers in the affirmative, with the proviso that appropriate planning and support is required (The World Bank 2000, p. 136).

At an overarching theoretical level, municipal entrepreneurship is a vital facet in any city strategy for exploiting the advantages of agglomeration economies, which constitute "the source of urban efficiency" (The World Bank 2000, p. 126). For organizations, agglomeration economies are the spillover effects, deriving from proximity to similar competitors. They involve benefits that can accrue from being located within a cluster of organizations in the same industry (see, for example, Baum and Mezias 1992; Ingram and Inman 1996; Porter 1998). These benefits are variously described as "localization economies" (The World Bank 2000, p. 127). At the city/urban area level, agglomeration economies encompass not only localization economies but also "urbanization economies," which are "benefits that derive from proximity to many different economic actors" (The World Bank 2000, p. 127). Agglomeration in large urban areas also results in a diversified economic base that can act as a buffer against economic fluctuations with employment being able to flow within different sectors and industries in the locale, thus keeping down the average rate of unemployment. For consumers, the concentration of services and entertainment opportunities within cities are also a benefit of agglomeration (The World Bank 2000, p. 127). The greater the extent of agglomeration economies of an area, the larger the capacity to offset any additional costs of conducting activity in that area against an alternative location and the higher the productivity of activity in the area.

We may argue that successful sister-city relationships are one manifestation of municipal entrepreneurship and inasmuch as they make a contribution to the economic and social dynamism of cities, they indirectly contribute to reinforcement and magnification of agglomeration economies. The whole sister-city movement offers ample scope for the exercise of municipal entrepreneurship, albeit at a more subtle and relatively low financial cost level. Spending on the relationships by local governments in New Zealand approximately averaged US$12,000 in 1995 (Ramasamy and Cremer 1998, p. 454). While the setting up of the overall institutional framework for the twinning pact is an initial first step, to carry the agreement forward requires commitment and proactive nurturing by local government officials to build trust, cooperation and tangible yield as well as less tangible and measurable economic and social benefits. The distinguishing feature for the viability and success of the arrangement, however, is that it also requires significant community activism. It is this mix of community and municipal level action to tap into the opportunities that the sister-city arrangement presents for the mutual advantage of economic and social actors in both cities that we conceive as a hybrid entrepreneurialism we term "municipal-community entrepreneurship."

The notion of entrepreneurship here is a simple one, used to convey the specific, proactive steps to organize, establish, maintain and foster relationships and opportunities that directly or indirectly present at various levels within the sister-city arrangement. Thus for instance, at the lower community tier, school student exchanges and visits between sister cities are common. These require a great deal of time and commitment initially on the part of those members of the school staff and local government who are involved with arranging each visit, usually followed by fund-raising activity by students and parents to finance the visit and a myriad of other efforts, trivial though they appear to the non-involved outside observer, to ensure the smooth running of the event. The combination of all these actions are entrepreneurial in that they are taken in order to avail of opportunities, in this case educational, afforded by the sister-city arrangement. Thus entrepreneurship in the context of this paper entails actively tapping into the opportunities for beneficial links under the sister-city umbrella.

Elsewhere we have developed the concept of "community entrepreneurship" and provided New Zealand applications to illustrate community entrepreneurship in action (de Bruin and Dupuis 1995; de Bruin 1998). Our notion of community entrepreneurship has been seen as complementing the role of individual entrepreneurs in stimulating change and creating employment at a local level. It envisages the community supplying initiative and enterprise for the creation, transformation and expansion of employment creating ventures and is seen as a possible answer to both an initial lack of individual entrepreneurial skills and employment opportunities in labour market disadvantaged communities and for ethnic minority groups. It entails innovative community efforts as a catalyst for the growth of local employment opportunities particularly for ethnic minorities with low levels of human capital.

The concept of community entrepreneurship that we envisaged was quite deliberately focused on employment creation. As such, this entrepreneurship formulation does not convey adequately the wider spread of activity nor the more elementary style of entrepreneurship that the municipal-community entrepreneurship of successful sister-city relationships mainly exhibits. At this point, however, it must be noted that this does not mean that our hybrid concept of municipal-community entrepreneurship is peculiar to the sister-city case of this paper. Indeed the sister-city arrangement is merely the device used to empirically develop the concept. Thus we show in the dedicated example provided in Section V of this paper that positive benefits from twin city pacts involve both local government commitment as well as community activism on the part of a variety of community organizations, that is, municipal-community entrepreneurship. The concept itself hence may be adopted as a notion that epitomizes the importance of the partnership aspect in the maintenance of the dynamism of cities and other sites of localization. It also brings to specific prominence the forces of localization and decentralization/devolution of the role and responsibilities of state to sub-national tiers of government. Thus the inclusion of a dual terminology—"community" and "municipal"—effectively communicates the need for active community participation together with an explicit, overarching support provided at a local governmental level rather than that of central government. As Glaeser in his recent investigation into the question "Are Cities Dying?" points out, local governments are "crucial to the fate of cities" (1998, p. 141).[8]

It must also be mentioned that municipal-community entrepreneurship does not necessarily imply only a sense of basic entrepreneurialism commonly encompassed by sister-city activities. As with community entrepreneurship, municipal-community entrepreneurship can open new horizons through "market-leading" activity. Market-leading is described as a deliberately staged affair, unlike "market-following." The growth of the economy stimulates a market-following supply response from enterprises in order to satisfy new or additional demand. The relative price of labour and the elasticity of substitution between labour and capital will contribute to determining whether additional demand for labour will accompany this response and result in employment growth. By contrast, market-leading manages change to create demand and employment growth which would not otherwise have occurred. Market-leading may be likened to the Schumpeterian "creative response."[9] Market-following, on the other hand, is more in line with an "adaptive response." Similarly, market-leading community entrepreneurship or in this case municipal-community entrepreneurship is akin to Leibenstein's N-entrepreneurship, [10] since it engages in the creation and operation of ventures where the production function is not completely known (de Bruin 1998).

To conclude this section, we reiterate that municipal-community entrepreneurship is a concept that can be applied beyond the confines of the sister-city programme. However, an important benefit of our use of the sister-cities case, which by its inherently international nature overcomes the spatial propinquity usually associated with cities, to develop this concept is to highlight that this form of entrepreneurship can involve innovative action that transcends the local in order to take advantage of opportunities that present at a global level.

V

Dedicated Illustration

AS FURTHER ILLUSTRATION OF THE KEY POINTS discussed in Sections III and IV above, in this section of the paper we draw on a well established and successful sister-city relationship, that of the city of Hastings, New Zealand with Guilin in China. The selection of the Hastings–Guilin sister-city relationship was deliberate as it exhibits to a large extent the features we have put forward as intrinsic to the extended integrated approach that we see as fundamental in the development and maintenance of a successful sister-city relationship. These features are an initial person-to-person link; strong involvement of city officials, particularly the mayor; strong community support; a well developed strategic plan; a highly organized governance structure; and adequate funding.

The relationship between Hastings and Guilin, like many other successful sister-city programmes, had its roots in a person-to-person link. In this case the connection was established by the late Dr. Don McKenzie, a research scientist and New Zealand leader in the pipfruit industry,[11] who first proposed the Hastings–Guilin link in 1978. He identified a number of common areas of interest between the two cities, including horticulture and the rural-urban mix, and developed a range of contacts between the two cities. He also instigated the re-establishment and became the founding president of the New Zealand China Friendship Society in 1985 and launched a horticultural technician placement scheme. After his death in 1988, he was described in the Guilin newspaper as "the friendship messenger" (Hastings-Guilin Sister City Strategic Plan 1999, p. 2).

Acting on Dr. McKenzie's suggestion that a sister-city relationship with Guilin should be pursued, Hastings city officials took up the idea and approached the Chinese Embassy. In 1980 the mayor of Guilin invited a Hastings delegation to visit his city and discuss the proposal. The following year he made a reciprocal visit to Hastings, at which time the sister-city protocol was signed, including an agreement to "establish friendly city relations and to promote and foster goodwill and understanding" between the people of the two cities. It was also set out that friendship would be developed by "an interchange of all information in the fields of industry, agriculture, science and technology, city management and development, tourism, culture, education and trade" (Hastings-Guilin Sister City Strategic Plan 1999, p. 3). The mayoral support so necessary for these programmes to flourish was initially strong and is still highly visible today, with Hastings' current mayor also being the president of Sister Cities New Zealand Inc.

Hasting's strategic plan sets out plainly the mission statement and the objectives of the relationship. The latter include educational development through exchanges and curriculum programmes aimed primarily at children, students and professionals; cultural development, to be achieved in its broadest sense through people-to-people exchanges of all kinds; business links aimed at the facilitation of quality data, contacts, identification of opportunities and business links; and local government exchanges and information sharing.

Hastings' sister-city governance structure is clearly delineated and includes the Guilin Community Forum, the Sister City Board of Directors, three specialist link groups given over to education, culture and business and the Hastings District Council. The Guilin Community Forum provides a twice yearly opportunity for information sharing, education, networking, reporting back on activities, planning and reviewing. The Community Forum has a strong grassroots focus. The Board of Directors has promotional and overseeing responsibilities. It is also the key group in terms of pursuing the four major objectives of the sister-city relationship and devising and reviewing strategic planning for three to five year time periods. Board membership includes representatives from communities of interest including education, business, media, culture and iwi (Maori tribal groupings), the Chinese Association, the New Zealand China Friendly Society and the Hastings District Council.

The three specialist link groups were established to act as catalysts for establishing education, business and cultural links between the sister cities of Hastings and Guilin. These link programmes are strategically organized. For example, the education link group is charged with producing, reviewing and putting into action a three-year education plan and in liaising with its Guilin counterpart in supporting a similar program.

Adequate funding is always a concern for sister-city projects, although Hastings is better financed than most other such New Zealand projects. It has a local government contribution, community support in cash or in kind and delegation or group and individual visits to Guilin which are self-funding, as well as other grants from patrons such as Asia 2000 or the Lottery Board. The local government contribution amounts to $15,000, or approximately US$7,500. In addition, the Council supports sister-cities through a significant proportion of staff time, vehicle use, communications and administration, amounting to a further contribution of $16,200, or around US$8,100.

To conclude this section we need to make the point that the Hastings-Guilin relationship did not emerge from the flurry of East Asian sister-city contacts established in the 1990s. It demonstrates how local actors fostered the creation and nurturing of ties which now can be described as firmly embedded. It also amply illustrates the operation of vertical and horizontal multi-level ties. The dynamic flow of the vertical line of partnership incorporates, in a non-hierarchical fashion, the Guilin Community Forum, the Sister City Board of Directors, specialist link groups and the Hastings District Council. The imagery of the horizontal flow is apt in that it symbolizes the international outreach between the two cities. At each and every level of partnership there is evidence of aspects of the operation of municipal-community entrepreneurship.

VI

The Benefits of Sister-City Relationships

A WIDE RANGE OF BENEFITS, both tangible and intangible, accrue to cities involved in sister-city relationships. Among these are the benefits of international trade, cultural exchanges, educational exchanges, migration, investment and tourism. Within the sister-city movement it is widely thought that intangible benefits are derived from exposing the citizens of a city, particularly the city's youth, to different cultures. It is expected that the understandings developed and the connections gained through sustained face-to-face contact will enable people to better function in a world characterized by increasing globalization.

Sustaining sister-city relationships is something of a balancing act in New Zealand's current tight economic climate. The continuation of these relationships is often cast in local body political debate as more of a frills concern, rather than the core business of a city council. One way of discussing the benefits of sister-city relationships is to explore the criticisms made by detractors of the sister-city movement who do not see it as core business for a city council. Criticisms usually fall into three categories. The first suggests that people are either unaware or apathetic about these relationships. The second centers on the "strange choice" of the cities selected. A third commonly voiced criticism is that the sister-city connection represents little more than a "junket for politicians" financed from rate payers' money (Dupuis and de Bruin 2000).

In the absence of systematic New Zealand research gauging New Zealanders' awareness of sister-city relationships, we point to two examples which in themselves may not make the front pages of major daily newspapers but which are certainly highlighted in local publications and benefit, not necessarily in large scale or economic ways, people involved at the grass roots level. The first example highlights the unique contribution to the North Shore City[12] Libraries devised by visiting students from Konohana High School in Osaka, Japan. In association with sister-city exchanges, Konohana students have visited the North Shore almost yearly for the past nine years. For their visit, the Japanese students arrange for a bazaar to be set up on North Shore City's main street, where they sell to passersby the gifts and souvenirs they brought with them from Japan. The money raised, which has averaged $1,500 a time, is donated to strengthen the cultural sections of the North Shore Libraries. This is very significant in a city that boasts the second highest library patronage in New Zealand and in the context of the advertising North Shore libraries give this venture. The second example also involves high school students, though in this case that of New Zealand schoolchildren travelling to visit their sister-city counterparts. Since the inception of sister-city programmes in New

Zealand, many thousands of school students from New Zealand cities will have studied overseas, being hosted by families from another culture, attending school, enhancing their language skills and deepening their understandings of other cultures, thus fulfilling the initial aims of the sister-city movement. The wider significance of such exchanges cannot be underplayed. Not only the students involved but also their families, friends and teachers benefit from such broadening of experience and the increase in cultural understandings so developed.

The second common criticism of sister-cities has to do with the 'strange choice' of the cities selected. This idea explored more deeply highlights some salient features of sister-city relationships generally and points to mutual benefits that might not be obvious initially. An example should clarify this point. Waitakere City is one of the cities that make up Auckland. It is well known as an eco-city and has implemented a raft of innovative startegies for insuring a sustainable future and enhancing the lives of its citizens. Waitakere's sister-city is Ningbo, an important commercial city, and the second largest trading port in China. According to the signed sister-city agreement, the Waitakere City-Ningbo relationship is one of sharing ideas, knowledge and technology. Initially it might not appear there are similarities between the two cities, but Ningbo city officials, especially, saw themselves as facing similar problems to those of Waitakere City. Wanting to know more about sustainability issues, particularly those relating to sustainable building and sustainable technology, the sister-city relationship was initiated. While this relationship has an economic base beneficial to the two cities, it is broadening out to include cultural and work exchanges.

The third frequently heard criticism, that of sister-cities being little more than a "junket for politicians," perhaps reflects the politics of envy. While it is often the case that the cost of official delegations to sister-cities is met from local government coffers, the benefits that arise from the official nature of such visits cannot be overemphasized. City councils, whether New Zealand or overseas, do not enter into sister-city relationships lightly. After all, it is necessary for the mayors of both cities to sign a contract in order for the sister-city relationship to become formally established. An examination of North Shore City's sister-city contract with Taichung in Taiwan shows just how serious these agreements are. In this contract both cities agree to "establish lasting, friendly relations . . . strive to maintain their close alliance and improve bilateral understanding and trust" and "make every effort to contribute to the free and prosperous life of people in both Taichung and North Shore City." Both cities also agreed to "exchange experiences concerning municipal construction projects, to organize visits, and to learn from each other" and to "promote co-operation in the area of trade, cultural, economic affairs, education and social development to strengthen their binding ties." It is not surprising therefore that when Taichung recently suffered a disastrous earthquake, North Shore City sent its Civil Defence Chief to visit Taichung, not only as a gesture of sister-city support, but also to offer expertise and advice. As a result, an international conference on dealing with the impacts of earthquakes and disasters has been set up in North Shore City at the request of Taichung officials.

To conclude this section it must be conceded that any discussion of the benefits of sister-cities must acknowledge economic benefits. These however, are difficult to measure precisely because too many factors are involved and too few data exist on this level of analysis. Research on international trade, investment and tourism, though, leaves no doubt that these activities do not flourish unless they are accompanied by a supportive environment. As Cremer et al. comment, "business and tourism go where they feel welcome and supported." At the local level sister-city relationships can provide economic opportunities in a supportive environment (1996, p. 8). One key area where the economic benefits of sister-city relationships could possibly be effectively measured is that of tourism. According to Kearsley (2000, p. 1), tourism is a major global force that could be the world's biggest industry, consuming one in eight of all discretionary dollars spent. While urban tourism is a major component of overall tourism, as yet little is known about the tangible benefits of sister-city related tourism and few, if any, cities have deliberately promoted their city to their sister-city as a special and worthwhile place to visit. This aspect of the sister-city relationship however, provides considerable potential and is an aspect of the economics of sister-cities that could be readily measured.

VII

Conclusion

THE SISTER-CITY MOVEMENT MAY BE VIEWED as a small but potentially powerful element of the "'quiet revolution' in local governance" (The World Bank 2000, pp. 154–5), and a model of partnership that is deserving greater recognition in ensuring the sustainability of the economic and social vibrancy of cities. With successful sister-city relationships embodying a partnership that allows "synergy and the combining of resources among the public sector, international organizations, the voluntary and community sector, individuals and households" (The World Bank 2000, p. 155), and symbolizing the benefits that can accrue from bridging the global-local divide, they represent a crucial catalyst in the facilitation of urban well-being in the 21st century.

As a concluding observation, we stress that the concept of municipal-community entrepreneurship has wider applicability than merely the sister-city phenomenon. Current urban political landscapes, focusing as they do on decentralization and the rethinking of the role of local government, are increasingly highlighting the importance of multi-level partnerships for economic and social development. At the dawn of the new century we can foresee the value and strength of the concept of municipal-community entrepreneurship as an explanatory tool for analyzing the current urban condition. When operationalized, its potential for reaping agglomeration economies and hence enhancing the sustainability of cities should not be underestimated.

Notes

1. Precedents for helping conflict-ravaged cities had already been set after the First World War. For example, the city of Bristol in England financed the building of houses for war widows in Bethune, France (Brown 1998, p. 3)

2. There are a number of instances however, where agreements become dormant, are suspended or cancelled.

3. An example here is the case of the Stratford cities in Canada, the United States and New Zealand, all of which have a sister-city relationship with Stratford in England.

4. SCI is the national membership organization for sister-city, county and state programs in the United States and recognizes, registers and coordinates

American linkages with communities worldwide. The sister-city relationships American cities are involved in account for 2,191 affiliations or twinnings. In addition, there are a further 201 affiliations or twinnings associated with states, provinces and prefectures. In all, American communities are involved in 2,395 affiliations or twinnings worldwide (Sister Cities International 1999).

5. O'Toole terms the second type of sister-city relationship "reciprocative." This phase is characterized by the growth of educational exchange systems which provide a safe and relatively cheap way of running an exchange program, especially with homestay arrangements keeping costs to a minimum. O'Toole argues that education exchange programs are not limited to school and tertiary students, but also include professionals such as government employees who could also broaden their skills (O'Toole 1999, p. 2).

6. A similar push to establish sister-city links can be seen with New Zealand cities and those in Taiwan and South Korea.

7. We cannot emphasize this point too greatly. The Confucian culture of East Asia places great stress on personal relationships. East Asians devote time, patience and energy to foster good relationships. Face-to-face contact is an integral part in building such relationships.

8. It is also interesting to note here that conceptually Glaeser envisages a city as "just a dense agglomeration of people and firms." As such, "all of the benefits of cities come ultimately from reduced transport costs for goods, people and ideas" (1998, p. 140). These, the positive benefits, arise from agglomeration.

9. The role of the entrepreneur in the stimulation of dynamic growth was initially highlighted by Joseph Schumpeter early in this century. Under the Schumpeterian schema of capitalist development, the entrepreneur is the key agent of change. In a little known paper, *Comments on a Plan for the Study of Entrepreneurship,* thought to be written in 1946, Schumpeter identifies "creative response" in business activity with entrepreneurship. When the economy or a sector of the economy or some firms in an industry adapts to change by an expansion or contraction "within its existing practice," this is an "adaptive response." By contrast, if the reaction is "outside the range of existing practice," it is a creative response (Schumpeter 1991 [1946?]).

10. Leibenstein distinguishes between two broad types of entrepreneurship, namely routine entrepreneurship and Schumpeterian or "new type" or "N-entrepreneurship." Routine entrepreneurship involves the activities of coordinating and operating a firmly established enterprise in known and well defined markets, where "all the parts of the production function in use (and likely alternatives in current use) are well known." By contrast, N-entrepreneurship "involves the activities necessary to create or carry on an enterprise where not all the markets are well established or clearly defined and/or in which the relevant parts of the production function are not completely known" (Leibenstein 1968, p. 73).

11. Dr. McKenzie played a key role in establishing early scientific relations

with China which led to new kiwifruit plant material being introduced into New Zealand's breeding program. He is also credited with breeding the plant material for the recently released apples Pacific Rose and Southern Snap.

12. Auckland is made up of four major cities, Auckland City itself, North Shore City which extends from north of the Auckland Harbour Bridge to Rodney County, Waitakere City, commonly called West Auckland and Manukau City, located to the south and east of Auckland City itself.

References

Administration on Aging. 1996. "AoA Announces Partnership with Sister Cities International to Link Aging Services Across Nations." March 28. html. Accessed 24 March, 2000.

Baum, J. and Haveman, H. 1997. "Love thy Neighbor? Differentiation and Agglomeration in the Manhattan Hotel Industry: 1898–1990." *Administrative Science Quarterly* 42: 304–339.

Brown, M. 1998. "Towns that Build Bridges." *History Today* 48(8): 3–6.

Castells, M. 1977. *The Urban Question*. London: Edward Arnold.

———. 1978. *City, Class and Power*. London: Macmillan.

———. 1983. *The City and the Grassroots*. London: Edward Arnold.

Christchurch City Council (undated) "Christchurch's Sister Cities," html: Accessed 6 April, 2000.

Cremer, R., Gounder, R. and Ramasamy, B. 1996. "Guidelines for New Zealand-Asia Sister City Relationships: Economic Rationale for an Integrated Approach." Department of Economics, Massey University: Palmerston North, New Zealand.

Cross, B. 2000. "Council Relations with China." Porirua City Council Paper, Porirua, New Zealand.

Dear, M. 2000. *The Postmodern Urban Condition*. Oxford, UK: Blackwell.

de Bruin, A and Dupuis, A. 1995. "A Closer Look at New Zealand's Superior Economic Performance: Ethnic Employment Issues." *British Review of New Zealand Studies* 8: 85–97.

de Bruin, A. 1998. "Entrepreneurship in a New Phase of Capitalist Development." *Journal of Interdisciplinary Economics* 9(3): 185–200.

Dupuis, A. and de Bruin, A. 2000. "Face to Face Contacts Give Sister Cities Great Value." *New Zealand Herald* May 11: A17.

England, P. 1993. "The Separative Self: Androcentric Bias in Neoclassical Assumptions," in *Beyond Economic Man: Feminist Theory and Economics*. M. Ferber and J. Nelson, eds. Chicago: University of Chicago Press.

Fainstein, S. 1996. "The Changing Economy and Urban Restructuring," in *Readings in Urban Theory*. S. Fainstein and S. Campbell, eds. Cambridge, MA: Blackwell.

Glaeser, E. 1998. "Are Cities Dying?" *Journal of Economic Perspectives* 12(2): 139–160.

Granovetter, M. 1985. "Economic Action and Social Structure: The Problem of Embeddedness." *American Journal of Sociology* 91 (3): 481–510.

Harvey, D. 1989a. "From Managerialism to Entrepreneurialism: The Transformation of Urban Governance in Late Capitalism." *Geografiska Annaler,* 71B(1): 3–17.

———. 1989b. *The Urban Experience.* Oxford, UK: Basil Blackwell.

Hastings-Guilin Sister City Strategic Plan. 1999. Hastings City Council, Hastings, New Zealand.

Hepler, H. 1994. "Sister Cities Program Links Cultures, Businesses." *American City and Country* September: 22.

Ingram, P. and Inman, C. 1996. "Institutions, Intergroup Competition, and the Evolution of Hotel Populations around Niagara Falls." *Administrative Science Quarterly* 41: 629–659.

International Size Acceptance Association. Undated. "Sister Cities of Size Acceptance." html: Accessed 2 February 2000.

Kearsley, G. 2000. "Sister Cities and Tourism." University of Otago, Dunedin, New Zealand.

Lancaster, S. 1993. Taking the Initiative: Local Government Employment and Economic Development Initiative.Wellington: Local Government Association.

Leibenstein, H. 1968. "Entrepreneurship and Development." *American Economic Review* 58(2): 72–75.

Myers, S. 1995. "U.S. Cities Looking to Raise Cash are Taking to 'Selling' Themselves." *Minneapolis Star Tribune. July 16: 18A.*

O'Toole, K. 1999. "Sister Cities in Australia: A Survey Report." Centre for Regional Development, Deakin University.

Porter, Michael E. 1998. "The Adam Smith Address: Location, Clusters, and the 'New'" Microeconomics of Competition." *Business Economics 33:*7–14.

Ramasamy, B. and Cremer, R. 1998. "Cities, Commerce and Culture: The Economic Role of International Sister-City Relationships between New Zealand and Asia." *Journal of the Asia Pacific Economy* 3(3): 446–461.

Sassen, S. 1996. "The Global City," in *Readings in Urban Theory.* S. Fainstein and S. Campbell, eds. Cambridge, MA: Blackwell.

Saunders, P. 1986. *Social Theory and the Urban Question.* (2nd edition) London: Hutchinson.

Schumpeter, J. 1991. [1946?] "Comments on a Plan for the Study of Entrepreneurship," in *Joseph A. Schumpeter.* R. Swedberg, ed. Princeton: Princeton University Press.

Sister Cities International. 1999. "About SCI: History." html: Accessed 24 January, 2000.

Sister Cities New Zealand Inc. undated. *Guidelines for Developing a Sister Cities Programme.* Whakatane: SCNZ.

Sister Cities New Zealand. 1999. "Sister Cities – a Strategy for Success." May: 5.

The Economist. 1989. "Sister Sandinist." 312(7619): 28–29.

The World Bank. 2000. *World Development Report, 1999/2000: Entering the 21st Century.* New York: Oxford University Press.

Ward, J. 1995. "USCM's Crabb Takes Sister Cities Helm." *American City and Country* 110(2): 68.

Wellington City Council. 1999. *International Relations Annual Report 1998.* Wellington: New Zealand.

Zelinsky, W. 1990. "Sister City Alliance." *American Demographics* 12(6): 42–45.

———. 1991. "The Twinning of the World: Sister Cities in Geographic and Historical Perspective." *Annals of the Association of American Geographers.* 81(1): 1–31.

Zukin, S. 1995. *The Culture of Cities.* Cambridge, MA.

The Completely Decentralized City

The Case for Benefits Based Public Finance

By Fred E. Foldvary[*]

ABSTRACT. An alternative to centralized top-down city governance is a multi-level bottom-up structure based on small neighborhood contractual communities. This paper analyzes the voting rules and public finances of decentralized, contractual urban governance and the likely outcome of such a constitutional structure, substantially reduced transfer seeking or rent seeking. Tax and service substitution, with lower-level funding and services substituting for higher-level public finance, is the general process by which the governance would devolve. Land rent is the most feasible source of such decentralized public finance, and local communities could also engage in local currency and credit services. Some empirical examples demonstrate the implementation of some of these governance structures.

I

Governance

THIS PAPER PRESENTS AN ANALYSIS of a decentralized and voluntary contractual city governance.

Gordon Tullock (1994) theorizes that many urban services can be delegated to the neighborhood level, which could become a predominant level of government. Bryan and McClaughry (1989) also propose devolving much of government to a more local level, between the level of a village and a county. Tullock (1985) also proposes "associations with quasi-governmental power" which, like churches, would not necessarily have a unique geographical jurisdiction.

This paper carries the decentralist concept further, exploring the concept of a purely voluntary city based on neighborhood associations, in which all governance is voluntary and contractual. It exam-

*Department of Economics, Santa Clara University. His interests include public finance, governance theory, and economic philosophy. His recent publications include *Beyond Neoclassical Economics* (Edward Elgar, 1996). He is also a frequent contributor to this journal.

American Journal of Economics and Sociology, Vol. 60, No. 1 (January, 2001).

ines a voting structure, based on this governance, that would reduce the capability of special interests to capture the democratic process and shift funds to their special privileged benefits. The public finances suitable to voluntary territorial associations is then analyzed and the provision of local financial services is noted. A few brief case studies show how some of these principles have been implemented.

Ultimate power in a purely voluntary city would be completely decentralized, down to the individual household and family. Its governance structure would be bottom-up, power ultimately based on sovereign individuals. The distinction between the government and private sectors would disappear, as voluntary governance would be based on contracts among private members and property owners.

The dynamics of voluntary association can proceed in two ways, via evolution or devolution. The evolutionary method consists of the joining together of individual households into an association to provide services for the members. If there are more than a few households, it is efficient to create a governing body, a board or council elected by the members, who delegate some authority to the board. The financing of the services can come from equal dues or payments by the members, as done by some of the private communities in St. Louis, or by assessments based on the value of the real estate or land owned by the owners, or on some other basis such as income or wealth. Financing is discussed in Section II.

Devolution is the transfer of political authority, property, and programs from a higher level to a lower level of governance. The devolutionary method recognizes that any path to a voluntary city would start with the status quo of imposed government. Devolution would therefore consist of various degrees of secession and substitution of lower-level for higher-level governance, and the legal ability to create lower-level governance. We thus begin with a neighborhood which is part of a city and its government. Households as well as the owners of commercial property would be able to form a neighborhood association, which would then be recognized by the city as a lower-level governing agency, or even as a new separate jurisdiction. Authority, property, and programs would then be transferred to the association and the taxes that were imposed to fund these would be eliminated or reduced, to be replaced by the association financing.

Devolution can be partial, with residents of an association withdrawing only from some services such as schooling, and then not paying taxes for the state schools. Generally, "tax substitution" would allow residents to replace those services provided by the city with local services, with an equivalent reduction in tax liabilities. Some cities now do this for garbage collection; condominiums may contract with a private service and receive a tax rebate.

In the evolutionary model, the neighborhood associations would themselves federate into higher-level associations to facilitate the co-ordination of programs such as security and to provide services with economies of scale that make them more efficient to produce for a larger population or territory. The higher-level association would have a council or board which could either be directly elected by the households or by the neighborhood councils.

The election of representatives by a large number of voters, termed here "mass democracy," leads to the governance disease that economists have called "rent seeking" or "transfer seeking." Public choice, the branch of economics that studies choices made by voters and government officials, theorizes that when the benefits of transfer seeking are concentrated in a few recipients while the costs are spread thinly among consumers and voters, the incentives to organize are high for the beneficiaries and low for the payers. Also, since with mass democracy the voters are so numerous that they do not personally know their representatives, candidates rely on the mass media for their campaigns. Special interests can profit from providing much of the campaign financing in return for programs that transfer wealth to them. Mass democracy thus leads to the capture of the governance process by special interests. Besides the wealth lost by the consumers and taxpayers that is transferred to these interests, there is a social cost from the resources spent to obtain the transfers and from the disincentives created by taxes that pay for the transfers.

Mancur Olson (1971, p. 63) theorizes that while in large groups the incentive is lacking to provide collective goods, the voluntary incentives could be present in a federal group. This makes the problem of providing the good to a large area a small-numbers matter. The contrasting voting structure to mass democracy is small-group democracy, where all voting is done by small groups. The higher-level council or board is elected by the members of the neighborhood councils. For example, each lower-level council can elect one of its members to the higher-level council. To avoid being short a board member, the neighborhood voters can elect alternates who vote when the regular representative is absent. With this communitarian and cellular small-group voting, there is no need for media campaigns, hence little or no demand for campaign funds, since the voters personally know and have easy access to their next-level representatives.

The practice of government today is to have mass democracy for all levels of government, and thus a voter faces a long ballot with candidates for city council, mayor, county supervisors, state legislators, Congressional representatives, a Senator, and the President. Most voters do not bother to spend much time investigating all the candidates and vote either by a rule of thumb such as political party, or are swayed by campaign advertising that presents an image and a biased, superficial treatment of the issues. The practice by voluntary associations would more likely be small-group multi-level voting, avoiding the dysfunction of transfer seeking. (See the Columbia Association case study, described in Section V.) The voters at the lowest level would only vote for a few representatives to their neighborhood council. Those associations practicing mass democracy would be costlier and less effective than smaller groups, and competition with the more communitarian small-group associations would tend to favor them over mass democracy.

The association level above that of the neighborhood would in turn elect an association above it to federate the second-level associations for services with even greater economies of scale, and for coordination among the second-level associations. The associations would form a bottom-up small-group multi-level voting structure, the polity based on neighborhood cells, hence a "cellular democracy" as contrasted with mass democracy. The highest-level council could be that of a city, county, state, up to a continent and the entire planet. Spencer Heath (1957, p. 96), among others, envisioned such a structure, although he provided few details.

Since the lower-level associations voluntarily form the next higher-level association, they may also withdraw from it when the members no longer wish to be part of that association. The governance structure is thus entirely voluntary from the bottom to the top levels. Another feature that would reduce transfer seeking even more is to make the representatives recallable at any time. The absence of a guaranteed fixed term would reduce the potential to exploit the powers of the office, and the fact that each level is elected by a small number of electors would make it more feasible for the voters to monitor their representatives.

II

Finance and Public Goods

THE UNANIMITY IMPLIED BY PURELY voluntary governance poses two challenges to the associations: 1) funding their programs by voluntary means by those who benefit and 2) spending in ways that avoid major spillovers to non-members. This first challenge is due to the nature of public or collective goods, which are used by many persons at the same time. With a so-called "private" good, the amounts used by individuals are severable, each individual consuming a separate quantity. For collective goods, each individual uses or is impacted by the entire quantity of the item and once the good is provided, an individual may benefit without having to pay, unless he or she can be excluded from the domain of the good. Some economists have thus concluded that collective goods have a "market failure" in that firms will not provide the amounts wanted by the public if some individuals can refuse to pay.

The "market failure" argument sounds plausible only because it is presented in a way abstracted from realities such as space. The public goods typically alleged to be subject to market failure are civic goods typically provided by government, such as streets, parks, sewerage, street and traffic lights, public transportation, security, fire protection, the enforcement of contracts, and education. These services are basically territorial, serving the residents and visitors of a particular territory. To benefit from them, one must for the most part be located in that specific area.

In order to be located to benefit from civic goods, a person must pay rent for the use of space. If one buys the rights to some space, the site value is the capitalized value of the rents, so one is really buying the future benefits which have the rent as their market value. For owner-occupants, the economic rent of the space gets paid either as a mortgage or as the opportunity cost, what the space could have been rented out for, hence the foregone opportunity of having rented it out.

The presence of these civic works makes sites more desirable, increasing the demand and therefore the site rent. This marginal or extra rent makes the civic works self-financing. The civic goods generate rent, which then pays for the costs. The rent also provides a measure of whether the civic goods are worth providing. If they generate at least as much rent as they cost, then it is economical to provide them. The optimal rent is the quantity at which the marginal rent equals the marginal cost.

The rent enables the collective goods to be provided by the market process (Foldvary 1994). When developers, REITS (real-estate investment trusts), corporations, or civic associations own the land and provide the goods, they can collect the rent to pay for the cost. There are no free riders, since the users pay rent, or if they are guests, then their hosts pay the rent. The first challenge of collective goods is solved: those who benefit pay rent. Rent would be supplemented by user fees and profits from enterprises operated by the associations.

The second challenge, providing services in ways that avoid major spillovers to non-members, is solved by the multi-level association structure described in Section I. The civic goods are provided by the lowest level of association in which the spillovers to non-members is minimal. In practice, many civic goods do not have many economies of scale and can be provided locally, or local associations can cooperate for mutual benefit, such as by helping one another with law enforcement when criminals escape a jurisdiction. As noted by Hamilton (1991, p. 675), the evidence from several studies suggests that "we have no particular reason to believe that scale economies are an impediment to wide community choice." An analysis of economies of scale among St. Louis jurisdictions, which are among the most polycentric in the United States, has shown no significant evidence of diseconomy effects of size on per-capita expenditures, consistent with other findings (Parks and Oakerson 1988, p. 122).

To avoid free riding, a higher-level association contract can specify that if a lower-level association secedes from the higher-level association, some compensation or continuing payment be made for those services from which the lower-level still benefits. When only some households in a block wish to form a territorial association and maintain the local street or park and provide better security, the other services remaining directly under the city, then the city and the neighborhood can form a partnership, delegating some tasks to the association and sharing the costs. In this way, neither side is privileged. If the association members wish to adopt some rule or change (such as blocking off one end of the street) that the non-members do not favor, an arbitration board can assign compensation for the disfavored party. This then shares the social cost among the whole neighborhood rather than the majority imposing it on a minority. The association might decide that the compensation cost is not worth the benefit of the new rule. Either way, as Ronald Coase (1960) points out, economics suggests either win-win solutions or at least some sharing of costs rather than the win-lose method typical with imposed centralized government. Another option, as noted by Heath (1957, p. 136), if some owners can hold out, is that "they and their unincluded properties will naturally receive second consideration in all matters of public benefit or preferment. Unfranchised as owners, their influence and advantages all will be of second rate."

With multi-level associations, the financing is bottom-up, although the assessments can be top-down. A lower level is assessed by the higher level and pays assessments or fees only to the next higher level. The higher level may assess the payments according to the land value of the sites in the area, but the funds are collected and sent up starting with the lowest level. There could be special boards set up to assess rent and land value with representatives from several association levels, but the assessments performed by professional appraisers.

With freedom of association, there would be a great variety of association themes and services. Over time, people would move to the communities that are best suited to their interests and finances. Competition among communities, as described by Charles Tiebout (1956), would also induce efficiency in the provision of services.

III

Local Money and Banking

IN A WORLD WITH NO TRANSACTION COSTS and perfect knowledge, local-association money and banking would be redundant. Commercial firms and standard currency would be adequate for community needs. But in the real world, there can be cash and credit constraints that are overcome by voluntary civic institutions. Some communities have had success with local currencies, sometimes issued by local firms, which lend notes at a discount. The notes circulate and are later redeemed for goods. In Ithaca, New York, "Ithaca Hour Notes" circulate widely and are based on a labor hour (those providing more expensive labor can charge multiples of the base hour). Great Barrington, Massachusetts, has used "Deli Dollars" redeemable in food (Greco 1994).

Communities in several countries have also organized indirect exchange systems, most notably using the Local Exchange Trading System (LETS), which began in Canada in 1983. LETS is similar to a credit union, but members begin their account balances at zero and exchange with other members. Those who purchase goods incur a debit, while those who sell obtain a credit; debits and credits are denominated in the national currency. LETS enables a local economy lacking in cash and credit to provide mutual employment by creating a means for mutual credit and transactions without cash. As LETS expands, a wider market linking local systems can become feasible.

There can be multi-level LETS systems serving wider areas. Thus neighborhood associations can provide financial as well as civic services to their members (Greco 1994).

IV

Urban Problems

WE CAN NOW ANALYZE SOME urban problems to see how associations would compare with central city governments in handling them.

A) Crime

Security and criminal justice can be divided into two aspects, the front and the back ends. The front end is the prevention of crime by guards and equipment, as well as catching criminals. The back end consists of trials and punishment. Different agencies can handle the two ends. Already, much of crime prevention is done privately by households and businesses with guards, locks, alarms, and other security services.

Private neighborhoods in St. Louis often block off one end of a block, making it more difficult for criminals to escape. Associations provide for more control, more monitoring and involvement by the community, and a more difficult target. Judge Richard Neely (1990) has described how neighborhood associations are being set up for protection against crime, supplementing government policing.

On the back end, a devolution to local governance would retain constitutional protections for both criminals and victims, while emphasizing restitution where feasible. Arbitration as well as private courts already supplement the clogged civil courts. Bottom up governance would be supplemented by top-down higher-level constitutional requirements for justice and due process, but with local and private options such as contracting out prisons.

Crime itself is divided into two types, crimes with victims and victimless crimes. Decentralized governance would let the local voluntary association determine how it deals with victimless crimes. Some associations might wish to outlaw nudity, gambling, intoxicating and narcotic drugs, pornographic literature and performances, and prostitution, while others may wish to have some of these legal. Competitive communities would thus provide choice in law along with other collective goods. Communities which decriminalize victimless acts would have lower law enforcement costs as well as possibly less violent crime. The private provision of police services would in many instances be more focused on the protection of property and personal safety and less on the enforcement of cultural standards such as what people read or whether they spend money in gambling.

B) Slums and Poverty

Poverty, which is basically a low wage level, can be remedied by increasing labor productivity and reducing the cost of employment. Ways to do this include removing legal barriers to employment and enterprise, increasing skills and improving work habits, and eliminating taxes and other imposed costs on wages. By seceding from government with its restrictions and taxes, civic associations also withdraw from restrictions on enterprise and labor, such as not allowing jitneys or vans to provide for local transit (Klein et al. 1997). Devolution would also substitute local assessments and fees for income and sales taxes, a shift that would reduce the social burden of public revenues. This would include reducing the high tax rates for those escaping the welfare system, which adds the loss of benefits to the taxes on wages.

The property tax, as practiced in most of the world, imposes a burden on real-estate improvements. Whenever owners put up buildings or improve property, they get slapped with a tax increase, as though being punished for doing something bad. This is one reason why poor neighborhoods deteriorate. With control over their finances, a low-income community that chose to attract enterprise and development could exempt all buildings and other improvements from an assessment based on real estate.

As noted, increased productivity also comes from better human capital. If the city school system is costly or ineffective, families would be able to substitute private and home schooling, with tax substitution for the tuition. Some associations could provide schooling as well.

C) Sprawl

Urban sprawl consists of a wasteful use of land for urban expansion due to a greater amount of land usage than would exist in a pure free market. As defined here, sprawl is a function of interventionist policy which subsidizes land holding, rather than the result of purely voluntary choices to live in a low density environment.

Rather than develop compactly with gradually decreasing density, sprawl leapfrogs over developable land to further locations. Cities then build more costly infrastructure, and commuting times get longer and longer. With a low density, public transit is not economical, and there is more automobile congestion.

By definition, such sprawl is not a pure market outcome. Zoning contributes to sprawl, especially when it mandates a low density and precludes multiple-use real estate (Nelson 1977). Property taxes and government funding for public works also induce sprawl by creating dysfunctional land speculation. Speculation can serve a useful function in allocating goods over time and providing more buyers and sellers. But in cities today, government policy leads to inefficient and turbulent speculation. Government provides public works such as transit, streets, police and fire services, and schools. These services increase land rent and land values since the landowners pay only a small fraction of the cost. This constitutes a transfer of income from taxed workers to the landowners; developers thus become rent seekers. Speculators anticipate where the growth will be, accompanied or led by government-financed infrastructure. Lots held for speculation await higher prices, and so development leapfrogs over them to less expensive, further-away sites. Speculation can also induce malinvestments in real estate, buildings which turn out to be unprofitable. This especially occurs when monetary policy artificially makes interest rates low, leading to excessive investment in higher-order capital goods such as real-estate construction. Developers also expect a large part of their profits to come from increased land values. But those who build at the end of a real estate boom are left with vacancies, low rental income, and large loans to pay back (Foldvary 1997).

Cellular democracy and contractual communities would induce a more economical, since competition would induce a more rational system of financing public works and covenants would replace zoning. Association finance would follow the benefit principle, where those who benefit pay the costs. This would lead to a more compact development, since the profits from development would come from producing buildings and streets rather than from land values created by government works. Public utilities such as water would have a higher cost for users at the fringes who require longer piping and larger volumes from the source than do central-city users (Gaffney 1964).

D) Congestion

Since the streets and freeways in a city are free to the user, they tend to get overused during rush hour. A more compact development would ease the congestion with shorter distances and more urban transit, due to greater density. But also, privately provided thoroughfares would charge tolls which could vary according to congestion. Such peak-load pricing would reduce congestion. Some city associations might also provide public transit such as street cars, without excluding private alternatives such as vans and jitneys. The associations could fund the fixed cost from the rent assessments, since the transit increases rent, and users could pay the marginal costs.

While private streets are provided by many private communities and some firms run private toll roads, major avenues are typically operated at the city level. In St. Louis, however, some boulevards have been privately owned. An advantage of such ownership is the ability to control the utilities along the route (Beito and Smith 1990, p. 288).

V

Case Studies

COLUMBIA, MARYLAND IS AN EXAMPLE OF A large contractual community with both residential and commercial members, and which has decentralized its governance. It was developed during the 1960s. The population is about 100,000, with about 34,000 dwelling units. The Columbia Association runs an internal bus system, ColumBus, connecting the villages and the town center. The board is made up of one director from each of the ten villages. Each village has a governing board in charge of the local roads and grounds. Each resident, whether renter or owner, has a vote, as do non-resident owners. The Columbia villages are in turn divided into neighborhoods of between 600 and 800 dwelling units (see Foldvary 1994 for more details on Columbia and the cases below).

While Columbia is an example of successful multi-level organization, the model presented in this section would carry the concept further, to lowest-level neighborhoods of about 500 persons. Two examples of communities this size are the village of Arden in Delaware and the Fort Ellsworth condominium in Alexandria, Virginia.

Arden is an example of a land trust; in this case the land is owned by a nonprofit trust. The trust leases plots to households, who own the structures on the land. The lease rents pay for the expenses of the trust and the property tax as well as the village's budget. Unlike most residential associations, there are no restrictive covenants on the architecture in Arden, and it does not need them, since the houses are pleasantly different from one another, and very well maintained. There is no tax penalty for improving one's building, since the lease payment is only for the land and the property tax on the building is paid for by the trust. Indeed, Arden was deliberately founded on this principle in 1900 by followers of Henry George, as a model of a community funded from its site rents. The founders were also influenced by Ebenezer Howard (1965), who proposed "garden cities" which combine urban and rural features. Some 43 percent of Arden consists of greens, forests, and roads.

Arden is governed by town meetings and committees, with four regular town meetings per year. The village also elects a board of assessors to assess the lease rent. There are also many social, charitable, and recreational clubs. The Arden model was so successful that two similar communities were started nearby, Ardentown and Ardencroft. Arden demonstrates that a population of approximately 500 is sufficient to have community spirit, much activity, volunteers, and local civic goods. The village even had its own school until the state government forced it to give up local control in 1969. If it were much larger, town meetings would become unwieldy and the residents would be less well acquainted with one another.

The Fort Ellsworth Condominium Apartments in Alexandria, Virginia is an example of a private community within a city. Its 169 units were constructed in the early 1970s. There are five buildings, each four stories high, the buildings divided into sections with a stairwell, mail boxes, and a bulletin board. There is a Stairwell Captain for each section.

The governance at Fort Ellsworth consists of a board of directors and various committees, as well as an annual association meeting. The association also hires professional management. Though most residents do not take part in the association functions, there are about 50 volunteers, including renters, sufficient to run the committees and serve on the board, all without pay. If a community is too small, it might have trouble finding volunteers. Given some percentage of the population predisposed to community activism, a size of about 500 seems typically sufficient to provide members for the governing board and committees.

In the cases of Arden and Fort Ellsworth, the size of the land trust and the condominium land set the boundaries for the community. For neighborhood associations that devolve from city governments, the boundaries can be flexible so that the associations are just large enough to generate sufficient volunteers for the board or council as well as for committees, yet small enough so that candidates and board/council members still have close personal contacts with the members. But even associations of a few households would be feasible if the members are motivated enough to form their own community.

The "private places" of St. Louis are the best case studies of single-family housing in private associations in the midst of a city, integrated within the city of St. Louis and the towns of St. Louis County. In St. Louis, "street ownership [has] represented the means to control the 'commanding heights' of the local economy" (Beito 1989, p. 35). The fact that private neighborhoods persist despite a lack of tax substitution (there is no tax rebate or credit and, unlike property taxes, the association fees are not deductible from income taxes) demonstrates their value to the residents. Despite such handicaps, some streets that were not private have become so since World War II (Savage 1987, p. xi).

VI

Conclusion

THE PURELY VOLUNTARY CITY involves an integration of several political and economic concepts. Multi-level small-group governance would permit economies of scale while minimizing privilege seeking and keeping the power base centered on neighborhoods and households. Benefits-based public finance, based on user fees and site rents, is feasible in the local level and avoids the disincentives and burdens of taxes on productive effort. Tax substitution and degrees of secession and devolution from city government would provide an orderly way towards civic associations, respecting the right both of those who form associations and those who do not wish to join. Associations could also facilitate local exchange and credit operations that overcome institutional constraints.

Many urban problems could be confronted and remedied by civic associations which replace dysfunctional taxation and regulation with benefit-based financing and association covenants. Finally, the case studies point to actual successful implementations of some of these concepts. The conclusion seems to be warranted that a purely voluntary city is feasible and has the potential of replacing urban blight, congestion, and sprawl with the grandeur of free, prosperous, handsome, and well-governed centers of civilization.

References

Beito, David T. (1989). "Owning the 'Commanding Heights:' Historical Perspectives on Private Streets." In *Essays in Public Works History* 16 (December): 1–47.

Beito, David T., and Smith, Bruce. (1990). "The Formation of Urban Infrastructure Through Nongovernmental Planning: The Private Places of St. Louis, 1869–1920." *Journal of Urban History* 16, no. 3 (May): 263–303.

Bryan, Frank M., and McClaughry, John. (1989). *The Vermont Papers: Recreating Democracy on a Human Scale*. Chelsea, VT: Chelsea Green Publishing.

Coase, Ronald H. (1960). "The Problem of Social Cost." *Journal of Law and Economics* 3 (October): 1–44.

Fitzgerald, Randall. (1988). *When Government Goes Private*. New York: Universe Books.

Foldvary, Fred. (1994). *Public Goods and Private Communities*. Aldershot, UK: Edward Elgar Publishing.

———. (1996). "Rent Seeking in Communitarian Democracy," Paper presented at Western Economic Association, San Francisco, June 30.

———. (1997). "The Business Cycle: A Georgist-Austrian Synthesis." *American Journal of Economics and Sociology* 56 (4) (October): 521–541.

Gaffney, Mason. (1964). *Containment Policies for Urban Sprawl*. Lawrence, KS: University of Kansas Publications, Governmental Research Series No. 27.

Greco, Thomas. (1994). *New Money for Healthy Communities*. Tucson, AZ: Thomas H. Greco Publishing.

Hamilton, Bruce W. (1991 [1987]). "Tiebout Hypothesis." Pp. 672–677 in *The World of Economics*. Ed. John Eatwell, Murray Milgate, and Peter Newman. New York: W. W. Norton. First published in *The New Palgrave: A Dictionary of Economics*.

Heath, Spencer. (1957). *Citadel, Market and Altar*. Baltimore: Science of Society Foundation.

Howard, Ebenezer. (1965 [1902]). *Garden Cities of To-Morow*. Cambridge: M.I.T. Press.

Klein, Daniel, Adrian Moore, and Binyam Reja. (1997). *Curb Rights: A Foundation for Free Enterprise in Urban Transit*. Washington, DC: Brookings Institution Press.

Neely, Richard. (1990). *Take Back Your Neighborhood*. New York: Donald I. Fine.

Nelson, Robert H. (1977). *Zoning and Property Rights: An Analysis of the American System of Land Use Regulation.* Cambridge: MIT Press.

Olson, Mancur. (1971). *The Logic of Collective Action.* Cambridge: Harvard University Press.

Parks, Roger B., and Ronald J. Oakerson. (1988). *Metropolitan Organization: The St. Louis Case,* M-158. Washington, DC: ACIR (Advisory Commission on Intergovernmental Relations).

Savage, Charles C. (1987). *Architecture of the Private Streets of St. Louis.* Columbia, MO: University of Missouri Press.

Tiebout, Charles M. (1956). "A Pure Theory of Local Expenditure." *Journal of Political Economy* 64: 416–24.

Tullock, Gordon. (1985). "A New Proposal for Decentralizing Government Activity." Pp. 139–148 in *Rationale Wirtschaftspolitik in komplexen Gesellschaftern.* Stuttgart: Verlag W. Kohlhammer.

———. (1994). *The New Federalist.* Vancouver: Fraser Institute.

Index